ERIC SYKES was born in Oldham in 1923. He has enjoyed a distinguished career writing and performing as a master craftsman of visual comedy.

He has been given many awards of which the following are the most notable. In 1961 he received the Guild of TV Producers and Directors' Lifetime Achievement Award. In 1964 he was BBC TV Personality of the Year. In 1980 Sykes was given the PYE Colour TV Award and the Rose d'Or de Montreux for *The Plank*. In 1985 he was awarded the 25th Golden Rose of Montreux 'In sincere appreciation for his contribution to Television Entertainment'. In 1986 he was made an OBE and in 1988 he was admitted to the Freedom of the City of London.

In 1992 Sykes had a Lifetime Achievement Award from the Writers' Guild at the Comedy Awards. In 1997 he was recognised by the Variety Club of Great Britain for fifty years in the business. In 1998 he was given an Honorary Fellowship of the University of Lancaster and the Eric Morecambe Award by Comic Heritage. In 2001 the Grand Order of Water Rats gave Sykes a Lifetime Achievement Award and he received the Bernard Delfont Award for Outstanding Contribution to Show Business from the Variety Club. In 2002 he was Oldie of the Year and in 2004 he was made a CBE.

From the reviews of *If I Don't Write It, Nobody Else Will*:

'Anyone in love with the world of entertainment will find this a treasure-trove of material'   *Daily Telegraph*

By the same author:

Eric Sykes's Comedy Heroes
Sykes of Sebastopol Terrace
The Great Crime of Grapplewick
Smelling of Roses
UFOs are Coming Wednesday

ERIC SYKES

If I Don't Write It,
Nobody Else Will

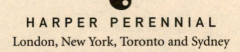

HARPER PERENNIAL
London, New York, Toronto and Sydney

Harper Perennial
An imprint of HarperCollins*Publishers*
77-85 Fulham Palace Road
Hammersmith
London W6 8JB

www.harperperennial.co.uk

This edition published by Harper Perennial 2006
1

First published by Fourth Estate 2005

A catalogue record for this book
is available from the British Library

ISBN-13 978-0-00-717785-1
ISBN-10 0-00-717785-2

Set in Minion and Serlio by
Rowland Phototypesetting Ltd, Bury St Edmunds, Suffolk

Printed and bound in Great Britain by Clays Ltd, St Ives plc

Picture credits:
Frankie Howerd © Popperfoto
Three Sisters © Catherine Ashmore
Bill Kenwright © Simon Turtle

For my mother

ACKNOWLEDGEMENTS

Thanks to:

My family, for all their love and support in enriching my home life; Norma Farnes, my umbrella when it's raining; Louise Haines, my editor *par excellence*; Chris Chism and her computer; and special thanks to Janet Spearman for her tireless efforts from the beginning to the end of this book.

And my thanks to Tom Courtenay for the title.

The most important person is missing...

UNDER STARTER'S ORDERS

On 4 May 1923 I was born, but in giving me life my mother sacrificed her own. Officially recorded as 'Harriet Sykes, née Stacey, died in childbirth', cold, clinical and final: cold and clinical yes, but final? We shall see. Although my mother had departed this life, she hadn't abandoned me. I know this to be true, from instances in my life too numerous to be passed off as mere coincidence, in fact some so inexplicable, so impossible, that they can only be described as miracles. As for my poor father, one can hardly imagine the depth of his despair, the rising panic as his whole world collapsed around him – his beloved Harriet in exchange for this red-faced wrinkled intruder. How was he to manage? He already had a two-year-old son, Vernon, and, good grief, at the time Father was only twenty-three years old, an ex-sergeant in the occupation forces in Germany and now, in this land fit for heroes, a lowly labourer in a cotton mill, which in those early post-war years was no more than being a white slave, the manacles being the need to eat.

Counsellors had yet to be invented, social workers didn't exist and the Citizens Advice Bureau was not even in the pipeline; but on the plus side, people cared more, and neighbours and anyone else who knew of the tragedy at 36 Leslie Street, Oldham, offered not only their condolences but, more to the point, food, and cast-off clothing; and apparently one old lady offered a kitten. It was heart-warming but it didn't solve the problem. Before long the cavalry arrived, as my distraught father knew they would, his parents, Granddad and Grandma Sykes, and my late mother's family, the Staceys, were not far behind.

It must have been a very sombre get-together. What was to be done? Most likely I was asleep at the time, so I can only surmise what happened next. Grandma Stacey was to take Vernon – after all, he was two years old and house-trained – but she refused point blank to take me as well. I discovered many years later that Grandma Stacey had been against the marriage in the first place, and Father was *persona non grata* in her house. However Mother used to visit regularly with her small son Vernon and ergo he was the only memory of their daughter Harriet had left them, whereas in their eyes I was partly responsible for the loss, and in truth I probably was.

What then should be done with me? My father couldn't take me with him to the cotton mill every morning and crèches were unheard of in those days. However after a time a solution was found. I was to be deposited with a kind spinster called Miss Redfern who lived in Davies Street, or it may have been Miss Davies of Redfern Street – I didn't keep a diary in those days. I'm now in my eighties and I still haven't got round to it.

Of the two years of my displacement I have only vague memories, of my surrogate mother's house: the smell of furniture polish, and above my cot a huge parrot that squawked incessantly from the time the black cloth was taken off the cage until it was mercifully covered up again at bedtime. It was my constant companion until eventually I was returned to the custody of my father at 36 Leslie Street, much less salubrious, with no smell of furniture polish (we didn't have enough furniture to warrant the extravagance), but at least it was home. In later years my father told me that neither he nor anyone else could understand what I was babbling about. Hardly surprising, as I'd never learned English, but spoke fluent parrot. At two years old I was incontinent, and still unsteady on my pins, because learning to walk too early was not encouraged in case it led to rickets.

Cataclysmic changes had taken place during my absence at Redfern/Davies's. My father had married again and already I wasn't the youngest in the family: I had a little brother, John. He was still only at the sleeping and eating stage of development, but already I'd taken to him. It was the beginning of a close, warm-hearted friendship that was to last a lifetime. Apparently I hovered round his cot most of the day, impatient for him to grow up so that we could play together. When John was twelve months old or thereabouts we'd hold conversations. I would come out with something and when I'd finished he'd wait for a moment or two before the penny dropped that it was his turn to speak, and when he obviously couldn't he'd gurgle, splutter and blow raspberries, making both of us laugh with sheer joy. It must have been the first time in my life that I laughed – the parrot must have found me a very dull ha'p'orth.

Two or three years later John was growing into a beautiful little boy, and one of the highlights for me was John's bedtime. Mother cradled him in her arms, then, sitting herself down in the rocking chair, she would begin singing. Softly she sang a hymn, the same one every time, but she didn't sing the words. It was 'bee bough, bee bough, bee bough, bee bough', each word synchronised to each rock, and a gentle patting in the same tempo; she 'bee boughed' in an absent-minded voice, staring into space as if I wasn't there. I don't think I was jealous, envious, or left out. It never even occurred to me that no one had ever sung me to sleep, embraced me or kissed me; I accepted as a natural progression that in our house I was last in the pecking order, and strangely enough it didn't bother me at all. Although I was unaware of it at the time, being a non-playing lodger relieved me from all responsibility and I was free to live in the fantasy world in my head, which transcended the hopelessness of the surrounding poverty and deprivation that typified most cotton towns in the late 1920s. Incidentally the hymn that Mother 'bee boughed' I discovered years afterwards was 'O God, our help in ages past'.

Another little incident occurred some months later. Vernon was not with us and John and I were still a-bed. I wasn't asleep; I'd just heard the front door close as Dad set off for work. Some minutes afterwards, Mother came into our bedroom, clambered over me and lay between us for a moment. Then she turned on her side to cuddle John. The sight of Mother's back was as if I'd had a door slammed in my face. A few moments went by, and I had an over-whelming urge to put my arm around her, but I was too shy, so I turned my back on her and worried about my pet tortoise, which had been missing for several days. Perhaps I had no need to worry: Dad had reassured me that tortoises hibernated, then, realising that he'd lost me with the word 'hibernate', he explained to me that my tortoise had stolen away to a safe place in order to sleep through the winter. Half mollified, I accepted his explanation, although it never occurred to me at the time that it wasn't yet July. I must have dozed, because when I opened my eyes again Mother had gone and so had John, and I then began to wonder if I'd dreamed about her turning her back on me to cuddle him. I was much too young to understand my silent cry for help, my desperate yearning to belong, to be acknowledged – even a smile would have sufficed.

I must have been about six when I woke up one cold autumn morning feeling different. Somewhere at the back of my mind a hazy thought began to take shape. I had the stub of a pencil some-where and I could buy a small notebook from the little shop on Ward Street. Then I forgot what these preparations were for, but then suddenly it all clicked into place. It was a brilliant idea: I was going to take down motor-car numbers, and I wouldn't tell anybody about it because if I did they'd all be at it. I couldn't wait to get started. Bolting down only half a Shredded Wheat, I dashed upstairs for the stub of pencil, down again, and then out of the door as if the house was on fire, stopping at the corner shop to buy a small notebook, which cost a penny (incidentally my entire fortune), and in less than five minutes I was sitting on the edge of the pavement. No one ever referred to the pavement: they were 't'flags', and the street or thoroughfare was 't'cart road', and so from the shop I ran down to Featherstall Road and sat on 't'flags' with my feet in 't'cart road'. Once settled, I opened my little notebook, pencil poised for action – so far so good. My head swivelled from side to side in case I missed a number and I made a mental note that when I'd collected fifty numbers it would be enough.

I wasn't being over-optimistic: after all, this was the main highway from Rochdale to Manchester. However, time passed and I reluctantly reduced my original aim of fifty motor-car numbers to twenty. It was coming up to dinnertime and now the cold, gusty wind was beginning to dampen my enthusiasm. I shivered, but sat on, book held stoically in one hand, pencil not quite so poised. I decided to abandon the enterprise if a motor car didn't appear before the next tram . . . Three trams later there was one coal cart, wearily pulled by a dozing horse, reins loosely held by a sleeping driver; sometime later a large cart coming the other way, carrying enormous barrels, the heavy load drawn by two off-white, huge beasts, trotting proudly on big hairy feet. Turning my head to the right, I disinterestedly watched yet another tram wrenching itself round the corner from Oldham Road into Featherstall Road to rattle and grind its way down the single track to the loop, where it stopped to allow an 'up-tram' to pass in order to join the one track to Royton, and from there made a sharp turn right to Shaw Wrens Nest or to carry on to Rochdale. But alas, there was not a motor car for miles. Pencil, notebook and hands now deep in jacket pockets, feet drumming against the road to coax a bit of warmth back into them, I must have looked a picture of abject misery, and hungry with it, when a voice behind and above me broke into my self-imposed despondency. ''Allo, 'allo, 'allo,' and I recognised the brogue of our local bobby or, to give him his full title, Constable Matty Lally. He was an imposing figure of a man, built like a full-grown water buffalo, which gave a great sense of security to the law-abiding and made him a fearful presence in the darker side of the community.

'What are you doing there, lad?' he said. 'I've had my eye on you for the last half hour.'

'I'm collecting motor-car numbers,' I said, as if I'd been directed to do a survey.

He shook his head sadly. 'You'll get piles sitting there,' he said, and moved himself off.

As I watched him go, the import of his words hit me. When Matty Lally spoke, everybody listened, and hadn't he just told me

I'd get piles? I assumed that he meant that piles of motor cars would be along any minute and my enthusiasm returned. So I renewed my vigilance, having finally decided that one motor car would be enough. How was I, six or seven years old, to know that Matty Lally had been referring to a nasty bottom problem and not piles of motor cars?

However, the enterprise was not a write-off. As I was about to leave, a ramshackle boneshaker turned the corner and trundled towards me. It was moving so slowly that I was able to walk alongside it while taking the number, BU something or other – I forget now, but it's not important.

We lads who lived in Leslie Street considered ourselves fortunate in having the Mucky Broos right outside our front doors. 'Broos' were small hills, and these were 'Mucky' because they were just a large expanse of dirt; rare blades of sickly grass struggled to exist and even though the rain was frequent, the soil was worked out – even weeds preferred to take their chances in the cracks on the pavement. Most days the Mucky Broos were just two acres of slippery, glutinous mud, but they had dry periods as well. The area was triangular in shape, bordered at the top end by Ward Street Central School and on the other side by Ward Street itself, with Leslie Street the base of the triangle. Not very inspiring, but the Mucky Broos were our playground. My best mate was Richard Branwood, whose little sister Martha was used when required in a supporting role.

On one occasion we dug a trench and, with poles for rifles, re-enacted the Battle of the Somme. A couple more lads joined us as we leapt out of the trench and then charged towards the imaginary Germans, only to retreat and sprawl on the ground to have our wounds attended to. Martha, the little sister of mercy, knelt by me, stroking my forehead gently, a sad smile on her face. I liked this bit: it left me with a pleasant, warm feeling that I'd never experienced before, and I couldn't wait to be wounded again when we repeated the whole process. It was exciting, but after a few more sorties we all wanted to be dead, so we all lay spreadeagled in the dirt, exhausted. After a time I raised my head and discovered that it was not only getting dark but Richard and the other lads had gone and, more importantly, so had the nursing staff, so I went as well.

However, that wasn't the end of the matter. The following morning an irate neighbour called at our house and demanded we fill the trench in, as it was a danger to man and beast. He claimed that on his way home last night he'd fallen in, and he rolled up his trouser leg to show my father a nasty graze. Dad sucked in his breath and sent me off to fill in the trench.

Reluctantly I did as I was told. No more mock battles of the Somme, no more charging over the top – but if the truth were known, what I would miss most of all would be the little nurse with the sad smile stroking my forehead. It was the first time in my young life that anyone had shown me tenderness, awakening emotions in me beyond my understanding but taken for granted by most children.

Fortunately my cup was always half full and never half empty, so in five minutes I had forgotten all about the Somme and I was galloping over the dips and hollows of Texas, pointing my two fingers like six shooters and cleaning up the bad lands. On another day with some of the lads, off-white hankies tucked into the backs of our caps to shield our necks from the pitiless sun, although there wasn't much of that in Lancashire, we were in the French Foreign Legion and with poles over our shoulders we marched over the burning sands – to us the sands were burning whatever the weather. When we had tired of the desert, we had lots of other pursuits. One of my favourite games was Ducky Funny Whip. How it got this name is a mystery, but we certainly didn't make it up. A 'ducky' is a smooth stone, and there were plenty of them scattered about the Mucky Broos. We each picked one out; the size was immaterial, provided you were strong enough to throw it. Having each found our own ducky, we stood in a queue while whoever was 'It' placed half bricks on top of one another to about three feet high, finally putting his own ducky on top. Then the game commenced. One by one we hurled our duckies to try to knock the column of bricks over. When a lucky throw brought the target down, we all picked up our duckies and ran away to hide amongst the dips and slight rises of our Mucky Broos. When 'It' had rebuilt his pile of bricks and put his ducky on top, he endeavoured to find someone, and when he did he tapped them and ran back to his column of bricks and cocked his leg over it, and he wasn't 'It' any more. However, if the unfortunate who'd been spotted managed to beat 'It' back to the target and knock the column down before 'It' could cock his leg over it, everyone ran away to hide again and the process continued. Older people will understand and forgive the dog's breakfast I've made in trying to explain what was, in fact, a very simple pastime, not as mentally challenging as chess but to us urchins infinitely more enjoyable. Ducky Funny Whip was a team game best played when the nights were drawing in, as lying in the shadows made it more difficult for 'It'.

Dad and most other working men hated Mondays, and looked forward to Friday night and a wage packet; above all Friday was the gateway to the greener grass of the weekend. Naturally young children had a different aspect to the week; we fought to keep heavy eyes open as bedtime approached, because that would end another day, but every morning was a new adventure. However, as for the grown-ups Friday night was our favourite, as for John and me it was our bath night.

First the rumbling in the backyard as Dad lifted the tin bath from the nail on the wall, staggering through the door with it on his back like a tortoise from outer space while Mother closed the door behind him to keep out the cold. There is nothing so soothing and delicious as a warm soapy bath in front of a blazing fire and even when soap got into our eyes it was a small price to pay for this weekly luxury. Once we were out of the bath, everything was warm – the towels, the milk – and best of all we felt clean and shiny. Roll on next Friday. If only we could carry these moments of happiness and contentment into adulthood.

Another pal of mine was John Broome, and when I was a little older his mother kindly gave me an overcoat, grey and much too large. When I wore it, only the top of my head and my feet were visible, but it kept me warm through two winters, when it finally fell to pieces before it could be handed down again.

It was an unwritten law that to qualify for use of the Mucky Broos one either lived in Ward Street or Leslie Street. We regarded it as our private and exclusive play area, and as far as I can remember no stranger ever played there or attempted to take it from us, which is hardly surprising, really, as there were thousands of Mucky Broos in Oldham and ours was well down the list of much sought-after properties. We played cricket in the summer with a pile of coats for the wicket and football in the winter with two piles of coats for the goalposts; an old tennis ball sufficed for both sports. In the soft summer evenings quite a few people in Ward Street sat out on chairs watching our games; folks who lived on Leslie Street stood in the doorways, as they didn't have the advantage of a pavement on which to place their chairs. For them it was only dirt but to us lads they were an appreciative audience and they spurred us on to ludicrous heights, and we played whatever game we were into with extra panache. We lads were all mentally in an England shirt and the couple of dozen watchers were a packed Wembley.

When it was completely dark, we wandered over to Ward Street for another of our distractions. Whoever was 'It' faced the wall of a house and shouted "M-I-L-K, MILK" and at the same time we advanced slowly towards him from across the street. A clever 'It' would start slowly with 'M' and then rush 'I-L-K', whirling round, and anybody caught moving took his place. This game was illuminated by the light from the toffee-shop window, a shop which never seemed to close in case somebody wanted a box of matches or a jar of pickles or even toffees. When we had money we were in the shop like a flash, with a coin on the counter and asking for a ha'p'orth of 'all round-the-window', which meant that the lady took a toffee from each of the boxes on display. When the lamplighter approached with his long pole to touch the gas mantle in the lamp opposite we had added illumination. The game continued until Mother's high-pitched voice called into the darkness, 'Eriiiiic', and sadly that was the end of my night's entertainment.

Of course it wasn't all play. I had my day job helping to lay the table and sometimes drying a plate during the washing-up, but my most important assignment of all was being responsible for cutting old newspapers into squares to hang on a nail in the lavatory at the bottom of the garden.

I can't remember John ever taking part in our rough and tumbles on the Mucky Broos. Although he was now old enough, Mother wanted to keep an eye on him and I was quite happy with this arrangement. After all, John was the centre of her universe and, much as I enjoyed his company indoors, during our games I was glad to be relieved of the responsibility of looking after him. I couldn't anyway as I was too busy enjoying myself.

Some Saturday mornings Mother gave us tuppence each to go to the Imperial, the picture house better known as 'the Fleapit'. It wasn't too far away, on Featherstall Road, almost opposite my numberplate collection station. She gave us tuppence so that we could afford the best seats and wouldn't have to mix with the scruffbags in the penny seats. John and I had other ideas: we didn't mind sitting with the 'untouchables' so that we had the other penny to spend on toffees.

There was always a cacophony of noise before the programme started, whistles and laughter, and scallywags running up and down the aisles, but the babble dwindled quickly when the lights went down. Usually there was a serial every Saturday morning. The most scary one I remember was called *The Shadow*. Two men were talking together or, to be more accurate, miming talking together – what they were discussing was written at the bottom of the picture. Then suddenly the music went into low menacing phrases. It wasn't really an orchestra but a woman at the piano in the pit, and as she pounded out a crescendo the shadow of a hooded person crept along the wall towards the two men. This was nail-biting stuff. We all knew what was going to happen, but nobody closed their mouth. Slowly the shadow raised an arm, holding the shadow of a weapon, to bring it crashing down on the head of the nearest man, who collapsed immediately. His colleague whirled round, drew his pistol and fired at the shadow, which was useless, it seemed, because the shadow, completely oblivious, sidled off the screen. There were, of course, no sounds of gun shots – after all, most films were silent in those days – but the lady pianist was working herself into a frenzy to build up to the 'to be continued next week'. The lights went on again before the next effort, but conversation was now subdued as *The Shadow* was discussed.

Sometimes the serial was followed by a comedy, but romance was anathema to us and a couple kissing was greeted with whistles, boos and showers of orange peel being hurled at the screen until the lights went up and the manager walked on stage and immediately we were subdued. He had a rough voice and he threatened us all with expulsion if we didn't behave. Meanwhile the film was still running, partly behind him on the silver screen but mostly on him as he spoke, and by the time he left the stage the offending scene was well past, or at least indecipherable until the lights went down and the lady pianist began again with sloppy arpeggios. Romantic films weren't often shown but whenever there was a kissing sequence it invariably provoked this situation. Sometimes I felt sorry for the manager: he probably had to show what he was given, films that a decent cinema would reject out of hand. But we still looked forward to the next Saturday morning.

Already I am now seven years old and still haven't decided what my career is going to be, although grown-ups always seem to ask me what am I going to be when I grow up. In truth, I haven't given it a thought – I have enough problems enjoying my childhood.

Wakes Week in the cotton towns of Lancashire was the annual holiday. These holidays were staggered – for instance, Royton's Wakes followed Oldham Wakes, and Rochdale's Wakes came after Royton's and so on, the reason for staggering obviously being so that only one town would be closed down at a time and Lancashire's cotton production would continue with hardly a hiccup.

Naturally we all looked forward to Oldham's Wakes. A travelling fair visited Oldham for the week, and the stalls of Tommyfield market were removed and replaced by the fair. The biggest attractions were the roundabouts, with prancing horses moving up and down under garish lights as they whirled round the mechanical orchestra belting out brassy cymbalised melodies; screams and laughter from the dodgems; coconut shies; hoopla stalls; roll a penny. There was usually a boxing booth, outside which two tough, battered characters dressed for the boxing ring stood on a raised platform with their arms folded. Next to them, only half their size but twice their IQ, the barker spoke through a megaphone, announcing that any contender lasting three rounds with either of his roughnecks would receive a pound. Many a brave lad accepted the challenge, and took off his shirt and vest to have his boxing gloves laced while the crowds bustled in to surround the ring. When the place was full, the barker fastened the tent flap and climbed through the ropes to announce the first bout. I was too young to go into the booth, but I asked Dad what went on inside. He shuddered and told me that few of the young hopefuls survived even into round two: most of them, blood-spattered with shocked eyes, were helped from the ring by their mates, and others, more prudent, chickened out before they had a chance of stardom. Dad swore that he would never set foot in a boxing booth again. He said it was a human abattoir and just to watch left him feeling sick and debased. All that remained in my mind was what is an abattoir?

One Wakes Week Dad had an exciting surprise for us. He told us that we were going to Blackpool for four days. To say we were delighted would be putting it mildly. For us Blackpool was our Shangri-La, our fairyland wherein it was Wakes all the year round.

John and I had never been on a train before, so having a compartment to ourselves on the Blackpool train didn't register until Dad said he thought it would have been crowded during Wakes Week. Mother and Dad sat opposite each other by the window but we didn't sit anywhere as we were too excited to be still. There were so many things to see: hedgerows whizzing past, meadows dotted with cows intent on cropping the grass, some raising their heads to glance curiously at the train, a black horse in the next field; and in the split second it took to vanish behind us we searched frantically for a white one, which was worth a toffee in one of our competitions that made the journey more exciting, as if we needed more excitement.

Then my father bent towards us and pointed to the horizon, and together we screamed, 'Blackpool Tower.' This was the highlight of our journey and we staggered and lurched on to the seats as we began to slow down and soon the train huffed importantly into Blackpool Central station. We were overawed by the sheer immensity of this austere Victorian building, with arches high above the concourse and hurrying passengers alighting from the train. It had never entered my head that there were others besides us making their way to Blackpool, so wrapped up were we in wonder in our own private compartment. As we passed the engine driver, Dad said, 'Thank you', and the engine driver, leaning out of his cab and wiping his hands on an oily rag, nodded and winked at John and me, while behind the engine driver a huge sweating man in a singlet, shovelled coal to feed the insatiable appetite of the boiler, his face lit by the glow. I backed out of the station, my eyes never leaving the old train driver enjoying his pipe, and I decided there and then that one day I would drive the Blackpool train.

Dad determined to take us along the promenade so that we could get a closer look at the fabulous tower, but unfortunately as we turned into the Golden Mile we were targeted by the screaming wind, which made progress almost impossible as we made our way to the boarding house. The waves were hurling themselves at the sea walls, flinging white spray into the air that was gleefully accepted by the wind and helped across the road to drench anybody stupid enough to be out on a day like this.

Without hesitation, Dad lifted John into his arms and Mother grasped my hand, and we all staggered into the shelter of the nearest side street. The calm and peace not ten yards from the frantic onslaught of the wind and sea were unnerving. As Dad wiped John's face with his hankie, a policeman strolled across to us.

'Been swimming?' he enquired sarcastically.

Dad puffed out his cheeks and replied, 'It's a force-ten gale out there.'

The policeman shook his head. 'Bit of a blow, that's all. It'll be all right tomorrow.'

Well, he was certainly correct in his weather forecast. On the morrow there was no wind to speak of, just the odd gust; but it was quite cold – 'bracing', the landlady said. So John and I paddled in the pools by the sea wall left by the receding tide. Mother kept a watchful eye on us while Dad took a tram to a place called Uncle Tom's Cabin to see if any of his mates were there. This was a favourite watering hole and he may well have met someone he knew: after all, it was Oldham's Wakes Week and visitors to Blackpool would most likely be Oldhamers.

The next day Mother took us down to the Pleasure Ground on the south shore. This was ten times bigger and more awesome than the travelling fairground that toured the Lancashire cotton towns. John and I rolled a penny each down the slots but won nothing, and Mother yanked us away before we got the bug. We had a ride on the prancing horses in between eating candy floss – we didn't eat any supper when we got home and in fact during that visit we ate enough candy floss between us to stuff a medium-sized mattress. Dad spent the day at Uncle Tom's Cabin and so we only saw him long enough to say, 'Bye, Dad.'

On the Wednesday Mother took us by tram to Bispham and I had the feeling that if it hadn't been too expensive we would have gone as far as Fleetwood, where Dad said you could get the best kippers in the world. Incidentally he wasn't with us, as he spent the day at Uncle Tom's Cabin again. On the last day it absolutely threw it down – the rain was unbelievable – and against the rules of the boarding house we were allowed to stay indoors and play draughts and snakes and ladders. We would have played ludo, only we needed four players and Dad wasn't present as he was at Uncle Tom's Cabin. By and large we had a marvellous holiday. Even Dad was over the moon, as he'd won a shilling at darts in Uncle Tom's Cabin. And so our wonderful few days by the sea came to an end, and now my ambition was to be a train driver on the promenade at Blackpool.

One Sunday Mother got John and me ready and told us that we were going to Grandma Stacey's for tea. It was the first I'd heard of Grandma Stacey, but in those days little boys didn't ask silly questions like 'Who's Grandma Stacey?' We took the tram to a much posher part of Oldham, a world we'd never seen, and I remember thinking that the further we travelled the more austere our surroundings were. When we finally arrived at our destination, I was overawed by the quiet, aloof elegance of the Victorian terraces. We were aliens in a land of privilege as we walked furtively uphill to the address of Grandma Stacey.

The front door was opened by an old lady whose bottom jaw trembled as if she was cold, with a long black dress ornamented only by a cameo brooch at her throat and hair swept up at the back and held tightly in place by a large comb. This turned out to be Great-grandma Wilson. She didn't speak, even after Mother's 'Good afternoon'; she just opened the door wider, turned and floated along the passage, to disappear in a room, and after a moment she reappeared and looked at us, whereupon Mother ushered us forward and we went into a more cheerful atmosphere.

A fire was burning brightly in the grate and an old man in a pillbox hat with a tassel was seesawing slowly back and forward in a rocking chair, busily puffing on a white clay pipe, which had a lid on it, his eyes never leaving the burning coals. We three stood around, hardly breathing in case he turned to look in our direction. In front of us there was a table covered by a startlingly white cloth and on it a small plateful of sandwiches and three bowls of prunes. Then the little old lady with the quivering jaw entered with a jug full of hot custard and poured it over the prunes, after which she made a silent exit and we never saw her again on that visit; nor did the old man in the rocking chair interrupt his quiet vigil over the fire. When we'd finished we stood around in silence, which was oppressive and broken only by the hissing and spluttering of the fire and, more dominating, the sonorous ticking of an old polished grandfather clock sneering down at us. Mother said, 'Well, er . . . we'll be off then,' and glared at us until in unison we said, 'Thank you for my tea,' and that was the end of the ordeal.

On the tram going home Mother told us that the old lady was not Grandma Stacey: she was not at home today, and neither was my brother Vernon. The old couple we'd met were Grandma Stacey's parents, Great-grandpa and Great-grandma Wilson. She also explained why they didn't speak: it was simply because they were both in their nineties. I must confess that this remark had me puzzled for days. If you were over ninety, were you not allowed to speak? Or, more worryingly, perhaps at that impossible age they'd forgotten how it was done.

Subsequently we went to tea for three more Sundays. On the last visit I think Mother must have taken John to the lavatory for I was left alone with Great-grandpa Wilson, still rocking, still puffing and glaring at the fire. I just stood and watched him. I was good at standing and watching – I'd had enough practice at home. Then Great-grandpa Wilson took the pipe out of his mouth and the old man I'd previously thought incapable of speech broke his silence, but it was as if I wasn't there – I'd had enough practice at that as well. Taking the pipe out of his mouth, he said, 'Last night she didn't come home till after nine o'clock.' He put his pipe back in his mouth, puffed for a while, took it out again and said, 'I reckon she's got a fancy man somewhere,' and that was the end of what could scarcely be described as a conversation – in fact I wouldn't have dared open my mouth. I just stood and watched, and his stare never left the fire. Many, many years later, when I was working for my living, Great-grandpa Wilson's words came back to me, and with a flash of insight I realised that he had been referring to Grandma Stacey, who was seventy-two at the time; and on mulling over those awful prunes-and-custard ordeals I realised that Great-grandpa Wilson must have been born in about 1836. What a wealth of memories must have been staring back at him from the fire! Victoria was Queen when he was young, but did Great-grandpa Wilson know this? After all, there was no such thing as a wireless in those far-off days; he would have been middle-aged before it had been invented. He must have been aware that Prince Albert, Victoria's consort, was German, but when Albert died an early death and the whole country mourned, how would Great-grandpa Wilson have learned of this tragic event? There were few newspapers and probably none at all in Oldham, which in those days was mostly forest and grassland, and certainly there were no newsagents. Perhaps information was conveyed by the town crier, but then would Oldham have been big enough to warrant such a luxury, and how did the town crier get the news in the first place? Questions, questions, questions. In the middle of the nineteenth century there were no such 'get-abouts' as the motor car, trams were yet to come, and there would have been no roads for them to travel on; horses and coaches were the only means of transport and then only for the gentry. To be abroad at night when there were no lights to illuminate the paths was to make oneself vulnerable to rogues and vagabonds. What a rich tapestry of first-hand knowledge stared back at Grandpa Wilson from the fire! I would have sat at his feet just to listen, anything, yet the only time he spoke to me was to slag off Grandma Stacey, his seventy-two-year-old daughter who hadn't come home till after nine o'clock. What was he afraid of – a highwayman? Oh, what a missed opportunity!

The next time I saw Great-grandpa Wilson was when Grandma Stacey took me by the hand and led me into a quiet bedroom to pay my respects to him as he lay peacefully in his coffin. Other people whom I'd never met stood around in quiet groups, but no one seemed particularly upset. When Grandma Stacey took me back downstairs, a different drama was taking place. I was fascinated as I watched one of the mourners – a large, untidy man in a bowler hat, with a large pointed nose with a large dewdrop hanging on the end of it reluctant to leave home – rummaging in the shelves of a magnificent bookcase, occasionally stuffing his pockets with anything that took his fancy. It later turned out that he was one of the uncles – so my father told me about a week after the funeral. Staring into the fire he said bitterly, 'Your Great-grandpa Wilson promised me the harmonium.' As there were only the two of us present,

I assumed he was addressing me. After a time he went on, 'Your Uncle Albert pinched it,' and, as if to clinch his case, he added, 'He was seen pushing a hand cart up Waterloo Street and that harmonium was roped on to it.' I remember thinking, 'Thank God for Uncle Albert': the last thing we needed at our house was a harmonium, and Dad struggling to play every night when he came home from work, his feet going up and down on the treadles like a demented cyclist on an exercise bike, his head bowed over a sheet of music he couldn't understand.

Some days later Dad's words came back to me. 'He promised me the harmonium', he'd said, and he'd stressed the word 'me' as if he was entitled to it, but to my knowledge he'd never met the Wilsons or Grandma Stacey; nor did he accompany us for our prunes and custard. More importantly, he hadn't gone with me to look at Great-grandpa Wilson in his coffin. So why should the old man promise him the harmonium? I gave up there, and I still didn't know who Grandma Stacey, Great-grandpa Wilson and Great-grandma Wilson belonged to.

Children when I was young were generally predictable. For instance, if we were walking sedately anywhere with a solemn expression on our faces it would be almost certain that we were on our way to school, church or the doctor – in other words a destination that was mundane, dutiful, boring or simply somewhere we weren't keen to arrive at; but if our target was pleasurable, we ran, and we enjoyed the run, full of excited, pleasant thoughts of where we were going.

So it was with John and me every Tuesday during the summer holidays, when Grandma Ashton baked bread and muffins. From home to Royton seemed to us like miles, and for little legs it was, but we ran all the way, up Featherstall Road, turning left at the Queens, along Oldham Road past Boundary Park Hospital and Sheep's Foot Lane, which led down to the workhouse next to the lunatic asylum and Boundary Park, the home ground of Oldham Athletic Football Club. We were now halfway to Houghton Street, where the Ashtons lived at the foot of Oldham Edge. As we turned into Houghton Street we could smell the warm loaves and muffins, which gave us a fillip for the last fifty yards. Breathless and flushed, we raced through the open door, John to fling his arms around the knees of Grandma Ashton, who held her arms wide so as not to embrace him in her flour-caked arms.

Grandma Ashton wasn't thin and austere like Grandma Stacey but dumpy and warm, always with a tired smile on her face, wearied by years of caring, feeding and bringing up her daughters, Auntie Emmy, Auntie Edna and of course our mother, Florrie. Her only son, Stanley, had been killed at Mons during the Great War and I don't think he had been twenty years old. Grandma Ashton was the rock upon which the whole family depended. Granddad Ashton always seemed to be sitting by the fireplace, even in summer, and like Great-grandpa Wilson, staring into the glowing coals, a lopsided grin on his face.

The fireplace was the focal point of most households then, and even some of the poorest managed to find coal. During the winter our mother and father sat on each side of the grate, us children standing, the gas mantle flickering behind us as the wind whistled malevolently through the keyhole of the back door. Sadly in the present day the fire has been replaced by central heating, paradoxically warm yet heartless, and the fireplace is no longer the focal point of a room. Again regretfully families now sit grouped round the television set and this modern world is no better for the change. In the burning coals you could see whatever picture you wished, but from a television you only get what you are given.

Now I've got that off my chest, back to Grandma Ashton's. Whenever she baked, there was always a small lump of dough for John and me, which we shaped into little men; currants for buttons and eyes, then into the oven with them. I really looked forward to going to Grandma Ashton's. It was fun, especially once when John and I stayed the night. It was a great adventure, sleeping in a strange bed, and when the night lightened into morning we were yacketing excitedly together when the door opened and Auntie Emmy and Auntie Edna, still in their nighties, sprang into the room, Auntie Edna wielding a sabre. We dived under the covers, shivering with fright, and screaming for Auntie Edna to spare us, while Auntie Emmy was laughing fit to bust.

The memory of that sabre has always fascinated me. I took for granted that it had once been issued to Granddad Ashton. It was the weapon of cavalry; ergo Granddad Ashton in his youth fought his battles on horseback – that is, if he had ever seen action. Perhaps he had been too young for the Charge of the Light Brigade, but surely he must have been in some other battle. Come to think of it, I never ever heard him say anything. In any case, I wasn't old enough to think of a question.

Apart from John, the only other person I'd ever really taken to was Auntie Emmy. She always looked upon me with kindness and understanding. Whenever I visited the Ashtons with John, Auntie Emmy invariably greeted me with a warm smile, as if we were two conspirators with a hidden agenda, although such a highfallutin philosophy never entered my head, let alone crossed my mind. Auntie Emmy must have known about my real mother's death; in fact everyone was in the know – except me. I was a rowing boat adrift on a foggy night in the busy shipping lanes of the channel. Perhaps that is why she took a special interest in me, though not, I must add, out of pity, and the rapport between us was genuine.

On one occasion when I had a raging toothache it was Auntie Emmy who took me to the dentist, an old man who must have gained his degree in the nineteenth century when possibly the only dental appliance was a pair of pliers. His surgery was the front room of his house, lit only by two gas mantles. He wore an old cardigan and a shirt fastened at the neck by a stud but with no collar.

Pushing his glasses on to his forehead, he gazed short-sightedly into my mouth. 'Which one is it?' he asked.

I looked across at Auntie Emmy.

'You have to show him,' she said helpfully.

I was at a loss for a moment. For most people visiting the dentist the toothache seems to disappear the moment they step over the threshold, and so it was with me, and I was afraid that I might point out the wrong one.

Luckily he put his finger in my mouth and waggled a tooth, and the pain was instantaneous. I jerked violently.

'I thought it was,' he said complacently, blissfully unaware of how close he'd come to losing a finger.

However, it was a quick, efficient extraction and triumphantly he held out the molar for me to see. There was a dark hole in it, no wonder it had caused me so much suffering. I was delighted and amazed that it had all been so quick and painless. I smiled at Auntie Emmy and was even more amazed when the dentist patted me on the head, called me a brave little man and gave me a toffee – a toffee of all things! He was probably looking forward to seeing me again in the very near future.

When we returned to Grandma Ashton's, I gave the toffee to John and then we had tea – well, they had tea, but I had to make do with a glass of milk because I was in no condition to eat. But my day wasn't ended. It was dark when Mother, John and I got on the tram. Mother was between John and me and I was squashed between her and a dozing old man. Why we had to sit there was beyond me; after all, apart from us and the conductor the tram was empty. No one spoke as the tram buckled and clattered up Oldham Road, and then almost imperceptibly the old man closed his eyes and began singing softly to himself in a cracked, tuneless voice. I was intrigued, and I turned my head to observe him more closely. Immediately Mother put her hand under my chin and whipped my head smartly to the front. After a short time I slowly turned to look at him again furtively and what impressed me most was his nose. It was large, round, extremely red and pockmarked, but before I could take a closer look my head was jerked back to neutral. The old man was still singing when we got off and straight away as the tram disappeared I asked Mother what was the matter with him, but Mother was reluctant to answer and I wondered if she'd heard me. Then she said, 'That's what you get from eating too much pork.' This explanation, brooking no argument, knocked me flat. I was so impressed that I never got round to asking about the man's nose; and it had such a profound effect on me that I avoided pork until I was well into my twenties, although I must have consumed buckets of alcohol since Dad bought me my first half a pint on my sixteenth birthday. The lesson to be learned here is: don't muck about with the truth when dealing with children.

Now in the year 2003 I'm at my desk wearing headphones as I listen to a programme on the radio. I sit back in my chair staring at the ceiling wherein lies inspiration when, half listening to the disembodied voice from the radio, a man is urging us to clean up our rivers. This doesn't particularly concern me as I don't own one but his next remark has my full attention. The voice mentions Manchester Ship Canal. Immediately my mind races back to when I was about ten years old and standing on the bank of the Manchester Ship Canal, clutching a damp towel round my thin white shoulders, my lips blue with cold, teeth chattering like a pair of demented castanets, and looking round occasionally in case there was an approaching bobby, because swimming, splashing about and especially diving or jumping off the lock gates were strictly forbidden. We weren't too bothered, though. In the event of a constable hurrying towards us, we'd simply jump into the water and swim to the opposite bank, and scrambling out we would pull faces at the sweating arm of the law, the width of the scum-laden, smelly canal protecting us. The police must have been aware of this tactic and wisely kept away – they had better things to do.

Deciding it might be warmer in the water, I was about to jump in when I noticed a small black object floating through the half-open, decaying lock gates. As it moved slowly towards the shrieking, juvenile, splashing mêlée, I was able to see what it was: a poor, dead dog floating majestically along, legs stiff and pointing to the sky. I quickly shouted a warning. I had to shout twice over the hullabaloo, pointing at the dog. When they realised what it was, there was panic as they parted to allow the dog unhindered passage to its Valhalla – just another incident on the turgid Manchester Ship Canal.

Returning to the present, I turn up the volume of my radio to hear the news that now at last the Manchester Ship Canal has been cleansed and purified, oxygenised or whatever, and for the first time in living memory can be enjoyed by the natural inhabitants, fish. But then the marine expert goes on to say, 'In the old days, anyone found frolicking about in the oil-scummed waters of the canal was unceremoniously hauled out and rushed off to hospital to have their stomach pumped.' On this note I switch off, and once again stare at the ceiling, recalling the dead-dog incident. It wasn't unusual – sometimes dead cats, rags of clothing and unmentionables floated calmly along – and when the weather was unusually hot there was always a gang of young herberts splashing about among the jetsam. To my knowledge none of us went down with malaria, typhoid, yellow fever or beri beri. The only real threat was hypothermia, and certainly no one was hauled out and rushed off to the infirmary to have their stomach pumped. I can only assume that in those days our bodies developed an immunity to diseases not yet known to man.

It's a good job my father didn't get to hear about my frolicking in the Manchester Ship Canal. He had never chastised me physically before, not even a slap round my bottom, but if he found out he would be driven to break the rule of a lifetime. Luckily for me he never showed any interest in where I'd been, who I'd been with or how I'd managed to rip my jersey. If he'd asked me, I would have answered him truthfully – we lived in a moral climate. However, I was apprehensive that day when I returned home from the Manchester Ship Canal, hair all damp and spiky, that he would say something like 'Where the dickens have you been?' and like George Washington I would have to tell him.

One Saturday morning I came running into the house, not because it was cold outside, nor because it was dinnertime. The explanation was simple: I hadn't been out for more than a couple of minutes and was idly chucking stones at the lamppost just outside when Jack had lolloped out of the ginnel and barked at me. Jack was a wirehaired brindle dog and we had a mutual dislike for each other. He'd never forgotten that I'd once hit him with a stick when he'd had his back to me. He'd been more shocked than hurt and, ashamed of his cowardice, he'd been after me ever since. It was an unfair contest, as he had teeth and could run faster than me. Luckily I wasn't too far from our vestibule door, but even as I slammed it on his slavering chops he kept up his barking and frantic scratching on the door.

I sauntered into the kitchen.

Mother said, 'Hark at that! What have you done to him now?'

And taking John by the hand, she brushed past me, opened the door and shooed Jack away, and he went without further argument. While she was gone I noticed a near stranger in the room. It was my brother Vernon, and he was looking at me as if he could smell something nobody else could. My father was sitting in front of the fire, reading *The Green Final*, a newspaper someone had left in the tram on his way home from work the night before. My father wasn't actually reading it as he was in the middle of an argument with Vernon, which I had inadvertently interrupted. Vernon was on one of his visits, and he always seemed to upset Dad, who was used to overlookers and managers berating him at work but was definitely against being taken to the cleaners by his eldest son.

'Dad,' said Vernon, 'you don't understand . . .'

I didn't wait to find out what was beyond my father's comprehension. I'd seen the signs on his face, which was the colour of a Cox's orange pippin.

I went to Mother and John at the front and listened attentively while she discussed the price of bread with Mrs Turner, our neighbour. I've no idea how the battle in the kitchen went, but for the next few days we were three in the bed. By the time Vernon came upstairs John and I were usually asleep, but what I did learn during his stay with us was that his real home was with his Grandma Stacey in a beautiful house where everyone had a chair to sit on at meals and he didn't have to stand at the table as we did to eat. The way Vernon had always spoken of Grandma Stacey, Great-grandpa and Great-grandma Wilson you'd think they were all closely related to royalty, and his disdain for 36 Leslie Street and all its occupants was plain for all to see. Poor deluded Vernon. It never crossed my mind that if he was related to the Staceys, so was I.

*   *   *

Birthdays came and went like any other day; we neither received nor sent cards, as they were unaffordable luxuries – in fact I don't think newsagents in our area even stocked them. But Christmas was something else. A few days before the 'big one', most houses began their preparations: sagging paper chains of merry colours criss-crossed the room from gas mantle to any other protuberance on the opposite wall, and small Christmas trees, festooned with tinsel and cotton wool, always sprouted in practically every home and certainly where there were children.

One particular Christmas Vernon, John and I had been saving for months to buy a present for Mother. Vernon was now permanently home but much more likeable, so he hadn't been completely brainwashed and he didn't argue with Dad as he would have in the past. On Christmas Eve the 'old 'uns' had gone out for the evening and with our pooled resources Vernon (ten), John (six) and I (eight) stole out of the house into the darkness of the Mucky Broos. Puffed, we dropped to a stroll by the chapel round by Robin Hill Baths and made an excited final burst up Barker Street to the lights of the shops. It was then that we received our first shock. There was a phalanx of people, almost a solid wall of Christmas Eve shoppers, all in good humour but unfortunately for us impenetrable. The three of us held hands tightly, John in the middle hemmed in by a sea of raincoats, great coats, long jerseys and scarves. To say we were frightened would be an understatement. It was only about seven o'clock and the shops didn't close till nine. To add to our folly, none of us had any idea what sort of present we were looking for. Panic-stricken, I held tightly on to John's hand – if I let go I might never see my brothers again. John wasn't tall enough to see above the midriffs and I wasn't tall enough to look anyone in the eye. Desperately we tried to retrace our steps – after all, we could always postpone giving a present until Easter – but there was no way out. There was a sudden surge of people behind us and we found ourselves in an ironmonger's shop. Thankfully it was fairly empty, which was hardly surprising, as nails, baths, hammers and bicycle chains are not at the top of everyone's Christmas shopping list, but it would do for us: the sooner we got back to the sanctity of the familiar and peaceful Leslie Street the better. Pointing to a saucepan up on a shelf, Vernon asked the price. He seemed to know what he was doing, and John and I watched him, our mouths agape with admiration. Vernon took a knotted hankie out of his pocket and watched the man count out the contents; Mother would have a Christmas present after all.

Our Christmas mornings were predictable yet wonderful. Like most other children on Christmas morning, we woke well before our normal reveilles in eager anticipation of the most exciting day of the year. Our stockings, which had hung over the fireplace the night before, were now at the foot of our bed. Kneeling quickly up in the bed, we took a stocking – it didn't matter which as they were all the same, each lumpy with an apple, an orange and some nuts. This was only the prelude: there would be more goodies under the tree downstairs. This Christmas morning, when it was light enough, we marched into Mother's bedroom – she was still in bed but Dad was downstairs lighting the fire – and Vernon and I pushed John forward. He proudly held out the saucepan as we all piped 'Merry Christmas, Mother.' After we were dressed, and it didn't take us long as we all slept in our shirts anyway, as we clattered downstairs we could see the rosy flickering on the kitchen wall reflected from the cheery fire in the grate. Dad hurried upstairs with a cup of tea for Mother and the hurly-burly of another Christmas Day began.

Every year our main present was always a Cadbury's Selection box, which we joyously received as if it was a surprise, but the real surprise was usually a present we could all share. This year it was a Meccano set, which we pounced upon eagerly because, according to the blurb, with Meccano we could build anything. For the rest of the morning screws and nuts littered the floor as we salivated at the delicious aroma coming from the stove as Mother cooked the dinner. And what a meal it turned out to be: Yorkshire pudding with onion gravy to start with, followed by rabbit, roast potatoes and cabbage. When the table was a ruin of bones, bits of cabbage and dirty plates, we all thanked Mother, who said it was much easier to cook now with a new saucepan. Even to this day I bet that if we were all granted a wish for something to eat our answer would be unanimous: a rabbit.

For the evening party we all went down to Grandma Ashton's for the traditional fun and games in which we children and the adults took part. When we arrived at 8 Houghton Street, there was already a Christmassy feel about the evening, with laughter, warm spicy smells, holly around the picture of Uncle Stanley, mistletoe in a strategic position over the door, and on the table Mint Imperials, mince pies and, best of all, luscious black Pontefract cakes like the buttons on an undertaker's overcoat. Cups of tea for the ladies, something stronger for the men; we had sarsaparilla from large stone bottles, which when empty would be filled with boiling water to warm many a cold bed.

The games were the same as last year, but who remembers, and what does it matter? We children were led one at a time into a darkened kitchen; I was the first to go. I was told to kneel, facing a large white cloth, behind which the light of a torch shone through, and was instructed in a sepulchral voice to put my nose against the light and follow its every movement. My nose never left the light, which I followed slowly up the cloth, and as my head cleared the top a cold, wet sponge was slapped into my face, I yelped, everybody in the kitchen laughed and I joined them. John and Vernon both yelped as I did, and I laughed before the grown-ups because I knew what was going to happen. This was turning out to be a really great Christmas.

Gleaming with excitement at the thought of the next romp, the three of us were in the kitchen, which was now lit by candles. Auntie Emmy started to blindfold me, and so I assumed that I was to be first again for whatever was in store. She led me from the kitchen into the front room, where I was helped to step up on to a plank of wood, and again the sepulchral voice informed me what was to happen: 'You are going on a flight and you must be very brave.' Already I was trembling, especially when the board I was standing on began to rise up and up and up, until finally I banged my head and the sepulchral voice went on, 'You have just hit the ceiling, and now you must jump.' I was petrified: I couldn't possibly jump down from where I was at the top of the room. But they urged me on, and eventually I took a deep breath and gave an almighty leap. There was a roar of laughter as Auntie Emmy took off the blindfold and the realisation dawned that I had only really been lifted about six inches. Sheepishly I smiled – it was such a simple mind-over-matter diversion. Auntie Emmy had been kneeling in front while I was blindfolded and as the three-foot plank was being slowly lifted by Dad and Joe Waterhouse, an uncle in waiting until he married Auntie Emmy, Auntie Edna had bumped a book on top of my head, which I took to be the ceiling, and the illusion was complete.

Vernon was next. He wasn't petrified at all and when Auntie Edna banged the book on top of his head, he just smiled and whipped off his blindfold to loud groans of disappointment – he must have remembered last year's party. John didn't have a go as he was already fast asleep, and it was time for us to be taken home, leaving the grown-ups to their own Christmas games.

Grandma Ashton's seemed to be a meeting place for all our relations. I recall evenings when Dad, Uncle Joe and two other men I cannot bring to mind played cribbage for a ha'penny a point. Before the cards were even shuffled, the curtains had to be drawn and the front door locked, as gambling was illegal – such was our respect for the police, which in this present day sounds over-cautious, as the players neither lost nor won more than tuppence an evening.

Northmoor Council School, built before the Boer War, was about half an hour's walk from across the Mucky Broos up Chadderton Road, past a huge black shiny boulder on the left, which was reputed to be a meteorite from outer space, awesome in itself and, even more frighteningly, said to be bewitched and evil. I never walked by it without crossing my fingers, looking straight ahead, although I watched it out of the corner of my eye in case it did something untoward. That was my daily journey to school, my first small step on the road to education, but after that fatuous fanfare I can recall only very little of my early schooldays.

Question: 'How old were you when you enrolled?'
Answer: 'Don't know.'
Question: 'What was the name of the headmaster?'
Answer: 'She was a headmistress.'
Question: 'What was her name?'
Answer: 'No idea.'

It would be a very dull interview indeed. I remember the head-mistress, a motherly, plumpish lady with white hair, for one unforgettable incident. Every morning, first thing, the whole school assembled for prayers, which culminated with a hymn: the headmistress stepped on to a podium, took up her baton and raised it – this was the only still moment of her performance – and then, crash, bang, wallop, we were off . . . Arms flailing about, she conducted with gusto in a way reminiscent of a flight controller on board an aircraft carrier guiding a drunken trainee pilot down on to the deck. Not only was it fascinating to watch, but on one particular occasion there was a highlight yet to come. So frenetic was her conducting that there was a flash of colour beneath the hem of her frock and a voluptuous red garter made its appearance, slid down her leg and rested round her ankle. We all waited for the other garter to appear, but we were disappointed. Sadly the garter never appeared again and I assumed she had bought herself a pair of braces. That is my only recollection of the headmistress. In fact I cannot bring to mind other members of the staff, even though they stood behind the headmistress at prayers.

I invariably looked forward to playtime, unless it was raining, when I would have to stand shivering under a sheltered bit of the schoolyard with the others who didn't possess raincoats. No one except the staff was allowed to remain in school during playtime. Worse still, we could see the teachers staring through the rain-spattered windows in order to keep an eye on us, steaming cups of tea in their hands, and biscuits. As we watched enviously there was a sound of thunder, but in fact it was the rumbling of a mass of small stomachs at the sight of the biscuits. When the weather was good playtime would be a blessing – a shrieking, screaming, laughing riot of sound, skipping ropes for the girls and tennis balls kicked all over the place by the lads. One of the more popular games was Jubby. Kneeling, we flipped marbles or glass alleys into a small dent in a corner of the school yard and then we – unfortunately I have forgotten what we did then, but we enjoyed it.

Alongside the 'Jubby bandits', another line of kneeling raga-muffins played in pairs a game of Skimmy On. This entailed skimming tab cards alternately at two other cards leaning up against the wall. If you knocked one over, you scooped up all the cards that had missed the target: then another card was placed up against the wall and round two was on. To see these lines of 'skimmers' and their intense concentration was like observing Northmoor's version of one-armed bandits in Las Vegas. Incidentally, those tab cards, better known as cigarette cards, came in most packets of cigarettes. They disappeared about fifty years ago, if not more, and as cigarettes are not politically correct I don't envisage those wonderful educational cigarette cards coming back, more's the pity.

Another memory of Northmoor's is when, after school had ended one day, I dashed out into the pouring rain. It was bucketing down and I was in two minds as to whether to run back into school or swim home. I did neither and, ducking my head, I raced across the street, only to find that the pavement was dry. When I turned round I discovered that the monsoon on the other side of the street was still pelting down. I stared at this phenomenon, a solid wall of rain two yards away. After a short time I rushed off home to relate this extraordinary experience. I expected amazement or at least astonishment, but all I got in reply was a bored, 'It didn't rain here.' That's all I can remember about Northmoor Council School ... funny about the garter, though.

Every Saturday morning Dad sent me up to Grandma Sykes to see if she wanted any errands to be done. This was odd, because he and Mother were reluctant to send me on errands at home. Many years later my father told me that he would never send me out on errands because of my woolly-headedness. I would very likely not remember which shop I was going to, and even if I arrived at the right place I would have forgotten why I was there. Why, then, did Father send me to Grandma Sykes to see if she wanted any errands done? It couldn't be because he disliked her – after all, she was his mother. Perhaps he just wanted me out of the way for a time. When I arrived at Grandma Sykes I asked her about it, but she just smiled, shook her head and sent me off on an errand, which was no answer at all. It must have been preying on my mind, because I went into the butcher's and asked for five pounds of King Edwards, and by the time I reached the greengrocer's I'd forgotten the potatoes and came out with a cabbage. Grandma sighed heavily, took the cabbage from me, donned a shawl over her head and we made our way to the shop together. As we walked, she casually remarked that she and Granddad Sykes together with Aunt Marie, Dad's younger sister, and Uncle Ernest, Dad's brother, would soon be moving in with us. This information was of such importance that it banished all the other rubbish from my mind.

Two or three days later, the invasion was upon us. They hadn't far to come, as they lived in Tilbury Street, which ran along the top of Leslie Street. Everything they owned was carried from their house to ours – the cost of a removal van would have been infinitely more than the value of their assets. My father and Granddad Sykes staggered down the path lugging a large double bed, followed by Grandma Sykes and a neighbour edging sideways holding a mattress between them as if inciting the watchers to jump out of their bedroom windows on to it, Aunt Marie, with an armful of blankets and not far behind Uncle Ernest, hidden under a moth-eaten armchair, slipping and slithering in front of me. 'Every little helps,' they said, handing me an ashtray – 'A Present from Hastings' – and a three-legged stool which must have been handed down through generations of farmers.

Stanley Taylor, who was walking out with Aunt Marie, lurched along the uneven ground with a ragged, worn-out carpet on his shoulder. Mercifully it was rolled up, and so its threadbare condition was hidden from the critical watchers. As the column made its way to number thirty-six it must have been reminiscent of

Dr Livingstone's first expedition into darkest Africa. Within a few more hours the Tilbury Street house was stripped bare, and that evening the changeover was complete. Granddad and Grandma Sykes, Aunt Marie and Uncle Ernest had finally made 36 Leslie Street their new home.

So now there were nine residents: Granddad Sykes's family in the front bedroom, and in the back bedroom Dad and Mother in their corner and John, me and Vernon in the bed opposite. Nowadays it would be deemed overcrowding but to Father it was halving the rent.

Our house, like millions of others, had four rooms, two up and two down, but the hub of all this domesticity, the nerve centre, the engine room, was the kitchen, the one room that was communal. Nine of us ate our staggered meals there. Washing up, washing clothes and washing ourselves took place at the sink, which was next to the stove. Breakfast time was the busiest period before the workers left. No one wide awake enough to converse muttered 'Look at the time' or 'Is there any Shredded Wheat?' It was feverish, like a railway buffet when the train is due in. During melancholy moments I fervently wished we could have our kitchen back and our own bedroom, but almost immediately I would be ashamed of my uncharitable thoughts.

Grandma Sykes was my favourite. Once I returned home from my primary school, stiff-legged, tearful and as far down in the depths of despair as I'd ever been because I'd messed my pants and had been sent home to get myself cleaned up; it was this disgusted dismissal in front of the class that had been the final straw. However, when I entered our front door I was met by Grandma Sykes. She was on her own and when she saw me she wasn't cross or anything. She just said, 'Come on, let's get you cleaned up.' Then she lifted me on to the draining board, and took off my shoes and stockings so that I could put my feet in the sink. 'By jingo,' she remarked as she peeled off my pants. 'What have you been eating? Any farmer would pay good money for this lot.' In spite of myself I chuckled, and by the time I'd been cleaned and dried, and had half a slice of bread and dripping in my hand, I felt a wave of warm affection for her. I stood in front of the fire, watching the steam rising from my damp, clean pants, and when everybody came home that evening Grandma didn't utter a word about the drama that had taken place earlier in the afternoon; it was our secret. So as far as I was concerned, I'd be happy for Granny to stay with us for ever.

Granddad didn't say much. He and Uncle Ernest worked at the same place, and when they came home in the evening, Granddad washed his hands and face at the sink, followed by Uncle Ernest. Then they'd sit down for their supper, which was usually a plateful of baked beans, and as I had eaten much earlier the sight of Granddad and Uncle Ernest slurping their way through those delicious baked beans had me salivating. To be hungry was the norm, but it didn't help to be constantly reminded of it.

I saw very little of Aunt Marie. She was very rarely home by the time I went to bed. She worked in a shoe shop along with a man called Stan Taylor, and it wasn't long before they were courting. She never brought him home to meet her parents, but that was understandable – where would he sit? And a meal was out of the question, unless he brought his own. Many, many months later they were married and the mystery man became my Uncle Stan. I met him for the first time at some family gathering or other and I took a shine to him from that moment. I secretly observed him standing in a little group of relatives. He had a perpetual smile on his lips, and occasionally he would nod at something.

The discussion was apparently about Stanley Baldwin, our Prime Minister – I knew that because Granddad talked of little else. Everyone put in his four pence except Stan. He didn't utter a word, but nodded now and again, raising his eyebrows at something or other. I was waiting for him to join in but he didn't, and I came to the conclusion that he must be a very wise man who kept his counsel; or to look at it another way he could be stone deaf and couldn't hear a word anybody said. Anyway, Aunt Marie was the first to spread her wings. When she and Stan married they went to live in a little village called New Longton, not too far from Preston, away from Oldham for privacy but close enough in case of emergencies.

Uncle Ernest was next to go. Still in his mid-teens, he enlisted in the Royal Navy and in peacetime that seemed like a pretty smart move – sailing the high seas, three meals a day, not much pay but regular, and when he'd served his twelve years he'd still be young enough and with sufficient skills to obtain a steady job ashore. So his departure from 36 Leslie Street left only Granddad and Grandma. Two down and two to go, but already I was missing Aunt Marie and Uncle Ernest. Is there anything so fickle as a child's thoughts?

As a child I was a very sickly specimen. In fact my father told me many years later that a doctor, shaking his head sadly as he looked at me, said, 'You'll never rear him.' Naturally, being but a few months old, I was totally unaware of the doctor's opinion and I simply continued to live. On the other hand when John came into the world he must have shone like the evening star. He was a beautiful baby, radiant, healthy and, judging by his ever-present smile, comfortable with his surroundings. It was inconceivable that any germ or virus would defile such a perfectly healthy child. Hospitals weren't full of little 'uns like John; the wards were more likely to be occupied by people like me. On the other hand, it is all clearly logical if you think about it: what self-respecting germ is going to be satisfied with a stale crust when there's a leg of lamb on the table? Poor John happened to be the latter, and he was carried off to hospital with scarlet fever. I was mortified, and the atmosphere at home was dark and sombre, as if the gas mantle had gone out and we didn't have enough for the meter. Weeks seemed like months, but it all ended happily when Mother collected him from hospital, and although it was foggy outside the sun was in our hearts. But it left me with a sobering thought: if scarlet fever could happen to John, was I next in line, and would Dad start worrying all over again if it was possible to rear me?

Illness struck once more, and to everyone's astonishment it wasn't me. It was Vernon this time and, more serious than scarlet fever, he had the dreaded diphtheria, which was high up on the mortality list. Why Vernon? He'd always looked pretty healthy to me – after all, he'd virtually been brought up at the Staceys' on a more balanced diet, too costly for Leslie Street. Prunes and custard don't encourage diphtheria, so why him? Truthfully if I could have changed places with Vernon I would not have hesitated. I felt better equipped to deal with illness than either John or Vernon.

On that black day the clang of the ambulance bell opened practically every front door in Leslie Street, not out of idle curiosity but because the residents were bonded together by a genuine concern and sympathy for the grieving household. Inside 36 Leslie Street, as we waited apprehensively while a burly ambulance man was upstairs preparing Vernon for his admittance, something extraordinary happened: a little black bird flew in through the open front door into the kitchen, turned and flew out again. My stomach was gripped by a cold foreboding. It was a bad omen. A few moments later, the ambulance man made his way carefully downstairs, carrying Vernon, wrapped in a blanket, his face white and bloodless, and his eyes closed as his head lolled against the ambulance man's chest. I was convinced that I'd never see Vernon again, but, God be praised, as usual I was being over-dramatic. After some weeks, or it may have been longer, Vernon was cured and discharged from hospital. Dad walked him home and what a joy it was when he arrived! Mother, John and I shared a huge smile of welcome. In those long-forgotten days in the north-west we were certainly not demonstrative, but our faces said it all. We were a whole family again. It had been a harrowing time – first John smitten by scarlet fever, and then Vernon struck down with diphtheria – and the most I could contribute was a runny nose.

Oddly enough for a delicate child, I never saw the inside of a hospital, not even to visit John and Vernon; but I hadn't escaped completely unscathed. I was laid low for a few days with mandatory mumps, and I must say I quite enjoyed the experience, propped up in the bed with hot milk; and, best of all, Grandma Sykes brought me a comic to read every day, wiped my face with a warm flannel and combed my hair. I'd never had such personal care and attention in my life.

On the day of the doctor's visit, Grandma Sykes was like a nervous chicken awaiting a fox, plumping up the pillows, giving my face an extra shine, stuffing the comic in a drawer, even running a damp cloth over knobs on the bed rail until there was a rat-a-tat-tat on the front door. Grandma smoothed her apron and gave me a warning look as if to say, 'Don't go away.'

Dr Law was respected by the whole community, where it was generally accepted that he was a fine man. I'd seen him in his surgery a few times – once just to pick up a prescription for cough mixture, and on another occasion when John had pink eye and I went with him – and on each occasion Dr Law was seated behind his desk, which we had to go round so that he could examine little patients without having to bend down. On the two days when he had called at our house about the scarlet fever and diphtheria I hadn't been at home, and I'd never actually seen him standing up, so when he had to duck his head to enter the bedroom where I was prostrate with mumps I got quite a shock. He was immense, well over six feet tall; his brown hair had an off-centre parting, and he exuded good health and breeding in stark contrast to the pinched white faces of undernourished Lancashire.

As he approached the bed, he spoke in a deep, melodious Irish brogue. 'And how are you this morning, young man?'

Grandma, following him in, brought up a chair.

'Thank you,' he said in a dark velvet voice that made her blush, and he sat down to put his stethoscope on my chest. ''Tis a fine morning,' he said as he listened to my heartbeat.

I nodded, as it was still uncomfortable to speak.

He stood up and, placing his stethoscope in his bag, he said, 'You'll do.' Then he nodded and Grandma saw him out.

When they'd left the room, I slipped out of bed and wobbled over to the window. As Dr Law climbed into his trap, he said a last few words to Grandma, raised his trilby to her, and then slapped his reins on the pony's rump and clip-clopped to his next patient. Oh, if only I could grow up to be half as good a man as Dr Law.

There was only one drawback to the billeting arrangements. At five thirty every weekday morning, the knocker-up came, a man shouldering a long pole with wire prongs on the end of it with which he tapped on the front bedroom window like brushes on a snare drum to let my father know that it was time to rise and shine. However, Granddad was in the front bedroom now, and so he had to scramble out of bed in his shirt, tippy-toe to the window, push it up and stick his head out to let the knocker-up know that they'd got the message; then, pulling the window down, he tiptoed on the cold oil cloth into our bedroom to wake up my father. This done, he'd tiptoe back to his own still-warm bed, because his place of work was closer and he didn't have to get up until seven thirty – what luxury!

The services of the knocker-up cost my father a penny a week. Imagine: on those cold, dark, winter mornings, the unfortunate man would have to tap, tap on bedroom windows 240 times a week just to earn a pound, barely enough to keep him out of the workhouse. And by the way Granddad didn't tiptoe in order to be quiet: if he'd put his feet flat down in winter they might have stuck to the below-zero linoleum.

Talking of shirts: they were the standard sleep attire for males; the ladies wore nighties. We all knew about pyjamas, of course – we'd learned about them from American films. We were aware that the well-to-do brushed their teeth, but a toothbrush had yet to make its appearance in our house or in any other domicile on our patch. Most of the grown-ups ate with false teeth, their smiles a bright uniform plastic. These dentures were heirlooms and, like spectacles, were handed down. Using these was better than having porridge at each meal.

Across the road from the top of Houghton Street where the Ashtons lived was the start of Oldham Edge, a large area of sparsely grassed ups and downs that could have originally been a breakaway from the Pennine chain. It was bisected from the Royton end to the heights of Oldham by a straight road in desperate need of repair possibly, in fact almost certainly, built by the ancient Romans. The whole hilly, hummocky area rose to magnificent views of commercial Oldham. A dozen or more black factory chimneys belched dark smoke straight up on a rare calm day but in a capricious wind all the smoke would suddenly veer at right angles to the chimneys and then move as one in another direction like synchronised smoking. On Sundays, however, there was no such entertainment as the cotton mills enjoyed a day of rest and it was on these days that the workers – the younger ones, that is – got together for their sport on Oldham Edge. In the summer there was cricket, but there were not many matches because of the weather and because flat bits of Oldham Edge were sparse. In the winter there were games of football requiring unknown talents when dribbling along the side of the hill, which had piles of clothing at either end for goalposts.

I once played footie one Sunday when the light wasn't good and ominous dark clouds had been assembling since early morning until the whole of the sky was black. I can't remember how the game was afoot when the heavy leather ball flew over my head and before I could pull myself together I was trampled under a stampede of players. There must have been forty or fifty a side on that pitch, and as they were mostly young men wearing ordinary working clothes it was difficult to know who was on the opposing team. How I got involved in the first place, wearing my only shirt and an old pair of off-white army underpants over my own short pants, I'll never know. Then the ball went over my head again, this time in the opposite direction, and I was faced by a sweating mob chasing the ball. I didn't hesitate: I joined them. I could have been trampled to death. Then, to make matters worse, the monsoon broke, as heavy a deluge as I'd ever seen. Immediately the pace of the game eased up. It had to, as within a few minutes large areas of Oldham Edge were waterlogged and to kick a ball when it was floating was against all the rules of the game. Everything spluttered to a halt when one of the young bucks picked up the ball and walked disconsolately homewards, and everyone slouched off. It was too late for running and we were all wet through.

Hair plastered to my head, I went as well, but not home. The nearest port of call was 8 Houghton Street. When I knocked on the front door it was opened by Auntie Edna, and straight away she turned to shout into the room, 'Another survivor from the *Titanic*.'

I later discovered that I'd turned up at the wrong football match: I should have been enjoying a kickabout with other little boys half a mile away.

Standing on the bed one day, I found that I could just about reach the bulkhead, a small space beneath the rafters, and I was curious to know if anything was stored there. I wasn't tall enough to see, but by swinging my arm about I came into contact with a leather suitcase. I swept it down on to the bed in a cloud of dust. It wasn't heavy, and so at first I thought it must be empty, but when I opened it I found an old dog-eared hardback book, with a yellow cover, entitled *Tudor Kings and Queens of England*. I wasn't too interested, because my attention was drawn to the lining of the suitcase, which was an old newspaper. I opened it out and my eye was taken by drawings of slim young women advertising dresses buttoned at the neck but with skirts down to the calves – very daring, as the paper must have been at least ten years old and the present year was barely into the 1930s. It had the latest styles, mind you, all priced under a pound, and the most modern handbags from Italy, less than ten bob. There were no photographs in the newspaper just drawings. How I wish now that I'd kept it to the present day, but then again how many things would I have kept had I 'some power the giftie gie us' (Robbie Burns). I was just about to close the case and chuck it back when a sudden thought swept through my mind. *Tudor Kings and Queens of England*? I'd never read a book in my life but there's always a first time. Taking the book downstairs, I sat on a buffet and flipped through the pages. I realised that it was going to be a stiff test because it contained no pictures.

Chapter One and I embarked on my first literary expedition. Page two, page three – diligently I read every word, not understanding any of them. By dinnertime I was three parts through the turgid, boring kings and queens of England, but with a slice of bread buttered with condensed milk I pressed on. Dad, who was out of work in the depression of the thirties, came home after a fruitless job hunt, took off his cap, coat and scarf and, seeing that I was already eating my dinner, stuck a slice of bread on the end of the toasting fork and held it over the fire. I wished I'd thought of that, but then again condensed milk and toast was unthinkable. I went back to my book. I hadn't far to go now, and I was devouring the book page by page, reading every word religiously. I even read what some unknown had written on the bottom of page 163: in a spidery hand he'd scrawled, 'Remind Amy about Saturday.' I remember turning the corner of the page down in case I might want to read it again. It was intriguing . . . Perhaps Amy was his intended, or maybe they were already married and what was happening on Saturday? A dance, a football match . . . Ah, but could the writer be a girl and Amy her best friend? I stared unseeing at the page before me, and then I pulled myself together and concentrated – only a few more pages to go now.

Eventually near teatime I came to the most wonderful part of the book: just two words, 'The End'. Snapping the book shut I stood up and stretched. I'd been hunched for hours but it had been worth it.

I casually edged towards my father and said, 'Dad, I've just read a book,' as if I'd been awarded the Nobel Peace Prize.

He said, 'What's it about?'

I stared at him blankly. I was flummoxed. Wasn't it enough that I'd read it? After all, that was the achievement – surely I didn't have to understand it as well. On second thoughts it might have been better to have counted the words instead of reading them. Then I could have said, 'Dad, there are twenty-five thousand, four hundred and twenty-six words in this book, not counting the title.' I just looked at him. He was staring at me pitifully, as if I was slightly backward, and on reflection I think he had a point.

I can't ever recollect my father having a serious talk with me or anyone else for that matter. He was a quiet, gentle person and never, ever, did I hear Dad swear, to the day he died in 1972, but if provoked beyond all endurance he always used the same innocent alternative. It was 'broad lastic', uttered through gritted teeth. It scared the daylights out of us. I know it sounds innocuous, but throughout my life I probably heard as many expletives as any other veteran, and none as dangerous as 'broad lastic' when growled by my father.

He was a man of principles and on election day he would vote Conservative, the only one in a community of staunch, long-live, die-hard Labourites. Dad even put a photo of our local Tory candidate in the front window. This was unfortunate for John and me when on the day before the votes were counted the young sons of Labour supporters came out with rolled-up yellow paper bound by string, which they whirled about their heads, and lambasted us for betraying the working class. However, on the following day all was forgotten and we carried on playing together as if nothing had happened, which was true as the Liberals usually got in.

Every Sunday, while other tired, weary fathers lay a-bed till dinnertime, our dad was preparing himself for his morning's hobby: he was a campanologist or, in common parlance, a bell-ringer.

Whatever the weather, he would stride across the Mucky Broos to St Mary's Parish Church, not in his drab, worn, workaday clobber, but completely transformed in black bowler hat, overcoat – always unbuttoned – flapping behind him like an opera cloak, stiff white collar, black tie and highly polished shoes protected by pearl-grey spats, which intrigued me. I can remember watching him fastening them over his shoes, dexterously making them secure with a buttonhook, which he always replaced on the mantelpiece, out of my reach. Every time I watched him going to church my heart swelled with pride, even though I knew that in the lining of his bowler was rolled-up newspaper to prevent it from falling over his eyes, that his overcoat had only one button left and that his shoes once belonged to his father and had more balled-up newspaper in the toes to prevent him from walking out of them in the damp Broos. From a distance he was a real bobby-dazzler, but close up the rag-and-bone man wouldn't have given him fifteen bob for the lot. Anyway, what do fancy clothes matter? It's the man inside that drives the engine. Dad looked forward with excited anticipation to his stint in the belfry, just as a keen football supporter will push his way through the turnstiles at Boundary Park to stand for almost two hours on a cold, windy terrace to watch Oldham Athletic.

Arriving at the church opposite the war memorial, he strode over the gravestones, one of which was for a whole family: husband, wife and six children, who all died within a week in the year 1734. What a tragic story behind that! If this was the graveyard, how old was St Mary's Parish Church? I can imagine my father opening the great front door which led to the stone steps winding their way up to the belfry, 'Good mornings' to the seven other ringers, overcoats and jackets on hooks in the corner, sleeves rolled up as they approached their allocated places, a nod from the conductor, and then with a creak and a rattle of the bell ropes the Sunday morning silence shattered by the clamouring of the bells. The opening round was usually reasonable, but then the rot set in and the bells seemed to compete, jostling with each other for a piece of the action. It was as if a mighty hand from above had scooped up all the bells to fling them down to earth, clanging and banging as they bounced down Barker Street.

I don't wish to sound disloyal, but the bell-ringers cocooned in their sheltered belfry do not get the full benefits of their efforts. I've never mentioned this observation to a soul and to all campanologists, in spite of my uneducated criticism; and in fact I would never ever swap the bell-ringers for the soul-less chimes of a press-button carillon. As I was writing this I heard a loud grinding noise: it could have been my poor father turning over in his grave . . .

Vernon and I were in the old St Mary's Parish Church choir and John joined us when he was eight years old. Also in the choir was Dad's older sister, Aunt Mag, and an alto Aunt Marie, Dad's younger sister, who was the first lady bell-ringer in England. Mother was exempt because she was cooking the dinner. How's that for a family record? We almost outnumbered the congregation. While Dad and Aunt Marie were bouncing up and down on their ropes, Vernon, John and I were making our way to the church to bring joy and hallelujah to the faithful and this journey by Robin Hill Baths, up Barker Street, and through the Tommyfield market was at times an eerie experience. Every Sunday morning Oldham was a ghost town; it was as if the whole population had been spirited away to a distant planet.

Apart from the battle of the bells, the occasional distant cockcrow and the clacking of our footsteps, all was silent. Walking through a deserted Tommyfield was a depressing experience. The whole area was littered with the detritus of a hectic Saturday night – cardboard boxes, straw, wrapping paper, chip paper – disturbed from time to time by a marauding wind, but on days when it was really blowing the predominant noise was the flapping of the stall coverings, like the sails of a three-master crossing the Bay of Biscay in a force nine. This was bend-forward-and-hold-your-cap weather, which we preferred to the malignant calm as we made our way to church.

As for Saturday night, the market was a cacophony of voices, laughter and the constant shuffle of hundreds of feet tramping through the stalls lit garishly with single electric light bulbs or lamps, blue smoke busily curling through the lights from a chippy or a hot dog stand, candy floss machines for young and old. No two stalls were alike – clothing, footwear, crockery, herbal remedies, cheap jewellery; in fact that little world of Tommyfield market catered for almost everything, and if money was tight many people just shuffled round to enjoy the quick-fire repartee of the vendors. Strange as it may seem, the crockery stall invariably drew the biggest audience. A fat jolly man held a dozen dinner plates, slapping them as he announced, 'I am not going to ask you five shillings . . . I'm not even going to ask you four bob,' and then with a triumphant slap he would launch his punchline, 'Half-a-crown the lot.' There was a stirring in the crowd, and after a slight pause there was a surge forward, hands outstretched proffering half-crowns while two assistants busily wrapped dozens of plates in old newspaper. Most of the crowd would not even have house room for a dozen dinner plates, but it was Saturday night and what a bargain! There was more crockery to be had, more people to be had and above all there was entertainment. And now as the dawn of Sunday morning creeps silently over Tommyfield, what a contrast to the night before!

*   *   *

I was getting older by the day; in fact in a couple of years I'd be in double figures, so I should have known better . . . but my friend Richard and I were up to our old shenanigans after nightfall. It wasn't brilliant, it wasn't even funny, but you have to remember that in those days we didn't have wireless, let alone television. Here's what we did. We'd reach up and rat-a-tat the door knocker of a house in Ward Street, and then scoot across the cart road, flinging ourselves on the darkness of the Mucky Broos to watch the developments. Someone would invariably open the door, and look up and down the street, only to find it deserted. Then they'd close the door, wondering if they had imagined the whole thing. As I said, it wasn't brilliant, but when did a bit of mischief deter a child? We took it in turns to rat-a-tat another door and another until the game palled.

It couldn't possibly go on unchallenged and the more doors we knocked on the closer we were to discovery – and so it was on one particular night. It was my turn to rat-a-tat, which I did peremptorily, but there was no time to cross the street, as the door was opened immediately by a young athletic man. I was almost paralysed, scared out of my wits, and I ran panic-stricken for the corner of the street. Richard was already safe in the anonymity of the dark Broos. My little legs were no match for the confident stride of an angry man, and as I rounded the corner his heavy hand grasped my collar and lifted me off my feet, and I am sure he was about to do me serious damage when a deep Irish voice from the darkness shouted 'Oi!'. I was petrified, and more so when I recognised Constable Matty Lally. I could have survived a blow but not a custodial sentence. I wasn't too relieved when Matty Lally advised the man to go back home and leave it to the law. The man went off muttering – no one argued with the law – and when he'd gone I tensed for the well-deserved official wallop; but the policeman bent down to me and whispered, 'How many motor-car numbers did you get?' I hadn't the foggiest idea what he was talking about but it was a great let-off.

It wasn't until I was well tucked up in bed that I connected Constable Lally's 'How many motor-car numbers did you get?' to my motor-car spotting day on Featherstall Road – and I lay there wondering what a remarkable memory he had to recall an incident that must have taken place years ago. It was my last thought before sleep took over and sadly that was the last time I saw my new-found friend Constable Matty Lally.

Dad's hobby was mending pocket watches. Well-to-do men sported pocket watches chained across the front of their waistcoats – wrist watches were, as yet, an unknown in the cotton towns of the north-west – and so to see Dad bending over a backless watch, eyepiece screwed into his eye socket, was a fairly regular occurrence. But on one particular day he was immersed in a larger contraption with dials along the front. He was peering into the innards of the thing with such concentration that he didn't notice me. In fact if the house had fallen down he would still have been bent over his work, standing on the foundations. This isn't as far-fetched as it sounds because he was insulated from his surroundings by a large pair of earphones clamped round his head.

'It's a wireless set,' he said, answering my enquiry. 'A cat's whisker,' he added, which left me no wiser – what had all the wires and valves got to do with our Tiddles? 'There's something there but I can't make out what it is.'

'Can't you make it louder?' I said helpfully.

He took off his earphones and pointed through the window at the house opposite, in whose backyard was a tall mast as high again as the house. As far as I was concerned it had always been there, but I had assumed that it was a flag pole, although on Remembrance or Empire Days I'd never seen a Union Jack fluttering from it. 'He can get signals from all over the world with that: it's a wireless mast.'

Then he stared into his own little contraption and I noticed one of the valves flashing a feeble light nervously, like a child attempting its first step. Quickly Dad slipped on his earphones and listened excitedly for a few moments; then he took off his headphones and transferred them to my head.

I listened intently, and then with a shriek I yelled, 'It's a band, it's a band.'

A moment of history marking the day I heard magic from the airwaves.

I don't know how, or from whom, or what day I learned that the one I thought was Mother was not my mother at all, and that in fact my real mother had died when I was born. I couldn't absorb it at first, and when I did it wasn't earth-shattering: I took it in my stride. It wasn't a catastrophe – after all, a catastrophe to a little boy is when he puts his hand in his pants pocket and finds a hole where his hard-earned penny should have been, so the news of my real mother was hardly a tremor on the Richter scale. However, a few days later when Dad and I were alone in the kitchen – it must have been Sunday morning because Dad was shaving at the sink, towel tucked into the top of his trousers as he stropped his razor and then pinched his nose to shave his top lip – taking the bull by the horns, I blurted, 'Dad, what was my real mother's name?'

He cut himself and after a 'broad lastic' he glanced round and, satisfied that we were alone, he muttered, 'Harriet.' Then he took a little piece of paper and stuck it on to his top lip to make the blood coagulate. Next he lifted his face to the ceiling and began scraping under his chin.

Thinking that I'd at last opened the door, I said, 'What was she like?' and he cut himself again. Why didn't he just go to the barber's?

Exasperated, he put down his razor and sent me out to play, and that was the end of the matter. But I didn't let go. Every time we were alone together and I approached him he found some excuse to forestall any question. I had to know why it had been kept secret from me for so long but as I cleared my throat to ask, the drawbridge came down with a bang – it was a 'no-go' area. Nevertheless in the mess of half-formed thoughts and ideas lurking at the back of my head questions as yet unformed required answers.

A few mornings later, I was luxuriating in bed between sleep and full awareness, John not yet awake by my side, the beginning of a perfect day – when suddenly a roller blind in my head shot up, illuminating my mind. No questions or answers about my real mother but, more importantly, explanations! I knew now why the lady called Mother lavished so much love and attention on John: John was her son and I wasn't. I now understood why Dad was reluctant to even discuss my real mother: it would have been extremely tactless even to mention her name in front of Mother. His life began again when he married Florrie Ashton. The discovery also clarified the three sets of grandparents – the Staceys, the Ashtons and the Sykes – and here was a troubling thought: would I have to give up the Ashtons for my own kin and join Vernon at Grandma Stacey's? I shuddered. Grandma Ashton must have known about me for years but she'd always treated me with kindness and affection as John's best friend. It also made it clear why many people regarded me as an adoption gone wrong – a puzzling thought, but now I knew the reason I was strangely comforted.

Once when Mother was filling in a form to enrol John in something or other, John was at her elbow when she filled in 'name of applicant' and wrote 'John Stanley Sykes'.

'Who's Stanley?' he asked and she told him that Uncle Stanley was her brother who was killed at Mons during the Great War.

She said that most people had a middle name and some people had several names but they were mostly royalty. When she saw that John was still a little perplexed she told him that Vernon had three names as well, Vernon Wilson Sykes – Vernon after his father and Wilson the family name. Apparently when he asked what my middle name was she said, 'He hasn't got one', but with my newly acquired knowledge I knew the reason: all the relatives had been used up and there was no one left for me.

Some days later when John told me all this he said that he didn't think this was fair, and if I wanted to call myself 'Eric Stanley Sykes' he was more than willing to share. I thanked him but said I was quite happy with the name I had. Significantly, though, all through his life I never heard him refer to himself as 'John Stanley Sykes', nor sign his name as such, and here is the difference between my two brothers, for Vernon on the other hand was inordinately proud to sign himself V.-Wilson Sykes. Poor Vernon, he had left the Wilson household convinced he was better than the ménage at

36 Leslie Street and unfortunately it was an attitude he carried all through his career. He would take a job convinced that in two years he would become managing director and life, unlike Hollywood, doesn't work like that.

Not having a middle name didn't bother me at all, but my subconscious wasn't wholly satisfied until Joe Waterhouse and Auntie Emmy were married and they christened their only son Eric. God bless you, Auntie Emmy.

It appears that everyone had been party to the secret of my birth, but I wish they'd let me in on it. I wouldn't have told anybody. One thing is certain: I wasn't going to give up Granddad and Grandma Ashton. I was now an honorary member the Ashton family and John's mother was still mine as well, and if I left matters alone things would just carry on as before – and they did: Dad had his bellringing, and Mother cooked the meals, did the shopping, dusted and polished every day. My real mother was forgotten. As the saying goes, you never miss what you've never had. But somewhere in the great unknown a young woman called Harriet Stacey had other ideas.

In my exciting days of growing up, technology was desperately trying to keep pace with the introduction of motor cars as they began to proliferate, and for the first time an intriguing method of car control emerged. They were called traffic lights: red for stop, amber for wait a while and green to allow you to drive on. They would not change automatically to accomplish this. A car had to drive over a strip of rubber in the road about five yards before the lights, when the lights would turn to green and the car would drive on. The light would stay green until another car travelling in a diagonal direction went over its own rubber, changing the lights in front of it from red to green and the original lights from green to red. It was an ingenious invention and provided us children with hours of hilarity. On Sunday mornings when Oldham was a ghost town we ran from home to the traffic lights, which were at the bottom of Barker Street on our way to church, so as to have plenty of time to take turns at changing the colours, John jumping on one rubber strip while I stood in Barker Street ready to change the lights back. It was not as much fun as Ducky Funny Whip but it stretched our technical capabilities.

Every time I went out from our front door I only had to glance up to my left to see Ward Street Central School, an elegant red-brick building on two floors. All this austere magnificence I'd taken for granted as I played and romped through my early life. On my first day as a pupil there I could stand in the school yard looking down from a higher perspective and surveying all the familiar places. How small were the houses of Leslie and Ward Streets, and the Mucky Broos were not as vast as I'd thought they were. As I looked down at my old stamping ground I wondered if this was what they called higher education.

The headmaster, Mr Parker, was a tall, thin, cadaverous man with a face reminiscent of the Easter Island statues. We didn't see much of him most of the time, but when we marched along the corridor we instinctively dropped our voices as we passed his study. The door was never open; it was a room of mystery and the boys who'd been inside weren't very keen to go in again. If, for instance, the teacher considered your wrongdoing so appalling that three strokes of the strap would be insufficient to fit the crime, you would be sent to the headmaster's study, with words that were of the same gravity as a judge intoning, 'You will be taken to a place of execution . . .' Luckily in all my days at the school I experienced this ordeal only once.

What started off as an innocent prank led to thoughts of running away to join the French Foreign Legion. We had a teacher called Mr Barker and, as opposed to Mr Parker, he was overweight by many a ton and known to all the school as 'Fat Barker'. Unfortunately one afternoon while in his class I'd sketched a fair likeness of Mr Barker stark naked with his belly hanging out. In my drawing he was facing a woman also in the altogether, both of them with their hands down by their sides. It wasn't erotic – it wasn't meant to be. I thought it was funny and I was proud of the likeness. I showed it to my classmates and in no time at all Fat Barker became aware of the chortles and sniggers, and, spotting the paper being passed on, he intercepted the exchange and ordered it to be brought to him. He glanced at it, and then, as if he couldn't believe his eyes, he looked more closely, and without a word he hurried out, leaving the door open. I peered round at the class and everybody was suddenly interested in their exercise books. Typical, I thought: two minutes ago I was a hero and now I had the plague. Fat Barker returned and with a gesture despatched me to the headmaster's study. He stood back from the door as I passed him as if I might be contagious. There was no appeal, no call for explanation. He knew that the ludicrous figure was meant to be him; the woman could have been Miss Thomson, another teacher.

When I entered the headmaster's domain, the great man was looking at the sketch. After a time he folded it over until only the bottom of two pairs of legs were visible, held it out to me and said, 'Did you do this?'

I whispered, 'Yes, sir,' and that was it.

I got six strokes of the leather strap on my hand, but it really didn't hurt that much. He was getting on in years, and I suspect he did himself more damage in wielding the strap than he inflicted on me. But that was only the corporal punishment. What was so embarrassing, so shameful and degrading, was having my name entered in the punishment book. I had a criminal record already and, good grief, it might affect my job prospects if this became public – even worse should Dad get wind of it. As I returned to the class, Mr Barker was holding the strap and I thought for a minute I was going to get a second helping, but he ignored me and I slunk to my desk, an outcast.

Secretly I was glad that Mr Barker hadn't administered the punishment himself, as he really knew how to hurt you. I remember in glorious Technicolor my first larruping from him. I forget what I'd done to deserve it but there I was in front of the class while F. B. measured his distance. It was to be the first of three. I braced myself and as the leather came whistling down I moved my hand and he caught himself an almighty whack on his knee. This brought a great smothered snigger from the class and three more strokes were added to my original sentence. As Mr Barker taught a mixed class, we lads had to show a bit of bravado whenever we were about to be chastised. It was unmanly to cry in front of the girls, but to tuck your right hand under your left armpit after the punishment was acceptable. Girls were never punished, and I'm sure they secretly revelled in the spectacle as some poor devil held out his hand for the strap. Is this a trait in women? After all, during the French Revolution they took their picnic lunches and their knitting to enjoy the work of Madame Guillotine . . . But I digress.

One of the popular myths going the rounds regarding the strap was that a hair from one's head laid across the palm of the hand would take some of the sting out of the blow. It was worth a go, and I tried it a couple of times, but it didn't work for me, so I packed it in. Had it been a success I could well have been bald before I left school.

Apart from daisies, dandelions and buttercups, I can't recall ever seeing any other flower. I wouldn't have recognised a bluebell if you'd rung it violently into my good ear. Even in Westwood Park the rhododendrons were not a riot of colour; they were in fact a dirty grey from the fallout of the factory chimneys of the cotton mills, which caught me at a disadvantage when some joker or other named a festival Beautiful Oldham. Every year schoolchildren had to paint or draw a daffodil and those judged to be winners had the satisfaction of having their efforts pinned round the walls of Werneth Fire Station. The doors were opened to the proud public, and talented offspring pointed out their own contribution to their parents – in my case 'Eric Sykes, aged twelve years, Ward Street Central School'. It was a marvellous exhilarating day out, culminating in a walk through Werneth Park all in our Sunday best. The daffodils round the walls were at least all yellow but back in the classrooms where we had all competed it would have been a psychiatrist's nightmare. Most of us had never seen a daffodil and like a rumour some of the entries were greatly distorted.

I'm not sure, but I think we only had one lady teacher at Ward

Street Central, Miss Thomson, blonde, medium-sized but bulging. As I think back she reminds me of Miss Piggy in *The Muppet Show*. Anyway on one occasion I was kept in class to write out some lines before I was dismissed. Head bowed, I was writing 'I must not do . . .' whatever it was for about the hundredth time, with four hundred more to go, when a shadow fell over me. I looked up and Miss Thomson was perched on the edge of my desk, looking down at me in a peculiar way. She was hot and her make-up was beginning to cake, and little beads of perspiration dotted a faint moustache which I'd never noticed before. After a few moments she said, 'You have very long eyelashes for a boy.' I thanked her, she gave me a long peculiar look and, picking up my uncompleted lines, she said, 'That'll do,' and left the room. For some inexplicable reason my mind raced back over the years to when I lay wounded and the little nurse with the sad smile stroked my forehead.

Then there was Mr Wilton. He was our English teacher. I think he enjoyed listening to himself a darn sight more than we did. Well built, he wore a grey suit and for the street he wore a brown trilby with the left side of the brim turned down. I suppose that this was how he imagined a poet would wear his hat. Incidentally, why must we have an English teacher? I could have understood it if I'd been French or Greek but I not only spoke English fluently but could read it as well. Mr Wilson was groaning on about something or other and my interest in the lesson waned. I looked out of the window and my eyes were drawn to our house. One day, noting that the front door was closed, I turned my head to the house in Ward Street, where I made my abortive rat-a-tatting and had my last brush with Constable Matty Lally, and suddenly something extraordinary caught my eye: in the middle of the Mucky Broos two dogs were stuck together, bottom to bottom, trying to run in opposite directions. It was intriguing, and I was wondering what was going on when a woman came out of her house and threw a bucket of water over them, and they came apart, like greyhounds leaving the traps at the races. I turned back towards the blackboard and with a start I almost bumped my face against Mr Wilton's jacket. He had been leaning on my desk, baffled as I was, no doubt, by the goings-on outside. I thought he was about to discuss it, but I was way off the mark. 'Sykes,' he said, 'I am endeavouring, in my humble, stumbling way, to add a little knowledge to that treasure house above your eyebrows, but as you prefer to ogle lasciviously at a rutting perhaps you'd be more at home in the Zoological Gardens?'

I looked at him in wonder, thinking that to learn English could be an advantage.

Mr Sutcliffe was our sports master, a tidy, tall, black-haired man; it must be said, that in his sports jacket and flannels he looked ideal for the part. It was also rumoured that he played cricket for Werneth Second Eleven, which in my mind only was open to doubt. For one thing, he wore spectacles with lenses as thick as the bottom of a pop bottle, making his eyes look like blackcurrants; also he never seemed to like cricket. When we were all eager to be marched down to where we played our organised games, he would be looking at the sky, hoping for rain, or even bad light, in which case we spent the sports hour in the gym, practising imaginary cover drives, left-foot-forward off-drives, back on non-existent stumps for an imaginary short ball. We did all this synchronised to a record on a wind-up gramophone, usually of 'The Blue Danube'.

These exercises in the gymnasium were no substitute for the real cricket, at which Mr Sutcliffe was a semi-pro. Perhaps he was embarrassed to have to shepherd a crocodile of boisterous, happy schoolboys through the streets on the way to the cricket ground. This was in fact a large area of fairly flat ground, with goalposts at either end for footie; and, because there wasn't a blade of grass to be seen, our cricket was played on coconut matting. We didn't have two ends – in fact I don't think we had more than four stumps, but that was just right: three for the wickets and one for the bowler. There was only one pad, which was buckled on to the left leg, and if you happened to be left-handed, tough.

Mr Sutcliffe would throw the ball to someone, anyone, and point out somebody else to bat and the game began. Mr Sutcliffe looked on with a bored expression, occasionally glancing at his wrist watch so that he wouldn't be late getting back to the warm common room. However, in one particular session he took off his jacket, handed it to me and picked up the bat, which I'd laid down while I buckled on my pad. He threw the ball casually to one of the lads, and then he surveyed the fielders, gesturing for them to spread out more. It was obvious that he'd done this before on a much higher canvas. Nodding to the bowler, he took up his stance and we all crouched in readiness. What happened next was like a page out of comic cuts. It was an innocuous ball, not quick, but falling short, and then for some unaccountable reason the ball reared up and caught Mr Sutcliffe on the bridge of his nose. His glasses flew off, and he stumbled back, knocking his stumps over.

'Howzat?' screamed the bowler.

Mr Sutcliffe struggled unsteadily and glared myopically around him. The bowler was quick-witted and, seeing Mr Sutcliffe's glasses on the ground, took the opportunity of merging with the rest of the field.

'You stupid boy,' he yelled at nobody. 'I wasn't ready. What's your name?'

There was no answer and when I picked up his glasses and handed them to him he saw that there was no one at the other end. We all knew who the bowler was, but there wasn't a chance in a hundred that anyone would give him away.

One thing is certain, though: Mr Sutcliffe wasn't much of a cricketer. Any decent batsman for Werneth would have hooked the ball for six.

That was the end of cricket for the day, and so I didn't have my turn with the bat. Dissatisfied with the world in general, I limped off, although there was nothing wrong with my foot – my limp was because of the cricket pad buckled on to my left leg, obviously made for someone much taller than me. Ah well, I still maintain it was another century I never made.

Our classes weren't always mixed. For instance, the boys attended a carpentry class and the girls beavered away at domestic science, mainly cookery. Mr Barker's class, as I mentioned earlier, was mixed and to my shame I can't remember any of the girls, not even the one I was passionately in love with, although she didn't know it. I never approached or spoke to her but I recall following her home to the centre of Oldham, where she disappeared through the back door of a pub, and then with a great sigh I turned round and floated home in a euphoric haze.

My most vivid memory after school finished for the day was watching the staff going home. Mr Barker went hatless, dragged along by the weight of his stomach down Ward Street towards Featherstall Road in order to catch a tram to wherever he was going. The English master, Mr Wilton, would invariably be striding casually twenty yards behind him – perhaps they didn't like each other. Some of the teachers went the other way to board trams going in another direction. No member of the staff, not even the headmaster, possessed a car. Cars were still a rare sight and an expensive novelty, and teachers, as today, were underpaid; but even so all the male staff managed to wear suits with a collar and tie and Miss Thomson wore respectable frocks.

I may have treated the staff with a levity they don't deserve. Discipline was paramount and by and large they were all respected, and we pupils had no difficulty in addressing the masters as 'sir' and the lady teachers as 'miss'. Although I wasn't a credit to the school academically, when I finally left school, like every other pupil I could read, write, add up, subtract and divide. In other words, I had been equipped with the basic skills, preparing me for the next stage of the journey, and thankfully that did not include sex education – that was an adventure to come, as and when the bugle sounded. I have long had a theory that pupils who pass their leaving exams with high marks in every subject may be star pupils but when they face the real world they lose a lot of their sparkle and can be likened to a blind man whose guide dog has left home. On the other hand, many, many brilliant entrepreneurs, artists, writers, etc., proudly boast that their final reports were abysmal, so I wasn't as upset as my father when he read what the headmaster had written as a footnote to my school leaving report: 'Inclined to be scatterbrained'. Ho hum, you can't win 'em all.

My schooldays were over and presumably I was well equipped to take my place as a member of the working class. First, however, let me sum up the last fourteen years. They were mainly a pleasurable experience, although there were bad times as well, but I haven't included these simply because I can't remember them, and to my adolescent mind the bad times invariably happened to other people. For myself there were only two major problems: trying to keep warm during the cold winters which swept across the north-west for several months and staving off hunger, a condition endemic during the depression of the early thirties.

In looking back over my schooldays at Northmoor and Ward Street Central, I am appalled by my lack of attention to my education. For instance, when the history master declaimed that William the Conqueror invaded England in 1066 following the Battle of Hastings, that was the last thing I heard. But in my mind's eye I saw William beaching the long boat, French soldiers leaping into the surf to storm the beaches yelling Gallic obscenities at the British troops, and King Harold looking up towards a shower of arrows – a very silly thing to do – and his ostler, too late with his warning, gasping as King Harold said, 'Ooh', and slid from the saddle with an arrow in his eye – 'The King's copped it.' And just then I was brought back to the present day as the bell went for us to change classes, but whatever subject, maths or woodwork, my imagination still wove vivid pictures of the tale of the Battle of Hastings, until a geography lesson in which the mention of Mount Kilimanjaro had me halfway up the mountain pursued by Zulus before the bell rang for the end of the day.

So it is hardly surprising that academically I wasn't exactly a star pupil; in fact wallowed about for most of my schooldays at the bottom of the class. That is except in one subject, art, and the marks I got for this, year by year, were never less than ninety-eight out of a hundred.

During the last week of my school life, parents of the pupils about to enter the uncertain world of work were invited to a half-day visit to the school in order to wander round inspecting some of the projects their offspring had been engaged in. My parents couldn't be there because Dad was working in the Standard Mill in Rochdale while Mother had taken her old job back in the card room of another mill about three miles beyond Royton. What with their wages plus Vernon's and soon, hopefully, mine we would be able to afford rabbit every Sunday. Dad usually took a sandwich for his dinner in the factory but Mother fared better. Grandma Ashton cooked something nice and hot, put it in a basin, wrapped the whole thing in a red-spotted hankie and made her way to the tram stop. When the tram arrived, she handed Mother's dinner to the conductor and he put it on the floor by his feet; then 'ting ting' and off went the tram about three miles down the line to where Mother met it, the dinner was handed over to her and perhaps 'Smells good, missus' from the conductor and off to Rochdale. This private delivery service occurred every workday, no money, no 'What's this, then?' – all smiles, even when it was raining. Oh, what a gentle, caring age we lived in!

To return to parents' day at Ward Street Central School: as the star pupil in art, I was given a large sheet of rough paper, three feet by two, with carte blanche to paint whatever I fancied. Without hesitation I began to sketch a huge liner thrusting headway through a choppy sea. Parents filed into the classroom to watch my progress. I was completely enraptured – it was turning out to be a good painting. While wiping my hands on a rag, I surveyed my work, wondering if a couple of fish being thrown about would enhance the bow wave. I dismissed the thought as I still hadn't finished the superstructure. By this time the room was beginning to fill up with parents, and two teachers were enlisted to keep the crowd moving. I was daubing red paint on the paper, creating the first of three funnels, when a man's hand shot out, pointing to the bows and exclaiming that I'd forgotten to paint in the hole for the anchor. He was loud, and there was a crush of people eager to spot the mistake. I was pushed forward and in flinging out my arm to save myself inadvertently I upset the pot of red paint and my marathon work was over: Michelangelo had fallen off his pedestal and his floating Sistine Chapel disappeared under a spreading red sea. My hopes were dashed; I'd had visions of hanging it over the dresser in the kitchen. Optimistically I thought, There is plenty more where that came from, which just goes to show that you can't be right all the time.

In fact I was the only one in the school to be offered a scholarship to the Oldham College of Art, but that would have meant an extra two years of schooling, which was out of the question, as we couldn't afford the luxury. But it didn't bother me in the least. When I left Ward Street Central School at the age of fourteen I was eagerly looking forward to bringing home a wage packet earned manually in a workman's overalls.

In 1937 I walked through the gates of Ward Street Central School for the last time, fully equipped to make my contribution to the national debt. It was the same year that Aunt Marie and Uncle Stan were blessed with a child, a daughter Beryl. Our tribe was growing, and apart from my brother Vernon and my half-brother John I now had a beautiful baby cousin.

THE WORLD OF FLAT CAPS, OVERALLS AND BOOTS

Having left school, I still had no idea of what I wanted to do or how I should go about attaining an interview. It was the normal practice in those days for a father in a good steady job to recommend his son to the foreman, or even the manager, so as to ensure that the son followed in his father's footsteps. They could then make their way together to and from their place of employment and have their tea at the same time when they got home. However, no self-respecting father would push his son into a cotton mill and Dad was no exception. He had better plans for me, in short to put in an application for employment in the Post Office.

I greeted this suggestion in a lukewarm fashion. I'd often chided Vernon because he worked somewhere in an office. Polished shoes, collar and tie – that wasn't my idea of a workman. I wanted to work in overalls, sweep the streets, the chimneys, clean windows, anything as long as I could come home weary and dirty with a good day's work behind me. But the Post Office – I would go to work clean and tidy and come home in the same state, and I didn't consider selling stamps a proper job. However, my attitude changed when my father came home with a bit of newspaper he'd picked up on the tram and he smoothed it out to show me an advertisement urging school leavers to apply to the Post Office for positions of telegraph boys. My face lit up. The main argument in favour of the Post Office to Dad was a job for life, but for me, I was already sold on a uniform with a stiff peaked cap, a black belt and a pouch – all this and a bicycle too. Excitedly, I sent in two applications, both of which were ignored. Bitterly, I thought, 'It's typical of the Post Office – neither of them have been delivered.'

Meanwhile, not far from the top of Featherstall Road was Emmanuel Whittaker's Timber Merchant's, and I have no idea how it happened or who did what but all I know is that on Monday next I was to start work as a timber merchant. I had no inkling of what I was expected to do, but no doubt they'd tell me when I arrived.

So it was with outward calm and inward trepidation that I made my way up Featherstall Road, thrilled by my overalls washed many, many times to a faded blue, bought possibly from a sale at a second-hand or even a pawn shop. Had my overalls been new I would have looked like a raw beginner, if only I was old enough to shave. I crossed Featherstall Road at the exact spot where seven years ago I had attempted a career as a car number collector. There were other people making their way to work, some of them overalled like me; women were bound for offices or shops, and there was a man at the tram stop, in bowler hat, collar and tie, eyeing me as if he was superior. I tried to spit in order to make a point, but it wasn't too successful: it didn't go anywhere but just dribbled down my chin. I brushed it away, too late, and he was sniggering when he boarded the tram. Rounding the corner of Featherstall Road, I stopped suddenly as if I'd just walked into a brick wall. There on the other side of Oldham Road was the formidable office building of Emmanuel Whittaker's, and to the right the heavy iron entrance gates to a yard which housed countless orderly stacks of wood, some covered by huge tarpaulins. A daunting prospect loomed before me and it took all my willpower to approach this man's world.

Undecided, I was standing outside the gates, all courage gone, when two or three young bucks and one older, laughing at some joke or other, walked through the gates. The older one stopped and looked at me, and said, 'Hurry up, lad, or you'll be late.' All fears dispelled, I joined him and we walked in together.

My benefactor turned out to be my number one. He was on the cross-cutting bench. The wood on rollers moved towards him, he pulled the large circular saw through them, and then he pushed them along his bench to me. I hoisted these three-foot-long battens on to a large leather pad on my shoulder and carried them through to another shed, where two elderly men were nailing battens together to make crates, which would then be lorried down to the cotton mills to hold the cops – a cop being a cone of cotton thread wound on to a spindle. These two men rarely spoke – they couldn't, as I never saw either of them without a mouth full of nails – but by golly they could knock up a crate in the time it took me to bring another batch of battens. So for the next few loads I was striding out as if I was dropping back in a marathon and as the pile of battens began to get larger I was falling behind. Sweat was rolling down everywhere when my mate switched off his cross-cutting saw, helped to load me up and said, 'Now take it easy, otherwise by dinnertime we'll be having a whip-round for your parents.' It was kindly meant, but I was determined to earn my wages. However, when I got home that night I fell asleep in the middle of my baked beans on toast.

A few days later I learned a little dodge, which was the beginning of my indoctrination into the shady world of the working man. Rather than being sent to an early grave with a pile of battens on my leather pad, I was assigned to another job. This entailed going round the carpenters' shop to take their orders for dinner, which was usually a hot meat pie with a dollop of mash on top. My mouth watered at the thought of it but as it was sixpence it was out of my price range, and in any case I lived close enough to go home for midday meals.

As I wrote down their orders I also collected the money, and this is where my trade union education began. When I returned from the shop at dinnertime with an armful of sustenance I was met at the gates by my new mate on the cross-cutter.

He said, 'Did you get any change from the shop?'

I said, 'Yes, eight pence.'

Quickly looking over his shoulder to see if we were being observed, he folded my hand over the coins and hissed, 'Stick it in your pocket, lad.'

Perplexed, I looked at him. 'It doesn't belong to me,' I said guilelessly.

He shook his head sadly. 'Listen, lad,' he said. 'You're not the first to collect dinner money and you're not the first to get change from the shop but you will definitely be the first to hand over the money to that lot.' He jerked his thumb to the joiner's shop. I was about to object when he carried on, 'Some of the lads who collected dinner money before you are still working here.' I still couldn't get my head round the gist of his words. This must have been obvious from the blank look I gave him, for he sighed, 'If you start giving change back to them you'll be putting a noose round the heads of all the dinner lads before you.'

'But it would be dishonest.'

'Go ahead, then: sell your mates down the river. I give up.' And shaking his head, he strode away.

It didn't take me long to decide which path to go down and that night I went home eight pence richer, which was almost ten bob a week, but some of the blinkers had been taken from my eyes. I realised now that the working class I'd been so proud to join was not as far along the road to Jerusalem as I'd first imagined and secretly, and a little shamefaced, I accepted my corruption as my entrance fee to the world.

A few months later I found myself in a different location, opposite the cross-cutter. My new assignment was on a machine called the fore-cutter. The cross-cutter was a much older, capable and efficient man in a boiler suit and a very old trilby, sides pulled down to protect his head and neck from flying wood shavings and splinters. His job was to feed a dirty long plank of wood into the fore-cutter, where it would slowly move through the blades and emerge at the other end planed and shiny. It was up to me to take it off the rollers and stack it with the others in time for the next twelve-footer. It sounds simple enough but the storm of wood shavings and chippings flying from the machine was much greater in volume than it was at the front end so an old hat was found for me. Nowadays one would certainly wear gloves to protect the hands from splinters and goggles to protect the eyes, but in the early thirties at Emmanuel Whittaker's these had never even been considered. Every fifteen minutes or so the machinist would switch off to allow me to sweep the shavings through a square, two-foot opening in the floor, and at the break I would go down the ladder to spread the sawdust and chippings more evenly. When I got to the bottom of the ladder I was up to my waist in sweet-smelling wood, so it was a slow job to spread the load.

As I write this, it suddenly occurs to me what a fire hazard the sawdust and chippings must have been, but then I doubt that safety regulations were prevalent in those days. Come to think of it, I can remember at least three comrades with missing fingers.

Again I was moved to a different job. Whether I was up- or downgraded I've no idea, because my wage was the same. I was now a painter, but not exactly in the Van Gogh school. In fact I wasn't really a painter at all: my task was to prime the wooden window frames with a pink primer. At least my assignments seemed to be getting less onerous. Was the management experimenting, trying to find a job that would suit me, or, more likely, trying to find me a job I could do?

I threw myself into my new work. Proudly I returned home every night with my overalls stiff with almost as much paint as I applied to the window frames. After a couple of weeks I knew I had found my niche. No chance of losing fingers, no chance of a hernia from carrying more than my strength – it was going to be a pushover. But little did I know that splashing about with paint was a booby-trap. First I went down with painter's colic. This was not life threatening, but unfortunately the colic mushroomed into something more serious: exactly half of my face broke out in eczema, from the middle of my forehead, down the bridge of my nose and under my chin, while the other half of my face was completely unblemished.

Mother took me by tram to the skin hospital in Manchester. A middle-aged lady doctor treated the suppurating side of my face and my whole head was bandaged, with two holes cut into the bandage for my eyes and a slit for my mouth. Every Tuesday for months we made the journey, as in *Son of the Invisible Man*, to see the doctor, who would unwind the sticky bandage, view the affected area and shake her head in defeat. The eczema hadn't spread – it was down exactly half my face – but neither had it improved. She applied more lotions, bandaged me up again and told my mother that I would have to be admitted to the hospital. She should take me home now as there was no bed available and as soon as there was a vacancy the hospital would let us know. It shouldn't be too long a wait but if we had not heard we should report as usual to the outpatients' clinic on the following Tuesday.

When my mother told me what the situation was, I was horrified and waves of panic swept over me. For me it was a terrible week: I dreaded the days that followed and prayed that I would not be admitted. Every Tuesday for the past few months as we'd sat on the long benches in the outpatients', sometimes waiting for ages for our call, I had looked round me to see some terrible skin afflictions. One or two of these poor wretches were in dressing gowns, in-patients obviously, and some of those sights were horrendous. After a time I refused to look and just stared at the floor until my call came. At least I went home every night, but now the thought of lying along-side these nightmares in a hospital ward gave me the shivers.

Next Tuesday came and I was sitting opposite the lady doctor, listening as she told my mother that there still wasn't a bed vacant, and my spirits rose a little. Then she began to unwind the bandages and my self-pity evaporated somewhat; after all, this wonderful lady had to deal with skin diseases all the time and most likely much worse than mine. When the unveiling was complete, a cool breeze caressed my face and there was silence for a moment or two. Then the doctor beckoned Mother across and together they stared at me in amazement. The doctor nodded and said calmly, 'This is what I have been hoping for. It's the shock – it must have been.' She repeated herself: 'The shock of having to be admitted to the hospital is the trick,' and as I looked into the mirror I understood. There was not a blemish on my face; a pink tinge where the eczema had been but that was all. I was cured. No more eczema, no more bandages and certainly no more Emmanuel Whittaker's.

Once again Auntie Emmy came up trumps when she asked me if I would like to spend a week's holiday in New Brighton. She said it was Uncle Joe's idea, but I had a shrewd suspicion that she was being diplomatic. As far as I was concerned I couldn't wait to pack my swimming costume and a towel, a *Just William* book to read in bed and, naturally, a pullover.

So I went with Uncle Joe and Auntie Emmy to New Brighton, a place not renowned for its amusements, its main attractions being an open-air swimming pool with diving boards and a shopping arcade. In fact we spent every day at this manufactured oasis, except when it rained, which it did for a large chunk of our holiday, which we spent in bus shelters and shop doorways. Umbrellas were an unnecessary expense, affordable only by bank managers, local officials and the well-off. On sunny days Uncle Joe and Auntie Emmy lounged on deck chairs by the pool, and I sat on the grass beside them, ostensibly reading my book but all the time watching furtively the goings-on around me. We made an ideal holiday trio. Auntie Emmy sucked Mint Imperials from the bag on her lap, listening to the beat of a popular tune blaring from hidden loud-speakers, while Uncle Joe, knotted white hankie on his head, scanned any discarded newspaper he'd managed to scavenge on his way from the digs. As he was fair-complexioned, his only concession to sunbathing was to undo the top button of his shirt. But nobody went to New Brighton for a tan: although the sun was out it wasn't strong enough to cast a shadow.

People were splashing about in the pool but as yet no one had used the diving boards. I was a useful swimmer but my greater joy was high diving. As a young hopeful I had learned to dive from the lock gates on the Manchester Ship Canal and I had since improved from the top board at Robin Hill Baths, a few hundred yards from my home in Leslie Street. Now in New Brighton I eyed the top board by the pool. It was higher than anything I'd ever come across before, but I could manage a swallow dive, which was the nearest thing to flying, upwards and outwards, arms stretched out like wings and brought together for the final plunge: it was exhilarating, spectacular and fairly simple.

I stood up and announced that I was going for a swim, and Auntie Emmy said, 'All right then.'

Walking down to the pool, I was conscious of my thin, white, emaciated body. I was fifteen years old, midway between the round-ness of childhood and the chunky hardness of an adult, and I was fed up with the old gibe of many, who should know better, whenever I dived in the water at Robin Hall Baths: 'Who's thrown a pair of braces in?'

However, on this day, instead of diving off the side of the pool I made my way up the ladders to the highest board. On looking down, I had qualms as I saw the little figures below staring up at me, Auntie Emmy, shading her eyes from the sun, on her feet now. For a wild moment I thought of abandoning my madcap desire to show off, but then the thought of making my way down the ladders again was too shameful. I walked to the edge of the board, control-ling my breathing, I stared outward and the next moment I was floating down almost in slow motion, and when I brought my arms forward for the entry I looked along my body, I could see my legs and feet together and I plunged into the water. It was the most exciting dive I'd ever attempted, and when I heaved myself out of the pool I noticed that all the noise and shrieks from the bathers had ceased and they only had eyes for me: it was my moment of glory.

When I got back to Auntie Emmy she was wiping her eyes, as she'd been crying. 'Who learnt you to do that?' she said.

I was shivering so much that my shrug went unnoticed and as I towelled myself Uncle Joe remarked wryly, 'I can think of better ways to commit suicide.'

But the main memory of New Brighton eddies around my mind for one other landmark. On the day following my historic dive, a new entertainment visited the pool: eight beautiful girls, all blonde, same height – they might well have been octuplets. They were sponsored by a newspaper and announced as the Daily Mirror Eight. They danced to recorded music, perfectly synchronised. They were fantastic and I was mesmerised. Fifteen years old, and inno-cent, I was vaguely aware of the difference between men and women – this was made obvious when I watched them in their bathing costumes – but women had aroused no strange feelings in me until

I saw the Daily Mirror Eight. Auntie Emmy said they were going back to the digs and I said I wouldn't be long. In fact five minutes later I followed them, and as I walked through the streets in a haze of wonder a coach drew up alongside and, would you believe it, out stepped the first of the Daily Mirror Eight, the other seven close behind, making their way into a hotel. Not one of them noticed me, mouth agape, eyes shining with adulation. I hadn't expected them to look my way, and if they had I would only have blushed. I was in love with all eight of them and that was enough for me. What a wonderful place to live in!

Oldham was the major cotton town in Lancashire in my opinion. Others will undoubtedly disagree. Cotton towns all had one thing in common: they were tired, and weary, and it would take another few years to fill the gaps left by the bloodbath of the Great War. Oldham Town Hall was a quiet, austere Victorian building, with heavy, stone pillars at the front, and except for the dirty, smoked brickwork it could have been reminiscent of the Parthenon in Ancient Greece; in fact most town halls in northern towns seemed to have been constructed from the same blueprint. Across the wide roadway from the town hall in Oldham was the Cenotaph, an evergreen memorial to the young Oldham lads who would never again walk up West Street or Barker Street for a Saturday night out in the Tommyfield market; and overlooking the Cenotaph, St Mary's Parish Church.

It is poignant to bring to mind Armistice Day, the eleventh day of the eleventh month. Each year when the church clock struck the eleventh hour all traffic stopped, trams ground to a halt, horses pulling carts were reined to a standstill, and cyclists dismounted and stood to attention by their bikes. Every pedestrian remained where he or she was; men removed their hats and women bowed their heads. The silence was almost tangible. Then after two minutes a soldier on the roof over the church doors, head and shoulders visible above the black stone battlement, put a bugle to his lips and the melancholy, evocative strains of the 'Last Post' pierced the veil of silence. Not until the last note had faded away did the town re-activate itself.

Alongside the church was the commercial heart of Oldham: dress shops, chemists, solicitors, Burton's fifty-shilling tailors, Wool-worth's, Whitehead's Café and, squeezed in the middle of all this affluence, a brave little greengrocer's shop. It really was tiny, just one room crowded with a counter, a tap without a basin and no space for a lavatory, the nearest being the public toilets at the top of West Street – quite a distance for a weak bladder.

The over-worked proprietor was Sam Hellingoe, a round, dark-visaged man, not tall but compact. Alone he collected fruit and vegetables from the market in Manchester, laid out his daily pur-chases on a bench in front of the shop, and then hurried inside round the counter to serve his customers. If there weren't any he swept the floor, polished the apples or wiped the counter as if it made any difference. He was always busy, but sadly his age was beginning to slow him down and reluctantly he decided to take on the expense of an assistant. This was a momentous decision because money was tight, so his assistant would have to be willing, able and above all thick enough to toil every day except Sunday for a pittance – and that is how I came to work there.

Mr Hellingoe, was forever in a flat cap and brown dustcoat – as a matter of fact in all my time in his establishment I never saw him take his cap off, not even to scratch his head – and like a dutiful assistant I followed suit in a flat cap, brown dustcoat and, hallelujah, my first pair of long trousers. Beneath my overalls at Emmanuel Whittaker's I had still been in the short pants from my schooldays, but now I wore a pair of Vernon's cast-offs, a bit long in the leg with a shiny backside, but I didn't care: they were the bridge into manhood.

Each morning I met Mr Hellingoe on the Croft, where his small van was parked. We never exchanged 'Good mornings', we just nodded, and he squeezed himself into the driving seat, putting the gear shift into neutral before letting off the brake. Then I moved round the back of the van and when he gave me the thumbs up I began to push. It was hard work, but I'd only about a hundred yards to go to the top of West Street, where I gave him an extra running shove to set him off and the van slowly trundled down the hill. I watched it disappear like a very old tortoise on ice. It was all downhill to Manchester and that was his destination. Eight miles is a heck of a long way to freewheel, but I did say money was tight; after all, he had to pay me fifteen shillings a week – I had Tuesday afternoons off but worked until nine in the evenings on Saturdays – and petrol wasn't cheap.

As time went on, I grew accustomed to the work. Mr Hellingoe was away for longer periods and I became self-assured, looking after the shop on my own, weighing out potatoes, carrots and Brussels sprouts with fallible dexterity on the old scales, popping the goods in a paper bag, and then 'ting ting' on the till, 'There you are, missus, three pence change,' or whatever. One day, however, I overstepped myself. An old lady clutching a shiny purse was feeling the fruit, squeezing the bananas, smelling the cabbages. I watched her covertly as she turned her attention to a box of apples and suspiciously I wandered casually from behind the counter. If anybody was going to walk off with a Cox's pippin without paying it would be me, and why not? My wages weren't princely and to make up the deficit I ate more of the stock than my Friday night's wages were worth. Underneath the counter was a huge rubbish box. Over-ripe or beginning-to-smell fruit and vegetables found a quick exit into it, but amongst all this detritus there was quite a hefty amount of healthy apple cores, pears, some with only one bite out of them and banana skins, because while in charge of the shop I ate fruit by the sackful, but if a customer came in, wallop, the half-eaten fruit would find its way under the counter. But that's between you and me.

Getting back to the old lady, who was now outside the shop, eyeing the rabbits hanging there: having selected one, she brought it in and dumped it on the counter.

'How much?' she said, and I told her, and here's where I overstepped the mark.

Having watched Mr Hellingoe deftly skinning them, I blurted out, 'Would you like it skinned?'

She looked at me doubtfully and said, 'Can you manage?'

I winked at her and began the process. It was just like undressing a baby and she watched, probably marvelling at my dexterity – that is, until I came to the last bit. The rabbit was now stark naked and all I had to do was pull the last of the fur over its head.

'There you are, madam,' I said triumphantly, but when I jerked the fur over the rabbit's head I was horrified to see that the fur must have torn because there was still some left on his head like a crew cut.

'I'm not having that,' she said and stormed out in high dudgeon.

What was I to do with the naked rabbit? I couldn't chuck the whole thing in the rubbish box: Mr Hellingoe would know how many rabbits had been hanging outside. Then a smart wheeze crossed my mind. I still had the fur and all I had to do was to dress the rabbit again. The back legs were easy and I'd just got one of the forepaws clothed when Mr Hellingoe returned and I was caught literally red-handed. But instead of hitting the roof, he just smiled and said, 'Take that home to your mother. You can have it for your Sunday dinner.'

I was overjoyed and at the same time ashamed of the amount of fruit I'd got through illegally, and I made up my mind that anything I took from the stock I'd replace with money in the till. At that moment I would willingly have pushed Mr Hellingoe all the way to Manchester and, if it would have saved him petrol money, all the way uphill back to Oldham.

When I went home that night I was awash with good thoughts – and wide open for the sucker punch. It wasn't long in coming. I arrived home and casually tossed my wage packet on the table; then while Mother checked the contents, I pulled the rabbit from behind my back like Houdini at his best and said, '*Voilà*'.

She didn't smile. 'Why did you buy a rabbit?' she said, still holding my wages, and my heart plummeted. Mr Hellingoe had stopped it out of my wages – the crafty old devil. Mother didn't help matters when she said, 'And he's overcharged you as well.'

*   *   *

During the time I was helping to keep Mr Hellingoe's body and soul together something momentous was happening in an old building just in front of Tommyfield: a new Oldham Scout troop was being formed. As I passed it on the way home I decided to drop in. There were about twenty or so urchins in a circle round the edges of a fairly large room. Half of the boys were still at school but quite a few of us were working for a living. A tall figure in a black cassock down to his ankles stood in the middle and made a short speech, welcoming us all to the formation of the 113th Oldham Scout troop and I relaxed. I noticed three of the older ones holding kettle drums, and as there was one not being used on the floor by them I casually picked it up and stood with the other three. They handed me a drumstick and in no time at all we were marching round the room in single file to the beat of our four drumsticks. By the end of the evening we were all members of the 113th Oldham Scout troop and speaking for myself it was the best evening's work I'd ever done.

Scouting was to make me fitter and healthier, and give me self-assurance and the comradeship that had been so lacking in my past; but the most important part of this initiation was that I met Bobby Hall, a butcher's boy. He was also one of the drummers and there was an instant rapport between us. Neither of us could drum. We both showed promise, though; and in a matter of months a banner led the troop on church parade, with four drummers with white ropes hanging beneath our drums and a big drum, and to cap it all looking pretty smart in our new Scout uniforms. The troop was divided into four patrols and I had already been appointed patrol leader of the Peewits. Bobby was troop leader, next in line to the Scout master, who turned out to be the curate at St Mary's Parish Church. We never saw him in any uniform other than his cassock, but he was accepted nevertheless. The months went by and in that time I gained two armfuls of proficiency badges, all round cords; and my greatest achievement and the most coveted was that I became a King's Scout. I must have been an awesome figure to the spotty herberts of my Peewit patrol as I explained how to tie knots, put a tent up and recognise the mating call of an owl. I took great pleasure in helping my little band gain proficiency badges of their own, and in return they paid me the compliment of listening to me as if I was Baden-Powell's grandson.

I don't know what has happened to the Scout movement these days. I haven't seen a parade of Scouts for years but the writing was on the wall when I last saw a Scout jamboree on television. Gone were the broad-brimmed Scout hats, which were replaced by berets; and, worse, they all wore long trousers. Perhaps I should move with the times. Well, all I can say is tell that to the beefeaters.

It wasn't long after the rabbit fiasco that my employment in the grocery trade came to an end, my place being taken by Mr Hellingoe's daughter, a comely lass, I should think in her mid-twenties. I thought she was smashing but I wasn't old enough to fancy her. I felt a bit hurt at being given the elbow, but then again she was his daughter and perhaps she worked for nothing as it was all in the family.

I've no idea how I came to start work in Shaw, a far-distant cry from the fleshpots of Oldham. Whereas I used to walk to work at Hellingoe's, from Featherstall Road to Shaw was a fair tram ride. Even more extraordinarily, my new employment was at the Rutland Mill, a cotton mill, but thankfully not in the dark satanic part of it. I was to be the new office boy and I looked forward to it, completely forgetting how I sneered when my brother Vernon started to work in an office, but knowing him as I did I expect he aspired to an invitation to the boardroom table.

At least I had Saturdays off, and I put these rest days to good use, especially in the long summer days. Bobby Hall and I, now ex-Scouts, were still attracted by the lure of camping under the stars, miles from anywhere. For instance, on a typical Saturday afternoon we'd meet at the bus stop in the High Street of Oldham, both of us overloaded with heavy backpacks containing potatoes, eggs, bacon, bread and butter, cushioned by sleeping bags while our rolled blankets were tied securely on the top, frying pan and saucepans, enamel mugs hanging from the straps – we were always well prepared, living up to the Scouts' motto. From Oldham we went out into the country, perhaps Delph or Saddleworth. Having offloaded our kit and ourselves from the bus, we began our journey to our camping grounds. Our favourite destination was a place called Chew Valley, a massive terrain of huge boulders interspersed with trees and streams. We trekked anything from five to eight miles into this deserted landscape to a rare patch of grass about six feet from a fast-moving stream. We kept our eyes open for dead trees. Within sight of our tiny Shangri-La, and would hurl a rope over a long sapless branch and give it a quick tug to bring it crashing to the ground. Being so dry, it broke into manageable pieces, which we hauled the short distance to our camp.

The first thing was to put up the tent. Everything was then piled inside, in case of inclement weather. The fire was next and thanks to the deadness of the wood a saucepan full of water was soon heating while one of us peeled the potatoes. Then the light began to fade and the stars appeared until the whole of the blackness was crowded with a glittering, sparkling ceiling ... Sausage and mash had never tasted so good. A few minutes to digest it, tin plates rinsed in the stream, and then, relaxing on our backpacks, sipping our mugs of freshly brewed coffee, we sighed with happiness as we lit our first cigarettes of the day. Even now I feel blissful contentment overcoming my senses as I recall that first drag on a Woodbine. The silence of our surroundings was disturbed only by the spitting hot logs in the fire and the eternal symphony of the rushing stream's hypnotic melody. Sleep came easily as by and large it had been a hectic day. Being old hands, we knew that blankets piled on top don't keep you warm: it's the blankets underneath that do that, as cold comes up from the earth. Automatically now we pounded out a hollow in the ground for our hips – in fact no bed in the most expensive hotel in the world could have been as comfortable – and when the birds and the daylight opened our eyes on the Sunday morning, we were well rested, hungry and ready to enjoy the day. Light fire, wash in the stream, fry bacon and eggs, the whole breakfast including slices of bread toasted on the tip of green saplings and once again the enamel mugs of coffee, followed by . . . yes, you've guessed it, the first Woodbine – not a bad way to spend a summer weekend.

When I was working at the Rutland Mill in Shaw, Saturdays were once again bright and pristine; I no longer had to work till nine o'clock as I had done in the fruit trade. I was older, possibly wiser, although I wouldn't put money on it, and certainly a few shillings more affluent, and I had two stalwart mates. As well as Bobby Hall, Jack Cleaver was one of my pals. A strange lad, usually the target of our heartless humour, he wore glasses, steel-rimmed and held together by a strip of sticking plaster, and he had light straight hair which he pressed with open fingers to create waves. If the world was not exactly our oyster it was most definitely our winkle. Our main Saturday night attraction was the Gaumont cinema at the end of Union Street. As for the film, the question we first asked ourselves was, 'Is it a talkie?' and the second, 'Is it in colour?' This didn't bother us a bit: it was Saturday night, hey, lads, hey and the devil take the hindmost.

The Gaumont cinema was a large, luxurious emporium showing the latest films and up-to-date news, not forgetting Arthur Pules at the mighty Wurlitzer. For many Oldhamers the perfect panacea for the end of a stressful working week was a Saturday night at the pictures. Just relaxing into the armchair-like seats was an experience to savour. Uniformed usherettes busily showed patrons to their seats; one usherette stood against the orchestra pit, facing the audience with a smile as she sold crisps, peanuts, chocolates and soft drinks from a tray strapped round her shoulders; another usherette patrolled the aisles, selling various brands of cigarettes and matches from a similar tray. There was a general feeling of content in the audience, excitement slowly rising under a subdued babble of conversation. The audience were the same people who had gone off to work during the week in overalls, dustcoats, ragged clothing and slightly better garb for office workers, but at the Gaumont cinema they had all, without exception, dressed up for the occasion. All the men wore collars and ties and the ladies decent frocks and in many cases hats as well. What a turn around from my dear old flea-pit Imperial days; no running up and down the aisles chasing each other and certainly no whistling, booing or throwing orange peel at the screen during the sloppy kissing bits. In all fairness, though, I must add that that was only at the Saturday morning shows and we were children enjoying a few moments not under supervision or parental guidance. In fact when I was old enough to go to the Imperial for the evening films the audience even then dressed up and enjoyed the films in an adult fashion.

Back to the sublime at the Gaumont cinema; as the lights went down, so did the level of conversation. A spotlight hit the centre of the orchestra pit and slowly, like Aphrodite rising from the waves, the balding head of Arthur Pules would appear as he played his signature tune on the mighty Wurlitzer. He was a portly figure in immaculate white tie and tails, hands fluttering over the keys and shiny black pumps dancing over the pedals as he rose into full view, head swivelling from side to side, smiling and nodding to acknowledge the applause; but for all his splendid sartorial elegance, having his back to the audience was unfortunate as the relentless spotlight picked out the shape of his corsets. Regular patrons awaited this moment with glee, judging by the sniggers and pointing fingers. We were no exception: having all this pomp and circumstance brought down by the shape of a pair of common corsets on a man was always a good start to the evening's entertainment.

At this point the words of a popular melody would flash on to the screen – for instance, the 'in' song of the day, 'It Happened on the Beach at Bali Bali' – and, after a frilly arpeggio to give some of the audience time to put their glasses on, a little ball of light settled on the first word of the song. In this case the first word was 'It'; then it bounced on to 'Happened'; then it made three quick hops over 'on the Beach at'; and then it slowed down for 'Bali Bali'. The women sang with gusto and the men just smiled and nodded.

Happily this musical interlude didn't last too long. Arthur Pules, the organist, was lured back into his pit of darkness and the curtains opened on the big wide screen. The films at the Gaumont were a great improvement on the grainy pictures at the Imperial, and so they should have been: after all, the film industry had made great strides in the eight years since John and I had sat in the pennies, dry mouthed as the shadow moved across the wall to clobber one of the unsuspecting actors.

After two hours of heavy sighs and wet eyes 'The End' appeared on the screen and the lights in the auditorium came up, bringing us all to our feet as the drum roll eased into the National Anthem . . . no talking, no fidgeting, simply a mark of respect for our King and Queen.

From the cinema we made our way eagerly to the next port of call, the chippie at the top of Coldhurst Street, for our customary fish and chips sprinkled liberally with salt and vinegar, and salivated to the top of Belmont Street, where Bobby Hall lived. Conversation was on hold as we stood in a circle, the steam of the hot fish and chips mingling with our clouds of breath on the cold night air. Finally with sighs of satisfaction we saw Bobby to his door, and then Jack and I made tracks through the darkness to 36 Leslie Street.

Sunday evening was just as interesting. Our little gang met as usual and made our way down to Union Street, where hordes of people strolled down one side of the street to the end, crossed over the road and walked up the opposite side. It was habitual, the Sunday night *paseo*. Chatting and larking about, we joined the parade, just a few young blokes without a cogent thought between them, but this was not so – we were all of the same mind: GIRLS, GIRLS, GIRLS! We were growing up; it was the April of our lives. Should we come upon a linkage of girls we immediately locked on behind them, a decent space between us lads and our quarry. The girls threw covert glances over their shoulders and for our part we pretended to be oblivious to them, Bob and I laughing at nothing, and Jack staring ahead with what he perceived to be a steely glint, which didn't quite work because his eyes were slightly crossed to start with. And another weekend hit the dust.

The offices of the Rutland Mill were palatial, with high ceilings in the boardroom and the general office; these were separated by a washroom, which had two gleaming taps above the basin and at the far end a toilet. All the office doors were either mahogany or rosewood, with shiny cut-glass door knobs; the windows were long and curtained, the bottom half of frosted glass so that the workers would be unable to look in on their betters, and more importantly, we wouldn't have to look at them. In the first few weeks I felt embarrassed by the cheapness of my suit – Vernon had always been taller than me; but I did polish my shoes so that at least I could walk about the office with more confidence. Filling most of the space were two long desks. On one desk was a girl at one end and me at the other, and at the opposite side an older man facing me and a woman facing the girl, both more important than us; on the second desk a clerk even more important and facing him the big panjandrum, the boss man of us all, the secretary Edmund Taylor. From where he sat we were all within the orbit of his baleful gaze. As he looked at us over his glasses, we doubled our work rate. He never smiled and I surmised that he was either unhappy at home or nursing a grievance that he was grossly underpaid.

My duties were not too taxing. Most of my time was spent entering crate numbers of cops into an enormous ledger. The sheer size of this book gave me a sense of importance. Another duty of mine every week was to take the wages in a huge tray up to the mule room, where the big and little piecers queued for their hard-earned pittance. That was the only occasion I had to go into the mill, and for the first time my heart went out to my father, who was a big piecer at the Standard Mill in Rochdale. The treadwheel in old prisons would have been preferable to a few days in the mule room, where workers, barefoot on the oily, uneven floor, continuously walked up and down between the in-and-out movement of the mules piecing up cotton strands that broke with monotonous regularity; the heat was stultifying and the noise horrendous. Another regular duty of mine was to top up all the inkwells and distribute new blotting paper to the other members of staff.

When we acquired electricity at home is a mystery. It seems that one day we were holding the taper to the gas mantle to bring soft light to the room and the next we clicked a switch on the wall and a brighter light shone from a sixty-watt bulb. I can't recall any major upheavals in our lives at 36 Leslie Street – no electrician tearing up the skirting boards for wires and connections. Now we had a wireless plugged into the mains no less, and you can't do that with gas, but our listening was rationed because of the expense, unless it was something special; and on Sunday 3 September 1939, a fine, warmish day, sitting on the steps to the backyard, face turned upwards to the sun to take advantage of the passing summer, I heard Mr Neville Chamberlain, our Prime Minister, informing us all that from today we were at war with Germany. I was only sixteen years old, so I accepted the news with equanimity; I didn't honestly believe it concerned me. The next day the air-raid sirens wailed over the land and I still wasn't convinced it was real; in any case it was common knowledge that it would all be over by Christmas. Here a very strange thing occurred. Aunt Marie received a letter from her brother, Uncle Ernest, who was in the navy, assuring her that there would be no war. It was dated 21 August 1939, but ironically the letter was delivered the day after war was declared. In his letter Uncle Ernest told Aunt Marie that he was now serving on HMS *Adventure*, which in the past had been in reserve but now was commissioned on active service.

Contrary to popular expectation, the war was not all over by Christmas, and war in the air and on the high seas was taking a heavy toll of British lives; and at home Uncle Ernest was constantly in our thoughts.

During this moment of history, when I was still filling inkwells at the Rutland Mill, only once was I in trouble. Next to me, the girl on my desk was new, a little older than me but very self-assured. I didn't really get on with her, as she treated me like a minion – 'Bring this', or 'Pass me that' or, once when I sneezed, 'For heaven's sake, use a hankie'; and while I appreciated the fact that she was slightly superior in office seniority, she had been with us only for a few days whereas I was an old hand. Anyway, one dinnertime I happened to mention that the cotton mill was a frightening place at night, especially now that the war was in full swing and all the windows were blacked out. Ken Smith, the senior clerk, was about to leave the office and as he was passing he said that the mill was a frightening place during the day. Clever Clogs snorted. He looked at her and continued. 'Some time ago, he said, when he was doing my job, as he was about to enter the passage a man walked towards him carrying an arm on a piece of paper, followed by two other workers who were supporting the man who had lost it. He'd had an accident with a fan belt and there was blood all over that passage, and that was in the middle of the morning, he said, and some say that his ghost still comes along the passage at night. The story scared the pants off me. A cotton mill at night is never silent: it creaks and groans, and somewhere in the factory something falls to the floor. But when he'd gone she said she wasn't afraid of the dark.

'You're pathetic,' she said.

That did it. 'All right,' I replied. 'Go up into the mill tonight, then.'

She said she couldn't tonight as she was going to the pictures and that was that.

But the following night when everyone else had gone and the factory was deserted apart from us, as she was stamping the mail she gave the last stamp a violent thump, turned to me and said, 'I'll be back in ten minutes.' As she stormed out of the office, I thought, What's the matter with her? Then it all came back to me – my challenging her to go into the empty black mill. I dashed after her to the beginning of the long stone passage that led to the steps up to the card room and stared into the blackness, but it was too late: there was no sign of her. I hadn't a torch or anything – it had never really occurred to me that she would take up the dare. I gulped. Then again, she was so cocksure and I hadn't forced her. Tentatively I called her name. The silence was deafening, so I called again, louder, but to no avail. So I shrugged and wondered if she'd gone home, leaving me standing there like a bridegroom wondering if it isn't too late to call it off. But when I went back to the safety of the bright office, I saw her coat over the back of the chair, so I knew she had gone into the card room. Suddenly I'd had enough. If she wanted to play silly games, that was up to her. I had a tram to catch, and when she returned to the office full of triumph I wasn't going to be sitting there to applaud, and she could put that in her pipe and smoke it.

However, when morning inevitably came there was a strained atmosphere in the office when I arrived. The girl was not there, but more remarkably the secretary was, and he looked as if he'd had a serious illness and hadn't yet shaken it off. 'Come into the board-room,' he rasped, and I followed him into the hallowed magnificence reserved for the chosen few. He sat at the enormous table. 'What happened last night?' was his opening gambit. For a moment I didn't understand; then the events of the night before came back to me and I told him as much as I knew. In a quiet voice he filled in the rest. At about three o'clock in the morning he had been called out of bed by the police. The front door of the office was wide open and on entering they'd spotted the pile of mail unposted and the girl's coat slung over the back of the chair. The secretary dutifully posted the letters and put out the lights. Nobody gave going into the factory itself a thought and it was only when the women arrived in the morning to start work in the card room that the girl had been discovered in a half-full skip of bobbins, fast asleep. Again the secretary was called back to the mill and, observing that the girl was on the verge of a breakdown, instructed the other girl in the office to take her home and call a doctor. Then I arrived, the only one in Shaw apparently unaware of the calamity at the Rutland Mill.

The secretary gave me a severe rollicking, ending with the fatal words, 'Get your cards,' which in everyday parlance means, 'You're sacked.' I was appalled by what had happened to the girl and ashamed at my cowardice in not going to find her. Anyway, head down, I shuffled from the boardroom and sat at my desk, still in heavy shock. Then the secretary came back and sat in his place, and, probably from force of habit, on seeing him in his familiar seat I opened the enormous ledger and started, in a daze, to enter the numbers in the correct columns. The fact that I had just been given the sack never entered my mind and the secretary didn't press the matter; we both carried on as if it had never happened. The girl didn't return to work, so in all probability the secretary had concluded that he couldn't afford to lose two members of his staff in one day.

*   *   *

When I travel back in time to when I was just gone sixteen years of age, one particular incident in that historic year of 1939 springs immediately to mind. It was not the declaration of war but something more significant in my life than the inevitable conflict to come.

It all began to snowball one Sunday afternoon, when I found myself in a friend's house. How or why I was there I've completely forgotten, but one thing sticks in my mind: in the front room there was an upright piano and anything musical had always attracted me. I should add that I played the mouth organ, which hardly entitled me to call myself a musician. Any fool can press a piano key and get a result, and we all do it, but when my friend sat down to play, I listened with awe as he knocked out a popular dance tune. What impressed me more than anything was that he never once looked down at his hands, and without a break in the music he looked towards the door and said, 'Come in, Arthur.' Another youth entered, carrying a violin case, which he opened, and after a few tentative tuning notes they segued into 'The Blue Danube'. Then with more panache they went into a swing version of the same thing. I was transfixed, absolutely spellbound. If only I could play the guitar, we could form a British Hot Club de France. Surely the guitar wasn't too difficult to learn? I desperately wanted to be a part of the action and before I could stop myself I blurted out that I played the drums, which wasn't strictly accurate: all I possessed was a pair of drumsticks from my Scout days. The next Sunday afternoon I brought them along. I was the last to arrive and I was introduced to another member of the group, who played the bass, which belonged to his father, who fortunately was in hospital for a month or two. In a short time we were into the first few bars of 'Red Sails in the Sunset'. I was perched on the arm of the settee, drumming on the seat of a chair, and I'll tell you something: it wasn't at all bad – we were definitely in the groove. My friend on the piano had a healthy pile of sheet music and the rest of us busked it.

After a few more Sundays we were really swinging, to the extent that I was encouraged to do sixteen-bar breaks. I'd no idea where these came or how long were sixteen bars. I just beat time until they all stopped playing and the pianist said, 'Take it away, man,' and I went into a drum routine, starting on the chair seat, 'rack-a-tacket' on the back of the chair, on the linoleum part of the floor to the arm of the settee, all to the accompaniment of 'Yea, man, go for it.' It was heady stuff.

A couple of Sundays later we were at the stage of getting together a programme for dancing and suggesting names for the band. There was 'The Oldham Serenaders' and 'The Swinging Four', but the favourite was 'The Blue Rhythm Band'. I have no excuse for what happened next. Whatever possessed me to even consider we were ready for public scrutiny? But on the spur of the moment, unbeknownst to the rest of the band, I placed an advert in the *Oldham Evening Chronicle*: 'THE BLUE RHYTHM BAND WILL PLAY AT ANY FUNCTION, DANCES, WEDDINGS, ETC. MODERATE TERMS' and to my astonishment it was in the local paper that same evening. I couldn't wait to take the cutting with me to show the lads next Sunday. My troubles, however, were just beginning. On Wednesday, only two days after the advert had appeared, I received a reply. I was absolutely flummoxed: it had never entered my head that somebody would write back – my thought process had ended with the advert.

Fortunately the letter contained a telephone number. Good, I only had to tell them that we had another engagement on that particular Saturday. Yes, that was it – simple. Standing in a telephone booth, I dialled the number and a very attractive woman's voice answered. No, she hadn't sent the letter; she was only the secretary to Mr Flintock, the secretary of the club. Her voice was so pleasant and seductive that I found myself discussing terms for an evening of dancing at a municipal hall in Hollinwood. Having agreed a fee, I was now a worldly business tycoon and ended the conversation by saying I was looking forward to seeing her at the dance.

It wasn't till I'd walked halfway down the street that the enormity of my brashness came home to me. If only I had the address of the recruiting officer of the French Foreign Legion, I could be halfway to Sidi-Bel-Abbes by Sunday. Alas, this was not to be, and when I faced the lads on Sunday I confessed abjectly and fully. They looked at each other, and then the pianist said, 'We'd better get down to it.' We had only one Sunday left before we took to the road. Oh, how I loved my comrades at that moment, and how much I was looking forward to a week on Saturday! I was in the lofty realms of euphoria again, leaving myself wide open for the sucker punch. It was later that evening when the bombshell burst: I didn't have a drum kit. I certainly couldn't turn up at our debut with a pair of drumsticks and an old kitchen chair. Once more I fell on my feet. The pianist's brother ran a musical instrument shop and I hired the accoutrements for the Sunday only and on the condition that I returned them in good order. I agreed and walked away with as much as I could afford, which unfortunately didn't include a bass drum, but already I had an idea about that.

The days dominoed down to the fateful Saturday, and to seven o'clock in the evening, by which time the dancers were already changing their shoes in the cloakroom. The communal hall itself was a barn of a place, with chairs all round the dancing area and a stage where we would soon be performing. We were late, through no fault of our own: three trams had refused to take us on board. Normally tram conductors were in the main accommodating, but we were an odd collection. I was laden down with the big drum that I had borrowed from the Scout troop and a hired gold-glitter snare drum under my arm. The rest of the kit was packed in a suitcase crammed with the foot pedal for the big drum and a stand for the snare drum, not forgetting a carrier bag of sheet music. One witty conductor asked which one of us was Oscar Rabin.

Eventually thirty minutes later we were on the stage, busily sorting out our instruments. The bass player helped me with my stuff and picked up what he surmised was the stand for my snare drum. He looked at it curiously and then nudged me with it and whispered, 'What's this for?' Now he'd opened it out I understood. In my hurry to get out of the musical instrument shop I'd hired myself an ordinary music stand instead of the stand to hold my crowning glory, the gold-glitter snare drum, but the music stand would have to do for tonight.

I carried on tightening the ropes on the big drum, flicking my finger against the skin to satisfy myself that it was taut enough for a quick step. All this time there was a puzzled silence from the waiting dancers. They were mostly middle-aged women – it must have been some kind of Mothers' Union anniversary, or something like it. I fixed the foot pedal on to the big drum and balanced the gold-glitter snare drum on to the music stand, giving it two experimental taps to make sure that it didn't bounce off. The pianist had opened the lid of the upright piano before placing his pile of music on top within easy reach. Then with an arpeggio the tuning began, by which time the dance should have been in full swing, having started forty-five minutes ago.

Apart from us musicians the place was tight with the silence of amazement, even when the pianist nodded his head and opened with a Paul Jones. Usually this was just a preliminary so that everyone could get acquainted. The ladies went round in a circle, the men walked round the ladies in the opposite direction and when the music stopped couples facing each other were either delighted or lumbered as they then slid into a foxtrot or a waltz.

None of this mattered at this particular dance, though, as nobody left their seats to take the floor. They just sat stupefied all through our massacre of 'Here We Come Gathering Nuts in May'.

I was the first to crack. I had enough difficulty keeping the snare drum on the music stand, but a greater problem arose with the big drum. Every time I stamped on the foot pedal the big drum slid forward a few inches, and when the pianist had done about sixteen bars another calamity occurred: the pile of music on top of the piano dropped down into its innards, silencing the melody. We were left with only the thin whining of the fiddle for the tune, and only the Irish could dance to that. The situation was teetering dangerously close to farce. Stretched out almost flat on my back, looking as if I was on a recliner in my desperate attempt to get my toe on the foot pedal of the big drum before it ended up on the dance floor, I glanced fearfully at the immobile punters . . . Hostility, disbelief and outrage were the dominant expressions, directed at us maliciously. It was then that I noticed the secretary, who had met us on our belated arrival. He was standing in front of the stage, beckoning to me. I abandoned the big drum, went forward and bent down to hear what he had to say.

It was short and to the point. 'What are your expenses?' he hissed through gritted teeth.

I was so embarrassed that all I wanted at that moment was for a pile driver to trundle up and hammer me into the ground. I looked again at the lynch mob on the dance floor and whispered to him, 'Is there a back door to this place?'

'Behind you,' he replied curtly. Then he turned to the audience with a grovelling smile and asked, 'Is there anyone here who plays the piano?'

An old lady put up her hand and while we were feverishly struggling to collect our paraphernalia she was already thumping away at 'Carolina Moonbeams'. For a moment there was no response: the dancers were still shell shocked. Then, realising that they weren't going to get their money back, reluctantly they began to search out partners to express their grievances to as they shuffled round the floor.

After our escape we didn't wait for the tram and once we were at a safe distance from the communal hall we decided to walk home, – no mean feat, as it was all of three miles. Strange as it may seem, we were not downhearted. On the contrary, as we began to see the funny side of it I started to chuckle, which fathered a snigger and then a laugh, and soon we were all shrieking with maniacal laughter. Every so often we had to stop, offload and dry our eyes and our noses as we were shaken by another paroxysm of howling. It was carnival night at the asylum.

How could we have conceivably been a success with our amateurish blundering into a situation we were in no way competent to deal with? We had got away with it this time, but there'd be another and another until we were old enough to realise that all youth is not necessarily fireproof.

Meanwhile changes were taking place at the Rutland Mill. The storekeeper received his call-up papers and within a week he was serving in His Majesty's army. The next time he came to bid us farewell was on his embarkation leave, a hero. All we young bucks envied him and still very few shots had been fired in anger. His leaving the storekeeper's job left an important vacancy, and I wasn't going to let a chance like this pass by unnoticed. So from dogsbody in the office I became the new storekeeper, back in my beloved overalls, once more a worker, and I could sit on the upper deck of the tram and light up a Woodbine without embarrassment. My duties varied. I was responsible for all the goods that made a cotton mill operative. My storeroom was in the yard annexed to the main factory, a large airy room. On each wall but one there were wooden shelves about two feet in depth, divided into compartments three feet long and deep towering up to the eighteen-foot ceiling. These shelves were stocked with everything to keep the factory supplied with the necessities of life: different-coloured crayons to identify cops from the card room, electric light bulbs, nails, nuts and bolts, toilet rolls for the office staff and heads of departments – it was rather like a shop with everything costing only a signature.

I don't suppose for a moment that without a good storekeeper the factory would have ground to a halt, but it might have limped a bit. I didn't spend all my time in the storeroom. Whenever a lorry piled high with bales of cotton pulled up outside the warehouse, it was my job to offload it. Manipulating the hoist, I sent the clamps high into the air, where the lorry driver caught them in order to fix them round the bale. Then with a downward movement of the handle I lifted the load clear, lowering it gently on to a waiting trolley, where it was wheeled away into the maw of the cavernous warehouse. The next bale was clamped and the same procedure ensued, and so on.

It could be dangerous: in the unlikely event of the bale tearing itself free of the clamps and hurtling to the ground, if I happened to be underneath it, looking the other way, it would be goodnight Vienna, and I would be carted off to the mortuary with a very flat head, half my size and twice as wide. With the tall doors of the warehouse open it was a pleasant enough occupation. In the summer-time the warehouse was always the coolest department in the mill, but in winter a polar bear would have been in serious danger of hypothermia. I offloaded the bales wrapped up like one of the crew of Scott's Antarctic expedition. Blizzards in a Lancashire winter were frequent, but the bales still had to be unloaded until thankfully I closed the enormous twenty-foot doors and hurried off to a room adjoining the general offices, where a hot mug of tea helped to bring my circulation back to normal.

Nobody knew where I would be at any given moment, but hanging about in my storeroom wasn't an ideal way to pass time away, until I had a brainwave. I bought a lilo, hauled it up the shelves to the top one just under the ceiling, and laid it out so that I could lie comfortably, reading books or just resting. It was high enough to be unseen by anyone on the floor fifteen feet below, but a good vantage point for me to observe them. So that I would not fall off my perch if sleep overtook me, I nailed the long handle of a brush across the edge. It was the perfect bunk on an ocean-going liner. On one occasion, a labourer from the mule room poked his head round the door and called me. Had I been on the floor I would have asked him what he wanted and as long as he signed for it he could have taken away his articles; but when this particular man came in, he decided that I wasn't there, had a quick shufti round and then snatched two light bulbs and stuffed them in his pocket. He was about to leave when I shouted, 'Oi!' He stopped in his tracks, looking round. 'Put them bulbs back,' I yelled. He didn't hesitate: he put the bulbs back and ran out terrified. He was the gofer for the mule overlooker but he never entered the storeroom again without first knocking on the door, giving me time to climb down before shouting, 'Come in.'

In the course of my work I was able to visit any part of the mill to check on supplies. Sometimes I'd just be bored by long stretches in my secret bunk and in truth I had no object in mind but I walked purposefully with energy and foresight, ostensibly carrying out my duties. The operatives in the mill seemed to enjoy my passing through, exchanging cheery badinage. One morning I was chatting away to a couple of big piecers who were eulogising about Bing Crosby. My face lit up: Bing was my idol too. Spotting a bucket resting aimlessly in the corner, I picked it up, stuck my head in it and sang 'When the Blue of the Night Meets the Gold of the Day'. I finished off the song with a 'boo boo deo voihm' and when I lowered the bucket the couple of lads were now a dozen, obviously impressed by my rendering. With smiles all round, and like a seasoned artiste, I left them wanting more. Some of them started to call me 'Bing' and from then on there was always a bucket handy when I went up into the mule room. I vocalised other Bing offerings but the favourite was 'When the Blue of the Night'.

The bubble had to burst. Some of the big piecers were leaving their machines to gather round when I put my head in the bucket. I was in particularly good voice one morning and I finished up with the usual 'deo voihm', but when I took the bucket from my face the audience was not what I expected: it was the manager himself, all thin, six feet two of him. I attempted a sickly smile but he was unmoved. Either he didn't like Bing Crosby or in the last few weeks production at the mill had dropped disastrously. The manager, who must have been in his seventies, spoke in a quavering voice, but as always he was economical with his words. 'Get your cards,' he said, and he left, the mule room. I looked round but all my newfound fans were frantically busy at their machines.

This was the second time I'd been sacked from the Rutland Mill, but I'd learned the lesson from my first dismissal. I ignored it and continued to be the storekeeper. A few weeks later when the mule overlooker passed me in the yard he said, 'You must have a great guardian angel looking after you.' Naturally I didn't give it a second thought until the next time.

I must have been about sixteen when I had dancing lessons, not tap or ballet but ballroom dancing. I attended evening classes twice a week at Eddie Pollard's Dancing Academy, in Hollinwood. I never saw Eddie dance himself. He collected the fee at the door and put on the records, old seventy-eights, on an even older gramophone. Without wishing to boast, I was a pretty good dancer. I didn't get many partners, because I was a very young sixteen-year-old and like a fool I concentrated on learning to dance rather than assignations. I could do the fishtail and the running six and could even get round the floor without watching my feet. I wasn't too fussed about the waltz, and the foxtrot was OK. However, the quickstep was my metier. I don't quite know why I have mentioned all this, except now I'm a senior citizen I can still do a fishtail but in all my life I've never met a woman who can manage it.

One Sunday morning we had a very pleasant surprise. Uncle Ernest came to visit us on one of his leaves. What a fine figure of a man he cut in his navy uniform as he stood with his back to the fire, Vernon on his left and me on the other side! He spoke modestly of actions at sea in which he had taken part. Vernon and I drank in every word, watching him with admiring eyes. Obviously he couldn't tell us what ship he was serving on or where any operations took place. In fact he was reluctant to answer all our many questions and it was only when he had left that I realised that we should have talked about something else. As it was Sunday we had Yorkshire pudding and onion gravy, but today we all had a smaller portion in order to heap his plate, as the dinner was now in his honour.

Needless to say, we were all in the war as well. Firewatchers were introduced and once a week, according to a roster, a few of us spent the night on the roof of the factory with sand and stirrup pumps, in order to deal with any incendiary bombs released by the Luftwaffe. The Rutland Mill was situated on the edge of the moors, bordered by grassland, so at night on the factory roof we were surrounded by impenetrable blackness; the millions of stars above were the only visible proof that we were not upside down. The nearest target for the German bombers was the city of Manchester, ten miles to the south; and Liverpool was another danger area, much further away to the north-west. In all the time of our firewatches no one was called upon to put out an incendiary, no one even saw an incendiary and to be brutally honest none of us ever heard an aircraft, friend or foe – in fact Churchill and his war cabinet would have been much safer holding counsel in the boardroom of the Rutland Mill.

It was now clear that I would soon be called up to lend my shoulder to the wheel (what a useless choice of words). My mate Bobby Hall and I discussed which service we could volunteer for. We were both physically fit from our camping excursions and a brief dallying in Health and Strength, in which we had practised co-ordination of muscles, centralisation of the abdominal wall, pectorals, latissimus dorsi – we knew it all, almost as if we'd been preparing ourselves for the service of King and country. Bobby made up his mind to volunteer for the navy, but I had other plans: my ambition was to train as a fighter pilot. I desperately wanted to be one of the few who were owed so much by so many, according to Churchill, and that is why I would opt for the Royal Air Force – that is, if the war was still on.

How I came to regret that last thought about the duration of the war! On 25 November 1941 the flagship HMS *Barham* was torpedoed off the coast of Egypt, and five minutes later she capsized, exploded and sank. The War Office despatched over eight hundred telegrams expressing condolences to parents, wives or any next of kin. Granddad Sykes opened the buff-coloured envelope with dread in his heart. 'We regret to inform you that your son . . .' Now as for so many other grieving families the war had laid its clammy hands on 36 Leslie Street, and never again would we see Uncle Ernest, but to this day I can still visualise him standing with his back to the fire in the warm aroma of roast lamb.

As I sat in my storeroom one day, gazing at the blank whitewashed wall, an idea began to form. I took a handful of coloured chalks and began to sketch a flight sergeant pilot looking up into the sky. It was life sized from the waist up, with wings above his left breast pocket and three stripes on his upper arm topped by a crown. It wasn't bad – in fact people began to come into the storeroom on some pretext or other in order to see the sketch. The huge expanse of whitewashed wall was inviting and in a short time I'd sketched the head of the mule overlooker. His round, white, podgy face dominated by spectacles wasn't too difficult. More people came in and chuckled as they recognised the expressionless face.

Elated by my success, I added other bosses and even the secretary of the mill, my first boss, as I had an inexhaustible supply of crayons of many colours. The whole of the hierarchy was now on my wall, head-on or in profile, smiling or glowering, everyone recognisable. Word soon spread and each came into view the portraits and sheepishly give their own visage a cursory glance, and they came back again to examine their faces more closely when they thought I wasn't looking. It wasn't a storeroom any more; it was the portrait gallery of the Rutland Mill.

However, one face was missing: that autocratic phissog of the manager. There was an ideal space in the middle of his workforce, a perfect placing; and more than that, whereas the others were life size the manager, as befitting his rank, would be twice life size. I hadn't seen him since the bucket episode but he was an easy target. Some days later I was standing halfway up my ladder, shading in the wispy, white hair of his head, when there was a commotion outside the door. I was too wrapped up in my art to take notice, but then the door burst open and one of the workers in the warehouse crashed in, in a muck sweat, saw me up the ladders and said, 'There's three lorryloads stacked up waiting to be offloaded.' Turning, he was about to dash back when he stopped suddenly. He turned round and for the first time he saw that the man holding the ladder steady was the manager.

'Oh, I didn't see you, sir,' he said.

The manager, with his face sideways, so that I could sketch his profile, and without moving his lips, ordered the man to find somebody else to work the hoist.

The portraits remained long after I had left to serve my country and although the inside of the mill was painted twice a year, one wall remained inviolate. It was never painted over and when the mill finally closed in 1963 the flight sergeant, my first sketch, was still staring into the sky.

MY COUNTRY NEEDS ME

On or about my eighteenth birthday I left home to join the Royal Air Force, taking with me a carrier bag containing shaving kit, soap and a handkerchief, which for the few early years of my life had been pinned to the front of my jersey but had been hardly used when my sleeve was available. In addition I had a bag of Mint Imperials for the journey and half a crown for emergencies. I walked the five or six hundred yards from home until I reached the Methodist Chapel; then I stopped and looked back to 36 Leslie Street, just one of a row of ordinary houses, overlooked on the right by Ward Street Central School, with Ward Street on the left, all surrounding two acres of wasteland fondly known as the Mucky Broos, and at the far end of Ward Street, Featherstall Road. I swallowed a lump of nostalgia in my throat. It wasn't exactly the New Jerusalem, but it had been my own secure little world for seventeen years.

At Oldham Central station I am the only occupant of the windswept platform. A porter emerges from a door, a half-eaten sandwich in his hand. He takes out a huge pocket watch and looks down the line. Then he sees me and obviously comes to the conclusion that helping me on to the train with my carrier bag wouldn't warrant a tip and he disappears inside again to finish off his breakfast. Turning, I examine the Nestlé's chocolate machine but as I feel for some coppers a strident bell announces that a train is due, and at that moment, chugging asthmatically, it comes round a bend and squeals to a halt in the station. No one alights and I am the only passenger to get on. The guard's piercing whistle brings my head out of the window in time to see him wave his green flag before adroitly nipping back into his compartment, and with a hoot of indifference the train leaves Oldham, bearing me to the beginning of a new life in the Royal Air Force, cue music, go lights, stand by curtain. Every now and again I indulge myself in a spot of melodramatics, and believe me, there isn't a dry eye in the house – all, of course, in my imagination, which explains my sometimes vacuous expression.

Padgate was my destination, a collection point for new recruits. Naturally I didn't know anybody, and I was too shy to rectify this. Others more convivial hung about in groups, enjoying the start of a new adventure, all in civvies, the only piece of uniformity being cardboard boxes containing our civilian gas masks slung around the shoulder by a length of string. I remember standing open-mouthed, listening to a group whom I took to be Poles or Czechs. They were neither. I was about a couple of thousand miles wide of the target: they were all from Glasgow. Looking around at the motley collection of would-be heroes my heart sank. I knew that the war wasn't going well, but if they were enlisting the likes of us the situation was worse than I thought. By lights out I hadn't said a word to anybody. In fact the last time I'd spoken had been back at home when I said, 'Well, I'll be off then.'

I climbed into a top bunk and, stuffing my head into my rolled-up jacket, which was to be my pillow, I cried silently, tears pouring from me until I ran dry; stifled sobs racked my body in a bout of self-pity and homesickness. I hated change, but this wasn't just change, it was a monumental leap into the unknown. It never struck me that my misery was the ending of my youth and the beginning of my education, the door opening to manhood.

Lesson one came the following morning. Everyone had left the hut to parade outside, except that is the old sergeant, two smart characters in sports jackets and flannels, possibly thirtyish, and me, fascinated by the three of them whispering together. Then one of them took out his wallet and surreptitiously passed over something that crinkled into the sergeant's big hand. While it was disappearing into his trouser pocket, he glanced around to check that they were alone, and with a start he spotted me, and barked, 'Outside, you, or I'll have you on a fizzer.' I hurried out, followed by the irate NCO, but the two 'nudge, nudge, wink, winks' didn't leave the hut. Nor did they appear on any other subsequent parade and I learned my first lesson in the academy of life: there's always a way round everything if you have the wherewithal.

On one of our next parades we were all in uniform, well most of us, some partially fitted, some ill fitted and one or two fit only for the dustbin. We were being instructed in the art of forming fours, dressing, halting, about turning, etc. – not a taxing programme for us lads, but there's always one ... Ours was an obviously well-educated, well-connected youth, six feet four, with a podgy, lumpy body misshapen by three square meals a day since birth in houses where dinner was taken in the evening and not at midday. Apparently there wasn't a uniform to fit him, so when we all paraded he lined up with us in his civilian suit and his box gas mask held round his shoulders by string; the only bit of uniform was a forage cap, which was obviously too small and looked even more ludicrous when worn perfectly straight on top of his head. He viewed everything with disdain, as if he'd just woken up in a rubbish tip. But this wasn't all. He was dysfunctional: his legs and arms were strangers to the rest of his body, he couldn't march, his right arm went out with his right leg, and when the order came 'By the left, quick march,' out went his left foot and so did his left arm, so he marched with a sort of lopsided gait. The way he managed to keep his hat on defied all the laws of gravity. The loud bellowing, the cajoling, the demonstrations of the drill sergeant were useless. To put it simply, he was a misfit and no further use to the RAF, and within two days he was demobbed and back in civvy street. Poor lad, I felt sorry for him. On the other hand, I wish I'd thought of that – but then again I was happy where I was, and he undoubtedly enjoyed a much better life in his ancestral home than he did in our Nissen hut.

After a few days of spit-and-polished boots, button burnishing, inoculations and drill, we were ready for our first posting. It was ... Blackpool. When I read this information on the noticeboard my heart surged with joy. Sixteen weeks in Blackpool, the whole summer in Blackpool – I could scarcely believe it. Accommodation and food were free, and on top of that we received money to spend, so you can imagine my euphoria as I shouldered my pack and rifle to rough it in the land of my dreams.

On arrival at Blackpool Central station our intake was paraded so as to be informed of the allotment of billets, and once again my cup of happiness was dangerously near the top. We were not to live in barracks, Nissen huts or tents; we were billeted in bed-and-breakfast guesthouses a short walk from the tower and even shorter to the promenade. Perhaps this was a dream and I was still in Padgate with my head buried in the jacket.

As I made my way up the stairs of my guesthouse, carpeted stairs too – what a novelty, I stood at the door of the bedroom, wondering if I should knock. I could scarcely believe my eyes. Perhaps I should have taken my boots off before I entered. There was no tatty, torn linoleum on the floor but instead a thick wall-to-wall carpet, a rug in front of a dressing table – a dressing table no less, twin beds with white pillows, eiderdowns, bedside tables with lamps and a glistening chandelier above. It was more palatial than anything I had ever seen, even in films. I couldn't wait for bedtime, or maybe I should now say, 'Roll on lights out'. Apart from Padgate, it was the first time I'd had a bed to myself. Then an awful thought struck me: I had been sent to the wrong address and any minute now an irate air vice marshal in a dressing gown full of medals would walk in and bellow, 'What the devil are you doing here?' But it was no mistake.

The man sharing the room was slightly taller than me, with light floppy hair above a boyish, unlined face; even so I reckoned he must have been pushing thirty. He merged effortlessly with the room, moving gracefully as he unpacked an enormous suitcase and placed bottles of various potions on the dressing table, two monogrammed hairbrushes, even a box of powder. On removing the lid he dipped in a powder puff and patted his face, scrutinising every inch of it in the dressing-table mirror as if yesterday he was somebody else. Satisfied, he turned away from the mirror, looking over his shoulder to check that everything at the back was in order, and resumed his unpacking, placing a pair of purple pyjamas on one of the beds and thus claiming his territory. I placed my razor and a comb on my bedside table and the housewarming was over.

The following morning was a rude awakening. My room-mate, whose name I've quite forgotten, had already gone, leaving a heady smell of perfume behind him, and I realised that I was going to be late. I ran to the parade area and with a feeling of dread I saw ranks of blue in front of a flight sergeant standing on a low wall and addressing them in a loud commanding voice. I squeezed myself into the rear rank, but not carefully enough. I knew that when the flight sergeant, without any pause in his welcome speech, said, 'Take that man's name' he was referring to me, and that evening in the office of the CO (commanding officer) I was on a charge of being late on parade, for which damnable sin I was awarded four days jankers. In other words, each evening in full equipment, including backpack and tin hat, I was to be found kneeling to scrub the floor of the orderly room. From a distance I must have looked like Quasimodo searching for his contact lens. After four days of scrubbing the same piece of floor, my punishment was over and I learned my second lesson: if you are about to arrive late it is better not to arrive at all. When I spotted the whole mob lined up I should have gone back to bed; they wouldn't have missed me.

The most important part of our training was learning the Morse code, essential to wireless operators. Our schoolrooms were at the Winter Gardens, a venue I played many times years afterwards in a more peaceful, pleasurable age. Incidentally, the mastering of the Morse code was a doddle for me: I was already proficient and could send and receive in Morse code as fast, and in some cases faster, than some of the instructors. I'd mastered this skill when I was sixteen in order to be a wireless operator in the merchant navy. On reaching a fairly competent standard, I applied to the Marconi School of Wireless in Manchester and I'm sure they would have accepted me but for two monumental obstacles. First, not too difficult, I had to get my father's permission but the second, the impossible barrier, was in the small print: the course would cost fifty pounds, almost as much as our house was worth, so joining the merchant navy was out of the question, which was probably just as well because the war was imminent and, as I was to learn later, the German U-boat packs were no respecters of young British seamen and my chances of being seventeen would have considerably diminished.

However, here I was in an extraordinary, sunny Blackpool, marching, drilling, doing rifle practice and dozing through the lazy afternoons in the Winter Gardens, fitter than I'd ever been. I even enjoyed guard duties, standing as smartly turned out as the Grenadiers outside Buckingham Palace in tin hat and full blancoed webbing with bayoneted rifle, enduring endless box-Brownie camera snaps and trying not to blink when the shutter went.

The weeks rushed by too quickly for my liking. I was now conversing with my instructors at a speed too fast for ordinary erks. Physically I could have run to the top of the Matterhorn thanks to PT every day on the beach; I was suntanned to a deep walnut, clear eyed and bushy tailed; I even looked forward to guard duty, although we were only guarding Marks and Spencer's. Marching to the corner, clattering my boots on the pavement as I effected a copybook turn before marching smartly back to my clattering halt, left turn, order arms and a last stamp of standing at ease – awesome; all the holiday makers sitting outside their digs enjoyed watching my every movement and when I stood easy they all relaxed and lifted their newspapers or continued their interrupted conversations, the show over until the next time I got itchy feet.

It was heady stuff. I was a bulwark of the Empire, so enveloped in a world of self hero worship that I didn't hear the screaming child being dragged along by a harassed mother who stopped and pointed to my bayonet and snarled, 'If you don't shut up, I'll tell that man to stick his knife in you.' The lad wiped his snotty nose on his already overworked sleeve and then, taking a few steps up to me, he kicked me fiercely on the shin, wearing clogs. I was so startled that I let go of my rifle and it crashed to the pavement. The newspapers went down, all the talking stopped as if in a drill movement and all heads swivelled in my direction. I picked up my rifle just as the sergeant marched out to see what the commotion was all about, and again I was on a fizzer and an apple-sized bruise on my leg was no defence.

Apropos of nothing, I learned a very important wrinkle while on guard duty. At night, if you feel tiredness creeping into you, hold your rifle with the butt on the ground so that the point of the bayonet is under your chin. If tiredness seeps insidiously into your brain, your head begins to nod and ouch, you're wide awake again.

Strangely enough, I never saw my room-mate during the day, so he obviously wasn't a trainee wireless operator. No matter, we went out for a drink together some evenings to the Queen's Hotel. We never drank more than a half pint of bitter each, but I couldn't help noticing that whereas I took hefty swallows from my glass he sipped his daintily; and we never really conversed. His eyes furtively searched the customers as if he was looking for somebody and one evening as we made our way back to the digs he said, 'We nearly got off tonight.' I didn't answer because I hadn't the slightest idea what he was talking about, for as far as I could recollect there hadn't been a woman in the room except the one behind the bar and he always ignored her.

It must be remembered that I had spent all my life up to a few weeks before in Oldham, which was hardly the sophisticated centre of the universe; and in those days homosexuality was a word we had never come across, let alone understood. I was still an innocent abroad and I suspected nothing. My room-mate was a very pleasant, likeable fellow and even if he did use face cream and wear pyjamas it only went to show that he came from a well-to-do background in which his gentle, superior ways were the norm. Conversely he must have thought of me as one of the peasantry, a bumbling village idiot who went to bed without washing, clad in my RAF-issue vest and underpants. For my own part I felt lucky to have found such a delightful room-mate.

On one occasion I received a cake from home. The last one had been a disaster, as the mice had had most of it, although I'd put it in my kit bag to guard against such a catastrophe. This time, however, I stood on my bed and hung the cake in my shirt from the chandelier.

This way it would be out of reach of the little terrors. My room-mate was asleep, or I assumed he was. I turned off my bedside lamp and settled down on my back, hands behind my head, awaiting the sandman and wondering if I'd tied the cake bundle securely enough. My lids were getting heavy when suddenly I was wide awake. Inside my bed I sensed rather than felt something crawling towards my thigh. It could only be a mouse . . . Very gently and slowly, I withdrew my arm from the back of my head, and then crashed it down with all my strength – and my room-mate yelled, 'Ouch!' Quickly I put my lamp on and he was abject with apologies. I couldn't grasp what he'd been up to, sliding his hand into my bed. He must have been dreaming. He kept saying sorry and that he wasn't like other men: he had been a ballet dancer before he'd been called up, and he missed his friends. I didn't know what he was babbling on about. When I switched my light off and settled down, he was still talking and the penny still hadn't dropped about his motives; in fact I was only glad it hadn't been a mouse. I was no wiser when a few days later he was demobbed. Apparently he had turned up on parade wearing lipstick and mascara. What's so terrible about that? I'd known him for only a few weeks but I missed him when he'd gone and was glad that I'd not been born into the aristocracy and made to wear make-up.

However, on balance my training in Blackpool was idyllic, but nothing lasts for ever, and we marched and drilled to the band of the Royal Air Force in our passing-out parade on the forecourt of the Metropole Hotel. Filled with exultation, I considered signing on for a full twelve years – it wasn't such a bad career. After sixteen weeks of high summer in Blackpool, I was bronzed, fit and well out of the chrysalis I'd brought with me to Padgate. I thought the war was a doddle and felt privileged to have been invited to take part. But I didn't quite know it all: I still had a lot to learn and one of the hard rules of life is that when the birds are singing and the sun is shining and you are in a state of utter content, that's the danger signal and in the middle of a happy smile, wallop! The sucker punch.

Eagerly scanning the noticeboard every morning for the whereabouts of my posting, I didn't care where it was. Any operational airfield would suffice. At least I'd be sending and receiving messages that mattered, chatting up members of the WAAF (Women's Auxiliary Air Force), with aeroplanes taking off one after another for Berlin or the Ruhr, whatever was the target for the night, counting the aircraft as they returned in the lightening sky of early dawn, and with the WAAFs. The mess hall would be mixed – good grief, would I ever get time to sleep? Sadly, like so many of my optimistic fantasies of things to come, it bore little relation to the actuality, but I lived in hope and my heart leapt when I saw my name on the noticeboard the following day. It straightened itself out when I read my posting to a place in Herefordshire called Madley and, underneath, 'All personnel above report to guard room to collect travel warrants at fourteen hundred hours.' So at two o'clock I stood before the corporal in the guard room, which in peacetime had been the children's department in Marks and Spencer's. As he was making out my movement order, I asked him if Madley was a fighter or a bomber station.

Without looking up he said, 'If you see a fighter or a bomber at Madley, he's lost.' I didn't get it, and as he handed me my documents he took pity on me. 'All in good time, laddie. You're still in training and if I were you I wouldn't be in such a hurry to put my head on the bloc.' I didn't get that either. What it is to be ignorant!

Madley itself may be a delightful little town but the place where the three-ton lorries deposited us in the early darkness preceding the onset of winter, was barren and pockmarked by Nissen huts, corrugated iron and concrete floors – Blackpool had hardly prepared us for this. The first morning at Madley dawned cold and grey. It seemed like only yesterday we were in shirt sleeves, basking in the golden summer of Blackpool. How quickly the seasons change! Greatcoats now unpacked were the order of the day.

We were paraded and after a short address the commanding officer gave us a lot more information, which was mainly carried away on the brisk east wind; then he called four of us out and for some unknown reason I happened to be one of them, and we became class leaders. We were given black armbands with the letters 'CL' in white, and we had to wear them on our sleeve. Our duties were not too onerous. We had to line up our allotted section and then march them off to the classes. Afterwards we marched them back again, and when we shouted 'Halt' and 'Dismiss' our responsibility was at an end. Why we had been chosen to be unpaid, stripeless NCOs I will never know. There were quite a few sergeants and corporals better equipped to do our basic duties, but they were permanent staff and presumably had other duties such as counting the pencils after we'd left at the end of our course and replenishing stocks for the next intake. Secretly, though, I really enjoyed my taste of authority.

We were in Madley for further training. There were fewer drills, less marching, and no guard duty at all, but there was more about the complex inside of a wireless set and naturally a quicker, more competent way of receiving and sending messages in Morse Code, call signs, contacts, wavelengths – in fact everything a wireless operator should know.

I had not expected to be posted somewhere for further training; after all, I thought we'd passed out. At this rate we'd still be under instruction when the war ended. I was beginning to wonder when, and if ever, we would be posted on real active service. The only aircraft we'd seen up to now were Halifaxes, Blenheims, Messerschmitts, Dorniers and Spitfires, but unfortunately they were all hanging from the ceiling of one of the classrooms. When would we be close enough to touch a real one? When would we be posted to an aerodrome? I fervently hoped to fly as a wireless operator air gunner.

At last one grey, blustery morning the noticeboard was full with postings. The marching, saluting and PT were over, and we were about to be distributed into the real war. Eager faces scanned the board and there was an electricity in the wind, almost tangible, as the lads broke off to join mates who had been posted to the same destination. I found myself alone, searching the noticeboard for my name. It wasn't there. Carefully I went through all the lists, but I was definitely absent. It could only have been a clerical error and I wasn't unduly worried – after all, I was a much tougher hombre now, an 'old sweat'. But in fact these false premises didn't last. The next morning reality dawned when I saw a convoy of three-ton lorries and the whole intake, loaded with packs and kitbags, hopped on board to be transported to the railway station. My Jack the Lad attitude disappeared in a wave of abject panic. By midday the camp was deserted. I'd been abandoned, and was marooned in a ghost collection of empty Nissen huts. There was no babble of voices as the lads left the mess hall to douse their mess tins in a drum of greasy lukewarm water, or the odd burst of laughter; now all was as silent as the inside of a pyramid stranded on a dreary, windswept stretch of a forgotten part of Herefordshire. The officers, NCOs, cooks, etc. – the permanent staff – were still here, and I wandered about in an advanced state of shock, hoping to be noticed, but for all the attention paid to me I might just as well have climbed a tree and joined the rooks. I sat miserably on my bunk in the empty Nissen hut, shivering in my greatcoat with one of my blankets round my shoulders, as the stove was black and cold. I was sinking into the deepest depression I could remember. When I'd descended to the lowest point of despair, an idea hit me, so obvious that it surprised me that I hadn't thought of it before – I could have saved myself a whole lot of anguish.

Full of old madam, I strode in to the administration offices and demanded to see the CO. The corporal I addressed was startled out of his wits. This was quite out of order: no erk had ever marched in before and demanded to see the Lord God Almighty. Then his whole demeanour changed from bafflement to one of understanding.

'Are you 1522813 Sykes?' he said, looking at a form before him.

I said, 'Yes,' and the mystery was solved. He handed me a travel warrant for me to go home for seven days' leave. Transport had been arranged to take me to the station. When I asked why I hadn't gone with the others, he told me that they'd all passed out with the rank of AC2 whereas I had been promoted to AC1. Wonderful!

My next step up would be leading aircraftsman, and then corporal – my fantasies rattled on, and I was up to the rank of warrant officer, when the corporal rudely interrupted by handing me my travel warrant and instructing me to be at the transport section at fourteen hundred hours.

The mess for the 'other ranks' was closed as they'd all left, and as I was the only 'other rank' I ate in the sergeants' mess with the permanent staff. It made a pleasant change to eat Maconochie's stew off a plate rather than from a tin. I sat next to the sergeant who had been in charge of our intake, and as we munched he told me that he was a regular and had served overseas. He painted such graphic visions of desert, date palms, camel trains, sun and generally what a wonderful life he'd enjoyed in the RAF until Hitler came along. Again my life's ambition veered sharply in another direction: I would sign on as a regular in the RAF and wallow in the fleshpots of the world. I told him that I was being posted to an airfield in Swaffham, Norfolk, and he looked at me with a puzzled frown on his face.

'An airfield in Swaffham?' he repeated, and I showed him my travel warrant.

'Stay where you are,' he said. 'I'll make some enquiries.'

And he went over to the next table and jabbered earnestly to another sergeant. I couldn't hear what they were saying, but there was a lot of head shaking and pointing at me. Then the sergeant stood up, and at the same time carried on with another sergeant. I don't think my sergeant was making much headway, but when the performance began again, this time between him and one of the cooks, I decided that enough was enough and the train wouldn't wait, so I legged it to make my own enquiries.

After leaving Madeley with a light heart I went home for seven days' leave. When I arrived, the house seemed deserted. There was only Dad and Mother – John was now in the navy and Vernon, I believe, had been posted to Ireland; ergo on my seven days' leave I was the only sibling at home and I spent as little time as possible in residence. I strutted all over Oldham and Royton, buttons brassed, boots as shiny as a Nubian's bald head; I called in on everybody I knew and quite a few I didn't; I practically slept in my uniform, applying wet soap to the crease line inside my trousers, which I then carefully placed under my mattress so as to effect a razor-sharp crease for the next day's exhibition.

The seven days' heady admiration, as I like to think they were, soon came to an end and I boarded a train for Swaffham. When I arrived at my destination, I was briefed by the transport officer, and I discovered that seventeen other RAF wireless operators had arrived, and as they were all AC2s and I was an AC1, I was put in charge. When I asked the officer about the airfield, he replied that there wasn't one for miles, and he looked again at my travel vouchers. 'Yes, you're in the right place,' he said, 'but this is an army base,' so once again it seemed that my posting to an airfield had been put on hold.

As my duties entailed mainly marching them here and there, there was very little difference from when I was a class leader at Madley, except that this time I had the rank. It was a posting I didn't understand: surely the army had its own wireless operators? I wasn't an expert in army procedure, but I felt sure that they must have advanced from the heliograph and semaphore. I can't remember seeing any of my air force buddies from the course at Madley, and apparently no one recognised me, but as I was one grade above them they were probably under the misapprehension that I was an 'old sweat', and after my stint as class leader at Madley I was well versed in marching them from A to B with all the aplomb of a regular flight sergeant.

On our first day I was ordered to march our contingent to the parade ground to await the regimental sergeant major's inspection. We stood in line in desultory fashion until I saw him approach. He wasn't marching; he was walking casually as if he was leaving the senior NCOs' mess, but I was taking no chances. I brought the lads up to attention and to my surprise they did it. The sergeant major instructed them to 'stand easy' and then he made his way along the line, asking the odd question and, judging by his smile, receiving some very odd answers. Finally he came to me.

After looking me up and down, he asked, 'What's the difference between an AC1 and an AC2?'

I was flummoxed. He might just as well have asked me what was Vera Lynn's address. So I blurted out the first thing that came to mind, 'Sixpence a day, sir,' which I thought quite reasonable under the circumstances.

'Is that the way you look upon your war effort?' he asked.

'The only way, sir,' I replied.

He looked at me for a time and then almost to himself he muttered, 'It's going to be a long war.'

Well into the evening I wrestled with my answer. What *was* the difference between an AC1 and an AC2?

Each day I marched my seventeen-man contingent to a small place allocated as a classroom for us. Then at mealtimes I marched them to the mess hall. Afterwards I marched them back to our classroom. On the whole they marched pretty well in step, except for one youth, about six feet four. This tall pile of loose bones, with black-rimmed glasses, didn't actually march; he ambled, and that made me feel slightly uneasy. He was always reading some book or other on the march, and when I stared pointedly at him he'd raise his eyes from the book and give me a dazzling smile. What could I do? I had no real authority and in any case he was thoughtful enough always to march in the rear on his own so that the rest of the squad couldn't see him. That infectious smile hasn't changed to this day and we have remained friends. His name is Denis Norden.

Why we were attached to the Second Army was a mystery to all of us and I suspect also to the War Office. I assumed that the First Army were the desert rats in the North African campaign. Apart from these two armies there was the Fourteenth Army, known as the Chindits, fighting a hazardous war in the dark, steaming jungles of Burma, but that leaves eleven armies unaccounted for, and even if you include the Salvation Army there are still ten others in action. As far as the Second Army was concerned, we were being assembled for an assault on the coast of Europe known as the Second Front, and if we were being prepared for the Second Front, what was the First? Questions, questions, questions. What I found most difficult to digest, was how would our attachment of eighteen RAF wireless operators increase our chances of winning the war? But what did we know? We were a very small cog in a massive, unwieldy contraption called 'Hostilities'.

We were with the Second Army but not of it. They held their parades and we were not included; their every move was governed by King's rules and regulations, ours by whatever sprung to mind. The RAF pay structure was different from theirs: had I not been an honest idiot I could have put myself down for ten pounds a week – or perhaps not, but I doubt if the army CO was getting that sort of money.

Our schoolroom possessed a blackboard all along one wall. Again questions arose: why were we in a schoolroom and what was there to learn? We were all under the impression that we were fully trained. Another stumbling block was where we were to sit. There were three rows of desks, but they were for infants. It would be impossible for Denis Norden even to contemplate sitting there – we would never get him out. In the event he perched on the desk top, and most of the others followed his example. When they were all finally settled, fags lit up, one of them polishing his boots, and Denis of course engrossed in the pages of his latest book, the others eyed me with a kind of expectancy and I looked back at them, hoping for suggestions. It was then that I noticed a stick of white chalk in the gully beneath the blackboard and, without further thought, as if someone was pulling the strings, I sketched the innards of a wireless set, roughly remembered from a textbook we had had during our course at Madley. The diagram remained clear in my mind but what it represented I had not the faintest idea. It didn't really matter: it was all a subterfuge. If we were visited by the army CO or his adjutant, it would appear that I was instructing the class in the intricacies of a wireless set – please God they were as ignorant as I was. I explained the plot to the class. One of them would be a lookout to warn of any approaching brass hats and the rest could do as they pleased. It was unanimously accepted and immediately someone started shuffling a pack of cards, and even Denis lowered his book; but there was one exception – there's always one . . . In this case it was a little genius called Shackmaster. He was only about five feet four but intellectually he couldn't have been much behind Einstein. If, for instance, you were talking about the Suez Canal and you happened to mention it was almost forty miles long there would be a snort and Shackmaster would quietly exclaim, 'Exactly one hundred miles long. It was built by Lessops,' and before you knew he would be vouchsafing the height of the Sphinx. This we tolerated, but on subsequent days we were to be well in his debt.

Each day we marched from the mess hall to the schoolroom in order to relax and enjoy ourselves. My scheme for a holiday home was cruising along when a sudden cry from the lookout warned us that the CO and his adjutant were approaching. There was a flurry of frenzied activity and when the two officers entered the room the class was facing the blackboard in rapt attention. On seeing them I sprang to attention but the CO ordered me to carry on and I did. Tapping the blackboard with my knuckle, I said, 'Shackmaster, should this be a triode or a double diode triode?' Shackmaster was magnificent. He rattled off such verbal babble of technical mumbo-jumbo that Marconi must have wondered where he'd gone wrong, but when Shackmaster started on about electrical impulses bouncing off the stratosphere and megahertz, holding up my hand I stopped him, as, baffled and bewildered, the two officers had left. The cards were being dealt again, Denis opened his book at the marker and I rubbed the board clean and invited Shackmaster to chalk a different diagram on the board in case the two officers came back. Oh yes, you've got to be several jumps ahead to be a skiver!

I was still punch drunk at Shackmaster's grasp of the mysteries of a wireless set. He was, without a shadow of a doubt, streets ahead of anyone I'd ever met, but he was not perfect. Oh no, he was unable to see the funny side of anything, even when he looked in the mirror. Comedy to him was a frivolous waste of energy which left him open to ridicule. For instance, somebody might say, 'I saw a Blenheim yesterday with one of its four engines blazing.' You didn't have to address this to Shack, only make sure he heard it, and as usual his snort would be bang on cue and he would reply,

'It couldn't have been a Blenheim. A Blenheim only has two engines.' This would be greeted by cries of derision and send Shackmaster scrabbling in his pack for his book to prove his point; the trap was set and poor Shack was sniffing the cheese. Somebody else would pipe up, 'I saw it too. Shack's right – it wasn't a Blenheim, it was a single-engined Halifax.' By now Shackmaster would be almost apoplectic with rage. How could we describe a Halifax bomber as single-engined? On reflection I take no pride in how we baited the poor lad, but I think I learned a very important lesson in life. It doesn't matter how brilliant you are academically, top-class master of this and that: all these achievements must be sprinkled with humour or else your superior knowledge is worthless. I didn't tease Shack after that; you don't take a blind man to visit the Tate Gallery.

The schoolroom was situated on the edge of a largish forest and as the days were getting warmer I applied and got permission to carry on our refresher course outdoors. The next day we carried a large table deep into the wood, followed by benches to sit on around it and presumably to discuss wireless problems. The four people not at the table were the lookouts and we all carried on from where we left off in the schoolroom, except most of us were stripped to the waist in order to get ourselves a healthy tan.

But too much of a good thing is more than enough or, to put it another way, we were all getting a bit cheesed off with our daily shirk. Lying out in a sun-dappled wood, writing home, reading, playing poker and throwing darts at a board tacked on to a tree may be all very well for an elderly coachload on a mystery tour, but as far as we were concerned there was a war on and again, why were we here? It was painfully obvious that the army had no idea why we had been tacked on to their ration strength; they'd obviously had no instructions from above and frankly I'm sure we were becoming a source of embarrassment. We were billeted with the soldiers, and in the evenings we had drinks with them in the local, but as far as the war was concerned we were strangers.

It was then that an idea came to me. It was daring and risky, but at least it would be positive. I went to see the army commanding officer. I was shown into his office immediately and straightaway I came to the point by asking him what exactly we were supposed to be doing attached to the Second Army. He threw up his hands and said, 'I'm as much in the dark as you are,' which came as no surprise, so I fired my first salvo by suggesting that we should be sent on leave.

He pondered this for a minute or two and I took the opportunity to leap in with a reason for requesting leave. I told him that we hadn't been on leave for over six months. He was visibly taken aback by this and I wondered if I'd gone too far, because prior to our posting to Swaffham a few weeks ago I'd enjoyed seven days at home and I presumed that so had the rest of my lads. But I was worrying for nothing. The CO brightened and agreed that we should have leave; in fact I think he was glad to see the back of us for a week. The only stipulation he made was that we couldn't all be absent together and we would have to go two at a time.

Game, set and match. Five minutes later I was breaking the good news to the lads, asserting that as I'd gone out on a limb for this leave I would be one of the first pairing, and the other lucky erk would be drawn out of a hat. Folding up the names, I put them into my glengarry, and with all the mob following I took it into the next hut and asked one of the squaddies to pick out a name. Holding the cap at arm's length above my head, the army lad reached up and fumbled around and came out with a bit of paper, which I handed over to the nearest of our mob. Unfolding it, he read, 'Hoppy Holden'. Immediately there were cries of 'Fix', 'Stitch-up' and 'It's a fiddle', etc., because it was no secret that Hoppy and I were close mates. Then one of the lads blurted out, 'All the pieces of paper have the name Hoppy Holden written on them,' but when I up-turned the cap on the bed they could see that this was not the case – it was perfectly legitimate. However, there was a trick in it. Inside our forage caps was a ridge and having had a few words with the army wallah, backed up with a packet of fags, I'd made sure that all the other names were on one side of the ridge and Hoppy's name was on the other, *et voilà*!

When I walked into our house they wanted to know if I'd

deserted as it was only a few weeks ago that I was on seven days' leave, and to be quite honest the days dragged by. I was keen to get back to the rough and tumble of Swaffham. Sadly, when I returned all future leave was cancelled. There was a flap on and we were all issued with travel warrants for a place called Gatton Park just outside Reigate. Into my third year in the air force and although there were plenty of aircraft whizzing about the sky I had yet to see a plane on the ground, and I'd never even seen a WAAF.

From the bustling, busy little market town of Swaffham to the quiet gentility of Gatton Park – what a difference, what a contrast! As the lorry deposited me inside the gates, I was deeply moved by the rolling splendour. Perhaps I was dead and this was the first staging post to heaven. Acres of grassland surrounding a wood, stately trees from the saplings of Elizabethan days – I was enraptured. There wasn't a tree in sight in the part of Oldham near Featherstall Road. Had there been one we would have been up and down it like a squirrel with its tail on fire. The centrepiece of Gatton Park was an elegant Georgian mansion and, just a few strides away, a private chapel, the whole bordered by shiny manicured lawns, and I couldn't get over how green the grass was, a totally upper-class strain of the greyish blades sprouting from cracks in the Mucky Broos like the tufts of hair in an old man's ear. For the moment a wave of nostalgia swept through me, but it was only a moment. I just stood by my kitbag, pack still on my back, lost in wonder as I took in a section of bright sparkling water almost hidden by the house.

The home of the Colman's mustard family, Gatton Park, was their fiefdom. This I learned later from one of the estate workers who lived in a row of much humbler dwellings a discreet distance from the big house. This local, who turned out to be one of the gardeners, added. 'Isn't it amazing that all this splendour was built by the little bit of mustard you leave on the edge of your plate?' This I didn't understand. I'd never left a bit of mustard on the edge of my plate – in fact mustard and I had yet to be introduced.

With a sigh of content I accepted the fact that once again I'd fallen on my feet. Granted it wasn't the operational flying station I had been eagerly expecting, but then again there were more things in life besides the war. I was shaken out of my reverie when a voice yelled 'That man there.' I whirled round to see a sergeant beckoning to me. He was with a group of new intakes, milling around, kitbags at their feet, packs still not offloaded. To me they were all strangers and to each other, the only thing we had in common being the badge sewn on to the sleeve of our uniform of a fist clutching bolts of lightning denoting that we were all wireless operators.

After a meal, which would be better described as iron rations, suggesting that the cooks were new as well and didn't yet know where everything was, the sergeant led us down to a row of tents by the side of one of the roads. Eight of us were allotted to each one. It was only when we crouched in a huddle underneath the ridge pole that we realised that eight of us in the tent was going to be a tight squeeze; three of us would have been one too many. Perhaps if we left our kitbags outside?

It sounded like a good idea until one miserable git said, 'What if it rains?'

We looked at each other in dismay – there's always one in a group.

Then someone else piped up with, 'What if one of us is taken short in the night? Unless he's by the tent flap he won't be able to get out.'

Somebody else suggested getting a bucket, but he was overruled when somebody else said, 'There isn't room for a bucket.'

In the event it wasn't as catastrophic as we'd made out. Half the tent would be on watch while the other half slept. Had they told us this at the outset it would have saved a lot of aggro.

The Colman family were not now in residence, as the whole area of Gatton Park had been commandeered by the RAF for the duration of the war. Already there were several air force bods established on the estate – mainly administration, cooks, general duty men. Naturally officers had commandeered the beautiful home of the Colmans and, of course, the officers' mess, leaving the other ranks to occupy the cottages. Trust the base wallahs to get their feet under the table while the lads at the sharp end presumably had to make do with tents. We were under no illusions: when we were sent off to join the action they would remain at Gatton Park until they were evicted by the cessation of hostilities.

After a few days we were organised into watches, as we would be in wireless contact with satellite stations twenty-four hours a day. More menacing still, the transmissions would be made from the backs of Bedford trucks equipped as well, if not better, than a static wireless office. Another week passed and still we didn't have a CO, but our luck couldn't last for ever; nor did it.

I was on duty watch. I wasn't actually at my set – in fact I wasn't even in the truck. Stripped to the waist, I was sitting on the steps, face upturned to the warm sun. I wasn't entirely out of touch with my satellite stations: inside, the volume on my set was full up. Headphones hanging within earshot, I dozed gently, when suddenly a shadow fell over me.

Sleepily, I lifted my hand to shade my eyes when a harsh voice said, 'Where's your shirt?'

'It's in the van,' I replied, settling down again.

The voice, now affronted, spoke again, 'Well, put it on at once, and say "sir" when you address an officer.' My heart sank: it was the end of the holiday.

The following morning we were paraded to hear him make his commanding officer speech. He was only a flight lieutenant, a middle-aged man who had a perpetual look of surprise on his face. He wore an officer's peaked cap but he'd taken the stiffener out of it so that he would look like Jack the Lad, but he addressed us all as if he was expecting a raspberry at the end of each sentence. From now on there would be discipline; any misdemeanour, no matter how minor, would be punished; he was going to lick us into shape, etc. Most of it was delivered at me and I knew from that moment that he was going to be a problem, the enemy within.

Throughout my life I have followed courses of action on the spur of the moment when two minutes of rational thought might have dragged me back from the abyss. This was the case when one

Sunday morning in Gatton Park we were marched down to the chapel to attend the service. We halted opposite the arched doorway, and we were straggling forward, dragging off our headgear before we entered, when for some unknown reason I put my cap back on my head, broke ranks and stood at ease until the others were all inside and I was alone. I was motivated by a barrack-room lawyer memory that taking part in a church service was not obligatory, and if on religious grounds you objected to entering a church you would be excused. Why on earth did these idiotic ideas catapult me into situations beyond my control? But the die was cast.

One of the real sergeants sauntered over to me when all the rest were inside sorting out their hymnbooks. 'What's up with you?' he said in a world-weary voice as if I wasn't the only one that morning to come out with some crackpot notion.

'I'm not going into church, sergeant,' I replied with the assurance that I had a good case.

'Aren't you C. of E.?' he snapped at me.

Good grief, that was a critical flaw in my stance. Why had I requested Church of England to be stamped on my identity disc? There were lots of other religions I could have claimed: Muslim, Trappist monk, Buddhist. My brain raced as if I was an inept politician trying desperately not to answer a simple question, but before I could blurt out an adequate response he'd marched towards the door and entered the chapel, whipping off his glengarry just in time.

I realised I'd won the exchange. All I had to do now was to stand at ease and enjoy the warm summer breeze. I was looking the other way, so I didn't notice the approach of the senior officer until he spoke.

'What's the problem, lad?' he said in a quiet, fatherly voice.

I sprang to attention and spluttered the first thing that came to mind. 'I don't believe in it, sir, not with the war and people being killed.' Actually I'm sure these words bear not the slightest relation to what I actually said – it poured out in fluent gabble.

He looked at me uncertainly, and then reasonably he said, 'Why not give it one more try?' and as he said it he gently propelled me into the chapel.

It was embarrassing to say the least. All heads were turned towards the entrance as we came in. Then the senior officer, his arm still round my shoulder in case I made a break for it, led me to a place next to him on the front pew – 'Officers only'.

As we sat, the padre came over to where I was sitting, and, laying his hands on the ledge in front of me, he began a lecture on why it was imperative that everyone should be Christian. After a few minutes he took his eyes from me and to the chapel in general he said, 'Let us pray for all our wayward lambs.' There was a shuffling as the congregation knelt and I did the same, blushing like an eastern sunset as my thoughts sped off at a right angle, as I noticed that, being in the officer's pew, I had a hassock to kneel on and I am sure the erks were on bare boards, ha, ha.

Perhaps that lunatic action of mine was responsible – but I shall never know. If my memory serves me right, I can't recall any more church services at Gatton Park.

One night I was on the midnight-to-eight watch, waiting for the welcome sound of the lorry bringing our relief from the camp. After the formalities of handing over were complete, we'd board the lorry, which would then take us back to camp for breakfast and, best of all, a few hours of blissful oblivion in our blankets. The night watch had been particularly draining, but the sun was strong and the birds were twittering 'Good mornings'. What a pity to waste such a glorious summer asleep! On impulse I waved the lads off – there'd be plenty of time to sleep when we're dead – and I started the long walk downhill to the town. Reigate was still unexplored, as far as I was concerned, but at least I knew where the WVS was (the Women's Voluntary Service), a canteen run by bright-eyed, tweedy women with perpetual smiles who dished out tea and buns, rock cakes, sweets, and cigarettes to anyone in uniform who happened to drop by. These surrogate mothers giving up their free time for their highly valued war effort were a different world from the exhausted, shawled women of the Lancashire cotton towns. I banished the thought. They probably had a WVS in Oldham too, but somehow I doubted it.

Contentedly I munched on a bun – it was a good idea of mine

– and sipped my tea. It tasted much better drunk from pottery. Also it was a well-known fact that the tea we drank at the camp was liberally dosed with bromide in order to dampen our appreciation of the opposite sex. The things we believed . . . Sighing with content, I continued to munch. Who needs sleep? I was feeling warm and comfortable and in a strange way the incessant babble of conversation was receding, as if someone was turning down the volume. The next thing I knew was that I was jerked out of a state of well-being by a crashing snore, and it was only when I noticed other servicemen staring at me that I realised that the snore had been mine, ruefully answering my cocky assertion, 'Who needs sleep?'

I couldn't stay in the WVS any longer. I put down my half-eaten bun and hurried into the fresh air. It was invigorating and once again I was wide awake and Reigate was my oyster. I took in my surroundings. Reigate itself was a flurry of activity during the day, with masses of servicemen – RAF, army, Poles, ATS (Auxiliary Territorial Service), a veritable league of nations. The British drove sedate old three-ton Bedfords, which pulled up at traffic lights with an apologetic wince of brakes; and now there were Chevrolets pulling up at the lights, doing at least forty miles an hour, stopping dead when they pressed the foot pedal with a triumphant chooooo of the airbrakes, shattering all the gentility of this lovely old town – the Canadian Army had arrived, careering everywhere, giving the impression that there was no speed limit in Toronto and beyond. But the envy of all the young bloods were the Canadian despatch riders. Even these weren't just men on motorbikes: they rode Harley Davidsons, the nearest thing to a horse on wheels.

The realisation hit me that I was still only twenty yards or so from the WVS and I'd been standing on one spot for the last twenty minutes, gawping like a hayseed from the mountain country. Then a motor horn peeped and a Bedford pulled up by the kerb. I hadn't even seen it arrive and had no idea why he was tooting. Could I have been asleep on my feet? He called out 'Eric.' Oh, blessed chariot! I dozed through the third gear of Reigate Hill and when we arrived back at camp I took off my boots, and that's all I could manage before sleep overtook me.

All the wireless operators were relieved of duties, two at a time, in order to take driving lessons. The cars were ordinary family saloons and the instructors all civilians, and for the next few weeks we shuddered and stuttered, veering erratically and at times bumping on to the pavement. Fortunately we were taught the rudiments of driving on the quieter roads surrounding Reigate. It was hairy, but I was quite pleased with myself, considering I'd only sat in the front of a vehicle once before. I was only ten at the time and that was when the lunatic who drove the bread van offered me a lift. He was obviously a racing fanatic, because he had me clutching on to my seat as he made his way up Oldham Road, crouching over the wheel, his foot flat on the accelerator, double declutching, making louder engine noises with his mouth than the motor itself; then, with spittle swinging from his lips, he stamped on the brake so suddenly that I slid down under the dashboard. 'Don't go away,' he said as he plunged through the shop door with an armful of loaves, but I'd had enough and when he emerged I'd gone. I almost perspire now at the thought of that crazy half mile. On reflection we couldn't have been doing more than thirty miles an hour, but that was unsafe for a bread van.

Anyway, when we were considered proficient enough as drivers to be tested, we were trucked off to Croydon – busier than Reigate – to be examined by a senior civilian instructor. I passed my test, but I think only just, because as I stepped out of the car he said, 'As a driver you'd make a good commando.' I never discovered whether this was praise or sarcasm.

A very interesting interlude, but that was only the first course; the main dish was driving a three-ton Bedford. We were chucked in at the deep end, at the wheel, in convoy and, if that wasn't hazardous enough, at night. It wasn't too bad once I could change gears without having to fiddle for the lever. The tricky part was keeping a distance of thirty yards between me and the tail light of the lorry in front. A lapse of concentration could be at the least embarrassing. The hooded headlights didn't make matters easier; a half-inch strip of illumination doesn't give a driver confidence. When I learned the reason for this crash course (unfortunate choice of words), that if, when we were in action, anything happened to the driver we would be able to take over, enabling the war to continue, this led to much conjecture at our camp at Gatton Park. We were now sure in our minds that we were a new innovation in the RAF, the first of its kind: an MSU or mobile signals unit. At least we knew now that we'd be mobile, but where would we be going?

The Second Front was now openly discussed. This was to be an invasion of Europe, a landing on the coast of France, something the Russians had been agitating for during the last twelve months: an all-or-nothing attempt to push the Germans back to Deutschland. It was dicey because we would have to overcome the cream of the Wehrmacht, who were heavily entrenched on the French coast. It was the most high-risk strategy of the war. It would be bloody and it would be final. No wonder the Russians were impatient for the assault to begin – they wouldn't be in it. As a prelude to this historic event, there was an exercise in the south of England under the name of Spartan, a mock battle between British and Canadian forces. In the event we didn't see anything of the battle, nor the Canadians, but for us it was a memorable evening.

Our MSU, 589A, left Gatton Park at twenty-one hundred hours in convoy. Several lorries carried personnel, our generator and a six-ton Crossley, and leading the convoy was the fifteen-hundredweight carrying the CO and his driver. The CO was the only one who knew our destination, and on hindsight this was the first mistake, for if he became the first casualty the whole convoy would be wandering about like 'It' in a game of blind man's buff. As it was only an exercise, however, such a situation eventually was, thank goodness, hypothetical. All our intrepid CO had to do was find his way to our destination but, give him his due, this was not an enviable task: following a map laid out on his knees through towns, villages and, at one hairy moment, a field, was almost impossible. One must remember that we were a blacked-out land, with no signposts, no traffic lights; the only illumination at the CO's disposal was a shaded torch with which he scanned his map, but doubtless he'd spent hours in his tent perusing and memorising the shortest, quickest route. Incidentally, it couldn't have included the field. I say 'doubtless', but on reflection the only thing that he would have been likely to peruse in his tent was the magazine *Lilliput*. At almost every turning we stopped and after hesitation and obvious indecision we turned either right or left. In the top of the cab of the three-ton Bedford was a hole and if I stood on the seat the top half of me was in the open air. At the sharp end of the service I would be armed with a Bren gun, but these hadn't yet been issued to us, and as this was only an exercise, I was able to enjoy the pleasant, cool night until we occasionally reached nearly forty miles an hour. This was exhilarating for the first few miles, but now it was almost midnight. Our destination could well be in Scotland, or more likely I wouldn't be surprised to find we were still in Gatton Park.

At one of our interminable stops I ducked down into the cab. The driver was half asleep, but I belted him on the shoulder and he sat upright quickly, as if he'd found the answer to something. All the wagons had switched off their engines, mainly, I think, to conserve petrol for our way back. Then we heard the sound of a motorbike. I popped up again through the hole in the cab top and leaned out. Our despatch rider was making his way from the direction of the CO's transport, stopping to say something to each driver. He puttered up to our wagon and I leaned down to hear him over the clattering of his machine.

'Anybody live round here?' he yelled.

Somebody poked his head round the canvas at the rear of the wagon and shouted, 'We're in Maidenhead.'

'Come with me,' said the despatch rider.

Nobby jumped from the back of the lorry and rode pillion down to the CO. He didn't return and the convoy moved off confidently this time because Nobby was crouching in the back of the fifteen-hundredweight shouting directions into the driver's ear; and, some-time later, we were back in camp. It was then that Nobby recounted what had happened. The CO, sitting next to the driver, poured himself a hot coffee from his thermos flask – coffee was a rarity, so he didn't offer it round – and when we arrived back at Gatton Park about three quarters of an hour later the CO was fast asleep. Nobby never even got a 'thanks' for our swift, safe return. Much more seriously, however, the CO's competence in map reading didn't bear scrutiny and boded ill for the future.

Whenever I got an evening free, Reigate was my target. I strolled from the camp, downhill, full of hope, but coming back it was different: I was full of best English bitter and I struggled to the top breathless and unable to walk another step. Occasionally, weary, sleepy and broke, I flopped down in the lush, sweet-smelling grass, staring up at a sky full of twinkling stars winking at each other, now and then a maverick comet falling out of formation, until my eyelids became too heavy to cope and I was asleep. After one such night of heavy slumber I was thrust into a new bright morning by the sound of aircraft engines. I sat up, fully awake. Two Spitfires flew past and the wonder of it all, from my vantage point on the hill, was that they had flown past below me – yes, I was actually looking down on them. I could clearly see the RAF roundels on the upper side of their wings. What a wonderful start to the day! I even forgot to have a hangover. I stood up and gazed down at the magnificent panorama, and my heart was full. Ours was a country to be proud of and with Churchill in the driving seat no German was going to goosestep this land into a suburb of Hitler's Third Reich.

On one of his rare visits back to camp the CO sent for me, and for the first time he actually smiled as he handed over travel documents for the Isle of Weight and dismissed me with a sarcastic 'Bon voyage!' His smile wasn't reassuring; for a start you could tell his face wasn't used to it, and it was the expression of a cat creeping up with eager anticipation behind a deaf mouse. The 'Bon voyage!' bit bothered me: that usually meant a cruise of some sort. It was baffling. Here was I, an RAF wireless operator who'd never seen an aerodrome and knew even less about the sea.

On the Isle of Wight I was met by another RAF wireless operator and together we were whisked off in a fifteen-hundredweight driven by a naval driver, who dropped us off at the foot of a gangplank. For the first time I was now certain that our destination would be somewhere at sea. On the dock we hesitated at the foot of the gangplank, unsure of our next move, until a voice from aboard shouted, 'What are you waiting for, the band of the Royal Marines?'

We were ushered down below to join a jabbering crowd, all talking at once in several different languages. In the dim light I looked around me and I assumed that this must be a converted cargo hold of a merchant ship. Who were all these people? Some were uniformed, some were in civvies. It was rather like a scene from a very busy mainline railway station when the train is over half an hour late and the milling commuters have no idea if indeed it will arrive at all. Then a cold shiver ran through me. Could this be a prison ship? I was about to put this thought into words when I was saved by the crackle of a tannoy. Immediately all heads swivelled round to discover where it was coming from, which is silly really – one didn't have to look at it. All one had to do was to stand still and listen while a disembodied voice gave us our instructions. Everyone was allotted a hammock and then we were lined up to be issued with a doorstep sandwich and a mug of char, after which we were given permission to turn in. But the question on everybody's mind was still unanswered – this was Swaffham all over again: what the dickens were we doing here?

As it was too early to turn in, we made our way up to the deck. Other men had had the same idea, and there was a long dark line of them, elbows on the rail, staring at the sea and thinking their individual thoughts, and an aroma of Woodbine and naval-issue Players hung in the air. Everybody was a smoker, their cigarettes shielded by horny hands. This seemed to be a little over-cautious – after all, there was not a whisper of an aircraft, unless they'd been bombing the Isle of Wight from gliders. Nobody spoke, so after a couple more cigarettes we made our way below to wrestle with our hammocks.

In the morning we were led to another cargo hold, which had been transformed into a huge wireless room. A shelf ran the whole way round three of the sides; there were wireless sets at yard intervals, a Morse key, and pads and pencils by each set. A three-badge naval rating showed us each to our allotted set. Almost every other seat was occupied, and what an odd lot we were, all in pairs, one to operate the set while his oppo stood behind the chair to take over if necessary: wireless operators from various army units, commandos, Canadians, merchant navy men, policemen, railwaymen and naturally a pair of Royal Navy men, and a lot of other uniforms I couldn't make out, nor the language they spoke. In all I suppose we were a job lot; it seemed that every one of our allies was represented. One thing we had in common was that we were all wireless operators. Excitement gripped me: this, then, was the prelude to the invasion of France.

I put on my headphones and tapped out the call sign I had been allotted and I waited. It was a blustery day and the ship was lurching from side to side, and again I tapped out my call sign. Our seats were weighted at the base so that they wouldn't fall over, but it didn't stop them sliding back and forward to the roll of the ship. I continued tapping dots and dashes on the Morse key while the chair slid slowly away from the set. Holding on to the ledge with my left hand, I waited a moment before the seat slid forward crushing me against the ledge, then back again, arm at full stretch as I held on – and never a break in my transmission.

In front of me, just above my head, was a porthole and in one moment I could see bright blue sky as I slid backwards and then as we moved forward the porthole was sea green. To tell you the truth, I was really enjoying it. I'd no idea where we were bound or what was the reason for a score of clattering Morse keys, each operator in contact with their own particular branch, but at last I felt I was in active service and wholeheartedly revelling in the joys of a fusky sea voyage. But my moments of euphoria were short-lived. The same old veteran of the navy came up to my set and plonked down an enamel mug half full of navy rum. I took off my earphones and he said, 'Get that down you – it'll do you good.' Up to then I'd been in full control of my bodily functions, but when I got a whiff of sipper, as the navy called it, I was immediately queasy, and, to my horror, I was about to be seasick.

I handed the headphones to my oppo and the old navy wallah took me up to the deck and left me. Amazingly the cold air and lusty breezes brought me back to life. All malaise gone, I was able to take stock of my surroundings. As far as I could make out across the turbulent sea there was nothing, not another vessel, in sight; in fact all around us the sea was empty of other ships, which worried me slightly. If we were the Second Front we were definitely undermanned and would most certainly lose the war.

I went below again to the wireless room and relieved my oppo; taking over the headphones I was back in business. It was routine work and tedious. Thank goodness I had the porthole to relieve the monotony. After a couple of hours I handed over my headphones and went back on deck, and there ahead of us was the big solid bulk of the Isle of Wight moving ever closer. Our 'mystery tour' was over.

On returning to Gatton Park I went to the CO's tent to report back, and the expression on his face made my day: he had the look of a man who'd just fouled his trousers and in a flash I understood. When he'd sent me off to the Isle of Wight he must have thought he'd seen the back of me, and here I was looking better than when I left – the sea air had done me good.

Halfway down the hill to Reigate was an army establishment of mainly clerical staff. I had assumed that they were something to do with the pay corps or some like department because they seemed to work office hours, and most of the men wore spectacles and had the vacant, white faces of most office workers the world over. But on a walk down to the town we all gave this building the once-over as we passed and discovered that about half the army staff weren't bespectacled and unworldly: they were the ATS, the feminine branch of the army. As Gatton Park was an all-male establishment, anything in skirts was given the curious, expectant once-over, as if we were eunuchs peeping through the keyhole of the harem, and it was on one of my treks down the hill that I met a real bobby-dazzler, a Scots girl called Maud.

Though I'd had childish crushes on girls at school, I'd never really fancied any girl enough to give up my freedom, but now all that changed. She spoke with a soft Scottish burr and I couldn't believe my luck. I've never considered myself attractive to the opposite sex and with my broad Lancashire accent I'd thought that my only chance was a half-blind Lancashire lass, and now I really thought my ship had come in.

So serious was our affair that I bought her a diamond engagement ring. Granted it had only one diamond so small that it could have been overlooked by a cursory glance, but I'd bought it in a reputable pawnshop. However, this togetherness was frowned upon by the authorities, so it was our secret. In fact although we spent off-duty hours together she didn't even put her arm through mine; we just strolled happily along the streets of Reigate with a decent separation between us. It was the age of innocence when a kiss was the best we lads could hope for, when to embrace and gaze into each other's eyes was a silent declaration of serious intent, in which case a passionate kiss was acceptable. So comfortable were we both in our plans for the future that when I came up for seven days' leave she arranged a seven-day break for herself.

We spent the week together at her parents' home in a little village just outside Edinburgh – very genteel, a quiet backwater, mainly elderly because practically all the young men and women were in the services. I assumed that all the young men would be officers in the army, navy or air force; later I discovered that my assumptions were not far off the mark and on leave it was considered bad taste to swan around in uniform. Unfortunately I had no civvies to change into and I was regarded with a certain amount of reservation, tempered only by the fact that I was merely an erk and therefore lacking in good taste. I felt that the parents of my intended were welcoming but guarded; nevertheless when I was ushered into the study for an interview with Daddy I wasn't too worried: I'd been quizzed by authority once or twice before, the only difference for this interview being that I was seated in front of his desk, whereas before I'd had to stand to attention.

I can only remember three questions. The first one was 'What are your prospects?' and I got away with a mumble. The next was, 'What does your father do?' to which I replied with a straight face that he was in cotton. He brightened a little at that, but I didn't elaborate. His last question was 'Do you have any money?' Hello,

hello, I thought. He was probably hard up and wanted a little to tide him over. Eagerly I thrust my hand into my trouser pocket, where I had two pounds and a bit of silver. He put up his hand to stop me, and, realising I hadn't quite got the drift, he asked me, if I had money in the bank. I now understood, but I didn't know how to reply. A bank? It was ludicrous. The cash in my trouser pocket was all my worldly goods.

On the train back Maud happily reported that I'd made quite an impression on Daddy. However, secretly I didn't agree and I was convinced I'd blown it with the bank question. Unbeknownst to me the investigation into my suitability as a son-in-law was continuing. Accepting an invitation to spend a weekend in Scotland, Dad and Mother were even more of a walking embarrassment than I'd been. On Sunday morning the two sets of parents went to church. As Dad had already revealed that he was a labourer at the Standard Mill in Rochdale, my future marriage was extremely doubtful, and on returning from the church he was brought to task politely, and told that the differences in their two family lifestyles were incompatible and that a sports jacket was not the accepted way to turn out for a visit to church. Dad didn't stay for the roast lamb; they were on the first train back to Manchester. They couldn't wait to get home in order to return the jacket to Uncle Joe. Meanwhile, enjoying our war in Reigate, Maud and I, blissfully unaware of the differences between our parents, enjoyed each other's company – long walks, coffee and rock cakes with the WVS and occasional dances where we waltzed with me singing impressions of Bing Crosby in her lovely ear. But the war was moving inexorably to a climax and although we were both unaware of it at the time our happy hours of companionship were about to be rudely interrupted.

I had volunteered to join the RAF when I was eighteen years old and now on my twenty-first birthday, 4 May, I was a fully trained wireless operator who had never set foot on an operational aerodrome. For some time I'd accepted the fact that I never would. Mobile signals units attached to the Second Army had about as much to do with flying as the navy lads who went to sea in submarines. Another important factor was that the wireless operators on operational air fields were not trained to fire Bren guns as we had been – not only to fire one but also to take it to pieces and reassemble it even in the dark. So what was to be our role in the near future?

The air about us was forever cluttered with thoughts, rumours, more rumours and speculations. There was a frenetic build-up of tanks, artillery, and battalions of troops of mixed nationalities, and it all pointed to only one conclusion: – the Second Front was imminent. May was half over and Maud and her comrades found little time to relax in Reigate; their workload was increasing by the day. As far as we in Gatton Park were concerned the whole of 589A MSU was gripped by a feeling of anticipation and the sense that impending events would at least answer the question uppermost in our minds: what part had we been allotted in the history to come?

As May drew to a close our convoy rolled out of Gatton Park for the last time and rumbled down the hill towards Reigate. Having been confined to camp for some days now, I had no way of con-tacting Maud. As I passed her workplace I stared hard at it, hoping to get a glimpse of her, but we passed in a flash with no joy.

The roads to the south were an almost continuous stream of military traffic: huge tanks on transporters, armoured cars, jeeps and lorries crammed with military personnel. We left the main road and arrived at a place called Cosham, and made camp in the middle of a fairly big wood. No communications to the outside world were allowed – no letters or phone calls – and once again we were confined to camp. For how long? It was anybody's guess.

One morning, looking up from my mess tin, breakfast lumping my cheek, I watched spellbound as four low-flying aircraft zoomed towards the coast – more aeroplanes than I'd ever seen at one time, and although they weren't on the ground they weren't far off it. But this wasn't just an ordinary flight: in place of the familiar RAF roundels the aircraft had white stripes underneath their wings. They were the first sign that the British troops landing in France were already engulfed in the bloody carnage of what we later learned was D-Day.

We in 589A, confined to a wood on the outskirts of Cosham, were both puzzled and frustrated. We should have been in France and here we were picking up bits of paper, any other litter and, as we were nearly all smokers, spent matches – chores invented to keep us occupied. Later we discovered that our sister unit, 589B, did land on D-Day, and we followed them shortly afterwards.

We embarked on an LCV (landing craft vehicle), skippered by a young naval lieutenant who looked younger than me, leaning on his elbows on the bridge rail looking down on us as if we were a collection of tourists on a package holiday. When all our vehicles were secured, our CO made his way up to the bridge, and when he was halfway up, the young naval lieutenant, who turned out to be the captain, enquired in a bored voice, where did he think he was going? All conversation ceased as we turned to watch the drama.

'I'm coming up to the bridge,' the CO said lamely.

Still leaning nonchalantly on the rail, the lieutenant said, 'Not on my bridge you're not. Get back on deck.'

Blushing, the CO did as he was ordered; we all turned away, embarrassed, and confidence in our hapless CO plummeted – not an auspicious beginning to our war.

Out of sight of land, the flat-bottomed barge began to roll. It wasn't rough sea; it was just a stomach-wrenching swell. One or two of the lads were leaning over the rail and I don't think they were studying marine life. On the fore deck the cooks had two dixies full of soup simmering nicely. The steam from the Maconochies, scattered every which way by the gusting wind, was too much for one of the cooks, and with his apron clasped across his mouth he stumbled to the side. The other cook, being a good trade union man, came out with him and I was left, mess tin in my hand, at the head of what should have been a hungry queue. I wasn't going without, so I helped myself. I was just blowing on my second spoonful when I heard a soft, polite cough behind me. It was one of the lads. I filled his mess tin and together we supped and slurped through our Maconochies. This done, I shouted, 'Come and get it,' and rattled the ladle against a dixie, but it was obvious that there would be no takers, so we emptied the rest of the stew overboard, tied a rope on to the handles of the dixies and dropped over the stern and let the sea do the cleansing.

One of the lads from the transport section explained to me that the Whitehall mandarins who had arranged this cruise to France had planned that as the unit held out their mess tins they were to be issued five cigarettes and two boiled sweets. I looked at him, puzzled: what was he on about? He jerked his head to a large cardboard box and I looked in to see four cartons of cigarettes and three jars of boiled sweets. As all the rest of the unit had their backs towards us, and were gazing over the rail at the grey sea, we hastily stuffed the cigarettes down the front of our battle blouses, leaving the boiled sweets to the young naval skipper and his crew.

The sun was hot, tempered only by a soft sea breeze as we approached the Normandy beach, almost deserted now a week after D-Day. What a contrast to that historic pre-dawn of 6 June, when a great phalanx of ghostly ships steamed towards France . . . My reverie was shattered when the CO ordered us to mount our vehicles. What did he think we were – a bunch of Cossacks? The engines exploded into life and the ramp of our LCV splashed into the surf. Immediately the first three-tonner rolled slowly down it into about three feet of water, followed by the second and so on till we were all ashore. In our short immersion between the LCV and Sword Beach, there were no disasters and the transport section must have breathed a sigh of relief: all their dirty, gruelling work with Bostik and the extensions of the exhaust pipes had done the trick. We ponderously drove up the beach in second gear, ignoring a group of soldiers who, with frantic arm waving, were trying to speed us on our way. On leaving the beach the convoy halted, possibly so that the CO could receive his instructions from the harbour master and silently I gazed around me. To the left was a single, forlorn café, but they would not be serving tea there ever again, as the building was now a pockmarked ruin with only the word 'café' to identify it. The LCV was now just a dot out at sea.

Although the beach itself had been cleared, just off the sandy stretches was the detritus of war. What sacrifices had been made on that horrendous landing! A cold shiver ran down my spine when I looked into a burnt-out Bren carrier. A couple of brave lads had been the target for the German defences, and half a charred

When 36 Leslie Street was our castle and Dad was king.

The beach was thronged
with our family.

Paddling was all the rage.

In case one of us didn't
survive the war.

A bland face as yet
unlined by experience.

Pitchoune (right) and a girlfriend.

Pitchoune, sophisticated and beautiful, and me, unsure and unaware that this first meeting was the overture to a most important chapter in my education.

Bill Fraser, Ron Rich and Rick Allan in our after the war concert party.

Just before demob: (from right to left) Bob Errington, Steve Stephenson and Boots. Not a bad life, this.

First allied troops to set foot in Denmark.

Oldham Repertory Theatre Club.

THE COLISEUM

All Evening Performances commence at 7

Matinees Tuesday at 2-30 p.m. and
Saturday at 4-15 p.m.

"ALL THIS IS ENDED"

A Play in Three Acts by Jack Alldridge.

PROGRAMME — TWOPENCE.

Holt, Richardson & Co., 310, Middleton Rd., Oldham.

Week commencing March 31st, 1947.

"ALL THIS IS ENDED"

A Play in Three Acts by Jack Alldridge.

CHARACTERS (in order of appearance):—

Corporal Marks (" Benny ")	Douglas Emery
Private White (" Chalky ")	... Arthur Hall
Private Jones (" Lucky ")	Eric Longworth
Private Nicholls (" Lenny ")	Brian Carleton
William	David Champion
Lester Ratcliffe, War Correspondent ...	...Harry Lomax
Captain Pringle	... David Callan
PFC Michael O'Brien, an American ...	... Eric Sykes
Major Owen	Antony Oakley
The Padre	Maurice Hansard
A German soldier	... Paul Morgan

The scene throughout appears to be the living-room of
an Italian villa. Spring, 1944.

ACT 1. Twilight.

ACT 2. The same evening.

ACT 3. Before Dawn.

The Play is Produced by Douglas Emery.

Stage-Director, Arthur Hall.
Décor by Douglas Emery.
Scenic-Artist, L. S. Siddall.
Master Carpenter, Jock Dorran.
Electrician, William Haigh.

Cigarettes by Abdulla.

Next Week—" THE POLTERGEIST "

ABOVE: Theatre programme from my first professional performance, 31 March 1947.

LEFT: The Coliseum.

ABOVE: Now with an Equity card to prove I'm a professional actor in a repertory company in Darwen, near Blackburn.

BELOW: Peter Brough and Archie Andrews and the unseen cast for the weekly read-through. As for the nurse … read on.

Archie Andrews, (with Peter Brough), radio's most romantic scene-stealer, monopolised the attention of Nurse Milbradt at the Royal Alexandra Hospital, London, yesterday. Real patient is script-writer Eric Sykes.

Archie falls—and UP goes his temperature

ABOVE: Our wedding day and now, after fifty-three years together, I'm still smiling.

BELOW: With our two youngest, Julie and David, and a lily pond – idyllic … or was it?

boot and the bones of a foot remained on one of the pedals. My thoughts of the Bren carrier episode in Swaffham diminished and shamed me.

As 589A was given the order to roll, the convoy left the beach head. I stood on the seat of one of our three-tonners, my upper body through the hole in the roof of the cab, with a grandstand view of France as we made our way through Cruelly and the historic town of Bayeux. When we finally arrived at our camp, the tents were already erected. After we'd slung our kit in them, we were immediately ordered to sling our kit out again, and it was explained to us that our first job was to dig slit trenches for ourselves and our equipment inside the tent. We had a meal which had been prepared. So far the splendid organisation of Whitehall was spot on but the slit trenches inside the tent were puzzling.

Up to now it had been a beautiful summer's day, but it was a fool's paradise. As daylight dimmed into night the bombardment began. It was our baptism into war, a catastrophe no training could prepare raw innocents like us for; the continuous cacophony was mind deadening. I don't think I was afraid. I was numb with shock, as the barrage of noise – bangs, booms, explosions with no pauses, hour after hour – assaulted our eardrums. There was no respite. This was our first night and we accepted our slit trenches with gratitude.

As the darkness lightened, the barrage ceased as abruptly as it had begun. Near by we heard the roar of aeroplane engines as they warmed up for their first sortie of the day. This was the pattern for the next few weeks: night barrage, daylight Spitfire engines. At about seven o'clock I emerged fearfully from my tent, looking round for the carnage brought about by last night's bombardment – but there was none. People were going about their business as if it was a bank holiday, and the sun was shining against a backcloth of unruffled sky, but at the back of my mind an uneasiness lurked; something was missing, something was odd. Then it came to me: no birds sang. Where had they all gone? A deep sadness came over me. What a depressing world it would be without the chirping of our feathered friends!

There was an all-pervading, cloying stench of putrefaction, and I noticed in a nearby field the bloated bodies of cows and horses, stiff legs pointing skywards. These were partly responsible for this smell of death, and there was a whiff of something I couldn't identify at the time, which subsequently turned out to be camembert. Apart from this it was a pleasant day, but as the light faded into evening I was already lying in my slit trench. Would there be a repeat of the horrendous firework display tonight? I was prepared: my slit trench was six inches deeper, and I had found for extra protection a curved sheet of corrugated iron, which gave me adequate cover for the upper part of my body, while my tin hat guarded my private parts. Then, as if Zeus, or Thor, had flicked a switch, the bombardment erupted.

As I lay prone in my bassinet the walls of the tent were constantly by the nightly barrage from dusk onwards. No one slept until the dawn chorus of the warming-up of the engines of the aeroplanes. However, as familiarity breeds contempt, I was bold enough to step out of my tent in order to watch this fantastic display of pyrotechnics and I found that I was not alone: several others were already standing around as if it was Guy Fawkes Day. There was no panic, or desultory remarks, and to me it seemed safer than lying in my slit trench imagining what was going on outside. The black sky was lit up by a constant traffic of high explosives, glaring wide streams of red; the stars were outshone and invisible above the carnage. It was then that I noticed that the projectiles were flaming against each other. The dark shape next to me explained that it was a British naval bombardment aimed at Caen and the reply from the enemy was directed right back to the ships off the coast – it was a madman's game of tennis.

Troops, equipment, ammunition, letters from home, etc. continued to pour into Normandy, only to pile up behind the Allied infantry and artillery surrounding the walls of Caen. Bombarding Caen was an objective which would surely be swept aside ere long, but ere long turned out to be another month. Nevertheless the forward plans of the War Office were unstoppable. Each day more troops, more equipment, etc. were rushed up the sandy beaches as if the forward elements were already on the borders of Germany. Thus Normandy became crowded as if by an audience without tickets to listen to a concert from hell.

As 589B, our sister unit, had landed on D-Day, our unit was sent across a few days later in order to leapfrog them. It was a pretty poor leapfrog, as our camp was only about two hundred yards from theirs – at this rate we would be leapfrogging each other for several years before we got out of Normandy. The great brains of Whitehall had not bargained for the hold-up. On paper we should now have been well on the way to Belgium, but the Germans defending Caen had other ideas. They were crack troops, having the advantage of cover, slightly more than a hiccup in Whitehall's grand strategy.

One man intrigued me. He was a secretive person, with grey hair, although I imagine he was in his early thirties, and twinkling blue eyes, as if he treated the whole of life as a bad joke. He rarely used two words when one would suffice. He was Sam Irwin, familiarly known as 'Jock', and that is about as much as anyone knew of him. I noticed him on one or two occasions in camp, diligently trying to avoid being collared for anything physical or collared to do anything for that matter. So it was completely out of character when, on our morning parade, the duty sergeant, having called the roll, asked anyone who played the piano to step forward, and of course nobody moved – one of the basic rules in the military was don't volunteer for anything – but as the squad was looking furtively at everybody else Jock moved one pace forward. To say we were astonished would be an understatement; bowled over, knocked out, would all be applicable. As for the sergeant, his mouth was open, his brain in neutral, as if Jock had yelled 'Heil Hitler'. More often than I care to remember I've been prone to leap into situations on an impulse, and this was one of those times. I too took a step forward. The sergeant dismissed the rest of parade except Jock and me, and in five minutes we were in the back of a three-tonner to Cruelly to load a piano which was to be offloaded in a big marquee a few hundred yards down the road.

As the lorry left the camp I asked Jock if he really did play the piano. He shook his head as if it was a stupid question.

My follow-up was more pertinent. 'Why did you volunteer?'

To which he replied, 'All we have to do is lift a piano on to the back of the lorry and lift it off at the other end.' He paused and went on, 'Not a bad day's work.' It was the longest speech I'd ever heard him make.

The piano, a decrepit upright, was picked up from an old hall, loaded on to the lorry and driven to a large marquee in a field, where it was offloaded. When Jock slapped the top of the piano and nodded his approval, I realised that it was the only time he'd laid hands on it. I and four others had done the heaving and sweating to get the pathetic thing up and down and off the lorry. It was pandemonium inside the marquee – potted plants, long tables with wine glasses, pint beer glasses, folding chairs and more comfortable ones – because this shindig was a farewell party for some very high brass prior to his return to Blighty.

The driver of our transport had to wait for Jock and me, and we were in no hurry to get back. Sometime later when Jock jerked his head towards the entrance it was time to go. On reaching the camp he said, 'Get your mug,' and only when we were sitting comfortably in the back of one of the Bedfords did Jock, with the ease of a master illusionist, produce a bottle of gin from his battledress. It was incredible; it was as if he'd planned the whole thing, from volunteering to hanging around the marquee long enough to half-inch this bottle of Beefeaters. I didn't pursue this line of enquiry, as my brains were already scrambled with alcohol; neat gin from an enamel mug is not to be recommended.

As the evening handed over to night, I was maudlin drunk and I made up what was left of my mind to walk back to the marquee and return with tomorrow night's booze. Jock tried to dissuade me, but this was too much even for him and together we staggered back to the party. It wasn't a boisterous knees-up – quite the opposite: officers in groups or pairs were standing outside the marquee smoking quietly. Our only cover was the night, but it was obvious that we were in no condition to slip into the marquee unnoticed.

We were about to abort when I bumped into what turned out to be a barrel. Next to it was another barrel up on stocks, the back end outside and the end with the tap inside the marquee. They were barrels of beer. It was better than nothing. We couldn't leave empty-handed; that would be a defeat, and the gin in us wouldn't allow that. So, as if we did this for a living, we rolled the full barrel slowly across the grass, a yard at a time in case we were spotted and so as to be careful not to roll it into a group of officers. We cleared the field with great sighs of relief, but it took us almost an hour to reach our camp. We must have sweated out most of the gin – or perhaps not, because as far as I was concerned our mission was accomplished and, this being so, I lay down by the barrel in a blissful dreamless sleep. What happened next is only a hazy recollection. Of course getting the barrel into our bailiwick was only stage one, and here is where Jock's organising brilliance took over. Where he got his energy from for stage two or the ability to think clearly under the influence of half a bottle of neat Beefeaters I don't know; I can only put it down to his Scottish heritage – roaming over the Highlands, barefoot and kilted, playing his tam-o'-shanter in a blizzard.

I was rudely awakened when he splashed a five-gallon can of water into my face. He had organised four or five of the lads to help, all carrying water cans. As they unscrewed the caps, I was on my rubbery legs like a shot; Jock had already baptised me and I didn't want a bath as well. These water cans were to be the receptacles for our barrel of beer. Jock had them lift the barrel on to the back of a three-ton lorry and bashed in the bung, and in line the lads filled the cans. I think we must have filled about six cans in all, more than enough, so we left the barrel to empty itself while the lads filled their water bottles. Mission accomplished, but again I was jumping the gun. Jock had the barrel lifted down and they all bashed and smashed it to pieces. The nightly barrage covered all our actions – ah yes, destroy the evidence, good thinking Jock. The lads gathered up all the remains of what had once been the pride of the barrel makers' union and carted them off to where our tents were pitched. I staggered along in their wake, marvelling at Jock's capacity for organisation, and when I arrived at the tent, mildly puzzled by its familiarity – no doubt about it, it was my tent – all the debris of the barrel had been dumped in my slit trench, and

I watched as they covered up the whole lot with shovelfuls of earth. As they were doing this, Jock, standing at the foot of the trench, put his hands together and intoned, 'Ashes to ashes, dust to dust,' which I thought was hilarious. My hilarity lasted until they had left, and I was faced with a problem: when I spread out my blankets on top of the earth pile, I was not protected by my slit trench – far from it. I went to sleep above ground – and I didn't care.

With a sick head, I was on the morning watch. Each of the wireless lorries had a small window above the set, and once when I stood to stretch I glanced out and my blood froze. About a hundred yards away, two red caps of the military police were straining at the leashes of two large dogs. Thoughts flashed through my mind as in a fast-forward film: I would desert, plead insanity, hang myself, the game was up, twelve months in the glasshouse, that is if the powers that be had sent a glasshouse over – they'd brought everything else; the dogs had sniffed the trail from the start of the roll-out of the barrel to where it had been smashed to pieces, it wasn't fair, they'd no right to bring dogs with them. I sank back into my chair. Oh, what I'd give for a direct hit from an 88. Half an hour later I stood and looked furtively out again. They were still there, but with a difference: one of the dogs was sitting down and the other one was standing next to his handler, and the two military police seemed to have lost interest as well. The weight of the world fell from my shoulders. Of course the barrel was under blankets, so the spoor was cold. The dogs had found the spot where the barrel was destroyed and there the trail ended; thanks again to Jock and his machiavellian brain, we had got away with it, and although I'd aged considerably Jock seemed unperturbed. It was to be the forerunner of more escapades to come. As for the beer barrel incident, it wasn't until the war was over that I was able to get it off my chest, but that will be several chapters ahead.

After I'd got away with it again, I was newly born. What a crass, childish piece of bravado to steal the barrel in the first place. And to be quite honest, the beer wasn't up to much in any case, thin and polluted with sediment. I smiled wryly at the embarrassment of all my escape theories. Firstly to desert – ludicrous when I considered it in the cold light of reason. Where would I desert to? I was in Normandy, for heaven's sake, I didn't speak French and, if that wasn't enough, I was in uniform – good grief, I'd stand out like a dandelion on the centre court at Wimbledon. As for my second option, to plead insanity is inadmissible; it has validity only if put forward in your defence by a learned psychiatrist. I've no doubt that several of my comrades and the CO – especially the CO – would have been only too eager to plead insanity on my behalf. Why are some of my thought processes so imaginative yet so useless? Another person being nailed by the red caps would simply deny all knowledge of the incident, but that was a thought that never entered my head.

I can't recall the day a weird-looking aircraft, small and black, flew low over our camp, spluttering seawards. We didn't know it at the time but this was the first of what were to be known as doodlebugs, the much-feared V-1s. Fired from a German base, and packed with explosives, these were programmed to create havoc in London and the south-east. The roughness of their engines provoked anxiety amongst the people on the ground, but when the engine cut out anxiety was replaced by the urgent need to take cover, as the buzz bombs fell to the ground indiscriminately, wreaking destruction everywhere, whether it be residential areas, hospitals or offices. It was a new innovation of war, designed to sap the morale of the non-combatant citizens of London, a crude device only to be replaced by a more fearsome lethal contraption called the V-2. This was a rocket-propelled bomb with a much longer range than the buzz bombs.

In fact one of these fearsome monstrosities plummeted to earth in a little suburb of Oldham. Abbeyhills was not much of a place, situated on the edge of the moors; a few bungalows and a monument spring to mind. When the V-2 exploded, the only recollection of the old people of Abbeyhills was an almighty bang. The following morning they ventured out and were astonished to find an enormous smoking crater on a large expanse of nothing.

Years later when I was a civilian, Granddad and Grandma Sykes, who lived in one of the bungalows in Abbeyhills, related the coming of the V-2; and after a decent pause they related it all over again, with slight embellishments – Grandma, on hearing the bang, 'had dropped a cup', 'Not even a window was cracked', and 'Nobody ventured out for the rest of the night in case they sent over another one.' In fact every time I paid them a visit they not only told me the story again but forced me to put on my cap and go and view the hole. They lived out their lives in Abbeyhills, and although the crater had not quite grassed itself over the tale of the night of the V-2 was as green as ever.

Incidentally, in writing of the Abbeyhills V-2 incident I recall that as we were busy liberating Europe, from my familiar vantage point out of the hole in the roof of the cab as we sped in convoy I watched in amazement as a V-2 rocket was launched, flames belching from its tail, straight up to disappear in the overcast sky. It must have been about five miles away, in a place we learned later was called Peenemunde, and I wonder if that rocket was the one addressed to Granddad and Grandma Sykes.

Now back to Normandy. Not far from our camp there were two roads, one east to west and the other north to south, and every morning at precisely ten minutes to ten the military police halted all traffic approaching the crossroads. At ten o'clock the Germans shelled the crossing, pretty well bang on target, bombardment not ceasing until the ration of missiles was used up. Immediately the sappers moved in to fill in the craters, which were liable to impede the flow of traffic, and when this was done the red caps waved the traffic on and the roads were busy again until the next morning. It was as if the war was waged by numbers. Fortunately this harassment lasted only a few days, but it was a salutary lesson concerning the predictability of the German character.

On 27 June we were reinforced by more wireless operators. Why we required reinforcements was beyond me; we hadn't lost anybody. In fact we hadn't done anything as yet. One of the new intake entered the tent and slung down his kitbag. He was a Scotsman, not very tall but sassy, and he looked curiously at my slit trench.

'Is that compulsory?' he said sarcastically, as he spread his blankets on the ground next to my trench.

'Nope,' I replied cheerfully, waiting eagerly for full darkness . . .
The shades of night fell and the bombardment began immediately.
It was ear-splitting, as if we'd come out of a sound-proofed cubicle
and entered the engine room of a battleship going full speed ahead.
I began to whistle 'O God, our help in ages past' and not ten
minutes later a small Scots voice fearfully asked if he could come
in with me. I replied he was welcome to it and left the tent to watch
the proceedings. It was chilly and, realising that I was only in my
vest and pants, I went back into the tent and rolled myself in the
Scotsman's blankets; and in spite of the din I was asleep inside two
minutes. When I awoke it was daylight, quiet now, and the Scotsman was looking down at me.

'How can you manage to sleep through all that?'

'You get used to it,' I said laconically, and almost before I left
his blankets he'd thrown them aside and was digging his own slit
trench, shovelling tons of earth outside the tent as if he'd just
discovered oil.

Some days later, in the last light of early evening, we heard the
drone of several hundred engines, getting louder by the minute and
rising to a climax as a large concentration of Lancaster bombers
passed over the beach towards the already battered but impregnable
city of Caen. On the ground we waved our tin hats as they passed
overhead at no great height, cheering and whooping. It was a magnificent, chilling display of air power, such as most of us had never
seen nor were ever likely to see again. We witnessed the inevitable
reply from Caen in the distance: all their anti-aircraft guns opened
up as the armada of British bombers passed overhead. From our
standpoint the concentrated enemy flak from the beleaguered city
appeared to rush up to meet them like fairway sprinklers lit by the
rays of the sun, innocuous but deadly. It seemed impossible for
any of the aircraft to survive the barrage, but after releasing their
bombloads they banked and turned back towards the sea leisurely,
as if in no particular haste. It was a brilliant display of precision
flying and incredibly in that hail of death from the 88s in Caen I
only recall seeing one Lancaster in trouble.

Eventually the raid was over, but with disbelief we watched a lone Lancaster flying in circles, seeming to disregard the lethal barrage of the anti-aircraft guns – we could only assume he was taking photographs. Miraculously unscathed, he banked for home, and as he passed he got the loudest cheer of them all. It was a very moving moment. What a banquet for our reinforcements in the few days they'd been with us! What a performance they had witnessed from the best seats in the house – the nightly cacophony of high explosives, buzz bombs bound for England by day and top of the bill the mighty formation of Lancaster Bombers . . . Surely this was the end of the beginning? That precision bombing raid had been a stark reminder to the beleaguered German defenders that it was time to go home; and for us it was the starting pistol for our mystery tour of Europe, the finishing post being Berlin.

Shortly afterwards, the small convoy of 589A MSU picked its way gingerly through the devastation that had once been the city of Caen. It was an eerie experience. There was no road; a path had been bulldozed between high piles of rubble. We later discovered that this was known as the Falaise Gap, the gateway to war. The first intimation of this was when, on leaving the city, we came on to a narrow road, only to see sappers probing the verges with mine detectors, and I couldn't help thinking we'd been a bit quick off the blocks.

For the next few miles, though, all was tranquil meadows and hedges, oblivious and unravaged by war. I began to enjoy myself; I was Rommel, the 'Desert Fox', inspecting his Africa Corps. Then the driver slapped my leg, and my peace of mind was blown to bits when on either side of the road we spotted heavy tanks. I breathed a sigh of relief – ours, thank God. They were in line, astern and on either side of us, two hundred yards from the road, their hatches open, men relaxed. They waved to us and of course we waved back. As we left them behind, an awful thought struck me and I bobbed my head into the cab and said, 'You do realise that those tanks were the spearhead of the Second Army.' The driver gulped and stared fixedly ahead, and I popped up again, thinking no doubt as most of the lads, and our CO in his fifteen-hundredweight at the head of the convoy, that the situation was somewhat more fraught than exercise Spartan: this was for real. If he had difficulty reading a map, he would be unable to stop as he had at Maidenhead and enquire if anybody lived round here.

On we went, without seeing a soul; there was nothing to disturb the sun-kissed scenery. But I had a sinking feeling it wouldn't last and it didn't . . . We came upon a long steep hill, and slowly ground our way up in bottom gear until the CO at the front stopped and high above us in the sky we saw two Typhoons. I didn't identify them at the time, as they were fairly new off the assembly line, but we all recognised the stripes under the wings: they were ours. Then, as I watched, horrified, they dived, and the leading Typhoon fired off rockets, again an innovation to me. What was happening? We were a static target and yet they'd missed us altogether; in any case we had white stars on the top of all our vehicles – surely they could see we were on the same side? It was only after the next pass that I realised that we were not the target. That was something out of our sight on the other side of the hill.

It couldn't have been more than five minutes since we had stopped and now the Typhoons had broken off to return to base. Warily we started up again for the crest of the hill, fearful of what was on the other side. We didn't have long to wait. What met our eyes was a scene out of Dante's *Inferno*, a still flaming, devastated German convoy, or more likely the sweepings of one. It couldn't have been a very long convoy; there was an assortment of vehicles, rolling stock, mainly carts, even a small armoured vehicle probably delegated to guard the whole motley collection of forlorn hope. Not one transport had escaped attention. A dead horse blown out of the shaft of a blazing cart; the small armoured vehicle, smoke and flames pouring out of it, a German soldier draped over the edge of the open hatch; limbs, torsos and, oddly in all this carnage, a dog lying apparently unhurt but dead – even dogs don't sleep with their eyes wide open. However, a dozen or so German soldiers were still alive. Not one of them was standing; they were either lying by the side of the road or sitting, arms leaning on knees with heads bent, all totally shell-shocked.

We didn't stop but rattled and bobbed over bodies, limbs and debris; there was nothing we could do to help in any case. There were no more incidents in the next few miles, but neither did we meet any of our mob. As the light was leaving the sky, our convoy pulled off the road and drew in close to the trees of what seemed to be a large wood. Before I'd even jumped out of the cab, a bullet ricocheted off a piece of the engine; other lads heard it too. The shot had come from the wood but now it was too dark to see anything. We stampeded to lie under the wagons, Sten guns thrust out before us, and there was the clatter of magazines being pushed home, followed by the clicks of safety catches off. This was a very fine welcome indeed. We didn't fire back because there were no targets, and in any case we didn't want a fire fight – we hadn't been trained for it. Thankfully the order to hold fire was passed on to us from the CO.

It was a long night, with a few desultory incoming rounds just to keep us awake. Nobody left the protection of the wagons, but as the sun burst into the morning a slight movement was discerned in the woods. We were all wide awake now, eyes bulging, throats dry. Then puzzlement became the popular expression as a man appeared in a top hat and tailcoat with a sash around his shoulder like a bandolier, clutching a bottle of wine in one hand while with the other he held the hand of a pretty little girl in white, holding a bunch of flowers. Uncertainly at first, they approached and we struggled from under our cover and awaited our visitors. Obviously relieved, our CO stepped forward and saluted. Then the man with the sash raised his hat and rattled off something in French. Subsequently the whole story came out. The Frenchman was the mayor of the nearby town and the bottle contained wine, which he handed to the CO. The little girl, who was the mayor's daughter, held out the flowers to the CO, who had the grace to say 'merci'. As for the shooting, that had come from the local Maquis (French freedom fighters). Because of the bad light and our air force uniforms being coated with dust, they had wrongly come to the conclusion that we were the rearguard of the German army. As I mused on this idea, a very disconcerting assumption around on the fringes of my mind: if we had been mistaken for the remnants of the German army we must, therefore, be the most forward troops of our advancing army . . . Not a very assuring thought for the day. I decided to keep it to myself.

With the entente cordiales over and apologies accepted, the Mayor and his daughter disappeared back into the wood and we wandered aimlessly to the centre of the field. Too tired to say anything, we stared vacantly at nothing; quite a few of the lads lay down in the grass – had we been a herd of cows I would have said it was going to rain. The cooks were the only ones who knew what they were doing. They busily prepared breakfast, which at least encouraged us to collect our mess tins lethargically and walk like zombies to the steaming dixies to form a queue. The transport section was carrying out minor repairs, mainly as an exercise in looking busy; then they refuelled their vehicles, awaiting the order to move, or the order to stand down, or any order. In fact we were all of the same mind: if we went forward, God knows what lay in wait for us, but we certainly couldn't retreat, as we were British. Reluctantly I came to the conclusion that the War Office in White-hall was totally unaware that 589A MSU was stranded in a field somewhere in France, well ahead of the main force and, more to the point, ill equipped to take on the German army.

On the following day, however, we took matters into our own hands. A fifty-gallon drum of water was heated on a blazing log fire, clothes lines were rigged and most of the lads stripped to the waist, and, clasping their dirty laundry, queued for their turn. By the middle of the afternoon, vests, underpants, socks and shorts hung steaming on the clothes lines. They dried quickly under the hot July sun, although one of the lads who worked in a laundry in civvy street said you couldn't beat a stiff breeze. We were more relaxed now, not having seen another human being, apart from each other, since the visit of the French legation. Somebody produced a tennis ball and with a piece of wood baseball was organised; the war was forgotten, and there were not even passing planes to break the state of well-being – oh happy days.

But it couldn't last. As if the film had broken down, everybody froze into stillness as we heard the noise of an approaching vehicle.

Hardly daring to breathe, we watched as it sped up the road. It was enormous, and heavily armoured, but it wasn't a tank. It travelled on thick, tyred wheels on either side, six or eight of them in place of caterpillar tracks with a large white star on the side. We identified it as one of ours. As it drew level with our frolics, it stopped. What a sight we must have been! Yards and yards of washing hanging innocently on the lines, all of us staring incredulously at the vehicle as if it had just come from another planet. Inside, the crew must have been reassured by the identical white stars on our vehicles. After what seemed ages three British soldiers leapt down from what we learned later was a scout car. They had machine guns, which made our Stens look as if they belonged in the Natural History Museum.

One of them, an officer asked, 'What are you doing here?'

To which we replied, 'We've been here for two days.'

The officer pushed back his tin hat and said, 'That's impossible. We are the recce patrol of the Second Army.'

It was only then that we realised that all our half-hidden fears were justified. Shaking his head, the young lieutenant waved his men back to their vehicle and we watched with admiration as they climbed back into their contraption and sped off, just as our CO bounded across the field, probably to ask them to join him in a cup of tea, or more likely to enquire if anyone lived round here – we were never to forget exercise Spartan and Maidenhead.

The recce patrol was the subject of excited discussion. At least we were now relieved of the dicey responsibility of leading the advance. We relaxed even more when about two hours later a huge convoy of vehicles of all shapes and sizes followed in the tracks of the recce patrol. This, then, was the main body of the Second Army, seemingly eager to make up time lost by the battle to overcome Caen.

Seeing the enormity of what was happening before his eyes, the CO ordered us to prepare to depart. Our holiday was over and within an hour we were formed up to join in the convoy. We spent that night in a field near Beauvais but it was only a brief respite: at 4.00 a.m. as dawn was lightening the sky, we took to the road again.

But where was the Second Army? Off we set, and I only hoped that we were facing the right way – otherwise in a week's time we would be back in Normandy. As we passed over the border into Belgium my fears receded, and what a welcome awaited us! Cheering crowds lining the route, throwing flowers, handing up bottles of wine, children running alongside, girls blowing kisses – I basked in all the adulation as I stood on the seat waving, accepting their gifts as if I was Montgomery himself. Mind you, I looked like a warrior: leather sleeveless jerkin over my battle blouse, woollen cap at a rakish angle, unshaven, as we had been on the road since dawn and it was now late afternoon. Add to this a thick coating of white dust over everything and you had the perfect liberators. As I leaned out to touch their hands, blowing kisses to the younger women, smiling at the old, you'd have thought I was a parliamentary candidate on the eve of polling day.

After a few more miles of the Belgian welcome, we finally entered Brussels. The acclamation was awesome. We'd done the marathon and now we were entering the stadium. Apparently we'd followed the Welsh Armoured Division into this maelstrom of joy, but the army lads had pressing business in Louvain, where there was a pocket of resistance to be dealt with, and so were unable to bask in a leisurely dalliance with the hero-worshipping citizens – it is impossible to stop a line of tanks. We, of course, were a horse of a different colour, and we were mobbed by ecstatic Belgians surging forward to clamber on to our transports. I jumped from the cab in order to stretch my legs and immediately a bottle of wine was thrust at me. I took a healthy swig and they applauded. Another bottle appeared, but before it reached me I was hoisted on to broad shoulders and carted as a hero down a side street, where I was offloaded on to a large civilian lorry already crowded with a singing, boisterous mob; there were also an accordionist and a drummer doing their damnedest to play something.

The wagon stuttered off to the screams of the girls but after a short, juddering trip we stopped at a bistro and all the mob on the back of the lorry jumped down, taking me with them. We did a conga into the premises, where we knocked back schnapps, beer, wine and more schnapps – an awesome cocktail guaranteed to explode the brain. Then we conga'd out and staggered back on to the lorry, which poured us all out at the next café, where there was more of the same ... It was at this point that I must have flaked out, and I awoke shivering in the back of one of our own lorries, where I wasn't alone; other bodies of our unit were lying about next to me, engaged in a 'Who can snore the loudest?' contest. We were on the move and it was dark. We'd entered Brussels like lions and look at us now, a mobile doss house. I must have dozed off again, so I missed our triumphal entry into Holland.

Eindhoven was our journey's end, and it was to be home for the next few months.

It was the first time we'd slept with a roof over our heads since our attachment to the army in Swaffham, and this billet was a palace by contrast. Until our occupation it had been a convent, inhabited by nuns but thankfully they'd all been posted. It was luxury indeed. The floor would have been hard to sleep on, but even that difficulty had been taken care of: sacks were issued and an abundant amount of hay to stuff in them. This introduced the word palliasse into my vocabulary.

The following day we were assigned to our wireless watches. There was very little to transmit but there were hundreds of five-figure groups to receive. Rumour had it that these were the weather reports; however, we didn't know for sure because all these five-figure groups had to be deciphered.

Evidently Eindhoven was to be more than a whistle-stop because after a few weeks we were given Continental leave, which meant four days in Brussels. I was in the first group to go, and like exuberant schoolboys we clambered aboard the transport with our small kit (shaving gear, toothbrush, etc.) and, of course, rations for a week. It was a singing, laughing, excited trip into Belgium.

The driver lowered the tailboard and as we jumped down the passenger door of the cab opened and out stepped Jock Irwin. Of course I was delighted. It was uncanny: I hadn't seen him since

Normandy, and again I had to ask myself the question, how did he manage to keep coming up smelling of roses? I didn't ask him, and even if I had he'd probably have tapped the side of his nose and winked, leaving me to pick the bones out of that.

Brussels had settled down after the rapturous welcome we'd received on our first triumphal entry into the city. I don't know what we'd expected – certainly not indifference. Jock, however, didn't seem too bothered. He was looking up and down the street – ah, it seemed he'd found what he'd been looking for because he set off in a very positive way, and naturally we followed. He went into a food provision shop, where he emptied all his rations on to the counter. Each tin of something or other was closely scrutinised by the shopkeeper and an agreement was reached, whereupon the man pinged his till and handed Jock a bundle of banknotes. Naturally we all followed suit.

That evening five of us were in a nightclub. Jock wasn't with us; he said he'd catch us up, but he never did. At the next table sat a couple of ladies, beautifully dressed, one dark-haired and the other blonde. Straight away I was in my Errol Flynn mode, but they didn't seem to notice; or perhaps they were short-sighted and hadn't seen us at all. The fact is I wasn't sophisticated enough to do more than ogle, but one of the lads, who had been a lawyer in Liverpool before being called up and was polished and suave, had no hesitation in approaching them. What sort of conversation went on was beyond me, but before I knew what had transpired we were leaving the club in a body. Fortunately they both spoke English; in fact the dark-haired girl was voluble and amusing, and there was laughter and gesticulation to highlight anecdotes.

Now further behind, I sauntered, mostly in silence, with the blonde, who had introduced herself as Pitchoune. I didn't know her well enough to do an impression of Bing Crosby. With the group in front out of sight, we stopped by a large dark building and Pitchoune pressed the doorbell. Then she stepped back to look upwards to the top storey. Full of alcohol, I was under the impression when she put her head back that she was expecting me to kiss her, so I stepped forward, but incredulous she turned her head and said, 'I thought you were a gentleman.' And she looked skywards again, as a window was pushed up and a slightly balding man stuck his head out. Obviously recognising her, he ducked back into the room, and two minutes later the front door opened, and the man from above, in a long, comedy nightshirt, handed two bottles to Pitchoune. After a '*Merci, Paul*' from her and an ingratiating bow from him, the door was closed. I took the bottles from her and we continued to wherever.

The only words that passed between us occurred when she stopped and looked at me to say again earnestly, 'You are a gentleman, aren't you?'

There was only one reply and just as earnestly I said, 'Of course.'

There was still no contact between us; we walked sedately like two mourners at a funeral. We arrived finally at an imposing block of flats. Hers was the penthouse occupying the whole of the top floor, and I was impressed by the red carpet leading to her door. As she took out the key for her flat, we could hear much laughter from inside: a party was in full swing. Pitchoune raised her eyebrows and smiled, but the smile left her as she opened the door and saw the reason for all the hilarity. The dark-haired girl was wearing the RAF uniform of the lawyer from Liverpool and, even more incongruously, he was mincing about the place in her frock. Pitchoune was not amused and in a stream of French castigated her companion in a quiet, controlled voice. Personally I thought this was a bit over the top; they had not had the time for any hanky-panky and changing clothes wasn't a criminal offence. The poor girl, her head bowed and shoulders shaking, was taking it hard; I thought she was crying. I wasn't too pleased, because I thought that what had begun as a promising evening was now disappearing up the spout, but I was way off the mark. She wasn't crying at all; far from it, she was laughing, and before long we were all laughing. Even Pitchoune's face melted into a smile – normal service had been resumed. A few moments later I was handed a Scotch in a beautiful cut-glass tumbler. Standing in a circle, we all clinked our glasses in a toast to our hostesses, and the whisky hit my throat like prussic acid, bringing tears to my eyes. Then we toasted our King and Queen. Winston Churchill followed, and by that time I was having to blink hard to concentrate. I was losing my grip and from this moment on my recollection of events is hazy, to say the least.

However, I do remember my mates sitting around, shovelling down mouthfuls of delicious mince from plates on their knees. I vaguely remember sitting on a chair with, like my mates, a plate of mince balanced on my knees, the only difference being that Pitchoune, kneeling at my feet, was spoonfeeding me like a baby. Thankfully it was at this point the curtain came down.

When I awoke the following morning, I was extraordinarily clearheaded, considering the sherbet we'd knocked back, but where was I? Above me there was a glittering chandelier; moving only my eyes I beheld a large oil painting on the wall; raising my head I saw a dressing table, mirrored on three sides, with bottles of perfume and lotions. It slowly dawned on me that this was a ladies' bedroom. Then I remembered Pitchoune. Hardly breathing, I turned my head slowly to the pillow beside me. There was an indentation where another head had lain and at that moment Pitchoune entered, bearing a silver breakfast tray. I sat up guiltily as if I was an intruder.

'Good afternoon, milord,' she said, smiling happily. By golly, she was in a two-piece pinstripe with white blouse. I stared at her in open admiration. She was the same lady I had met at the club, but now she seemed more relaxed – why, and what was the score?

'Eat before it is cold,' she said and, sitting on the edge of the bed, she stretched across and kissed me on the cheek. Then she was gone. I picked up a slice of toast, but it could have been a table mat for all the notice I took; my scrambled thoughts were jostling each other for some sense of cohesion. This was Pitchoune's bedroom; ergo I'd slept with her – I'd actually slept with a woman for the very first time in my life. Marvelling at this, I suddenly realised that I was naked. This was another first in my life – even as a boy I'd always slept in my shirt. Who had undressed me and put me to bed? Then the thought struck me like a well-aimed brick: I'd been deflowered – good grief, apart from birth this was probably the most momentous event in my life, the gateway to manhood. According to books, the earth should have moved, violins crescendoing to a climax – and I'd missed it. I couldn't recall a thing. What a clot, what a stumbling, bumbling idiot! My toes curled with the embarrassment of it all. The sooner I left the better.

The bathroom was another revelation. There was a shower, two washbasins, and a toilet next to another toilet. The second was slightly different from the first and when I bent forward to experiment a jet of water shot straight into my face – a wet hello from my first bidet. Behind me was a huge bath, steaming with scented foam. I tested the water and before stepping in I glanced round this marble ablutions palace once more. There was something out of place: just by one of the washbasins, neatly laid out, was my small-kit – shaving brush, razor and toothbrush, a forlorn collection completely alien in all this magnificence. As I lay up to my chin in the bath, it came to me that this was the first bath I'd had since the mobile bath unit had visited us in Normandy and even that hadn't been a bath, just showers fenced by canvas walls for privacy. The bath dissipated my self-sorry state, and as I dressed I formulated my approach to Pitchoune. Thank her for the lovely evening and the use of her bathroom . . . I decided to play it by ear. I strode confidently into a large room to present myself to Pitchoune, and when she came in all my lingering doubts as to my welcome were swept aside by her lovely smile. Behind me her manservant entered with a bottle of champagne and two glasses, which he set down on a bar in the corner, and Pitchoune and I spent the day getting to know each other. It was as if we'd been close friends for years. We didn't discuss our histories; Pitchoune never once talked about herself, and for my part I never mentioned that my father was 'in cotton'. Our silences were as pleasurable as our conversation . . . Today was the beginning.

In the evening I said I was going out, on the off chance that I might bump into my mates and be able to let them know that I was OK. With gentle understanding, Pitchoune didn't ask if she could come with me; instead she went over to her escritoire and came back with a bundle of banknotes, which she offered me. Forestalling my objections, she said, 'I want you to have a good time, and buy all your friends a drink.'

Hell's bells, I was only going out for a couple of hours and here was enough moolah to buy me a month's luxury holiday in Blackpool. I was deeply touched by her generosity, but there was no way in the world I was going to accept it. I put the banknotes firmly into her hand and closed her fist over them, stopping all her protestations by the simple method of kissing her. Then I turned towards the door, but before I reached it she said, 'If you want a good time I can recommend a place,' and she gave me directions.

The atmosphere in the club as I walked in was warm and friendly, and I was shown to a table. The clientele was mainly civilians – they could have been the elite of Brussels society – and, apart from myself, there wasn't a uniform in sight. I began to have misgivings: two drinks would be all I could afford in this place. I was about to leave when a suave man in a dinner jacket came over to me, bowed and introduced himself as the manager. There was something familiar about his face; I knew I'd seen him before. Then it came to me in a flash: this was the man in the long nightie who had handed over two bottles to Pitchoune last night. I remembered that his name was Paul, and when he addressed me as 'Monsieur Eric' he had the drop on me as well. I was about to order a half of lager when he bent over me and, *sotto voce*, told me that I was his quest this evening and everything was, erm – he struggled for the next phrase and I helped him out: 'on the house', I suggested hopefully. He beamed and I'd made a new friend.

After a moment's consideration I asked for a bottle of white wine. It was good, with a nice fruity taste, but after one glass I wasn't sure that half a lager wouldn't have been the better choice. I smiled at the two couples on the next table, they smiled back and before I could say '*garçon*' they had joined me. A waiter brought over four glasses, which were filled from my bottle while I ordered half a lager. Fortunately they spoke English better than I did; we had a hilarious evening and my list of friends grew. When we finally called it a night, they accompanied me back to Pitchoune's apartment. This wasn't just food for thought; this was a four-course meal. How did they know where I was staying? And, how did the manager know that my name was Eric? Pitchoune reluctantly provided the answers. Yes, she'd telephoned Paul to tell him to expect me, and no, she wasn't about to settle my bill, she owned the joint – game, set and match.

The rest of my leave flew by all too quickly in a beautiful blur of happiness, and it was with a heavy heart that I clambered over the tailgate of the lorry. The journey back to Eindhoven was the first time I'd seen any of my mates since that memorable night when we'd all met Pitchoune and her friend. They'd obviously made the most of their four days' leave and it was a boisterous journey, each funny story better than the last. I laughed with them and the only time I intervened was to ask if any of them had seen Jock during their shenanigans. They told me they hadn't seen him since that first day. No one asked me how I'd spent my time and I was grateful. What had happened to me was a memory too precious to share.

I had come to accept that Jock was not of this world – his sources of information could have taught the intelligence in Whitehall a thing or two – so a few weeks later when he asked me if I fancied another visit to Brussels I knew immediately that he was in the process of carrying out some machiavellian plot of his own. As for me, wild horses wouldn't dissuade me from an evening with Pitchoune, and in less than fifteen minutes I was at the wheel of a three-tonner on the road to Belgium. It never once occurred to me to ask how he'd managed to hijack the Bedford or how he'd known I wasn't on duty until the next evening.

When we finally arrived in Brussels he directed me to a small café. 'Leave the truck here,' he said. 'See you tomorrow at about four o'clock.' Then he turned and entered the café.

Pitchie was overjoyed to see me. Oh, the radiance of her smile and the genuine warmth of her welcome! One would have thought I'd been away for years. I still found it difficult to understand what she could possibly see in me, at the same time blessing my good fortune. Just to see the happiness in Pitchoune's eyes was contagious – even the manservant smiled as he relieved me of my small-kit. The following morning we made our way down to the second-floor flat, which was in direct contrast to the penthouse with its modern outlook and furniture: here all was antique, with dark heavy furniture reminiscent possibly of an eighteenth-century mansion.

Pitchie had arranged a luncheon for me and had invited two couples to make up the party. 'They would like to meet you,' she said. 'I think you will like them.' They were a jolly lot, who spoke English, and when it was my turn to accept a glass of champagne from the proffered tray I said, '*Merci*,' and they all nodded their appreciation as if I was bilingual. I'd grown to like champagne, but before I could ask for a refill Pitchoune was seating the guests, placing me at the head of the table, facing her at the other end. Wine was poured into our glasses, and a buxom woman in black placed a plateful of roast chicken before each of us while a girl doled out potatoes. These tasks carried out with elegant efficiency, they both bowed and left.

When they had gone, there was an uncomfortable silence. They all seemed to be looking at me expectantly. I glanced down the table at Pitchie, who smiled and nodded as if something was expected of me. Were they waiting for me to say grace? Oh, to hell with it, I put down my pristine knife and fork, picked up a chicken leg and began to demolish it. The spell was broken. They laughed and applauded, and followed my example with gusto. Apparently I'd passed the test with flying colours. By jingo, that chicken was delicious and a new experience for me as it was the first I'd ever eaten in my life. One thing was for sure: it wouldn't be the last.

On the journey back to Eindhoven, Jock passed over a bundle of banknotes. 'For the petrol,' he said.

I slipped the money into my breast pocket. Physically I was driving the Bedford, but in my heart I was still with Pitchie. About twenty kilometres on I came back to reality. 'What petrol?' I said, and in a few words I learned that we had sold four five-gallon cans of petrol to the owner of the café. It transpired that the petrol had come from our own transport section, who had siphoned off 5 per cent on the transaction. Unwittingly I was now a black-market baron.

Life in Eindhoven was dull and monotonous, relieved only by thoughts of Brussels and Pitchoune. The next two weeks dragged by like a month's package tour in Bulgaria. Fortunately, as the saying goes, it is always darkest before the dawn, and when I saw Jock approaching it instantly became full daylight, so it was with a great beam on my face I was soon steering one of our trusty Bedfords down a now-familiar road to Belgium. Didn't anyone in the transport section ever tumble to the fact that at certain times they were always one wagon short?

Jock sat in the passenger seat, arms folded, head down, eyes closed. He was either asleep or preparing himself for the evening's petrol transaction, making sure that this plan had no chance to 'gang aft agley' (Robbie Burns). As we squealed to a stop in front of the café, he was instantly wide awake, as if he'd merely been examining the crease in his trousers, and he had entered the café before I had jumped down from the cab. I had just taken out the rotor arm to immobilise the vehicle when Jock beckoned. He wanted me to meet our opposition. This was unexpected. Mentally I was already in Pitchie's flat, but what the heck – my arrival was always a surprise, as there was no way I could foresee when my next trip would be, and even if I had known it would have been impossible to communicate with Pitchoune, so a few more minutes wouldn't make any difference.

Jock introduced me, not by name of course but as one of his mates, to three Canadian soldiers. Hard men with dead-pan expressions, they were also in the racket of black-market petrol from Canadian army dumps. Jock ordered drinks all round, which I paid for, and after the second round, which also came out of my pocket, the atmosphere had thawed enough for me to take my leave pleasantly as if I had enjoyed their company. I was champing at the bit; the light had been draining from the sky when I arrived but now full darkness had taken over, and it was nearly ten o'clock. With every step, a warm feeling of excitement was growing in my stomach, but when I arrived something totally unexpected happened. The manservant let me in, with a smile of welcome as he took my small-kit away. Pitchoune came into the hall and her face lit up when she saw me. Then, as she led me in, her face clouded for a moment, all serious now, as she told me that she had guests. I assured her that it was entirely my own fault that I had been held up, and she squeezed my hand and said, 'If you come at three in the morning, you only have to ring the bell.'

Her guests were army officers. They were grouped at the bar and their banter ceased as they watched curiously as Pitchoune sat me in an armchair. They were even more puzzled when Pitchie went behind the bar and brought out a cut-glass tumbler, a bottle of gin and one of tonic water, which she placed at my feet before returning to the bar to play hostess. Pouring myself a drink, I observed the guests. They were all officers, the lowest in rank being a major and the most senior having red tabs on his collar. I also deduced that they were probably the desert rats from North Africa; khaki tunics and cavalry twill trousers over brown suede shoes – pretty important stuff. I was just too far away to hear clearly what their stories were about, but they all seemed to go down well – even Pitchie smiled.

An hour later, my gin bottle half empty, I beckoned to Pitchie and when she came over I said, 'Get rid of 'em.' It was out of character, two parts me and eight parts Gordon's gin, but incredibly Pitchoune did just that.

Pitchie patted my hand, turned, and like me came straight to the point, 'Gentlemen, we have had a good evening but now it is last orders.'

They all laughed hesitantly and finished their drinks, and as they were leaving each muttered their thanks as they shook hands with Pitchoune; but their whole attention was focused on me, lolling in an armchair and sipping my gin and tonic – more than likely they'd heard my 'Get rid of 'em'. I thanked my lucky stars that they were army and that being air force I was outside their jurisdiction, but I had the uneasy feeling that they'd all mentally assembled my particulars, uniform, rank, height, colour of hair, etc. – enquiries would be made.

In the morning the manservant informed me that there was a telephone call. I remembered the army officers of last night and my stomach dropped to the seat of my underpants. I sidled up to the telephone as if it was booby-trapped. I'd seen enough films to know which end to speak into – like the bidet it was a first, my introduction to the telephone. A man's voice came through the earpiece, heavily accented, so my panic moved aside to admit curiosity.

'How are you enjoying Brussels?' he asked and he addressed me by name.

I mumbled a reply, and after a few more minutes of non-essential chat he rang off. Who was he and how did he know where to find me?

Half an hour later I had a similar call, this time from a lady enquiring about my health and how Pitchoune was.

Some minutes later when I put the phone down Pitchoune smiled happily. 'You are getting quite famous in Brussels,' she said, adding, 'Now they know you are with me.'

In this city Pitchoune was on a pedestal, and she was helping me up to be by her side. I would do my utmost to be a credit to her. But all my good intentions went out of the window when my involvement in the petrol caper kicked me in the stomach. I squared my shoulders and resolved there and then I'd have done with it. I owed Pitchoune that at least.

However, I needn't have bothered. On the journey back to Eindhoven Jock told me that the petrol racket was finished, kaput. We'd got out just in time, and the Canadians were packing it in as well. It appeared that the military police were getting too close. Jock never knew what a relief it was to me but I think he was glad to be shot of it himself. After a time he smiled and said, 'They were a tough bunch, those Canadians.' Knowing it was to be their last trip, they'd not only sold the petrol but, would you believe it, flogged their wagon as well.

Back at our base in Eindhoven, I began to wonder if I'd ever see Pitchoune again. After all, we couldn't stay in Holland indefinitely if we were serious about winning the war; we'd have to move into Germany, which would not be a picnic. The order to roll could come any day now, so rumour had it; but three weeks went by and still only rumour had it. Then out of the blue one of our officers approached me as I was rinsing my mess tins in a large drum of greasy water.

'I'm going down to Brussels this morning to pick up our monthly beer ration.'

I was perplexed. Why was he telling me? I wasn't his mother.

He went on, 'Do you fancy a lift?'

My perplexity grew, but my spirits rose – for a moment only. 'I can't come with you. I'm on watch at midday.'

'I'll soon fix that,' he said. He went into the orderly room, and in two shakes of a duck's whatnot he was out again. 'All fixed,' he said. 'Leaving in ten minutes.'

I couldn't believe my luck as I crouched in the back of a fifteen-hundredweight on the well-worn road to Brussels. But the incongruity of my unexpected trip never crossed my mind. I had long since given up questioning my good fortune; to me the abnormal was standard.

When we finally arrived in Brussels, we pulled up and the officer leaned back to say, 'Can you give the driver directions to where you want to be dropped off?'

I did so, and when we arrived I climbed over the tailboard. The officer got out as well and said, 'Aren't you going to invite me in?'

Pitchoune opened the door herself, her face alive with welcome, but seeing the officer she gave my hand a squeeze. Knowing her as I did, it was sufficient. She was too well bred to be demonstrative before strangers. I introduced him to Pitchoune and over a polite drink or two he said he'd pick me up at four o'clock. Then he was gone, but by golly, in the short time he'd sat making polite conversation with Pitchie his eyes had wandered round the room and he'd been impressed.

Was I hungry? Was I tired? Pitchie questioned me with deep concern. 'Would you like a hot bath?'

The last appealed to me, as winter was edging out the autumn and a hot bubble bath was a luxury the RAF didn't provide. I must have been tired as well. When Pitchie shook me gently awake the water was lukewarm and it was five minutes to four.

Eindhoven was white with snow and frost as Christmas drew near; it was a cold I'd never experienced before, crisp and clean, invigorating the body into a healthy glow.

'Hey, Tam.' I heard the familiar call and turned to meet Jock. I hadn't seen him since we'd given up our life of crime. Naturally I was pleased to see him and not in the least surprised when he took two glasses from his greatcoat pockets and a flat bottle of navy rum from his battle blouse, and in no time we were sitting in the back of the Bedford drinking each other's health '*à la* Normandy'. It was then that an idea flashed into my mind.

'What are the chances of a truck on Christmas Eve?'

The familiar twinkle came into his blue eyes. 'Brussels?' he queried.

I nodded and that was enough. No doubt Pitchoune would be surprised by my bringing along a guest, but I was in no doubt that she would handle the situation with her usual unflustered efficiency.

Once again on Christmas Eve 1944 we were on the road down to Brussels. It was a clear day, and driving easy indeed – for the first fifty or sixty kilometres we hadn't seen another vehicle. Suddenly, though, we were alert. At the sound of an aircraft I wound my window down and stuck my head out, and a Messerschmitt overtook us, only about thirty feet to our left, flying just about telegraph pole height. He waggled his wings as he passed. 'Cheeky sod,' muttered Jock as we watched it disappear into the far distance, but we were both sharing a thought: why didn't he shoot us up? Answer: he was out of ammunition. But if he was out of ammunition, why was he headed for Brussels? Questions and answers tumbled one after the other through our minds, and we finally came to the conclusion that someone up there liked us.

Jock, who had never met Pitchoune, was bowled over by her serenity and her beauty, as I knew he would be. In the drabness of war Pitchie was a twenty-carat diamond in a rubbish dump. When she excused herself to make a telephone call, leaving us sipping champagne in front of a cheery fire, Jock surveyed the opulence about him. Finally he looked at me, as if I was the only thing that didn't quite fit the surroundings. Pitchoune came back to announce that all the arrangements for a happy Christmas were now in place and she hoped that Jock would be pleased. 'Enchanted,' murmured Jock, kissing her hand, and the ice was broken. In less than half an hour Pitchoune's girlfriend arrived, the dark-haired one I'd last seen in RAF uniform on the day we'd all met. She greeted me warmly, and then Pitchoune introduced her to Jock.

It was the first time Jock had looked out of his depth; it was all too good to be true. I glanced at Pitchie and she looked at me totally innocently, as if she hadn't set the whole carousel in motion. Needless to say, we had a hilarious, glorious Christmas Eve, and wished Jock and his new-found friend all the best when they made their way down to the second floor and the austere flat where I'm sure they spent a very happy Noel.

Arriving back at Eindhoven that same Christmas Day, I looked around me and it was obvious that a good time had been had by all. Hardly anyone could stand, and had I not known Pitchie I would most certainly have been flat out in a drunken stupor, waking up on Boxing Day to share in the communal hangover. Instead I was gripped by a premonition, an unthinkable thought, that I would never see Pitchoune again. As long as we were in Eindhoven I always hoped that there might be another trip to Brussels and Pitchie, but sadly, my premonition became a reality when 589A MSU rolled out of Holland in the last stages of the war. The door was slammed in my face – slammed, bolted, locked . . . but not quite nailed shut.

Our advance stalled as we made our way to Nijmegen Bridge, where the infantry came up against stiff resistance from last-ditch German forces. This was only to be expected, as Nijmegen Bridge spanned the Rhine into the Fatherland, and from then on the Germans would be fighting in their own backyard. Our own unit was not far from the bridge, and my most vivid memory of this time was the cold, biting, incessant rain slashing our faces; it was impossible to keep dry. With memories of Brussels, I was in a fit of deep depression; and then, as at other times in my life when I've been at my lowest ebb, the sun came out, and it shone this day in the shape of a mud-spattered despatch rider, who presented me with a parcel. When I'd signed for it, he saluted and marched off to his bike. I'd never been saluted before; nor had I ever received a parcel. In the back of a wagon I tore off several wrappings of brown paper, wondering if this wasn't some kind of a joke, but it wasn't. To my astonishment I took out a thick woollen sweater and a bottle of brandy. Was it a Red Cross parcel, or the Salvation Army perhaps? Then I noticed a little note: 'I hope this will keep you warm. All my love, Pitchoune.'

Who was Pitchoune? For the next few days I could think of nothing else. I knew that she was in the top echelon of Brussels society and, remembering the night when high-ranking army officers were her guests, I knew that she must have had some influence with the brass hats, because it would take somebody of great seniority in the military to instigate enquiries as to my whereabouts in Germany. Obviously this had been successful (but I wished they'd let us know, as we weren't too certain where we were ourselves), and then authorisation had been given for a despatch rider to pick up a parcel from Brussels to deliver it into my hands . . . So again I came round to the question that has continued to nag me for years: who was Pitchoune? Typically, though, after posing the questions I was content to leave the answers to somebody else. Suffice it to say that Pitchoune was the epitome of goodness, wisdom and the meaning of love. I hope I filled a corner in her life; she built a mansion in mine.

Just before we left Eindhoven I received a letter from home which I did not open immediately. When I did, I found that it mostly concerned my brother Vernon. After reading it I relaxed and my mind went back to 1940, when Vernon first joined the RAF as a trainee pilot. How I admired him when he came home on leave with the white flash in his cap denoting that he was air crew in training! He went on to further instruction in Paignton, Devon, and was about to be posted to a flying school when he suddenly appeared in our front room. He wasn't on leave; he'd just had enough, so he had walked out, and if they wanted him back they'd have to come and fetch him . . . Which they did, personally. I think he walked out of the RAF base at Paignton because he'd been in uniform for two or three months and they still hadn't invited him to eat in the officers' mess.

I picked up the letter again and re-read it. Vernon was now a corporal on an RAF air sea rescue boat on Lough Erne in Ireland. I had to smile at this: trust him to find a cushy billet – there couldn't be too many air crews parachuting into Lough Erne, so I imagined he had plenty of time for fishing. He was a funny old cuss; his only drawback was that mentally he moved through life well beyond his station, travelling first class without a ticket.

Into his multi-coloured, expectant dreams came a small, gracious Irish lass called Eve. She was not a particularly ravishing beauty, but there was something about her that appealed to Vernon – something that was as yet indefinable, until Eve happened to mention that she was a classical pianist. How his heart must have leapt! All this I gleaned from Dad's letter. Vernon had also intimated that Eve's father was a landowner. I can visualise Vernon blowing all his meagre corporal's pay on wining and dining her, during which he would manage to serve an ace by telling her his own father was in cotton. Naturally they decided to tie the knot, both believing that they were marrying into gentry. There was only one irritating little cloud in an otherwise azure blue sky: Eve was a Roman Catholic and before they could marry Vernon would have to be of the same persuasion ... No problem: without hesitation Vernon resigned from the Church of England and in the twinkling of an eye the Pope was his best friend. After they were joined together Eve took her new husband to meet his father-in-law and here I can only imagine the disappointment that trampled all over his happy betrothal. The ancestral pile was nothing but a broken-down cottage held up by the front door and surrounded by barely enough land to supply peat for winter warmth. The plot thickened when Vernon eventually brought his bride to Oldham. Eve's reaction must have echoed Vernon's as he waved her over the threshold of 36 Leslie Street.

And there I left them both to concentrate on Nijmegen Bridge.

*   *   *

After crossing the Rhine, our convoy rolled on to the dry land of the Third Reich. Our triumphant days of liberation were behind us and from now on we were the invaders. Twilight slipped away with the onset of night as we moved forward towards a vast red glow reflected on the underbelly of the clouds. Our first German town, called Wesel, was ablaze. As there had been no air raid, we assumed that the fire was a deliberate act of sabotage and I don't think we were too wide of the mark. Our convoy halted on the outskirts as our road disappeared into a maelstrom of hungry flames. As I looked around me I spotted the first sign of life, a cow, silhouetted against the backdrop of the blazing inferno, bellowing piteously as it was driven on by the flailing sticks of two shadowy figures. A third man was beating off two hysterical Fraus, yelling and screaming loudly enough to be heard over the conflagration. On seeing our convoy, the two women broke off the unequal battle and ran towards us to elicit our help, yelling, pleading and pointing towards the three dark shadows endeavouring to make off with tomorrow's roast.

We got the message: the cow belonged to these two harridans, and probably the three rustlers were DPs (displaced persons), dispatched in cattle trucks unwillingly from their homeland to work as slave labour for the master race, and now that they were liberated that cow was part payment for their long overdue wages. I suspect that they had also had more than a hand in the inferno before us. We gathered all this from the pantomime and broken English, but there was nothing we could do. When we began to move off, the two Fraus turned all their invective against us, spitting and screaming as they ran alongside until we left them behind. Welcome to Germany.

Our war was virtually coming to a close. As at Caen and Nijmegen Bridge we were held up, but this time not through enemy opposition but because of a political decision made at Yalta between Roosevelt, Stalin and our leader, the indomitable Winston Churchill. The British and American forces were marking time in order to allow the Russians to enter Berlin first. Taking advantage of this standstill, a few of the lads were given seven days' leave. Not Continental leave: this time it was a week in Blighty. It was almost a year since

I had last seen home, and yet strangely enough I wasn't overjoyed. Here in Germany we were within spitting distance of the end of hostilities, and I wanted to be here with my mates to see the war through to the end. I'd no desire to be strutting down Featherstall Road being admired when the curtain came down.

Anyway, it was good to be home, although the journey through Europe by train was arduous. It took us more than a day to arrive at a channel port for embarkation and we eventually pulled into London Road station in Manchester at about four o'clock in the morning. From there I set out on the eight-mile hike to Oldham, fully loaded with backpack, side packs, gas mask and, if that wasn't enough, a bulging kitbag to top it all off. It was just getting light when I pulled our front-door key through the letter flap on its worn piece of string. I had to wake Dad and Mother up so that I could say, 'It's only me.'

Over breakfast they filled me in with all the local news. My younger brother John was away in South Africa with the navy and apparently, according to his letters, he was making out with a Cape Town girl and playing lots of tennis.

Dad was pleased to see me, but he said he'd only received one letter from me in nearly a year. I said, 'That's right, I only wrote one. It was from Normandy.' I had had to let them know where I was, but as all mail was censored I had put it in code. Dad took down my letter from the mantelpiece. It was only on a flimsy, dished out to us for writing short letters.

Dad told me it was nobbut a few lines and, putting on his glasses, he read, 'Our favourite song on the wireless is "I Can't Give You Anything but Love, Baby".'

Eagerly I snatched the letter from him. 'Don't you see?' I said. 'I spelt "can't" C-A-E-N.'

'Your Mother and I noticed that, but she said spelling wasn't your strongest suit.'

'But that's where I was, near Caen.'

'Ah,' said Dad. 'Where's that, then?'

I gave up. It jogged my memory, though, because I remembered that I'd brought Dad a present all the way from Normandy. My water bottle was half full of Calvados, which I presented to him as apple brandy. He was delighted, and he couldn't wait to unscrew the stopper. Then he sat comfortably in his armchair. 'Cheers,' he said, and he took a hefty swig. Immediately he sat bolt upright, eyes bulging, as he looked round for somewhere to offload. Then, jerking forward, he spat the mouthful of Calvados into the fire. The fire resented this invasion of its somnolence and retaliated, shooting out an angry tongue of flame that caused my father to fall back in the chair, beating his head as if it was burning. Luckily it wasn't, although his eyebrows were singed. He was breathing hard as if trying to cool his mouth and he was unconvinced that it was not colourless petrol.

Almost before I knew it, my leave was over. I didn't look forward to the long haul back to Germany. In fact as the hours sped by and we rattled for hour after hour in an overcrowded train, I began to feel under the weather. I was perspiring, and by the time I reached the camp in Germany I was feverish, and I had to be helped down from the back of the lorry, from where I made my way to see the MO (medical officer). He was standing in the middle of the field, with one or two boxes by his feet, and when I looked round there wasn't a tent in sight. However, the MO put his hand on my forehead.

'You've got flu,' he said, 'but there's nothing I can do, as we're moving out in a few minutes.' He gave me a handful of aspirins. 'Take one every two hours and when we get to where we're going, go straight to bed.'

Our destination turned out to be Luneberg Heath. As if we had been expected, it was awash with orderly lines of tents so glaring white that it was more like an advert for washing powder and within half an hour I was dozing in one of them, wrapped up in my two blankets and in and out of consciousness. That night, after one of the lads had brought me a mess tin full of hot soup, which I could barely keep down, I listened on and off to their excited chatter: 'Tomorrow the war will be officially over', and 'All the top brass of the defeated German forces will unconditionally surrender to Montgomery.' In my overheated state I couldn't have cared less, I must confess. I felt better when I woke in the morning, not better better, but better than I had been though not well enough to rise from my blankets. I had an aspirin for breakfast and settled down to enjoy my incapacity.

Later that day I ducked out of the tent on rubbery legs, only to discover that it was all over. Unconditional surrender had been accepted by the German delegates; our top brass had signed several papers; this done, the whole circus of VIPs had decamped and that was it ... Apparently all the history had been signed, sealed and accepted just before three o'clock that morning without my knowledge as I was blissfully enjoying an aspirin-induced recuperation. Another idle thought penetrated the haze. Why we had been rushed up to this historic stage was beyond me. Perhaps we would be ordered to pick up any litter or matchsticks as we'd been trained to do in the Cosham woods just before we embarked for Normandy. The war was over and the good guys had won. Shouldn't there at least be one hurray for this?

I gazed around me. As far as the eye could see there was grassland – no trees, no buildings of any kind. Tranquillity reigned, broken only by the sporadic crackle of Sten guns as – I learned later – one or two of the lads prowled the area for rabbits.

We were absolutely unaware that throughout the Western world there were noisy, raucous, exuberant fireworks and church bells in celebration of VE day. Hysterical crowds packed Trafalgar Square, and on the balcony of Buckingham Palace the King, Queen and two princesses appeared to cheers that could be heard as far away as Bayswater, rising to a fever pitch when Winston Churchill joined the royal party.

Meanwhile on Luneberg Heath this historic day was just like any other. All was peaceful, apart from the jangle of our mess tins as we queued up for our supper, after which we stood around in groups, smoking cigarettes and chatting softly until it was time to turn in. It was ironic being camped next to the marquee wherein peace had been signed for ... We were all of one mind that it had been a very dull ha'p'orth.

On the morrow we boarded our transport and once again we

were on the road for what I hoped would be our final journey, our destination Schleswig-Holstein. Peace at last, but not for us. From liberators to invaders, and now we were the occupiers.

Our convoy entered the suburbs of Schleswig-Holstein and as we neared the centre we passed a German naval hospital. It was then that we had a foretaste of what the next few weeks had in store for us. Just outside the gates of the hospital there was a large group of wounded, all bearing their misfortunes in white bandaged stumps where a limb should have been. They merely stood listlessly in the roadway, smoking, in one case a young lad leaning on his crutch to hold a cigarette to the mouth of an armless comrade. We drove slowly by, not out of respect but because not one of the wounded Germans had moved, leaving us very little room to pass. They turned their backs on us and stared at the ground, but those backs were more expressive than any words and it boiled down to one: HATE.

A few more pitted streets and we arrived at our destination, a huge barrack block, very nearly intact but for a few broken windows. In more triumphant days it had been a Luftwaffe base and, judging by the discarded thick, rough clothing and one huge, grey, padded boot that we found in one of the rooms, one didn't have to be the head of our Secret Service to deduce that Schleswig-Holstein, being a north German seaport, had been the billet of the high-flying, long-range Dornier aircrews shadowing our Russian convoys and transmitting course, speed and, more important, the number of ships in the convoy to their intelligence bases ashore. It was here that we were to while away our time until our demob. There was nothing to do: no wireless watches, no drills, nothing. In fact our greatest difficulty was staying out of trouble. Our orders had been that no one was to leave the billet alone and Sten guns were to be carried at all times. We were also advised by the wounded we had seen on our arrival not to venture down the street; they were allowed out of the hospital every afternoon but as they hadn't the energy to go anywhere they just stood outside the gates.

The next day two of us decided to acclimatise ourselves to our new surroundings. It was overcast, which didn't paint the town in an inviting light, but no matter. As we strode jauntily down the *Strasse*, Sten guns slung over our shoulders, the world was a slightly safer oyster. The German citizens avoided our eyes when we passed by them; there were not many of them about, but all of them looked underfed, shabby and demoralised – an ironic twist of fate for a nation once hailed as the master race.

The buildings on either side of the street had taken a battering. Windows were boarded up; doors hung open; a staircase led up to nowhere. Even so, I sensed that most of these ruins were occupied, and I shivered as I visualised eyes observing our every move. The next street was a replica of the first one; so too was the next. With a growing sense of unease, we looked around for a familiar landmark. There were no British uniforms in sight and we only had three or four words of German between us. The trick was to keep moving. Turning into the next street, we knew immediately where we were and shock froze our movement: we had almost walked slap bang into the middle of the patients of the naval hospital on their afternoon's outing.

The amputees turned slowly towards us and the sight of those drawn, hate-filled faces had me paralysed with fear. We just stared at each other, a frozen tableau needing only a spark. Then silently they began to shuffle towards us and the spell was broken. In a blind panic we both turned and stampeded round the corner and it wasn't until we'd covered a hundred yards that we considered ourselves safe enough to look back. The angry, frustrated wounded were just coming into view round the corner, where they limped to a stop, brandishing sticks and crutches in frustration. They didn't shout, but a spine-chilling howl echoed down the street – it wasn't human. Their white bandaged stumps were the visible signs of the horrors of war but more insidious was the invisible damage to those shattered minds. We kept a wary eye on them as we bent forwards, hands on knees, to get our breath back. Shyly, we looked at each other embarrassed by our headlong rush like a couple of silly schoolgirls; we could have strode away with dignity and still outpaced them.

As we grew more accustomed to our life of leisure, we became less timorous. Everything was up for grabs. If, for instance, we spotted an unattended civilian car, we lifted the bonnet, hot-wired it to start and had a gentle sightseeing tour round the port. It was some weeks before the powers that be put a stop to it, but there were other things that could be bought with the currency of cigarettes, chocolate, tins of food, etc., but mainly cigarettes. Fraternisation with the Germans was a chargeable offence, but we all fratted and I can't recall anyone being put on a fizzer.

In an idle conversation one day I discovered that Schleswig-Holstein had never been the springboard for highflying Dorniers: this, typically, was a figment of my overheated imagination. The truth was less gung-ho: it had been a seaplane base, a more mundane branch of the Luftwaffe. When I'd digested this let-down, an exciting idea sprang to mind and my brain went into overdrive. How many cigarettes and bars of chocolate would be required to purchase one of these slow-flying amphibians? It shouldn't be too difficult to get the hang of it. I could even go home on demob in one, albeit in a series of short hops. What am I talking about? As swiftly as this wild scheme had fired my thoughts, my enthusiasm drained away like the sand in an hourglass. My feet were back on the ground and I mentally lambasted myself, vowing that it was high time I grew out of these infantile fantasies. Little did I know then that thoughts such as these in future years would be my stock in trade. But for the time being here I was in Schleswig-Holstein. I didn't have much interest in watches or cameras but I was constantly on the lookout for a bargain.

One blustery day six of us found ourselves at a small harbour, and as I surveyed the windswept panorama of the coast I felt a light touch on my elbow. I turned to see a frail civilian in a leather coat that reached to his ankles. He stood on tiptoe to whisper in my ear. I replied, '*Ja*,' although I hadn't understood a word. However, it turned out to be the expected reply because he took me to the edge of the jetty, where I looked down at the water. Then a short bargaining took place. I surreptitiously slipped him forty Players and I had just bought myself a rowing boat. The other lads came up and admired the craft. It wasn't as big as the lifeboat on an ocean-going liner, but it was roomy enough for the six of us. It was only when one of the lads pointed out that there were no oars that I whipped round, only to see the long leather overcoat disappearing round a corner of a boathouse. I'd been foxed and, furious at my gullibility, I couldn't even sell the damn thing – who would buy a powerless rowing boat? And to cap it all, it started to rain – it was not heavy but wet enough to dampen my spirits. What a gloomy place was Schleswig-Holstein, when I thought back to just over a year ago in Normandy where every day was a scorcher; now although it was summer every day in these northern latitudes was mid-November.

A tall, thin, moustached man came out of one of the sheds, touched the peak of his cap and said, 'Guten Morgen.'

I shrugged and held out my hand to catch the rain.

He tapped his chest and exclaimed, 'Harbour master.'

We all brightened and one of the lads said to him loudly, 'No oars.'

He shook his head vigorously, but I ignored his dismissive gesture and, pointing to my boat, mimed rowing and then said, 'Nix!'

His face went slightly puce and he let loose a torrent of German, making sweeping gestures with his hands, shaking his head and pointing to the sky in reply. I stepped towards him and mimed rowing again. Immediately he turned on his heel, strode into a boathouse and a minute or two later returned with an armful of oars, which he flung down at my feet. I looked at him and then down at the oars. Up to now I had been prepared to give him a cigarette for his trouble, but his boorish behaviour didn't warrant such generosity – good grief, we'd won the war, hadn't we? He should have been more deferential. I looked round to the lads for support but they were eagerly fitting the oars in the rowlocks. It was only afterwards that we found out that he had not been averse to lending us the oars, nor was he against our little adventure. Quite the opposite: he was afraid for our safety should we row past the breakwater.

Pushing off from the steps, we had to row the gauntlet between the E-boats tied up to the jetty on either side of us. What was even worse was that their crews stood by their boats expectantly, waiting for a catastrophe to happen. They were the roughest, toughest bunch of characters I'd ever seen in my life. I know it was a dangerous, dicey job in their branch of the service, but these men were something else; with woollen caps, unshaven faces, thick, grey knitted polo-necked sweaters and gumboots they looked capable enough to take on the world. Pulling myself out of my awestruck daydream, I dipped the oar into the water, determined to put on a show. We weren't Oxford or Cambridge, but we were British, from the greatest seafaring nation in the world. All our heads were down so that we wouldn't have to look at a critical audience, although in all likelihood the E-boat crew's faces were expressionless – they'd seen lunatics before. By now we were nearing the end of the break-water. It wasn't too bad and soon we would be round the edge into the ocean – anything to get away from those flat, German faces turned into the North Sea.

What happened next was sudden and dramatic. The wind didn't moan as it had on the breakwater; it screamed as it took the boat and flung it out into a maelstrom that would have capsized the *Ark Royal*. Instantly we all scrabbled for handholds and most of the oars, free to leave the sinking ship, went flying into the boiling, seething mass of angry sea to fend for themselves. A huge wave crashed over the boat.

'Bale out,' I screamed, but with that howling wind I might just as well have sung 'Swanee River'.

The boat was being thrust further in to deeper water so that the bigger waves could have a go. It seemed that we had come all the way from Normandy without a scratch, only to be lost at sea a few yards off Schleswig-Holstein. Then suddenly the boat stopped as if it had run into a brick wall and we all ended up in a heap in the bottom of the boat. We had run fast and hard into a submerged sandbank and although the sea flung itself at us, it could not free the boat – thank God, as had we missed the bank we could have been washed ashore in Denmark.

After a gabble of solutions had been suggested it was decided that as it was my boat I should lower myself to stand on the sandbank and push the boat into deep water. There was nothing else for it, so I scrambled over the bows. The sea was bitterly cold as I shoved with all my strength, and I could have sworn that the boat moved a little. The lads were all hunched in the boat looking down at me, giving helpful advice, but then a mechanical voice bellowed through the storm: 'Stay where you are' and, bucking about like a frisky cow pony, an E-boat made headway towards us. I clambered back into my boat, landing amongst my crew like a heavy catch of Dover sole. When the E-boat was alongside, a rope snaked across to us and six pairs of hands went up to receive it. The result was catastrophic – sheer slapstick: we crashed together and one of us fell overboard. He struggled back, ignoring the proffered hands – he'd had enough embarrassment for one day. Shamefacedly, we were towed back into harbour, stern first. At least the E-boat crews watching didn't add to our misery, but they surely must have been thinking how the hell had they managed to lose the war – just as I had thought on first seeing them, How did we manage to win?

Even in these northern latitudes there were the odd days when the warm sun dominated a light blue sky, and on one of these unexpected glimpses of summer a few of us in short-sleeve order decided to spend the day in the countryside surrounding the port. It was a wise choice. Rich green grass waved languourously in a gentle breeze, greenery shimmered as far as the horizon and as we topped a grassy knoll we stopped dead in our tracks, unbelieving and speechless . . . Below us was a fairly large, sparkling lake, but all our eyes were riveted on the grassy banks. Dozens of frauleins were lying about in bras and panties, taking advantage of the unusually hot day – a veritable open-air harem . . . After six years of living on the breadline a swimming costume would have been an unnecessary luxury. In any case, we all preferred what they happened to be wearing, and as none of us had swimming trunks in our kitbags, our standard-issue underpants were decent enough for us. In less than ten minutes we were all splashing and frolicking around with the lasses, completely ignoring the rumours that we were under constant observation by military police lying in the tall grass overlooking the lake with binoculars to enforce the non-fraternisation ban. Nobody gave a toss. Hungry females and lusty young lads – to hell with the rumours . . . The hills were alive with the sound of music.

I can't remember when or why our first CO left us, but I'm almost sure that us washing our 'smalls' in a French field two days ahead of the recce patrols of the British assault force can't have enhanced his chances of promotion; or perhaps to give him the benefit of the doubt he'd simply been demobilised. We now had a new CO, who was older, certainly wiser, and probably a regular serving officer. Information had most certainly been passed on to him, because when I heard that my old mucker Jock Irwin had been posted to the Far East and immediately offered my own services to carry on the war in Japan, the CO shook his head and, leaning back in his chair, said, 'Not in a million years.'

I tried to intervene but he held up his hand and said, 'No way am I going to lumber some other poor CO by sending you and Irwin together.' So that was that – I didn't even get the chance to wish Jock good luck.

That wasn't the end of it. Fifty years later, Jock and I met again when he arrived unannounced at my office. I recognised him immediately. It was as if time had stood still: in all the intervening years he hadn't aged. His hair was grey like mine, but then his hair had always been that colour; his back was ramrod straight and his eyes still twinkled mischievously. Sadly, I never got around to asking him all those questions which hadn't yet come to mind, as at that time I had no intention of writing my memoirs. I never saw him again; nor did we correspond. Sometime later his son rang me to say that his father had passed away – probably the only event in his entire life for which he didn't have an answer. I am proud to have known him.

I had had enough of Schleswig-Holstein. I was getting bored and, as was customary, I scrutinised the noticeboard every morning. On one particular day it was no different – there was the usual bumph, a few names for demob, a couple of postings, kit inspections, etc. – and I was about to leave, when an announcement at the very bottom caught my eye: 'All those with theatrical experience report to . . . etc., etc.' I didn't even consider it; I picked up my small kit and made my way to 'etc. etc.' It was only when I arrived outside the building that I had a surge of misgiving, but as with many other emotions in my life I put it to one side, and I looked for the entrance. Opening a door, I increased the volume of chatter and laughter from an exuberant group of RAF, bods enjoying each other's company. From the badges on their sleeves it seemed that most of them were wireless operators like myself, but most certainly not of our unit 589A – there wasn't a familiar face amongst them. Closing the door behind me brought the cacophony to an abrupt end and they all turned to stare at me as if I was a member of the Waffen-SS. Ignoring them, I looked to my left, where an RAF officer was seated at a trestle table, and I made tracks towards him, listening to my own footsteps invading the silence. The officer, however, gave me a welcome smile and then held out his hand, which I shook. This was most unusual: the last time I'd faced an officer across a desk I had been hatless, accompanied by a flight sergeant.

'Good morning,' began the officer. 'Name?'

It was at this moment that the other me spoke. 'Rick Allen,' I said, surprised at my own temerity. What had possessed me to come out with a name like Rick Allen?

'Rick Allen?' repeated the officer, expecting more.

'Yes,' I replied. 'The Rick Allen,' and now I was conscious of a stirring of interest in the mob behind.

'I'm sorry, but I've never heard of Rick Allen,' said the officer, completely baffled.

I looked round at the lads as if I couldn't believe he'd never heard of me, but from their expressions I gathered that they hadn't heard of Rick Allen either, which is hardly surprising – three minutes ago I hadn't heard of him myself.

'I'm not very well up in the vaudeville theatre,' apologised the officer. 'Forgive me, but what do you do?'

Still in Fantasyland, I replied that I did a drunk act, adding, 'Eight minutes without saying a word.'

The officer's face brightened and I was in.

I have referred to the man behind the table as 'the officer', but he deserves more than anonymity, much more. He was Flight Lieutenant Bill Fraser.

In 1939 a revue opened in the West End of London entitled *New Faces*, a show designed to discover a hitherto unknown comedian to be dubbed 'The New Face of the Year'. Bill Fraser cantered past the winning post several lengths ahead of the field; the West End was at his feet and the key to every number – one dressing room was within his reach. Malevolently Lady Luck snatched the goblet from Bill's lips before he'd taken his first sip. There was another contender for 'Man of the Year': his name was Adolf Hitler. He didn't get as many laughs as Bill, but he had a much bigger following. I'm sure that his sabotage of Bill's 'top new star' status was coincidence and not a premeditated act, but when Hitler declared war, Bill Fraser, being the right age at the wrong time, was cast in a supporting role as a lowly officer in the Royal Air Force in order to bring the war to an end before Christmas. That was an over-optimistic assumption – the end was to be almost six Christmases on – and Bill Fraser was now a flight lieutenant and the Entertainments Officer. He had been responsible for producing two service revues, the first *Bags of Panic* and the second *It's in the Bag*, both performed when he was stationed in Eindhoven. Now in rehearsal was his third offering, unsurprisingly entitled *Three Bags Full*, and after a fruitless morning of auditions his only discovery had been Rick Allen, an eight-minute drunk act.

For the rest of that first day Rick Allen became the centre of adulation. I was also re-introduced to a tall lad with an infectious smile, whom immediately I remembered from the old Swaffham days in early 1943. His name was and is Denis Norden. He was co-writing the show with a lad called Ron Rich, who, incidentally, after his demob became a minister in the Methodist Church. I suppose being a writer of saucy revues was his way of sowing his wild oats.

It was in a euphoric frame of mind that I ended my first day in the theatre, once again leaving myself wide open for the sucker punch. It didn't take long to connect. The following day Denis handed me a sketch, for me to learn and then rehearse. It should have been a pushover for Rick Allen, but I was well out of my depth. It wasn't too difficult to acquaint myself with the words, as there weren't any – a doddle for Rick; but as far as I was concerned, I wished I'd never invented him. Briefly, the sketch opened on me seated under an umbrella outside a French café and a waiter was haranguing me in broken English. This part was played by Gordon Horsewell, the only pre-war professional besides Bill, and he was absolutely brilliant. Although his was the straight role, he was getting all the laughs from the lads, while my attempts at playing a drunk were greeted with stony silence. After each rehearsal, Gordon would take me on one side and try to coach me in the art of being inebriated. I could only watch in admiration as he explained and demonstrated the psychology of a drunk: it was simple but well beyond my capabilities.

Arrogantly, I had assumed that playing a drunk would be a doddle for me – after all, I thought, I was well qualified: hadn't I drunk my quota over the last few years? It must at least have put me in the frame. But here's the catch-22: when you are well and truly under the influence of drink, reeling, staggering and slurring words, you're in no condition to stand off and observe how it was done; in fact a teetotaller would be better qualified for the part. So it came as no surprise when Bill, slightly embarrassed, let me know that Gordon would be playing the drunk. As he thanked me for my enthusiasm we shook hands and I said how much I'd enjoyed the experience; and, waving goodbye to the lads, I picked up my small-kit and made my way to the door – I was out!

Just as I reached for the knob, I stopped dead. My body was on automatic pilot and mentally I'd been thrown a lifeline. I turned and went back to the guv'nor, who was just about to recommence rehearsal.

'Oh, by the way Bill,' I said, and he put down his script, 'I think I should mention that I was with a four-part harmony group.'

'Oh yes?' he replied, lifting one eyebrow, a trick that was one of his trademarks. 'What was the name of the group you were with, then?' he asked.

Quick as a flash, I shot back, 'The Four Aces'. He was impressed – I could see that. The Four Aces were probably the most famous close-harmony singers in England. For a dreadful moment I wondered if I'd over-reached myself.

'You were with the Four Aces?' Bill asked. I nodded and he stared at me for a long moment, ideas forming in both eyes. Then he came to a decision. 'Do you think you could form a harmony group out of this lot?' he said.

Quickly looking at the lads, I turned to him. 'I don't see why not.'

He patted my shoulder. 'It's all yours,' he said, and with a sigh of relief I put down my small-kit. I was back in the family.

It was heart-warming to be back in the fold, but as in many other instances in my life there was another twist to this happy reunion.

Gordon, the old pro, took me to one side and said quietly with a smile, 'You don't give up easily, do you?'

I was flabbergasted but reassured by his smile. 'What are you talking about?' I replied, matching the friendliness of his statement.

'You were never in the Four Aces.'

'How do you know?' I said.

He looked round to make sure that wouldn't be overheard and whispered in my ear, 'I know because I was one of the Four Aces.' Again I was on the back foot, but seeing my expression he put his arm round my shoulders and said, 'But I'm glad you're back,' and our friendship, born during the drunk sketch, was rekindled, especially when he added, 'So we've only got another two to find now, a couple of numbers from our old act, some from the Mills Brothers and we'll be cooking with gas.'

Thanks largely to Gordon, we did form a group and with all modesty I can reveal that we weren't at all bad.

By the time *Three Bags Full* opened I was performing bits in various sketches. The show was an immediate hit, mainly because of the excellent writing of Denis Norden and Ron Rich and especially under the direction and guidance of the guv'nor, Flight Lieutenant Fraser. For us, each performance was carnival night and as, apart from Bill Fraser and Gordon Horsewell, we were all amateurs, enjoying a once-in-a-lifetime opportunity to stand on a stage and show off in front of captive audiences, it was no wonder that we were such a happy bunch.

What a wonderful finale to our service life! After-show parties in sergeants' messes, parties in officers' messes, first-class accommodation in places where hotels had been undamaged by war ... We had no costumes – we all wore our own uniforms – so we could walk into the theatre and on to the stage and after the final curtain walk straight out into the transport that would take us to our nightly frolics. The day was ours to enjoy from the moment we got out of bed, which depended on how we felt. No reveille, no parades, no sentry duty, and we didn't salute our officer; in fact we didn't even address him as sir – to us he was simply Bill. To put it another way, we were a protected species.

We travelled by boat from Silt to Denmark and to our delighted surprise the welcome that awaited us should have been afforded only to royalty. It was spectacular. The dignitaries in Copenhagen greeted us in frock coats, top hats and all. It was only later that the red carpet treatment was explained to us: it was because we were the first detachment of British troops to set foot in Denmark. From the breakfast on the ferry to the centre of Copenhagen it seemed to us that the war had bypassed Denmark altogether.

The show that night was an eyeopener. All the dignitaries of Copenhagen occupied the first few seats and the rest of the house was full of beautifully dressed Danes. Diamond tiaras were the order of the day and could easily have out-sparkled the show. However, this was not the case and as usual our finale was greeted with rapturous applause. Hi diddly dee, an actor's life for me.

On another occasion in Flensburg, Germany, our show was followed by a famous ballet company. The next day would be Christmas Eve 1945 and as they were booked into our hotel, Bill came up with a brilliant idea: we would take over the lounge and give them a Christmas party.

Throughout the day, while the ballet company were rehearsing at the theatre for their evening show, we all mucked in to decorate the large austere room and give it some semblance of Christmas. Chairs and armchairs were requisitioned and assembled round the imposing stone fireplace. A grand piano stood miserably in the centre, reminiscent of happier days when the clientele had sipped schnapps while a pianist rippled out numbers like 'Mein Eine Kleine Leibling' and other maudlin favourites. At the table Bill mixed a cocktail in an enormous silver punchbowl, which he kept having to replenish as the day wore on and we got thirsty. Eventually the scene was set for a riotous Christmas party after the show.

We were all well oiled when the ballet company returned from the theatre that night, and from that moment the party was a flop. Even the fire in the great stone hearth didn't infuse warmth into their attitude. At least four chairs had gone towards that cheery blaze, but even so they reclined around it elegantly as only ballet dancers can. I found myself sitting on the floor, exchanging monosyllabic words with a girl draped on a chair who never once looked in my direction, bored out of her mind.

I turned round to find that I was the only one of our mob present. All the rest had got the message early and made themselves scarce. Excusing myself, I went in search of our company and after a couple of minutes I found them crowded in a bedroom drinking the health of Christmas Day in the fug of cigarette smoke. They all stood up and coughed their way back into the lounge to do their duty. Somebody bashed out an intro on the piano and we endeavoured to blow a spark of life into the dying party with 'Roll out the Barrel'. There was no response from the ballet. Even 'Bless 'em All' was totally ignored. Then the glass doors swung open and Bill made his entrance. After a second's stony silence, we were all helpless with laughter. Bill had glided in with the grace of Pavlova but with a slight difference: he was stark naked, holding a fern frond over his privates. Just standing there in first position, he wasn't a pretty sight, but after several minutes of uncontrollable laughter he regained some sense of decorum with an expression we all knew too well: it said, 'Enough is enough.' Then in a falsetto voice he declaimed a short poem that eulogised the Scottish fern. His last line was 'But nothing can compare with the good old English rose,' and as he said this he whipped the fern aside and round his pathetic drooper was wound a red rose. With one synchronised rise the whole of the ballet stood and swept out. Not a word, thank you, Merry Christmas, kiss my foot. I hoped that one or two of them had the twitch of a smile before clambering into their cold beds.

It was not idle curiosity that drew me to a visit to Belsen, one of the nefarious Nazi concentration camps. What had begun as a rumour became a stark reality as, following the end of the war, the abominations of Belsen, Auschwitz, Dachau and numerous other camps became clear.

Ron Rich, Denis Norden and I were totally unprepared for the sights that hit us between the eyes. Appalled, aghast, repelled – it is difficult to find words to express how we felt as we looked upon the degradation of some of the inmates not yet repatriated. As far as I could see, all these pitiable wrecks had one thing in common: none was standing. They squatted in their thin, striped uniforms, unmoving bony structures who could have been anywhere between thirty and sixty years old, staring ahead with dead, hopeless eyes and incapable of feeling any relief at their deliverance. Misguidedly, we returned to our billets and came back with chocolates, bread and anything else we could lay our hands on. It was a pathetic gesture and a dangerous one, and we were sternly rebuked by a British Army medic, for had these poor unfortunates had the strength to devour our offerings, the richness on their emaciated stomachs might well have been their executioner. The sight of them is a memory I will never, ever forget and nothing angers me more when some people today not only defend the Hitler regime but also deny that the horrific death camps ever existed.

We were all in a sombre mood after our visit to Belsen and our show lost some of its lustre that night, until Bill reminded us in the interval that the show must go on. Trite, but it did the trick.

It wasn't long afterwards that Bill left. Being the eldest and one of the first to be called up, naturally he was at the top of the list to be demobbed. One minute he was the centre of our universe and the next he was gone. No farewell party, no eulogies, no fuss, but that was Bill's way. Sadly, without him we were a one-legged man without a crutch. No one could replace Bill. Somebody tried when half-a-dozen ladies in khaki uniforms bearing ENSA flashes on their shoulders arrived, but by this time more of our lads were packing up in preparation for demob – Steve Stephenson, Bob Errington, Pete Fawcett, Denis Norden, Ron Rich – and with the departure of these last two stalwarts it was goodbye to the fun and laughter of the last nine months.

We poor devils left behind were touring in a drama called *I Killed the Count*, hardly comparable to the drama of six years of war. All ENSA ladies were professional actresses and we amateurs, the stars of yesterday, floundered about like goldfish in a piranha bowl. Nevertheless the play was moderately successful, since nobody actually shot at us. However, we gave them another opportunity when we followed up the first debacle with another drama, the title of which escapes me, not too difficult as I'd left the door wide open.

But sadly my enthusiasm for the bright lights was rapidly diminishing. I was even seriously thinking, Roll on demob, when something completely unexpected happened. For some inexplicable reason I was transferred to AWS (Army Welfare Services). There must have been some mistake because unsurprisingly, as the title suggests, all the personnel were army and I was in the RAF. I didn't question it, though; anything was better than another abortive attempt at being an actor.

Winsen was the headquarters of AWS. Major Day was the CO responsible for putting on the variety shows, hallelujah. He was at that moment casting for a lavish extravaganza called *Strictly off the Record* and, to my delight, I was appointed the principal compère.

I didn't question this either; when somebody thrusts a bundle of five-pound notes into your hand, it's best to say 'Thank you' and not enquire, 'What's this for?'

Strictly off the Record was mainly a big-band show, and the twenty or so musicians occupied the stage for most of the time. They were tremendous, all army lads from different units with one thing in common: before being called up they had been professional musicians with Ambrose, Jack Hylton, Jack Payne and several other famous bands. By crikey they were good, and I should know because I'd had experience with my own little combo, The Blue Rhythm Boys, so I was able to chat to the musicians as if I was one of them. All I had to do was pop on to the stage from time to time, get a few laughs and introduce the speciality acts. It was money for old rope, or it would have been had they paid me. I must admit that although I was still slightly inexperienced as a patter comic, my material was first-rate, one-liners, funny anecdotes, wit – it was brilliant, and so it should have been, as I'd knocked it all off from short-wave radio broadcasts, mainly American shows such as *Midnight in Munich* and *Duffle Bag*; not one word of my act was original, and even my delivery was bordering on mid-Atlantic American. But my appetite for the theatre was rekindled.

Unfortunately the show was taken off, suffering the ravages of demobilisation, but I couldn't have been so bad because when I got back to Winsen Major Day invited me to compère another show. Completely different from *Strictly off the Record*, this time it was the Tzigane Orchestra, a motley collection of every nationality in Europe: a Czech, an Estonian, a Russian, a Pole, a Dutchman and that was only the string section – in fact no two musicians spoke the same language, and to cap it all the *Kappel Meister* (orchestra leader) was German. Before taking on the job of managing the whole caboodle, I should at least have heard them play, but I was so green that I didn't even know that tzigane meant gypsy, although I can't ever imagine any one of them travelling up and down in a caravan. I was promoted to sergeant and although the three tapes were khaki I thought they struck the right note of authority to go with my red silk neckerchief.

The *Kappel Meister* possessed an elegant Opal Admiral, the German answer to the British Bentley – I clarify this in case some readers assume that the Opal Admiral is a species of butterfly – and my first perk in my role as bossman was to commandeer this magnificent monster as my personal transport. It was driven by the *Kappel Meister*'s son, while the *Kappel Meister* himself sat next to him, and as the car was a drophead, I lolled elegantly in the back seat like Goering in his younger days. Behind us, at a respectable distance, struggled an old yellow coach carrying the orchestra, specialities, stage crew and the band's instruments. This is how we travelled to our first few dates, during which I began to wonder what had possessed me to accept this horrendous assignment. To say of the show itself that it was mediocre would be a kindness. The musicians seldom spoke together – understandably because of the language barrier – and it was obvious that they disliked each other from the way they played – even I spotted that, and I'm not a musician, but then neither were some members of the orchestra. The cast weren't much better: a hard, blonde singer who mangled 'Love Here is my Heart' each performance with eyes closed, secretly mourning the passing of Hitler; a top-hatted conjuror who by rights should have been in an old people's home knitting socks for the troops; and, most heartbreaking to watch, the adagio dancers struggling to catch their breath. At the beginning of the act, the man flung his wife across the stage, where she landed in the splits. That was actually graceful; it was getting up that was the problem. Then she hastened to her husband and leapt at him, whereupon he caught her and lifted her above his head, gasping as he hoisted her, '*Mensch*', which is the German equivalent of 'cor blimey'. It was awful to watch each performance. As for myself, I used the same act as in *Strictly off the Record*, same delivery, same cheeky smile, the only difference being that I never got a titter.

One particular afternoon was to send my life in an entirely new direction. As I swept through the gates of an RAF camp, followed by the bus, a young flight lieutenant ran across to meet us, introducing himself as the Entertainments Officer. Stopping his hand halfway to a salute on seeing my stripes, he pointed out the sergeants' mess, where I was to be billeted; the others would be put up in the DP (Displaced Persons) camp some way down the road.

Until that moment I had been reclining in the back seat, but now I opened the door and stepped down to make an impression, and I must have succeeded, judging by all the attention our arrival had caused. I said to the Entertainments Officer, 'They will not go to the DP camp. Accommodation will be found for them here.'

'But they are DPs,' he blustered.

'They are not,' I replied firmly. 'They are artists and as such should be accorded the respect they deserve.'

But he was adamant, so I stepped back into the car, saying, 'In that case there will be no show tonight.'

Had I not spent those instructive weeks with *Three Bags Full*, I doubt if I would have had the bottle to address an officer in this peremptory manner, but it worked: they were found accommodation in the camp, and sadly there was a show.

On this particular night, the show was a disaster, from the moment the curtain went up – but then it would have been, wouldn't it, after I'd chucked my weight about with the Entertainments Officer? For a start, only half the Tzigane Orchestra was in place during the first number, an up-tempo, fiery piece of gypsy dancing which had everything except the melody as the rest of the members furtively took their seats. If that wasn't enough, the rest of the show was worse. It was one hiatus after another, the whole show performed to dead, condemning silence, during which, in an effort to breathe some life into this thoroughly dead corpse, I bounded on to the stage with 'Hello folks' and immediately dried, stone dead, much too inexperienced to recover. In any case, the audience were shuffling out in the hope of salvaging what was left of the evening.

But that was only the beginning of my troubles. That shambles of a show was probably the most embarrassing episode in my short theatre life, but had I known what the morrow would bring I would have been several miles away when dawn lightened the eastern sky the next morning.

* * *

The door of my hut crashed open, wakening me, and I sat up on my bunk. Framed in the doorway was a short, portly WO (warrant officer).

'You,' he bellowed. 'Out.'

I glanced at my watch: it wasn't yet ten o'clock.

'Never mind what time it is,' he snapped. 'Get some clothes on.'

My stomach rumbled disconcertingly. No doubt about it, I was in deep water and there was not a beach in sight . . . Buttoning my battle blouse, I hurried out into the compound to where he was tapping his swagger stick impatiently against his leg.

'Where's your cap?' he snapped irritably.

'It's in the hut,' I replied.

'Well, then,' he shouted. 'Go and get it.'

I went back, got my cap, finger-combed my hair, jammed the cap on my head and hastened to the WO, who looked approvingly at my cap and nodded. Then he marched me into the CO's office to stand before the desk of the officer commanding.

'Caps off,' the WO barked. I wished he'd make up his mind.

The CO looked me over, trying to decide how to open his attack – after all, it was not every day that a uniformed wireless operator with khaki sergeant's stripes on his arm and a red silk neckerchief confronted him. Clearing his throat, he began on neutral ground. 'Are you 1522813 Sykes, E.?'

I nodded.

'What's that mean? You've got a tongue in your head, haven't you?'

'Yes,' I replied.

'Yes what?' screamed the Warrant Officer.

It was on the tip of my tongue to reply, 'Yes, I've got a tongue in my head,' but it wasn't a comedy routine. 'Sir,' I said meekly, curious to find out where all this was leading.

'Where've you been since May?' the CO snapped.

For a moment I thought it might be a trick question, as it was now September – how time flies! I explained my whereabouts during my hectic theatre experiences, with both the RAF and now the AWS.

'Well, Sykes,' he broke in, 'You are due for demob and this is your unit.'

I left the CO's office on the sharp horns of a dilemma. Of course I wanted to be demobbed, but not from this place. I'd upset just about everybody from the CO down to last night's audience. I could imagine them all licking their chops in anticipation of bringing me down a peg or two. Even one day would be twenty-four hours too long. There was only one thing for it: flight! In a flurry of dust, the Opal Admiral, with me crouched in the back seat, followed by the coach, disappeared into the wide blue yonder in order to antagonise another audience with the Tzigane Orchestra. I suffered another three weeks before I'd had enough, and the thoughts of demob became an attractive option.

Back in Winsen, I said goodbye to Major Day and anybody else in the vicinity, and with all my gear in the boot of the Opal Admiral I set out to ingratiate myself with the CO, the Warrant Officer and the Entertainments Officer so that I would have a painless demobilisation.

As the kilometres flashed by, my spirits rose. In a few days I would be home, walking into 36 Leslie Street in my demob suit. That's what I thought, but as in so many incidents before, my troubles were just about to begin – will I never learn? My chin was metaphorically exposed, and the sucker punch was well on its way. As we came in sight of the camp, something was wrong and my growing sense of foreboding was vindicated: there was no sign of life anywhere. I knew it was the camp, because there was the flat arid surface of the parade ground and faint tyre tracks, but that was it; the telephone lines were down, there was no flag pole, even the gates had gone. It was a ghost camp.

Some hours later, back in Winsen, Major Day looked up from his desk to ask hadn't I gone yet. I explained that I'd been and was back again, and why. Then it was his turn to explain to me that the AWS was army and I was RAF, and therefore he had no authorisation to demob me. I had to admit that I'd been hoisted by my own cowardly petard, for had I had the courage to overcome a few days of unpleasantness I might now have been trying on my demob trilby. Slapping the desk, Major Day came up with a solution. He put a fifteen-hundredweight truck at my disposal so that I could visit the nearest RAF establishment, and with any luck I could be demobbed from there. Perfect. Once more I bade him farewell, and with all my gear on the back of my fifteen-hundredweight I proceeded to a camp in Guttersloe, a rather large, busy station.

In the orderly room I outlined my predicament to a curious corporal, giving him a detailed résumé of my activities from answering the announcement on the noticeboard in Schleswig-Holstein up to the Tzigane Orchestra, leaving out the juicy bits, of course. It took almost half an hour, in which time the corporal's mouth never closed. Only once when I'd finished did he gulp and close it.

'Hang on a minute,' he mumbled, and he backed out, no doubt thinking I was a right nutter.

In the event his minute turned into an hour. He finally returned with an officer, who explained to me that they were not in possession of my record, nor did I appear on any list and unfortunately they had no authority to demob me. I couldn't take it in at first. I'd looked forward to being supplied with my travel documents, a good meal and then off to Blighty. However, the officer, noticing my stripes, said that if I signed on at the sergeants' mess a billet would be found for the night. The sergeants were very hospitable, not only for the evening but also for the following morning. I was able to draw my sergeant's rations, which included a bottle of Johnny Walker Scotch, and with this I drove out of the station to my next air force establishment, about sixty kilometres away, a much smaller camp. Again disillusionment: no record, no demob. Again I drew sergeant's rations – Johnny Walker. At two more establishments I had the same negative response, the only difference being that as well as my sergeant's rations (Johnny Walker), I had now concocted a tale of not having been paid for about six months, the signings for this extra perk being more indecipherable. I began to despair. I didn't want to end up a middle-aged alcoholic destined to roam the Autobahns with money in my pocket I couldn't spend. In any case, I had a premonition that the net was closing. I came to this conclusion on the next trip to an RAF base.

As I walked into the orderly room, the erk behind the desk became excited, shouting over his shoulder, 'Hey, Sergeant, this is him.'

And the alarm bells began to ring. Any minute now somebody might put two and two together about my sergeant's rations and, even more serious, my two handouts of back pay.

Major Day looked up as I walked into his office and said, 'It's not another farewell, is it?'

I didn't even laugh, but he bucked me up when he outlined his solution: although it was not in his remit to demob me, he would send me back to England on compassionate leave and once there I could sort it out for myself. A week later I was back home among my beloved Mucky Broos.

I'd had the usual interminable train journey from Germany to the Channel ports, but on the bright side by the time I stepped ashore I'd made my plans, or to be more accurate, plan. It was to contact my Member of Parliament and get him to sort out my demob. The best stratagems are always the simplest, and I was right; in fact my plan turned out to be inspirational. What a relief to hand over my burden! In less than a week, a letter arrived for me, and what a letter! With all the pageantry of government, the notepaper was headed 'House of Commons' and, more to my amazement, it was from Geoffrey de Freitas, the Minister of War, in his own handwriting. He apologised for my unfortunate predicament, saying that it had only happened once before to an airman in India. If I would present myself at the Air Ministry in Kingsway, my demobilisation would be speedily carried out. It wouldn't have surprised me if he'd signed it 'Geoff', but that was too much to ask. Bingo, jackpot – all my troubles were over. But once again there were a couple more hurdles before I passed the two-furlong marker.

When I arrived at the Air Ministry building, a sergeant, seated at a desk, spoke into a phone and almost immediately a young air force officer entered the hall and proffered his hand, which I shook. All this and I hadn't opened my mouth once, so I knew immediately that I'd been expected.

'Sorry about all your problems,' gushed the officer, smiling as he went through the motions of washing his hands. Had he been a civilian I would have been certain that he was about to sell me some insurance.

'We've located your unit,' he went on triumphantly. 'It's in Guttersloe.'

I waited for more but there wasn't any.

'First of all,' I said, 'Guttersloe was my first port of call and I didn't belong then, and secondly, Guttersloe is in Germany and I'm not travelling all the way back there just to be demobbed.'

I could see indecision in his eyes. He glanced quickly at the papers in his hand, which I deduced were my travel documents.

'You want to be demobbed, don't you?' he asked pettishly, striving to assert his officer status.

'Yes,' I replied, 'but I can quite well be demobbed in England.'

'I'm not in a position to authorise such a move.'

'Then get somebody who is in that position,' I said.

The officer departed in a huff. I was now beginning to enjoy myself. In my breast pocket I had the letter from the Minister of War giving me immunity from bureaucracy and if that young sprog of an officer had plans to become an air vice marshal in the future he'd prepare new travel warrants to somewhere close by, and this is exactly what happened: I was to be demobilised from RAF Hornchurch.

As I staggered through the gates of Hornchurch, which had been a fighter station during the war, it came to me that this was the first time since joining the RAF that I had set foot in a real flying establishment.

Lost in my scrambled thoughts, I heard a voice but didn't realise that the words were addressed to me. 'That man there.'

I turned to see a red-faced warrant officer beckoning to me. At the same time I realised my first mistake: what I should have done was report to the guard room, which was situated just inside the gates, but I hadn't seen it because the kitbag on my shoulder had obscured it.

Once we were inside, the warrant officer looked me up and down, before bellowing, 'Get your hair cut.'

When I refused, on the grounds that I was an actor, he whirled round and pointed to the corporal behind the desk, who was as bald as a boiled egg. 'He's an actor too.' It was a joke and he was so pleased with himself that he quite forgot to remark on my red silk neckerchief.

Again I had to explain that I was six months overdue for demob, I'd been to the Air Ministry in Kingsway and they'd directed me here, in order for me to be restored to civvy street. He was now uncertain of his ground, and when I disclosed to him that I had been a wireless operator by trade his face lit up. 'We could use you,' he said and he directed me to one of the huts.

A sudden sense of déjà vu enveloped me. I had kaleidoscope flashes of the morning after the debacle of the Tzigane Orchestra in Germany, with the CO informing me in a cold voice I was due for demob and this was my unit. Now here in Hornchurch this bombastic little warrant officer was a continuation of that day in far-off Germany. Dejectedly I made my way to the hut, determined to spend one night only enjoying the dubious hospitality of military life.

On entering the hut to which I'd been directed, I observed on each side two-tier bunks, with three-part mattresses topped by neatly folded blankets. Just inside the doorway to my left about half-a-dozen white-faced recruits, awkward in their new uniforms, huddled together, bewildered at my appearance. I looked them over – children, they should still be home with their mothers – and, striding the length of the hut, I slung my kitbag on the top bunk, as far away as possible from the bewildered, homesick conscripts now called National Servicemen. They just stood and stared at my red silk neckerchief, khaki sergeant's stripes and medal ribbons on my chest. Yes, I was worth a bit of awe, but enough was enough and to share a hut with this new intake was more than I could stomach. I shrugged on my greatcoat, put on all my equipment and, hoisting my kitbag on my shoulder, I left the hut and marched purposefully out of the front gates. In an hour I was aboard the London-to-Manchester express.

After a few days at home, I received a telegram instructing me to report to Padgate for demob. Rather a fitting end, I thought, as Padgate was where it all began.

THE BEGINNING OF
WHAT'S LEFT

Finally, after all the kerfuffle, I was a civilian again, but the suit they handed over to me at Padgate was reminiscent of the clobber doled out to the old men and women at the workhouse in Sheepfoot Lane. The only saving grace was that everyone else was wearing the same thing. When I got home my father admired it and was over the moon when I said he could have it. That worried me: only forty-six years old and his eyesight must have been going, or his mind. Thank God, it was neither. The next time I came home, about a month later, I noticed the suit draped along the bottom of the back door. At least they had found a use for it. It was ideal for keeping out the cold, icy blast of wind from Siberia that scoured the northern latitudes.

Soon after I returned home, I decided to exchange the squalor and dirt of Oldham for a new life in the squalor and dirt of London. As the train arrogantly huffed slowly from London Road station, I mentally bid my hometown goodbye. By the time it chugged busily through Stockport, my arms were beginning to ache, as I had been holding *The Times* newspaper in front of my face. I hadn't read a word and was afraid even to turn to page two in case someone tried to engage me in conversation. From the sound of the babble of unintelligible chatter, punctuated by inane bursts of laughter, the passengers were obviously at home with each other – cotton salesmen, businessmen, managers, men of substance who travelled often between London and Manchester.

I must have dozed, because when I opened my eyes the train was in the station and the fat cats of commerce were edging slowly towards the door. All stern now, all laughter gone, they had arrived in London and until the next journey back to Manchester they were in business mode. Following them out, I stood on the station platform, lost and forlorn, panic lurking in my stomach at the sheer pace and cacophony of my surroundings, the clacking of thousands of scurrying feet, the incomprehensible announcements on the tannoy, the guards' whistles followed by the slamming of doors, the rumbling of porters' trolleys, the anxious anonymous faces flashing past on either side of me in desperate haste to reach various platforms in time to catch a train, or in many cases to miss it. Feeling despondent, I was overwhelmed by the hopelessness of my predicament. I tried to think rationally. The first part of my plan was accomplished – I was in London – but I hadn't thought beyond that. So what do we do now, clever dick? I gripped my suitcase and from then on I was practically rushed haphazardly out of Euston and deposited unceremoniously in the street.

I shivered. What I wouldn't have given for an overcoat? My suit, even though it had cost five pounds from Burton's fifty-shilling tailors, wasn't designed for arctic wear. For an extra ten bob I could have had a waistcoat to go over my pullover. In the station itself it had been cold, damp and cloying like the flagstoned area of an ice-cream factory, but out here it must have been below zero. I should have hung on to my RAF greatcoat. Even the demob suit would have been warmer than the one I was wearing. I turned up my collar, which made little difference. The malevolent cold took my breath away and I had to move while I still had the power, but a sudden gust of icy wind pushed me back apace. It was something else, this bitter onslaught, right off the Steppes. I looked up to the sleet hurtling through the yellow nimbus of a street light, in two minds as to whether to catch the next train back home. At that moment a sudden surge of passengers exploded from the station exit behind me and I was propelled over the pavement and across the wide expanse of a busy highway, where the crowd separated right and left while I carried on straight ahead to avoid being trampled to death.

A man walked past me and entered a house, and I watched him enviously as the door closed behind him. My gaze panned over to the window and my spirits rose, for the notice said 'Bed and Breakfast'. Hallelujah, praise the Lord.

Standing before what passed for a reception desk, I had trouble answering the man's questions as he took down my particulars, for my face had frozen, making it difficult to enunciate. This, coupled with my broad Lancashire accent, apparently persuaded him that I must be Scandinavian, because he wrote down my name not as Eric but as Ulrich, and when I pointed to the name on my ration book he nodded and said loudly and distinctly, 'ration book'. Then he handed over a large key and pointed to the ceiling.

After struggling up five narrow flights of stairs, I reached the attic. It must be my room, I thought, as any further and I'd be spending the night on the roof. On entering I was struck by the chill. With a small, single bed in the centre and a cracked, brown-stained washbasin close by, and no wardrobe, just a hook on the wall, the room was no more than a cupboard, and I made a mental note that I could lie in bed and flip the ash off my cigarette into the washbasin without having to stretch, but it was cold – I would have been just as well off dossing down on platform one on Euston station. By jingo it was cold. What I wouldn't give for a nice hot bath, but I wasn't about to make the expedition down the stairs to face the receptionist again with 'Have you a bath in this hotel?' I looked towards the washbasin. I wouldn't be able to have a bath in that, but at least I could sit on the bed and put both feet in hot water, the idea of which was now rapidly developing into an obsession. I turned on the tap marked 'hot'. Immediately there was a frenetic juddering of pipes, and then the noise petered out and trickle of brown, cold water dripped pathetically into the basin, about enough to half fill an egg cup; then that too dried up.

I sat on the bed in deep despair. What on earth had induced me to exchange the warmth and security of my home for this indoor igloo? Sinking even lower, I suddenly realised that I was hungry. I hadn't eaten since I'd had a slice of toast and a delicious hot mug of tea for breakfast, which had been several hours ago. Dismissing my pangs of hunger, I concentrated on my main concern, which was to avoid frostbite. Quickly, in order to retain what little body heat I still possessed, I tore off my jacket and tie, and, kicking off my shoes, I leapt into bed. Good grief, the sheets were damp and icy. Covered only by two blankets, the same as those issued to us during the war, I curled up in the foetal position, hand between my thighs. It was a mite warmer. Encouraged by this, I slipped out of my pullover and wrapped it round my stockinged feet . . . Better, except that now my top half was colder.

I dozed, I shivered, I sneezed, and then before I became refrigerated I leapt out of bed, threw on my clothes in a frenzy of activity, and sat on the bed, waiting until the watery dawn leered in at me through the skylight. It was then that I heard the house stirring. Hunger drove me downstairs and I stopped outside the breakfast room, opening the door a crack . . . I was amazed, and a little disconcerted, to see that five or six decently dressed men were already getting stuck into whatever it was – fried spam, powdered egg, tinned bacon. I couldn't possibly join them – my shyness wouldn't allow it – but I couldn't stand outside the breakfast room drooling either.

Squaring my shoulders, I burst in and keeping my eyes averted from the eaters, I opened the front door and disappeared into the gloom of a winter morning, hoping that my hurried exit through the dining room would be interpreted as my being late for an appointment at the Foreign Office perhaps. I'd only spent one night there, but I hated the place and made a mental note that when I was internationally famous, my face on every billboard, this was one bed and breakfast that I would not be patronising. This thought cheered me as I made my way to the nearest tube station. I had no fixed idea of where I was going but at least the Underground would be warmer than the freezing street above.

During my first day on the tube, I began to thaw out. I was thrilled by the posters advertising the shows – I must have been on the Circle Line because I saw the posters several times on my joyride. I stretched my legs from time to time by getting out of the train and walking to the next compartment, settling down in my seat to await my next round trip. Eventually, though, hunger began to drive me up the wall and when the evening came I made my way up the stairs into the cold world of north London and searched wolfishly for an eating place. I found a Greek restaurant, completely empty, which should have warned me that it wasn't the best eatery in London. The food proved it, and though it was a plateful it was certainly not enough – I could have eaten it all again, whatever it was; but thankfully it was cheap and hot. I made my way back to my icebox on the top floor.

This was the pattern of my next few days. Although I didn't realise it at the time, I sank lower and lower, and my thoughts became woolly and disjointed, the future too bleak to contemplate; by Friday evening I had lost the power of thought altogether, and I was a robot. It wasn't as cold as it had been, mainly because London was blanketed by a 'pea-souper' of a fog, a miasma so thick that if you had stretched your arm out you would have been unable to count your fingers. It was a silent world, with no sounds of traffic or pedestrians.

I was merely putting one foot before the other, but where I was going was anybody's guess . . . when a shadow passed me, and then someone called my name. I turned to look at the voice and I recognised who it was, but I was too far gone to be astonished: it was Bill Fraser, Flight Lieutenant Bill Fraser of the long-ago 'Bag' shows.

He was starring in a revue called *Between Ourselves* at the Playhouse Theatre, only a short distance away. Apparently I had been walking along the Embankment; how, or why, or where I was going eluded me – I was past caring. Bill was on his way to the theatre for his evening performance and he asked me if I would go with him. Had he suggested it would be a good idea to jump in the Thames I would have agreed – at least it was something positive.

In his dressing room I sat watching Bill make up for his performance and he stared at me through the mirror. After a time he mentioned that before the show, he usually had smoked salmon sandwiches from the delicatessen next door. He gave me a pound and said would I get some for him. This I did. Ten minutes later, when I placed the plate before him, I sat down, disinterested. But when Bill asked me to help myself, it was like offering a thirst-crazed

Bedouin a glass of water. Bill pushed the plate towards me and I helped myself to a sandwich, and then another one, and before he'd finished his eyes I'd scoffed the lot. Those sandwiches were like a shot of adrenalin and I slowly began to come back to the world. This must have been obvious to Bill, because in a casual voice he threw me out another lifeline by asking me if I would write for him, but I hadn't recovered that much, so I just stared at him, not quite comprehending.

'Comedy material, I mean,' said Bill.

And although I had never written anything before, I said, 'Yes.'

He handed me a white, crisp, five-pound note, my first week's salary as a writer.

What is even more extraordinary about our meeting was the fact that it was Friday night and on the Saturday I had to settle my bill at the bed and breakfast. That was a laugh – I had only one penny in my trouser pocket. By golly, on reflection it's hard to realise to what depths I'd sunk. I was in Bill's employ as a writer for three weeks but he never once asked me to write anything. The five pounds a week was my salvation; without a shadow of a doubt Bill saved my life and I will always be in his debt.

Back home in Oldham, I spent the first two weeks in bed suffering from a load of stuff that had the doctor baffled: malnutrition, sores on my head, an inability to focus properly. I suspect that after another week in that ice-ridden bed and breakfast in London I would have had hypothermia as well. As soon as I was on my feet again, I wrote to the Oldham repertory company for an interview. One of the things that Bill had taught me was the correct way to apply for a position in the theatre, and he must have been right because two days later I received a reply, granting me an interview.

The Oldham repertory company at the Coliseum was hidden away in a side street off the main road, and it was here I was interviewed by the chairman and the director, whose name I later discovered was Douglas Emery. I hadn't expected things to go this far, because I loved vaudeville and the scars of my own inability to act were still fresh in my memory. I outlined my career and experience such as it was in the 'Bag' shows, followed by *Strictly off the Record*; I even gave the Tzigane Orchestra a plug. When I'd finished declaring, Douglas Emery shook his head.

'That is all very well, but it's not acting, is it?'

'No,' I replied hotly. 'But it was on stage in front of audiences.'

They looked at each other. Then the director said, 'OK, we'll let you know.'

I stood up, thanked them and walked to the door. Then the other me inside spoke. 'Don't say you'll let me know and then the minute I leave this room forget all about me.'

The chairman and the director were stunned at this affront. Then Douglas uttered lamely, 'We'll let you know.'

And with that I left, secretly pleased that my parting shot had made some impression.

Imagine my surprise when I received a telegram the very next day requesting that I report for a read-through of a new play on Monday. I was in two minds as to whether to attend or to forget it, but in my heart of hearts I knew that I would go. To a starving man half a slice of cold toast is a feast.

On the fateful day we read through a new play entitled *All This is Ended*. It was a war play concerning the afterlife of soldiers who had been killed in battle, and for some reason or other I had been cast as an American GI. This was a doddle for me, because during my war service I had got myself out of a couple of scrapes by pretending to be a Canadian, and the accent was not too far removed from my Lancashire one; and on the Friday night I drew my first salary ever as a professional actor. This gave me enormous satisfaction, even though it was only three pounds a week, but who cares about money? It was only a matter of time before they put a star on my door. It was only later that I found that the three pounds a week applied only when I was in the play, because I was not a member of the regular cast and was called upon only when they needed extra bods. On the other hand, I had no living expenses; I stayed at home, rent free.

Oldham repertory company was in the premier league, along

with Birmingham rep and one or two others, attracting guest artists such as Flora Robson and Robert Newton. In fact I had a small part in a play in which he starred, working in close proximity with the great man. I learned something very important to me: either you are an actor or you're not, and I wasn't.

After a few weeks my father said, 'Eric, lad, you only get three pounds a week when you work, so on average you've earned less than a pound.'

I hadn't quite thought of it like that.

In a reasonable voice he went on, 'Why don't you get yourself a proper job until something turns up?'

I was tempted, but then I came out with something so erudite, so out of character that I've remembered it almost word for word. I said, 'Dad, I know myself well enough to know that if I got a proper job, as you say, I would do it to the best of my ability but all my life I'd be eating my heart out by throwing away my theatrical ambitions.'

Dad looked at me for a moment and said, 'It's your life, Eric,' and he lent me two pounds to tide me over.

Sometimes one tends not to see what is under your nose, and in my case that was a life saver in the shape of a very old theatre, the Theatre Royal (would you believe it not a hundred yards from the Coliseum), where they also employed a repertory company. I applied for a job and with my experience at the Coliseum I was accepted with open arms. What's more, my salary would be five pounds a week when I worked, so between the two reps I was almost a full-time professional and making almost enough to buy my father a pint on Friday nights.

The standard of acting at the Theatre Royal was not a patch on that at the Coliseum. It was brash and undisciplined; it must have been bad because I outshone the whole bunch. But five pounds a week overrode my principles. One week when working at the Coliseum I approached the chairman with a request for a rise. I'd been on three pounds for some time and felt I was worth four. He readily agreed, strangely enough, and I wished I'd asked for ten. However, on the next pay day my pay was still three pounds.

Straight away I was in the office to remind the chairman of his promise to pay me four pounds.

'We can't afford it,' he snapped coldly and he bent over his paper.

I was dismissed, but I didn't go. I leaned over his desk and said, 'In that case I resign,' secure in the knowledge that I had five pounds a week to fall back on at the Theatre Royal. He didn't even look up as I left.

I walked across the car park, sad in a way at leaving the prestige of the Coliseum, but it was their loss . . . I tried the stage door of the Theatre Royal, but it was locked. I wasn't too perturbed, as they couldn't afford a full-time stage door keeper. However, when I went round to the front I couldn't believe my eyes: a large notice was pasted on to the doors, bearing the gut-stopping legend 'CLOSED'.

Nevertheless, all wasn't lost. A couple of the actors from the Theatre Royal were about to join Fortescue's repertory company and assured me that I would be most welcome to go with them. Not all were bitten by the theatre bug and one who was fed up with the profession sold me his evening dress for four pounds. It was a bargain, except he only came up to my chin and I hadn't even considered this. However, when you applied for a job as an actor you usually sent a photograph and your height, weight, colour of eyes and usually 'own dinner jacket' on the back, and in my case I would be able to say 'own evening dress', hoping to God that I wouldn't be asked to wear it.

I was accepted by Fortescue's repertory company for the princely salary of eight pounds. For this I was stage manager/small-part actor and call boy, the latter a demeaning part of the job, I thought, for a man of my experience, but the money was good. To be a stage manager and to act small roles at the same time required a degree of improvisation. For instance, on more than one occasion I had to say the tag line of the scene, sidle off and pull on the rope to close the curtains. My busiest week was when we performed *The Two Mrs Carrols*, a drama set on the French Corniche, in which the maid was changed to a valet so that I could play the part. Because it was a drama, not a pantomime, the part in itself wasn't very taxing but together with the stage managing it was a nightmare.

In the prompt corner I had a desk, over which was the first-aid box, and following the script I banged the door of the first-aid cabinet, whereupon one of the players on stage said, 'Those damn shutters are driving me mad.' Then, bending down, I cranked the handle of a wind machine and somebody or other on stage mentioned the mistral. I reached up to bang the door of the first-aid box again, and then – the tricky part – I lowered the needle on to a groove on a special effects record of a car arriving. On stage, 'I wonder who that can be?'

Off with the gramophone needle, press the doorbell, smoothe down my jacket and enter down left to answer it.

By Saturday night I must have lost a stone through worry and effort. My fingers-crossed bit was the arrival of the car on the special effects record – one slight mistake and the band of the Coldstream Guards could be marching up the drive. There was a bright side as well: the local critic paid me a compliment by saying that I had an innate sense of the stage, made obvious by the quietness of the scene when I entered to answer the door . . . People were talking.

I was rapidly being turned into a repertory actor, which was not what I had envisaged when I signed on. The theatre was a large drafty barn of a place, which was not helped by the fact that there were never more than fifty people in it at a time, but at least I was able to commute there from 36 Leslie Street. The routine varied little: leave home at 5.00 p.m., do the show and catch the bus back, and this six days a week. It was not boring – I can sidestep boredom – but just dull; my life was about as exciting as a slow-motion replay of the boat race. But there was one particular play called *Frieda* that gave my flagging spirits a twitch.

In weekly rep it was important to be able to change one's appearance by a wig, cotton wool in the mouth or the skilful application of make-up. In *Frieda* I was called upon to make an appearance at the French windows upstage and say hello in a German accent and run round the side of the set to pull the curtains together for the interval, and if that wasn't enough the directions in the script indicated that I had a scar over one eye. This was indeed a challenge. I sat in my dressing room, staring intently at my reflection . . . Then bingo! I had it. Cutting inches from a roll of plaster, I stuck one end just above my eyebrow and the other to my bottom eyelid, which I'd pulled down. This done, I applied a black wavy line over the plaster and the effect was horrifying. It was also uncomfortable, but then one suffers sometimes for one's art. At the end of the Monday night's performance I peeled off the plaster with great relief. The eye was bloodshot and weepy, but I persisted – after all, it wasn't everyone who could get mileage out of 'Hello' in guttural German.

So pleased was I with my performance that when it came to Thursday I suggested Dad and Mother come with me to watch the show. In my dressing room I applied my make-up with a little more ferocity than usual, before feeling my way down to stage level, already half-blind. Peeping through a rent in the curtain with my good eye, I spotted them immediately; they were the only ones in the audience. This didn't matter: there was still a quarter of an hour before curtain up, and the Accrington public were notorious for their late arrival. Five minutes to curtain up and I was thrilled to hear a low murmur of conversation. Putting my good eye to the curtain again I was heartened: there must have been almost thirty people out there in the stalls – the dress circle and the upper circle had been closed longer than anyone could remember. I took a deep breath and hauled on the rope; the curtains parted and scene one commenced. Although I say it myself, my appearance at the French windows caused a bit of a stir. With only one eye to guide me, I couldn't find the door handle, but when I did my 'Hello' I was brilliant. I really felt the part and I was thrilled that my parents were in front to see my moment of triumph.

In my dressing room after the show I peeled off the plaster (what a relief!) took off my make-up and dressed for the street. I knew that I had time; my dressing room being on the top floor, my parents would be only halfway up the steps. I had a pang of guilt at asking them to come to the dressing room, wondering if the steps would be too much for them; after all, they weren't chickens any more – my father was nearly forty-seven. But I needn't have worried: eventually there was a knock on the door – they had arrived.

'It's a good play, Eric,' said my father, while Mother looked critically around at the flaking walls, the cobwebs and the brown-stained basin. Neither of them mentioned the scar over my eye, so I decided to give them a little nudge.

'How'd you like the German at the French windows?'

Mother said, 'Oh, that was you, was it?'

I looked at her in the mirror and, trying to collect the shattered fragments of my ego, I pressed on. 'I had a scar over my eye,' I said.

My father leaned over my shoulder to examine the eye in the mirror; he patted me soothingly on my arm and said, 'Don't worry, lad, it didn't show from the front.'

On the bus going home I was more despondent than I could ever remember being.

Darwen, near Blackburn, barely a town, population not many, was important primarily because it was on the main road from Bolton to Blackburn; houses, shops, a couple of tea rooms and pubs stretched in two rows on either side of this main thoroughfare. But for all its size, Darwen boasted a cinema and, most importantly, the reason for our being there, a theatre – to be more exact the Tudor Theatre, a building that might have been erected originally as a meeting house, a factory or even a large shop, but fortuitously was now a theatre with a stage, seating and a box office. This was the launching pad for the Darwen repertory company.

It was also the fading-away place of the old actor-manager. A lovely old gentleman in his middle seventies, with sparkling eyes under the protection of two bushy eyebrows well in need of pruning, and a skin made smooth by a lifetime of the vanishing cream most actors used to wipe off the greasepaint, he was still entrenched in the mid-nineteenth-century method of acting. Dolly, his wife, was about the same age, specialising now in elderly duchesses and char-women. They were a kindly, gentle couple but I suspect that they secretly abhorred the new wave of 'reality acting'. Others in the cast were a leading man and lady; an old actor, probably in his late eighties, who played occasional small parts, helped to change the set, ran errands, made the tea and was called Will Power, obviously a stage name that might conceivably have amused Queen Victoria; and myself, the last member, known in repertory jargon as a jobbing actor.

Being far from home, I had to find digs, and by some incredible stroke of fortune I found myself full boarding at Harry Kershaw's farm about twenty minutes' walk from the theatre. For a townie like me this was an unattainable dream, a purposeful, rangy old house surrounded by fields and meadows, with stables across the yard from the house and a huge byre, the winter quarters for Harry Kershaw's Friesian herd until they were released to munch away the summer in one of the adjoining fields.

This was the time of rationing, and food concerned every household in the country. Food coupons had to be handed over the shop counter in exchange for rationed foods – a mouthful of meat, one egg, a pathetic rasher of bacon per person a week. It was strict and without the appropriate coupon there was nothing else for it but to go hungry. At the Kershaws' farm, however, food coupons were unknown. Every morning a breakfast of two eggs, bacon or ham, toast smeared thickly with fresh butter – half-a-dozen people's rations in one meal, and that was only breakfast. Dinner and a hot meal before the theatre were just as scornful of the ration regime.

As for the theatre, the plays were selected and directed by our old actor-manager, who was naturally more at ease with plays such as *East Lynne*, *Camille*, and *Svengali*. Sadly we were not too well patronised for a small theatre, only a quarter full at best, and from the day we opened our heads were just above the surface. You can only tread water for so long and the end was inevitable; economics kicked in and when the notice went up no one was surprised.

The leading man left the company to seek stardom in the West End of London and was never heard of again. The rest of the cast opened in Warminster, Somerset – a far cry from Darwen, but that's repertory for you. We opened the season with *The Shop at Sly Corner*. We'd already done this melodrama in Darwen, where I'd played Archie Fellowes, a slimy, ne'er-do-well, but on this occasion

I was given the role of a young naval lieutenant, originally played by our leading man. The old actor-manager played the father of a beautiful daughter to whom I was engaged. The play was going reasonably well, as far as I could tell – none of the audience had walked out as yet – until a critical point in the play, just before the interval. I discover that my future father-in-law is a crook and when I present him with the proof he decides to end it all by thrusting a poisoned thorn into his thumb. He snarls, 'This is curare and it kills in fourteen seconds,' and then he dies. I say, 'He's dead.' Curtain for the interval. Nothing to it – except on that first night . . . At that bit with the thorn steeped in curare, it all went to pot.

Having thrust the thorn into his thumb, the old actor-manager rose in anguish, staggered to the prompt corner and then lurched back to centre stage, moaning.

I took a tentative step forward but he shook his head and fell to his knees.

Again I stepped forward.

'Not yet, laddie,' he snarled.

What was I to do? He'd already had his fourteen seconds; in fact he'd been dying for the best part of three minutes, and when he finally stretched his length on the floor he was still twitching. Then he nodded slightly. I couldn't help myself. My line 'He's dead' should have been delivered with dignity tinged with shock, but instead my old vaudeville yearnings surfaced and, looking straight at the audience, I said, 'He's dead,' in a voice full of surprise. The laugh was tremendous and it warmed me: for months I'd been starved of this audience reaction and as the curtain came down they were applauding. I got to my feet and helped the old trooper to his and he was livid. Never before had I seen him in such a tizzy; his face showed angry red through his make-up.

'I'll show you,' he said through gritted teeth as he stomped off to his dressing room, and before I left that night he'd given me such a telling off and an instruction to be at the theatre the following morning at 'ten o'clock sharp'.

At ten o'clock sharp I walked on to the stage, where he was sitting behind the desk with the script in front of him.

'Learn that,' he said. 'It's all underlined.'

I opened the script and I couldn't believe my eyes. The part he was referring to was his, the old scumbag with the beautiful daughter. He was going to play the young naval lieutenant to whom she was engaged. This wasn't a farce, but it would be if he had his way.

'I'll show you how it should be done,' he said. 'You have till two o'clock this afternoon to learn it.'

We rehearsed our scenes together until only half an hour before the seven-thirty curtain-up, which left me little time to age my face. With old granny spectacles borrowed from the landlady, streaks of white from a stick of twenty giving me distinction and stooping a bit, in all truth I wasn't bad. He was the problem, in my uniform, which pulled dangerously at the brass buttons and sleeves with the gold braid two inches higher than regulations permitted; and when he made his first entrance he walked stiff-legged to avoid splitting my trousers. We were probably just about getting away with it when we came to the bit that had caused the bother.

Rising from my chair, I said in an old, quavery voice, 'This is curare, and it kills in fourteen seconds.'

I pricked my thumb and was about to groan my way across the stage when he said, 'Get on with it, laddie.'

And I did. I collapsed on the floor with at least three seconds to spare, died and awaited the punchline. He knelt by me, put his head on my chest listening for a heartbeat, and then took up my hand and searched for a pulse. Finally he took a white handkerchief from his breast pocket, placed it over my face and in an anguished voice cried, 'He's dead.'

As the curtain came down, he started to rise to his feet, and that's when my trousers split with a resounding note of criticism. Thank God, the curtain was down. As I got to my feet, he said airily, 'That's how it should be done,' and I proudly walked to the wings with a tongue of white shirt flap sticking out through the rent in my uniform trousers.

I thought it was funny then, but now I am ashamed. I was at fault. What arrogance to behave as I had done with only a few months' theatrical experience behind me; to take this gentle, old actor as a doddering old fool, a man in his prime even before my father was born! Forgive us, for we know not what we do.

Recalling my professional theatrical career is not a very inspiring thought. Oldham rep was the first and most prestigious beginning anyone could wish for, but in my innocence I assumed there were plenty more where that came from. The repertory company at the Theatre Royal was a colossal step down, the only advantage being a two-pound rise in my salary. Accrington was even worse, a vast, cold, inhospitable theatre, and my biggest mistake had been to invite my mother and Dad, as the experience confirmed their worst fears that I was doomed. Darwen was a happier experience, but that was largely due to Harry Kershaw. Theatrewise I was paddling a leaking canoe up Niagara Falls.

Now in the local rep at Warminster, I found myself looking back at my performances with uncomfortable self-analysis, but one thing is certain: the thought of leaving the theatre to be part of the real world never once entered my head. At the back of my mind I still believed that repertory would be a circuitous route to variety. In fact some weeks between plays I'd made a few appearances in the northern music halls with a pathetic act consisting mainly of trying to do a crossword puzzle.

In those days it was customary to have a few words on the bills outside the theatre, a short description of your act, for instance. One performer was billed as 'Kardomah', and underneath there were the words 'He fills the stage with flags'; there was also 'Mushy', the forest-bred lion. Another act was 'the man with a xylophonic skull', an act where from one side of the stage a bald-headed man in a dinner jacket walked on and from the other another man walked on with beaters such as those used to play the xylophone; then the bald-headed man bent his head and the other rat-a-tatted on his skull and played snatches of various melodies. How he didn't suffer from migraines for the rest of his life is beyond me. And, if my old friend Les Dawson was to be believed, other acts included 'Baldwin's Catholic Geese' and 'McElwayne's Jumping Infants'.

My own bill matter displayed the name 'Rick Allen' (my stage name), and underneath were the words 'You may have heard him on *Variety Bandbox*'. *Variety Bandbox* was the most popular show on the wireless every Sunday night, presenting new post-war comics. I'd never appeared on *Variety Bandbox*, but my bill matter didn't lie. Nobody had heard of me on *Variety Bandbox*, of course, but the words made them assume that I must have been on and they'd missed me. Incidentally the show's unprecedentedly high ratings were largely due to a comedian and an ex-army man called Frankie Howerd. He was brilliant and I looked forward to hearing him on Sunday nights, when I would be completely spellbound by his hilarious handling of an audience and his vocal range. In my opinion he will never be surpassed.

Although I was doing a job I loved, my career was in the doldrums and there was no sign of a breeze. I even began to wonder if my job was still open at the Rutland Mill. O ye of little faith! It wasn't a breeze that moved me on it was a force-ten gale in the guise of a telephone call.

After one particularly funny, side-splitting Sunday night listening to Frankie Howerd, I was more depressed than ever as I laid out the props for our weekly play. The stage-door keeper popped his head on stage and told me that I was wanted on the telephone. I approached the telephone warily – I still wasn't completely at ease with this contraption.

'Hello,' I said tentatively.

The voice came back, 'Is that Eric?' and without replying to my nod he went on, 'Gordon Horsewell.'

'Oh, Gordon,' I yelped, a surge of pleasure lifting my flagging spirits.

'Yes,' he said, 'only now my stage name is Vic Gordon. I'm doing a double act with Peter Colville.'

'Great,' I said, although I'd no idea who Peter Colville was. I would never forget Gordon and all the help and encouragement he'd given me in *Three Bags Full*. As Gordon was talking I was wondering how he'd managed to trace me, and so I was only half listening to him. I was about to ask my question when something in his last few words caused my heart to beat like a road mender's drill.

'Hello,' came his voice faintly and I realised that I'd lowered the telephone in astonishment.

Clapping it back to my ear, I blurted, 'What did you say?'

'Oh, I thought you'd hung up,' and he repeated what I thought he'd said: 'Frankie Howerd would like you to give him a ring.'

I took down the number Gordon passed on and hung up, not quite with it. I couldn't take it in; it was as if I'd just been told I'd won the Irish sweepstake. When I returned to the stage, the old actor-manager asked me if I was all right. He might just as well have spoken in a foreign language.

'Have you got change for a shilling?' was how I answered him.

Over the telephone I heard that unmistakable fruity delivery, so to ask if he was Frankie Howerd was unnecessary, but I asked him all the same.

In a nutshell, Frankie Howerd had been in Army Welfare Services in Germany at the same time as me: he was principal comedian in a show called *The Waggoners* while I was with *Strictly off the Record* at another theatre – and although during my period in Winsen I'd never met, seen or heard of *The Waggoners* he'd obviously seen me because he was now asking if he could use some of my material on *Variety Bandbox*. This rather put me on the spot because firstly, as I have explained, it wasn't my material – most of it had been pirated from America on the short-wave frequency – and secondly I wouldn't have been able to remember it even if it had been all my own. Nevertheless the next day I was on the train to Leeds, where Frankie Howerd was in pantomime.

Listening to him on the wireless, I had never envisaged a physical shape behind the voice, so I was neither surprised nor disappointed when I met him in his dressing room: he was simply Frankie Howerd. I explained that my act when I was with AWS was the sweepings of American one-liners far removed from his warm, domesticated style of delivery, and as I sat in a corner of the room watching Frank slapping the five and nines on to his face, then his eyeliner, making several expressions to himself in the mirror, I was in an exalted state of hero worship. Here was I from the Mucky Broos in Oldham, rabbiting away, unaware of what I was saying, while he made grimaces to a hand-held mirror.

'Do you think you could write for me?' he said through a cloud of face powder.

Strangely enough, my other self beat my brain to it as I replied, 'Have you got anything to write on?'

He pointed to a pile of foolscap on another table and at the same time the tannoy called him to the stage. I started to write, slowly at first, but quickening with inspiration, until my pen was dancing joyously across the paper. What is astonishing is that I wasn't at least surprised at the ease with which it poured out of my brain; it was as if I'd been writing Frank's scripts all my life.

When he came back to the dressing room, breathing heavily, he flopped down in a chair and mopped his face. I didn't ask him to read my script, but with a passable impression I read it to him. There were no jokes; it was purely situation. In it Frank was explaining to the audience his adventures as a messenger boy whose first assignment involved taking two elephants to Crewe. The script was peppered with 'No ... ah ... Listen. No. Listen' in Frank's own punctuation, and delivered in the outraged, gossip style of a neighbour leaning over the garden wall.

When I'd finished, he said, 'What do you suggest for the next one?'

And my career had taken an enormous leap forward. Apart from a few lines in a letter home, this was the first thing I'd ever written and in less than an hour I'd earned myself five pounds, in those days two weeks' rent.

My second script came as easily as the first one. The premise was simple: think of a ludicrous situation and then write it. For instance, in my second script Frank was talking about an interview he'd had with the head of the BBC, who had explained to an incredulous Frank that the effects department had the sound of everything on record, from doors opening to storms at sea, and even footsteps going up and down a stepladder – he was actually rather proud of this last effect because the footsteps had been his, long before he was head of the BBC of course; then he had quickly come to the point and said that the one effect they had yet to include in the archives was the sound of an eagle laying an egg. Everything had been arranged, and Frank, along with a tape recorder, was to catch the next plane to Ecuador to see what he could do about it . . .

The more eccentric the scripts, the more Frank enjoyed delivering them; and for me it wasn't work but a joy, and the scripts were surprisingly easy to write. After a few more scripts, Frank suggested I join him on a permanent basis at ten pounds a week (a month's rent). Things were looking up. I couldn't wait to kiss my repertory aspirations goodbye; I was on the Yellow Brick Road.

At that time scriptwriters were still in the chrysalis, just beginning to emerge. Obviously there had always been many a humorist scripting patter and sketches for comedians, but the names of these backroom stalwarts was a closely guarded secret. They were in a backroom under a forty-watt bulb. But because of Frank's enormous popularity other comics became aware that he couldn't possibly be making it up as he went along, and so somebody in the backroom had changed the bulb to something brighter. This being the case, people began to ask Frank for permission to contact me with a view to me writing material for them. The first one, who became a lifelong friend, was Max Bygraves; I wrote also for Alfred Marks, Harry Secombe and Norman Wisdom. Another of my happy associations was with the Australian and irrepressible Bill Kerr – you could tell him a joke in Piccadilly and his laugh would be heard in Tottenham Court Road. I was churning for this crop of post-war comics as if I was in a fun factory. I was still unknown to the general public, but just to be the man responsible for putting the words into the mouth of Frank, who breathed new life into them and enthralled nearly half the population every Sunday night, was a good secret to keep.

One balmy summer's evening in Oldham, I was strolling back home from somewhere or other when it occurred to me that this was Sunday night. I looked at my watch. In a few minutes, *Variety*

Bandbox would be on the air – little wonder, then, that the streets in the area were deserted. I had never realised before that this must be happening all over the country whenever Frankie Howerd was about to begin his ramblings. I doubt if anyone else had ever attained such a peak of popularity. I started to walk more quickly so that I could hear the show at home, but as I passed an open door I heard the introductory music and I slowed down again. It being a warm evening, all the doors along the street were wide open, so I was able to follow the show as I walked along, and I listened as it blared out from each and every doorway. At the end of the street at Frankie's 'Ladies and gentlemen' I turned to retrace my steps. I knew what each line was going to be before he uttered it, and I basked in the roars of laughter coming through the wireless. I wanted to shout out at the top of my voice that I knew what he was going to say next, but I didn't: it was enough to feel proud and exhilarated by being a small cog in the wheel.

When I got home, the first thing Dad said to me was, 'You missed a good show, Eric. Frankie Howerd had me in fits.' And he began to regale me with a particularly funny line. I laughed with him as if I'd heard it for the first time. One day he would know that I was responsible for the words, but ironically that would greatly diminish his enjoyment in listening to Frankie Howerd.

Frank's appreciation figures were still topping the ratings and the BBC, more astute in those days, offered him three spots in the show as opposed to his present one: the opening act an exchange of words with Billy Ternent, the band leader; the middle spot an act with a famous celebrity, and the third, to end the show, his normal act. Frank agreed, and I now had to write three spots for each show, but my ten pounds a week remained static. That didn't bother me in the slightest; money was way down on my list of priorities – good grief, I had nothing to complain about, as because of my association with Frank doors were now opening, and indeed had I been asked I would gladly have taken a cut. But don't get me wrong: I wasn't a pushover either.

Frank's three spots turned out to be extraordinarily successful. It was a hectic life for me, as Frank was doing a summer season in

Blackpool, and so each week I had to travel up with the opening spot and his own act at the end already written, and wait until the BBC phoned to pass on the name of the celebrity guest. When I'd written that, I was free as a bird, and Blackpool was a very attractive tree.

On one of these occasions, after visiting several watering places along the front, I went along to the theatre, where Frank and a friend were just about to leave. He'd had a wonderful offer from Derby Baths, who had agreed that the pool would open again after closing in order that Frank could have the facilities to himself without the harassment of public bathers. It sounded like a good idea, so I went along too, borrowing a pair of swimming trunks from the attendant at the baths, who was waiting to lock up. I dived into the pool and swam to the other side, in a deliberate attempt to sober up. Frank and his friend were splashing about in the shallow end and once again I felt the urge to show off. Apparently Johnny Weismuller, a bygone star of the *Tarzan* films, had dived off the top board and with breathtaking ease I decided to emulate his feat. It almost proved fatal. I still shudder at my utter stupidity. I left the board in my familiar swallow dive but in my befuddled state I straightened too early and arched backwards, hitting the water with a colossal smack. I floated to the surface while the attendant threw me a lifebelt and I almost laughed – a lifebelt? For God's sake, we were at the Derby Baths, Blackpool, not on the *Titanic*. However, I was in great pain, and was convinced that I'd broken my back. What a blessed relief it was when the attendant helped me out, and I felt to find that there was no permanent damage!

At the end of the series there was a celebration, which was attended by some of the BBC's top brass. I thought the time was right and asked Brian Sears, the producer, if in future it would be possible for me to have a credit in the *Radio Times* – something like 'Frankie Howerd's script by Eric Sykes'. He patted me on the shoulder and he smiled the smile of a hungry crocodile, and then he said, 'All Frank's fans believe he makes it up as he goes along. Ergo, if they had an inkling that it was all written for him he'd lose an awful lot of his fans.' Appealing to my better nature, he delivered the *coup de grâce* when he said, 'And you wouldn't want that would you?' I didn't even think about it. After the opportunity that Frank had given me, there was only one answer, and I withdrew my suggestion.

I did tell my father, though, but I don't think he quite believed me; he truly thought that Frankie made most of it up as he went along and I didn't correct him – Frankie Howerd was Dad's hero and I wasn't about to disillusion him. Had I been given a script credit, I would have been one of the first in the business to be acknowledged in print. What a difference these days, when the script credits are so long that there's time to make a pot of tea before they've finished, and just when you think they have we get the additional dialogue credits, which are sometimes as long as the first lot.

Two ambitions of mine were yet to be fulfilled, number one being to possess my own overcoat, which would keep me warm through the winter, and number two being, when rationing was a thing of the past, to live a life of thickly buttered toast. Now I was within reach of my first goal, the overcoat. I was measured carefully in a tailor's emporium in Hanover Square and you couldn't do better than that, according to the royal coat of arms over the door. It was to be dark blue, my favourite colour, with two side pockets and one at my breast for a handkerchief if needs must. Three fittings were required until the day of the launch, when it was all ready. When I tried it on, it was soft and warm and hung beautifully, as the tailor had vouchsafed. He was about to help me off with it in order to wrap it up, but I was affronted, as I wanted to wear it, not carry it under my arm like a bundle of dirty washing. So, with a last proud look in the long mirror, I stepped out into the square and made my way to the Klackan, a pub just off Regent Street which was my regular stamping ground. By the time I arrived, I was sweating profusely, as it was only just after opening time during an unseasonable week of hot weather in May, and it struck me that all the stares to which I'd been subjected during my walk from Hanover Square were stares not of admiration for the overcoat but expressing surprise – why the dickens was I wearing one during one of the hottest Mays on record? Thankfully I shrugged out of it as I entered the pub and slung it on the pinball machine by the door before strolling up to the bar.

'Hello, Eric, you're early tonight.'

'Yes,' I replied. 'The usual.'

And as Jack, which was his name, pulled me a pint of best bitter, I leaned on the bar to glance lovingly at my new overcoat, and saw that it was just disappearing through the door on the arm of a stranger.

'Hoy!' I shouted, and I chased after him, but my quest was hopeless: in a crowded Regent Street during the rush hour: it was impossible to pin down a man I'd never seen, his only recognisable feature being my overcoat.

The following day I made a formal complaint to the police, who obviously thought knowing me it was some sort of skylark, but when I insisted that I was serious, I was invited to Scotland Yard so that I could give them more details. Sitting at a desk, they opened a large volume in front of me of mugshots of criminals. It was only when I'd gone through several pages that I asked if this was really necessary, and very seriously they informed me that I only had to pick the villain and he'd have his collar felt within the hour. I closed the photo album sadly, saying that I couldn't describe him because I only saw half of his back as he vanished through the door, but I would gladly give them a description of the overcoat.

After six months of regular contact with a detective inspector at Scotland Yard, I finally gave up hope of ever seeing my beloved overcoat again. So much for ambition number one.

In the grey, oppressive atmosphere of a weary, bewildered, rationed nation appeared a tiny prick of light in the form of a production entitled *Ta Ra Ra Boom De Ay*, an extravaganza so bright, so full of talent, that it lit a spark in all the audiences who packed the theatres for two hours of optimism.

Jean Adrienne and Eddie Leslie, a comedy duo, were top of the bill, which surprised me, as I had assumed that Frankie Howerd –

who also took part – would have been the favourite, but then this was the real world of entertainment, the beginning of my education. John Hanson, a very presentable young tenor with an army of devotees, mostly elderly ladies who toured the country to worship from the stalls, sang romantic ballads, backed by a bevy of statuesque beauties exquisitely gowned in sparkling long evening dresses. These were the showgirls, who only had to walk up and down the stage looking beautiful, and were totally different from the chorus line, whose high-kicking legs were worth the price of admission alone. And of course there were three comedy sketches. Interspersed in this glittering array of talent was music provided by a full orchestra in the pit, under the baton of Don Ernesto, a cheery Spanish gentleman who smiled a lot, in order, I suspect, to show off the gold in his teeth to the audience as they greeted his entrance to the pit with the obligatory applause. The sets for a dozen or more scenes enhanced the production, from those for the comedy sketches to the elegant backgrounds of the more exotic showpieces. No expense had been spared, except in Frank's salary, and added to all this outlay were the hidden production costs of transporting the elaborate sets from this town to that, which was a formidable achievement.

Fortunately this gamble succeeded beyond the wildest dreams of the producer, Dean Moray, and after a few weeks on the road he had regained all his costs – the show was now in profit. Frequently Dean, with his expensive overcoat draped round his shoulders (a sure sign of success), his wife and entourage popped into the theatre and afterwards to the dressing rooms for a cheery word. Always he carried a Pekinese under his arm, the little dog a celebrity in its own right, having appeared in a national newspaper, being the only dog with false teeth. When the show finally closed, Dean Moray was a very wealthy man and in my mind he deserved it: he'd taken an almighty gamble which had not only paid dividends but had put the theatre back on the post-war map.

One night, back in the Klackan, which was just a brisk walk from the Palladium stage door, less if you're thirsty, I was swapping wartime yarns with the Canadian barman, explaining how we'd landed on the wrong beach at Normandy, when I became aware of a tall, lugubrious man in a long black overcoat at my elbow. The pub was half empty and there was lots of space for him to stand somewhere else. Perhaps he was lonely, and possibly a war historian interested in our discussion; or more likely he was just a harassed undertaker, worried that people were living longer.

'I'm Tommy Cooper,' he said, and at the time I thought it was an odd name for an undertaker. 'I know who you are,' he went on. 'You do Frankie Howerd's scripts,' and in the same breath he said, 'Can I buy you a drink?'

'I'm OK,' I said. 'No thanks.'

He relaxed immediately, and it was only many years later when we were close mates that I appreciated the enormous compliment he had paid me when he uttered those words in the pub – because I cannot recall him ever putting his hand in his pocket to buy a round. On other matters he was a most generous man; he just seemed to have a phobia about buying drinks. That reminds me of one occasion – true incidentally – when Tom stepped out of a taxi, paid the cabbie the exact fare and then stuffed something crinkly into his top pocket.

'Have a drink on me,' he said.

'God bless you, Tom,' shouted the delighted cabbie as he drove off, hoping it was a fiver or, praise the Lord, a tenner. He felt in his pocket and pulled out a teabag!

That was Tom, and such was his popularity that it wouldn't surprise me if that teabag, in a glass case, is now on the cabbie's mantelpiece.

But getting back to the pub in Kingley Street: by the time we left, we were best mates, full of bonhomie and Glenmorangie. I knew now that he was a conjuror and he was appearing that night at a club called the Bag of Nails. I offered to carry his suitcase, which he told me was full of his props. It was enormous and so heavy that I couldn't help thinking that it must be a long act. Thankfully, the Bag of Nails was only down the street. I remember clearly the black door and for a moment I thought he lived there – it couldn't possibly be a nightclub. Tommy knocked in a strange way, and a panel in the door slid open and a face appeared. The panel snapped shut and the door opened. Tommy took his suitcase and went in and the door was slammed in my face. I remember wondering if I'd ever see him again or, for that matter, if anybody would ever see him again.

From little acorns mighty oaks grow. Although Tom and I saw little of each other for the next few years, the tree grew well above ground and by the time we made *The Plank* some years later together it was fully grown.

Extraordinarily, Dean Moray, a shrewd operator, decided to mount a follow-up to *Ta Ra Ra Boom De Ay*, entitled, not surprisingly, *Ta Ra Ra Booms Again*. This again was a high-risk venture, but Frank would not be in the show. This decision to me was sheer lunacy: the theatres had been packed because of Frank's reputation and he didn't let any audience down, and so to replace him with a very much lesser-known comedian called Leon Cortez was a short-cut to bankruptcy. Assuming that Frank would be in the show, I had already agreed to write the sketches and I wasn't about to leave it there, but my heated pleas to Jack Payne, Frank's agent, fell on deaf ears, and as Jack was one of our leading bandleaders a deaf ear is no recommendation in his profession. Bill Lyon Shaw, the director and an old friend of mine, agreed with me, but as he was looking forward to directing the show, he wasn't about to rock the boat; even Dean Moray wouldn't be convinced, although I patted his dog. I limped out of the battle zone, bloody and bowed. Having already signed my contract to write the sketches, I was trapped. It was as if I'd jumped out of the aeroplane only to find that I'd left my parachute at home.

Bill did his utmost to giftwrap the show in gold paper tied up with a blue ribbon, but sadly without Frankie Howerd it was a case of batteries not included. My sympathies were with the cast; in my opinion their zing and enthusiasm had been rehearsed out of them. I felt even more depressed when Bill broke the news that the tenor – not John Hanson, I hasten to add – had lost his voice and would not be in the opening show. This was a catastrophe too far but 'things could not possibly get worse' was a statement well wide of the mark. My suspicions were confirmed when Bill came up to me, put his arm round my shoulders and, wheedling in a soft voice, said that as the tenor was not now able to appear in the comedy sketches, and as fortunately the tenor and I were about the same build, and I had written the sketches, would I take his place? How could I refuse? Bill was the captain of the ship, all the lifeboats had gone and the sea was lapping around our ankles. I'd made plans to watch the show from the back of the stalls, from where I could beat a hasty retreat if the natives got restless. All I could hope for now was a massive power failure over the whole of Wales, the first night being in Swansea.

The audience filled the theatre, bubbling with excitement as all first-nighters should. The show began, bright, pacey and promising a lot, rather like a newly elected government, and the first few scenes were passable; but the rot began during the first of the comedy sketches, which I thought went rather well, except that there was one very important omission: there were no laughs. Even the delivery of the tag line of the sketch, so hilarious at rehearsal, was greeted by a silence that was almost palpable. When I thought back to what had gone wrong, I remembered that in one moment during my stint on stage I had noted the white perplexed faces of the audience, and that the place was packed from the stalls to the gods, and my heart sank: the fewer people who saw what was on offer the better. But in the event we hadn't yet reached bottom; and regrettably I was to be the cause of it all.

As I left the stage, I was whisked up to wardrobe, a room of frenzied activity as overworked, perspiring dressers helped the men into nineteenth-century uniforms and the girls into sparkling dresses and crinolines. At any other time I would have enjoyed being able to be a voyeur, but before I could settle an elderly couple tore off my suit, leaving me in my vest and underpants, and one of them came back with a lion tamer's costume on a hanger. I asked the lady what this was for, but she couldn't speak for a mouthful of pins.

'The Kron Prinz,' gasped the man, as he struggled to fasten my trousers, adding that it was for the finale of the first half.

'What am I supposed to do?' I asked in rising panic.

He looked up from attaching spurs to my boots and said, 'Ask

Eva.' Then, standing back, he gave me the once-over and disappeared amongst the costumes.

By the time I'd found out that Eva was the stooge for Leon Cortez, the opening bars of 'Salute to Strauss' were coming over the tannoy, cutting out when a calm voice said, 'Mr Sykes to the stage, please.'

I hurried to the wings, where Eva was fretting impatiently, and as I joined her the curtain rose on a sumptuous palace scene. A couple twittered on from the opposite side towards us, the lady curtseying and the man bowing before backing off to make way for another couple, who repeated the bowing and scraping. A few more pairs came to grovel, and I was beginning to enjoy myself when Eva grasped my arm and I got the message that we were to cross the stage and receive more guests entering from our first positions. But crossing the stage wasn't as simple as it sounds. Eva was wearing an enormous crinoline and walking by her side across the stage with her arm linked in mine was to say the least a hazard, rather like wheeling a bicycle loaded with shopping. Luckily I was upstage of Eva, so much of my eccentric dancing must have gone unnoticed.

Eventually all the cast had made their obeisances to the background of Strauss waltzes. The scene must have looked impressive from the front as the principals formed a line across the stage, Eva manoeuvring me into the middle of it and us all swaying to the music. It was my greatest hour, shattered only by Eva pinching my bottom, Eddie Leslie to my right frantically trying to pass me a message by wiggling his eyebrows and, after every 'oom-pa-pa, oom-pa-pa', Don Ernesto from the orchestra pit pointing his baton at me frantically. I glanced down, but my tunic was covering my flies, so it wasn't that. Behind me I heard a stifled giggle, and at that moment realisation dawned. I remembered vaguely the tenor at rehearsals singing 'I was born in Vienna' – surely they didn't expect me to sing it? But they did and, after another round of 'oom-pa-pa's, I stepped forward and in a strangulated voice began, 'I was born in Vienna'. As it was the only line I knew, I sang it again, only this time with more expression, as if there'd been some dispute as to my birth.

Once more I sang, 'I was born in Vienna', and for one fleeting moment I considered whistling the next bit, but my courage failed me. By this time the orchestra (always the first to go when there's a disaster on stage) were having difficulty with their instruments and mercifully, before I could break into a tap dance, the curtain came down to the first laugh so far – but only on my side of the curtain: as I passed the stage manager in the prompt corner, tears were rolling down his cheeks as he chuckled, 'You should have been a comedian.'

The next day the critics panned the show (which surprised no one), selecting me for a special mention. I was described as a walking disaster, which wasn't very complimentary, but it was worse for the real tenor as because of the rush in substituting me there had not been time to change his name in the programme; nor had the powers that be deemed it necessary to make an announcement before the show. To make matters worse, the critic had simply called me 'the tenor'. Inwardly we all knew that the show was hurtling rapidly towards the waste-paper basket.

But having started with a dull thud, the day was also one that was to have a profound effect on the rest of my life.

About fifteen or more of us shared the same digs and as we were all nibbling at breakfast as if it was a wake, the landlady ushered in a little old woman dressed in black. She was introduced to us as a fortune teller and, this being Wales, we couldn't help but be impressed. Show-business people being the most insecure and superstitious bunch, a lot of silver would cross her palm by lunchtime.

When my turn came she took my hand and stared at it intently. 'Your mother's dead, isn't she?'

I nodded. It was probably a stock revelation.

'She died in childbirth and you were the child.'

I was floored. Now I was more interested.

She followed up with, 'Do you ever feel a slight touch on your shoulder?'

'Yes', I replied, although I couldn't recall any such feeling.

'That's your mother guiding you,' she went on. I didn't take too much notice of this.

'You will be famous one day,' she continued.

I was bucked. She certainly knew her onions. I'd already forgotten about my mother but the famous bit had all my attention. I reckoned that my shilling that had crossed her palm was cheap at the price. I had no objection to being famous, but with her next remark she demolished that house of cards.

'As a singer.'

One thing was certain: she couldn't have been at the show last night.

Strangely enough, I didn't attach much importance to the reading of the lines on my palm. My mother's death, the touch on my shoulder – I pushed them into the bottom drawer of my mind, but I was soon to have an awakening.

Ta Ra Booms Again limped on for another three weeks before the notice went up. Nobody was surprised, but for Dean Moray it was a disaster: his first venture had made him a fortune, only for it to be squandered by its sequel.

The next time I saw Dean was an occasion when I was a member of the panel on *What's My Line* on television. We were sitting on the bench awaiting the red light when a tall, sad-faced floor manager wearing earphones tiptoed across to us and whispered, 'Thirty seconds.' It was Dean Moray.

Now that my bank manager and I were on nodding terms, I managed to rent a room in a large terraced house in Longridge Road, Earls Court. Again right at the top of the building, the room was small – not quite as large as a prison cell – but it contained a stove, a washbasin, a single bed, a table and a chair and, hallelujah, a two-bar electric fire in the wall, just in time for winter – and all this for just two pounds ten shillings a week. There was only one snag: the bathroom was two floors down, but that wouldn't be too much of a hardship once a week.

In a splurge of extravagance I'd bought myself a second-hand reconstituted Ford Ten for three hundred pounds. It was only when I drove it to the garage and the pump attendant offered me fifty pounds for it, that I realised I'd been done. Granted, it had a six-inch hole in the floorboard, so as I was driving along I could watch the road go by between my feet.

On Christmas Day I decided to go home and surprise everybody with my new-found affluence. The engine, being a new one, still had to be run in, which meant that my speed must not exceed forty miles an hour, and with black icy roads and a blizzard over the first two counties, the journey from Earls Court to Waterloo Street, Oldham, took me nine hours. The party that year was given by my Aunt Maggie, Dad's eldest sister, and on hearing the car they all poured out to see me sitting in the driving seat. They had to rub my hands because my fingers were frozen round the steering wheel. Helping me inside, they sat me in front of the fire and handed me a glass of port. Dad patted my cheeks and brother John took my shoes and socks off to rub my feet, while Vernon came round and put a paper hat on my head. That was the last I remembered: with the warmth of the fire I must have dozed off, because when I came to it was Boxing Day . . . Another Christmas had passed me by unnoticed.

Life was sweeping me along in an ever-stronger current of exciting prospects and as these horizons became attainable so my thoughts of the family in Oldham receded, until I was jerked back to earth when on 27 March 1948 John was married to Irene Dyson. I vaguely remembered Irene's name – of course, she was in my mixed class at Ward Street Central School – but I couldn't put a face to the name. In fact I can't recall any girl at school, although I have a clear recollection of teachers and especially the headmaster, but at fourteen girls were as yet an alien species still to be discovered.

Unfortunately I couldn't attend the wedding and it was to be a month before I was able to offer my congratulations personally. I recognised Irene immediately, and she quickly transported me back to Ward Street Central School and my eccentricities in Mr Barker's class. I was amazed at her revelations, not believing half of them. She told me that one of my escapades had been to write comedy verses and leave them on our desks for the class to enjoy. One of them she had never forgotten:

'Tell me, tiger,' said Elizabeth Stranks,
'Have you always had stripes on your flanks?'
The tiger said, 'No,
I'm ambitious and so
I worked my way up from the ranks.'

I now remember writing yards of doggerel verse, amazed at the ease with which I turned them out; and one memory begets another. It happened one night when I was in bed between Vernon and John that I was awakened by the sound of guffaws from downstairs. Another belt of laughter, and I clambered over Vernon and tiptoed to the top of the stairs, where I sat down to hear more. My heart surged as I heard my father's voice reading one of my limericks. Not the best, I thought, but on the last line there was a howl of laughter from Dad's cronies, and to be honest it sounded funnier than when I had put it down on paper. Silently I sat on the freezing oilcloth, hugging myself with excitement as I mouthed the words Dad was reading, warmed by the laughter. Most writers, poets and artists crave the oxygen of recognition – otherwise how do they know that they are artistically blessed? – and to me the boisterous laughter was my reward. Finally I heard goodnights being exchanged, and I crept back to bed, starry-eyed and too excited to sleep. My father never referred to the successful poetry reading and I never told him that I'd heard most of it from a seat in the dress circle; and as with many a youngster who looks forward to tomorrow, yesterday is cold turkey and my night of triumph was erased from my memory, or more accurately it was placed on the back burner to be exhumed seventy years later.

Back to John and Irene. The newlyweds were now domiciled in Turf Lane, near Shaw Road End, only a couple of hundred yards from where Dad and Mother, having moved from 36 Leslie Street, now lived and a three-minute walk from 8 Houghton Street, the home of Granddad and Grandma Ashton. So in this small triangle the tribe had now re-grouped and I felt further away than ever.

*   *   *

Theatre is a village, especially in the West End of London, and apart from Frank I was now writing for several budding comedians and my name was becoming known. I was receiving invitations to this and that, well-known faces called me Mr Sykes as if it was their pleasure to meet me, and I was now writing for the stage as well as radio – in fact all the comedy sketches for the Palladium pantomime.

Apart from this heavy workload, I still found time to enjoy my mantle of notoriety and the next important episode was just around the corner.

Underneath the arches in Villiers Street was the Players Theatre. Hidden away off the beaten track, it was unique. The first I heard of it was in a letter inviting me to be their guest at one of the performances. I accepted with alacrity. What a change from Oldham, Accrington, Darwen and Warminster, where I could have walked through the streets in a sandwich board bearing my name and still have been unnoticed.

From the moment the manager escorted me into the Players Theatre I was enchanted. The atmosphere was warm and intimate, and instead of rows of seats there were simply wooden tables, around which sat the audience, the men guzzling pints of beer and the ladies something more delicate. The stage was a platform no more than a foot high, almost within reach of the front tables, and seated to one side, sartorially elegant in late-nineteenth-century evening clothes, was the Master of Ceremonies, who with a bang of his gavel brought us all to our feet to toast the health of Queen Victoria. This was done with the solemnity and respect due to the monarch. Once we were seated, the MC rapped the table once again and in florid, eloquent speech announced the first act.

All the artistes were costumed in the Old Music Hall tradition. There were comedians with patter applicable to the age, but still funny; a baritone who sang romantic ballads; a rubber man who went into impossible contortions; popular songs of the era in which the audience participated; and a couple of comedy vignettes as well. The Players Theatre was trapped in a time warp. In between all the entertainment we were gavelled to our feet to celebrate the Relief of Mafeking, and later we drank to General Gordon of Khartoum. It was great fun, but the high spot of my evening was yet to come. The show was nearing its end when the MC smacked his gavel enthusiastically on his table and, with glowing adjectives some of which were new to me, he introduced the finale. 'With your own, your very own, Miss Hattie Jacques.'

The place was in an uproar as a buxom, extremely attractive, young lady, gowned in the music-hall fashion of a high-spirited housewife holding a bird cage, came on stage. She sang 'My Old Man Said Follow the Van and Don't Dilly Dally on the Way', with such radiance and vitality that she took my breath away. She was the darling everyone had waited for and well deserved the standing ovation she received at the end of her song. She had to sing it again, and this time the audience joined in. Incredibly, at the end of the number, she leapt into the air and landed in the splits as softly as an autumn leaf.

Afterwards I was taken round the back to meet the cast. I thanked them all for a super evening but when I was shown into Miss Jacques's dressing room, I stuttered like a boy accepting a prize on Speech Day. Since leaving the Warminster repertory company, I had been mounting the steps of my career, pausing frequently on the landings to smell the coffee, but deep inside me I knew that this evening was to be the beginning of a new flight.

Television in those days was in its infancy. Not a brick had been laid on the derelict expanse of dirt, bicycle parts, bed railings and rags, the depressing piece of real estate in Shepherd's Bush that was destined to become White City – that architectural dream was still on the drawing board, as were the new breed of television producers. For the moment, television was run just a few hundred yards away from Lime Grove studios. The early television sets were small, black-and-white and capricious.

My Aunt Marie, Dad's younger sister, and her husband Stan, living in New Longton, a small village just outside Preston, were the first people there to own a television set and almost immediately her circle of friends increased out of all proportion. Each night she would invite a number of them round to stare wide-eyed at the magic box. They sat in two rows of chairs, with the curtains drawn to darken the room, and the picture had them spellbound. Every time a vehicle passed outside, a band of silver dots twinkled across the screen, but even that was greeted with eyes of wonder. Sometimes the picture would begin to fade, and when this happened the audience would ease forward like a Wakefield Trinity scrum. Had Aunt Marie charged for the privilege of viewing this magnificent invention, she might well have been able to move to a bigger house. A television was a status symbol, in as much as other householders would draw their curtains at six o'clock every evening to give the impression that they were about to commence their nightly viewing while in truth they didn't possess a set.

Here I must explain that on television there was only one channel and the actual output was but a few hours a day – news, talks, the first television chef, Philip Harben, and more news and talks. Interspersed between the items was a shot of Richmond riverbank edged by trees, with birds twittering and the word 'Interlude' superimposed on it, and this was watched with the same rapt attention afforded to the news, talks, etc. There was also an alternative interlude, a potter's wheel scene, in which a watery lump of clay whirled round while a pair of hands shaped it into we never found out what; viewers watched it every night without fail, and for many it was their favourite piece of the evening. Each night the evening programme was brought to a close by a rendering of the National Anthem, and there must have been many viewers up and down the land who rose from their chairs and stood silently to attention in respect.

After his sensational romp in *Variety Bandbox*, Frankie Howerd was a natural subject for fledgling television; he would be a great improvement on news, talks and Philip Harben. When an offer arrived, Frank was wary and before he agreed to take this monumental leap into the future he asked me if I was free to write something. What a question! Had I not been free I would have wriggled out of any on-going obligation to write Frank's first venture into the world of pictures in the home. Inside a week I'd written a comedy playlet, and Frank was delighted, judging by the way he chuckled as I read it to him. The premise was simply a springboard from which to launch him to the trainee viewers.

The opening scene is a lawyer's office, where the last will and testament of the late Obadiah Howerd is being explained by a solicitor to Obadiah's three sons, one of which is Frank. The lawyer is about to clarify some of the stipulated requirements of the sons in order to qualify for the lion's share of their father's estate, but they are interrupted when an elderly lady, wearing a large, stylish, brimmed hat, enters the room through the French windows. She is carrying a basket of roses.

> LADY Oh, isn't it hot again today? [Pause, then to Frank] Is your father up yet?
>
> FRANK [to audience] I don't remember this bit.

Frank goes on to tell her that he hasn't seen her at rehearsals, to which she replies that there was no necessity for her to attend since she had been on the West End stage for over forty years and she always entered through the French windows with a basket of roses and 'Is your father up yet?' Frank addresses the director out of shot.

> FRANK Can we have the interlude please?

The screen immediately changes to Richmond riverbank, interposed on which is the word 'Interlude'. Behind this idyllic scene we hear the voices of Frank and the lady still arguing the toss. When she finally exits, Frank's voice is heard saying, with some relief, 'Thank God she's gone,' followed by, 'Thank you' (loudly), whereupon the interlude is off and we're back in the solicitor's office. More dialogue from solicitor, and then the lady reappears, spouting some other domestic inanity. Frank turns to the front and calls for the interlude. Once again the picture of Richmond riverbank appears and as before we hear Frank and the lady chewing the fat. When she goes, Frank shouts, 'Thank you', 'Interlude' disappears and we continue the scene. This time the lady enters immediately. Frank despairingly shouts, 'Interlude,' but without speaking the lady exits through the French windows.

FRANK Well, that makes a change.

As he says this, the Interlude picture fills the screen. We hear Frank say, 'Thank you, it's OK – she's gone,' but the Interlude is still showing. After another, louder 'Thank you' from Frank there is no change. Then, after a short pause, Frank runs into the picture of Richmond riverbank and waves his arms to camera, shouting, 'Thank you.' 'Interlude' leaves the screen and we are back in the lawyer's office, where the solicitor is reading a newspaper. He guiltily puts it down as Frank enters breathlessly.

FRANK It's a long way from Richmond.

This little scene was my pièce de résistance, using television pictures as they had never been used before – hardly surprising considering that television was still in its infancy; and, more importantly, Frank was as enthusiastic as I was at this inspired piece of lunacy.

However, being highly sceptical of comedy producers from sound who, after a short course on panning, tracking, zoom in and zoom out, were transferred to television to follow in the footsteps of Cecil B. De Mille, Frank was decidedly wary. There weren't too many of this new breed in those days. The more experienced radio producers were either overlooked or preferred to meander through sound radio until they were retired on a healthy pension. Frank was taking no chances and he agreed to accept on the proviso that the playlet would be produced by the drama department. The BBC agreed to this with alacrity – and that was the beginning of my troubles.

The first ripple in the pond came with the arrival of a letter from the drama department, assuring me that we had given the 'green light' to the enterprise, their only suggestion being that the three brothers became identical triplets instead, thus enabling Mr Howerd to play all the parts himself. Oh yes, I thought, it wasn't an artistic suggestion, it was economical; they wanted to get three actors for the price of one. But on reflection I thought it wasn't a bad idea, so I rewrote parts of the play and sent it off.

A week later I was summoned to a meeting at Lime Grove in a cramped little office, with no pictures on the walls, no carpets, just a table, at which sat one of the high-ups in drama with my script before him; and standing behind his shoulder was the one I assumed would be directing my piece. I came to the conclusion that he was standing because I was sitting on the only other chair in the room. I was particularly proud of my first pages, especially the interruptions by the lady with the roses. I began to read, and was so wrapped up in my rendition that I was unaware of the stony silence from the other side of the table until I looked up and saw that they were staring at me as if they were senior officers of the Serious Crime Squad, listening to my confession of insanity.

During the pause, the bossman cleared his throat and said, 'While we've stopped – would there be French windows in a lawyer's office? It's out of character.'

I reminded him that it was a comedy.

They glanced at each other, but they didn't smile, so I carried on, and the lady with the basket of roses edged by without an objection, but I wasn't wholly at ease. I had the feeling that they'd let me off the hook on that one in order to keep their powder dry for the big salvo to come. All the interlude scenes ran the gauntlet, right up to Frank's 'It's a long way from Richmond', and it was there that they applied a match to the blue touchpaper.

'Hold it right there,' said the director. 'All those "Interlude" shots – they're not possible.'

'No,' I replied triumphantly. I wasn't intending to use the original Interlude. We would shoot our own riverbank scene, with Frank running into it.

'It is still not possible for us to shoot our own riverbank scenes,' said the director, 'because at this time of the year there'd be no leaves on the trees.' The man in the chair nodded at this *coup de grâce* and leaned back with a satisfied smirk.

'It doesn't matter,' I expostulated. 'Any shot of Richmond riverbank with the word "Interlude" superimposed on it will suffice.'

This had them perplexed.

'So,' I continued, 'we take our shot of Richmond riverbank and after a few moments Frank will run into the picture, waving his arms.'

This had obviously never occurred to them, but they re-loaded.

'Leave the technicalities to us,' said the director huffily, and then he played his ace. 'In any case,' he said reasonably. 'Frank couldn't possibly have got back from Richmond in that time.'

I closed my script. How in the world could I possibly get through to them?

The chief, wishing to pour oil on troubled water, spoke for the first time. 'Why can't we have Frankie ducking behind a bush on the stage?'

I accept that they couldn't understand what was in my mind, but that last suggestion still eludes me. Frank's first appearance never reached the rehearsal room. We hadn't been blown out of the water but I'd hoisted the white flag and scuttled the project. Ironically the pay-off came three weeks later, when I received a letter from the BBC demanding the return of the commissioning fee for the script. I didn't bother to reply – I'd already spent it on a round of drinks.

While I was flirting with the blossoming television, the heavy wheels of BBC radio were beginning to turn.

ARCHIVE

17 June 1949. The BBC Copyright Department noted a proposal to commission a twenty-minute trial radio script from Eric for a fee of ten guineas . . .

Not much in today's parlance, but in those days it was a month's rent. The BBC radio show was to be called *Educating Archie*, starring Peter Brough and Archie Andrews, Peter being a ventriloquist and Archie his dummy. It wasn't too difficult to write, as I treated Archie as a mischievous boy and Peter as his ward. Being hard and cynical, I decided that we were in the hands of the accountants and they were getting two voices for the price of one.

Peter was without a doubt one of the best-dressed men in London. He and his father ran a very successful cloth business and perhaps being a ventriloquist was a hobby he had inherited from his father, Whatever the case, if Archie Andrews decided to run away and join the French Foreign Legion the loss of income would make little difference to Peter's comfortable way of life, a fact for which I was to be eternally grateful: his warm-hearted generosity was later to save my life.

The BBC having accepted my pilot script, I was committed, but only then was I told that I would be co-writing the show with Sid Colin. Although I'd never met Sid, I was a great admirer of his work – there was no difficulty in that respect – but the news immediately put lines on my forehead. In all my short scriptwriting career I'd had the freedom to let my mind explore and wander into the realms of the abstract without let or hindrance, and so far it hadn't done me any harm. My worry was needless, because Sid turned out to be as independently minded as I was, and in order to avoid tripping each other up we agreed that Sid would do the opening sequence with Archie and his tutor, and I would script the rest. Already we were in harmony and that was such a tonic. As I came to know him better I realised that he wasn't a great conversationalist, but when he did speak it was worth waiting for.

On 6 June 1950 *Educating Archie* was launched. The spotlight beamed down on the immaculate Archie Andrews, not a hair out of place on his little wooden head down to his little shiny boots (if ever a dummy was born with a silver birch in his mouth it was Archie), with the backing of a very strong cast: Robert Moreton as the tutor, Max Bygraves as Archie's friend/handyman and, of course, my favourite, Hattie Jacques, who would play Agatha and any other female role that happened to crop up, not forgetting Peter Brough, Archie's ward. Musically we were strengthened by the Tanner Sisters, backed by the Hedley Ward Trio, and in our second interval by the very young, as yet unknown, Julie Andrews.

Not surprisingly, the first show attracted a very large audience, but it is the second one from which the offering can be better judged. Amazingly, the listening figures rose higher, and by the time the first series of six shows was completed we knew that we were a success – so much so that to our astonishment we won the prestigious radio award of Best Comedy of the Year, last year's winner being *Take it From Here*, written by Frank Muir and Denis Norden. After a year of ruling the roost, *Take it From Here* won the award back again, but incredibly we won it the following year – ho hum, it's a small world. I must not forget that I was able to let my visual ideas explode on the sound waves thanks to a wonderful effects department. The two boys working the sound effects enjoyed themselves immensely, because up to our show they had only been called upon to imitate thunder, wind, opening and closing doors, horses' hoofs and bird noises, but in *Educating Archie* they were given full rein for a number of outlandish situations. They were superb, and their spectacular sounds contributed greatly to our winning the award. Sid and I were over the moon and quietly we shared a bottle of champagne – he had a glass and I managed the rest.

ARCHIVE

2 November 1950. John McMillan sent a note to Michael Standing [radio's Head of Variety] suggesting that it was high time the BBC tied Eric to an exclusive contract in order to prevent the quality of his writing from being adversely affected by any extra work spent on 'some high-priced commercial series'.

Peter Madden, the announcer on *Educating Archie*, mentioned that during the breaks between series he and his girlfriend went to a little village called Bandol, a seaside resort in the south of France between Marseille and Toulon, and would I like to join them? Without hesitation I said I'd think about it. Peter said they would be leaving in two days' time, and so I went home to pack.

Some days later I was at the wheel of my little rattletrap, bowling down the Route Nationale in France. Peter, with the maps on his knees, sat in front with me, and his girlfriend sat in the back, squeezed beside their suitcases piled up to the roof. Good grief, we were only going on a two-week holiday but anyone would have thought they were emigrating. My small suitcase was in the boot, crushed underneath another pile of their worldly goods.

Peter's girlfriend spoke little on the journey through France, but when she did it was in a modulated, well-educated voice and I remembered that Peter had mentioned before we left that she was a high-born lady, in fact an Honourable, which I interpreted to mean that she was either a Member of Parliament or she'd never told a lie, and if that was the case she couldn't possibly have been a Member of Parliament.

It was a long, hot, dusty drive, but we finally made it to the Côte d'Azure and I thought that my little Ford Ten had behaved heroically, considering that it was her first trip abroad.

Bandol was breathtaking, worth every kilometre, a tiny little village with only two rows of houses, shops, cafés and bars right on the waterfront. Peter directed me to the pension, a delightful French bed and croissant, and said that he'd already booked a room, and for one awful moment I visualised the three of us dossing down together. I'd long since sussed out why Peter had invited me: I was the only one who possessed a car. I'd given them a lift from Earls Court to the south of France but although we'd stopped at innumerable petrol stations and they'd got out to stretch their legs, they didn't carry them even close to where one had to pay for the juice ... Ah, who cares? Anyway, if it hadn't been for Peter I'd never have discovered this pearl of a resort.

The days were idyllic: swimming in the warm blue bay; an underwater wonderworld to discover of coral reefs and formations of tiny fish who ignored my ponderous attempts to emulate them; striding up the soft silvery sand, light years away from the brown heavy stuff of Sword Beach in Normandy; lunch under an umbrella – grilled steak, *bien cuit* or *à point*, and lettuce which I've never liked, but there its coolness was refreshing; forty winks in the afternoon, a cold shower, and then dinner at one of the restaurants and drinks in one of two bars.

The very compactness of Bandol was its main attraction. There can't have been more than fifty local residents, so one quickly became acquainted with the ever-smiling villagers. It all seemed so tranquil, a paradise undreamed of in Oldham; but it also had its darker side, which I was to discover in due course. One sunny morning at about eleven o'clock I was sitting at a bar run by an Englishman and telling him how fortunate he was to live in this haven of peace and tranquillity, and I was about to expound further, when we were violently interrupted by the clattering cacophony of automatic gunfire. I rose from my stool but he pulled me back and shook his head. I tried to get back to my theme but things weren't so tranquil any more. I held up two fingers for a couple more beers – it was the only way to communicate over the racket – but just as suddenly as it had begun the terrifying rattle of shots ceased. Only then did we walk to the door, where we saw four, beefy, smartly dressed men emerge from another bar. They were in no hurry. Casually they walked to a car, opened the boot and stashed their smoking machine guns inside as easily as if they were loading up the week's shopping. That done, they drove off sedately. Only when the car disappeared in the heat haze did one or two locals warily approach the bar, and when there were enough of them for safety I decided to have a look for myself. Whole shelves of bottles behind the bar had been shattered and liquid was still pouring down in a tired cocktail; and, of course, the huge mirror behind the shelves had been shot to smithereens. A blue haze hung around the ceiling like a silk scarf and the smell of cordite was still prevalent. One of the local mobsters who worked in the bar was sweeping the broken glass into a corner, paying no heed to the critical stares of the onlookers. As nobody was dead or even wounded, they began to lose interest and drifted away in small groups.

I went back to the other bar and the Englishman filled me in. This happened about once a month, he told me. There were two rival gangs trafficking in anything illegal: drugs, cigarettes, alcohol, guns, cars – in fact anything of value that wasn't screwed down. The perpetrators of today's outrage lived in a nearby village and frequently visited Bandol to settle old scores, and shortly afterwards the Bandol mob would motor off into the blue to return the courtesy call. I was shocked. I had often had a drink in that bar, now closed for repair, and found them all rather jolly. The little man sweeping up the glass had befriended me, perhaps because I was English or, most likely, because a genuine customer was a novelty, and come to think of it I'd never actually seen anyone in that bar who didn't look as if he'd done five rounds with Joe Louis. It was with a sigh of relief that it struck me that by the time they got the place up and running I would be in the studios in London recording *Educating Archie*. So for now I would just get on with my holiday and put all this behind me – or so I thought.

I saw little of Peter and his girlfriend. Sometimes we lunched on the beach together, but the evenings were mine alone, except for one occasion when I was invited to dinner with them. Little did I know when I agreed that I was about to walk into a fireworks factory smoking a cigar. The restaurant was small, not much bigger than a lounge in an ordinary house; in fact it was probably a converted residence. There were only six tables and when we arrived a woman sitting at a table in the corner waved to us. Peter's girlfriend hurried over to her for a Gallic hug and a kiss on both cheeks, after which she introduced Peter and me, and the woman responded in perfect English, which is not so surprising as she came from Streatham. Peter took the chair next to his girlfriend, leaving me no option but to sit next to Peter's girlfriend's girlfriend – the alternative would have been to stand throughout the meal. Oh happy day! My evening was already in ruins, as although normally I get on quite well with ugly women this one was the exception, and she appeared to have a bluish lump on the side of her forehead. All the rest of the diners appeared to be tourists, mainly from Britain, judging by the way they stared intently at their tablecloths, whispering only occasionally and pointing out their orders from the menu to the doddery old waiter.

On looking round, I noticed a huge untidy bulk of a man standing in the doorway. His open-necked shirt could have done with a good wash and his light trousers looked as if they were holding up his stomach. He had obviously not come to dine. It was still light and the sight of him gave me a sense of foreboding. His angry eyes scanned the room and when he looked at our table I knew we were what he was looking for. He yelled a French equivalent of 'Hey you' and pointed at my companion, who uttered a tiny shriek before clasping her hand to her mouth. The man backed out of sight and the next moment my blind date was wobbling to the door on heels too high for a stampede. Peter's girlfriend leaned over and whispered. 'That's her Italian partner, Paolo. Oh God, she's in trouble – he's a beast.' Then a piercing scream echoed from the street. Everyone in the restaurant turned towards the open door and stared in a frozen tableau. There was the sound of scuffling and a lady's shoe hurtled past the doorway. As if on cue, all the diners swivelled round to observe my reaction. This was embarrassing: I didn't care what happened to the woman, but my audience didn't know that and what did they expect me to do? Resignedly I rose and walked out, with cold sweat dribbling down the inside of my arms.

I had no idea what might be required of me. Paolo was across the street, holding on to the woman's wrist while she struggled to get free. I crossed over and for the first time I saw that in his other hand he was holding a pistol. Now we were face to face and he thrust the pistol into my midriff. His woman had stopped struggling and was looking on, terrified. Speaking in a garbled patois, and using body language, he tried to get me to retreat but, as in the past when it came to checkmate, I froze. I was not afraid, I was just petrified. I stood my ground. Visions ran through my head at sixteen frames a second. I was English and it wasn't in our nature to retreat; after all, hadn't I liberated Europe? He must have realised that either he had to shoot me or we would be there all night, so he began to retreat, pulling the girl down an alleyway on to the sea front.

When I went back into the café, Peter said, 'You silly fool, why didn't you run?'

All the other diners were earwigging, so as coolly as I could I replied, 'The thought never occurred to me.'

I sat down and would have continued my dinner, but if I had let go of the tabletop my hands would have been shaking so erratically that I'd have missed my mouth. The stares from the other tables were beginning to rattle me, and so I rose and walked out, and went to my favourite English bar, where my car awaited me. But instead of driving off, I decided that a nightcap wasn't a bad idea – at least it would calm my shattered nerves. I ordered a Pernod. Watching my friend behind the bar pouring in a drop of water, I was fascinated by the Pernod changing into a milky liquid, but truthfully I wasn't about to lift the glass yet as my hands weren't steady enough. When I did, it tasted like nectar, but it wasn't enough, so I ordered another nightcap; in fact I finished up with my nightcaps for a week. Here is the mystic quality of Pernod: you don't feel drunk or even woozy – quite the contrary. Walking on water would be a doddle; standing on top of a high-rise block preparing to test your powers of flight was a very tempting prospect – you feel as if you are Superman.

Recollecting the scene with the hulking Italian, I resolutely stepped into my car and with headlights blazing I shot along the front with absolutely no idea of what was to happen next. I'd only gone about three hundred yards when the beams of my headlights picked out Paolo standing in the middle of the road, holding the pistol loosely by his side. I screeched to a halt a yard in front of him. We stared at each other in silence, but all the fire had gone out of him – he obviously didn't drink Pernod. I beckoned him with a peremptory wave of my hand, he moved slowly towards me as if he was sleepwalking and he just stood by the side of the car, looking down at me. I held out my hand and in a slow zombie-like movement he handed me the gun; and as if I had worked it all out I threw the gun over the sea wall into the Mediterranean. What I was expecting from him was anything but apathy, but that's what I got. I did a three-point turn and zoomed off back to the bar for a serious nightcap.

As I browse through the library of my mind, that scene on the waterfront of fifty years ago comes back to me in glorious Technicolor. What a pillock I must have been to even contemplate such a foolhardy stunt! It seemed melodramatic at the time, but as I look back it seems pathetic, like the last reel of the worst B picture ever made. I blame it on the Pernod. Perhaps my life is a B picture, in which case I'm glad to be in it.

I might have forgotten all about my scene with Paolo but the plot thickened. The following morning I was awakened by a frantic pounding on my door and before I could yell, 'Who is it?' Peter's girlfriend was at my bedside. From her excited demeanour I guessed that she had bad news. (Incidentally, I keep referring to her as Peter's girlfriend, but she wasn't a bimbo: in fact I would say she was pushing her late thirties and never lost her hauteur.) She asked me if I'd heard it, and I just looked at her blankly. She soon put me in the picture. What I hadn't heard was her friend's screaming through the night as Paolo had dragged her into the middle of the road, beating her and threatening to kill her. I must have been the only one in Bandol not to have heard anything; the locals could talk of nothing else.

The events of the previous night crowded into my mind. It didn't seem fair; I had been sucked into a situation for which I had no stomach. I had a sinking feeling that more was expected of me, but her next words dissolved all my apprehensions. 'I think we should leave Bandol as soon as possible, the sooner the better.' I readily agreed; the last thing I wanted was another run-in. But in every rose bush there's a thorn. Just as she reached the door, she turned and said, 'The trouble is she owes me money.' Then, in a wheedling tone no red-blooded man could ignore, she added, 'Do you think you could go and ask her for it before we leave?'

The Stun grenade she'd just lobbed at me was still in the air when she left. What was I to do? I'd got away with it the previous night, but my luck had already been stretched to the limit. Why me? What if he shot me? But that wasn't possible, as his gun was at the bottom of the Mediterranean. Why, oh why, had I accepted their invitation to dinner in the first place? Thinking about his gun, I knew instinctively that he wouldn't have shot me in front of a restaurant full of witnesses to spend the rest of his miserable life on Devil's Island. On the other hand, had he been unarmed I would have been really scared; he was taller than I was and a stone heavier, and a backhander from him would have sent me sprawling. There was no way I was going to get up for a second helping and that would have been the end of it. He could have dragged her off and I could have limped back into the café with my honour intact. There was only one thing that would persuade me to go and collect that debt.

An hour later I was sitting in the English bar having my breakfast – nothing solid, just four glasses of Pernod before I attained infallibility. Then I stepped out on to the seafront, and walked slowly down the middle, which to my amazement was deserted. On any other morning the front would have been bustling – with locals and a handful of tourists, greetings being exchanged, tables outside the few cafés, visitors enjoying their morning coffee – but not today. Already I was in a scene from a much better picture, *High Noon*. As I strolled slowly down the waterfront, the only person visible was one of the gangsters outside the bar. Wiping down a table, he glanced over his shoulder at me and then immediately turned back to double his efforts with his work.

When I arrived at the small garden gate, I yelled 'Paolo', making sure that everyone in the village heard me in case I needed help. The front door slowly opened. The blinds were drawn but in the darkened doorway I could make out his untidy shape. I pushed opened the gate and walked down the short path to face him. His partner, my dinner companion, was standing behind him; even in the gloom I recognised the puffy face, with one eye almost closed. We just stared at each other, waiting for one of us to speak. Then she sobbed, 'He had the dog shampooed yesterday. He loves it. Say something nice about it.' Incredulous, I looked down and noticed a black poodle by his feet. I told her that I hadn't come here to pat the dog; she owed some money and I was here to collect it. She looked at him as if to ask permission, but he obviously hadn't understood our exchange, so she backed off into the inner recesses of the house. This played into my hands; it seemed that when I had spoken to her in that authoritative manner I had hit exactly the right note. Paolo didn't understand the words, but he recognised a command. Who was I? A plainclothes policeman? Maybe I was with

Interpol. He immediately became abject. I pointed to a little room to the left of the door. It was a small bedroom. He went in and I followed, motioning to the bed. He sat on it, puzzled but wary. Then I began to castigate him, but with a smile. Raising my voice, hoping ears would be cocked along the waterfront, I patted him in a friendly way on the back and continued to give him the rough edge of my tongue, but with a friendly smile. In a few moments she came into the room and handed me an envelope. I took it from her. 'I hope it's all here,' I said, and her nod was eager. I was really enjoying myself; even she was beginning to believe that I wasn't just a tourist. At the gate on my way out I turned and declaimed, 'Tell him if he lays one more finger on you I'll be back.' It was a cheap shot, but as if to underline my superiority I left the gate open.

As I made my way back along the waterfront, people were emerging from their cafés, bars and shops, as if a monsoon had ceased and the sun was shining again. All wore smiles: they had all heard my diatribe. Some of the ladies kissed me on both cheeks and so did one or two of the men. The owner of the café where we hadn't eaten dinner last night came up to say, 'Tonight you are welcome, all is paid for.' The Pernod was still in my system and I made up my mind there and then to stay in Bandol. Who knows – on this wave of admiration within a few weeks I could be the mayor. And then I could really clean up the town.

As I approached the pension to tell Peter of my decision to stay, I was staggered to find that my room was sterile; there was not a stitch of mine to be seen. I went downstairs to be met by the landlady. With tears in her eyes, she kissed me on the lips as she crushed me to her enormous bosom, after which she presented me with the bill, which in turn brought tears to my eyes and a hole to my wallet. Peter and his girlfriend, hidden by her pile of luggage on the back seat, were fretting to be off. I sat behind the wheel, triumphantly handed the envelope over my shoulder and awaited the adulatory squeals of thanks. 'Never mind that,' she said. 'It's only a couple of pounds.' Did she not realise that I'd risked my life for that? Deflated, I turned the ignition key and we left the town that had lost its flavour to make our way back to the orderliness of Earls Court.

When I finally arrived on my home turf, I received an offer to write a three-part television series produced by Bill Lyon-Shaw and featuring Bill Fraser, Victor Platt, John Hanson and the Beverley Sisters called *The Howerd Crowd*. Naturally Frank would be the star, and apparently this prompted a memo from Peter Brough to Michael Standing, Head of Radio Comedy, asking that Eric be signed up for the entire run of *Educating Archie* and 'should not be called upon to write for anyone else during the run'.

The three episodes of *The Howerd Crowd* were very well received, but I suspect that Frank wasn't too pleased by the fact that Bill Fraser had a large slice of the cake – but then how could Frank possibly know how much I was in Bill's debt? For each episode I was paid sixty guineas, and the bank manager began to smile at me.

In November 1951, in between the *Educating Archie* series, I was asked to script a Christmas show for the British Forces Network in Hamburg to entertain the troops. The show would be simply Frankie Howerd and Betty Driver. Betty sang songs in a warm Lancashire accent reminiscent of Gracie Fields; she also possessed a wonderful sense of humour. So with Frank and Betty the show almost wrote itself. Incidentally, Betty Driver spent the latter part of her career as the barmaid in *Coronation Street*. Good on you, Betty.

One dull, rainy morning I woke up with a feeling to match the weather. I felt decidedly poorly and my right ear was hotter than the rest of me. Earache is one of the most painful afflictions, and worrying because the ear is very close to the brain – one doesn't need a first in biology to know this. Anyhow the throbbing in my right ear became so severe that I had to sort out a doctor in Notting

Hill Gate, an old man whose medical proficiency was suspect. In fact on my second visit to his surgery I wondered where he would apply the leeches. By now perspiration was pouring down my face and my brain was like a suet dumpling.

On my fourth visit in one week the old doctor was still mystified. He looked into my ear, and then he took my temperature, wrote out my particulars again as if it was the first time we'd met and finally took down a thick medical volume and thumbed through it, obviously searching for something he couldn't make head or tail of. Whatever it was wasn't there, so he gave me more pills and that was it.

The next day I had a visit from an old heartthrob of mine, Pat Bywater, one of the tall, exotic showgirls I'd met in *Ta Ra Ra Boom De Ay*. I hadn't seen her since the show and at any other time I would probably have gone down on one knee and proposed, but in my condition I would never have got up again. She must have noticed me hovering about the afterlife and she insisted that I see a doctor.

'What a good idea,' I said, but she was unmoved by my sarcasm and once more I found myself at the wheel of my decrepit Ford Ten on the way to salvation. However, the poor old doctor still couldn't decide whether it was beri beri, malaria or athlete's foot. Down came the book and I ended up with more pills. When I finally arrived back home, Pat, who had accompanied me, said, 'You're suffering from something much more serious and a handful of pills isn't going to cure it.' She went on, 'How we got back I'll never know. You drove down the middle of the road all the way,' and before she left she said, 'I'll be back to see you tomorrow.' But in the event that didn't happen.

It was early afternoon and I was in bed, the pillow drenched with sweat. If I had been conscious enough I would have realised that my temperature was outside the range of an ordinary thermometer, but in my condition I didn't care. The phone rang and it was Peter Brough. We talked for a while, and then I put the phone down, lay back and continued to stare at the ceiling. Sometime later I muttered, 'Come in' to a knock on the door. It was a chauffeur, peaked cap under his arm. 'I've come to take you to Harley Street,' he said, adding, 'on Mr Brough's instructions.'

In less than an hour I was seated in Mr Musgrove's consulting room. Mr Musgrove, unknown to me at the time, was considered to be one of the finest ear, nose and throat specialists of his day, but I was in no fit state to ask for his credentials. That evening I was confined to bed in a private room in the Homeopathic Hospital in Great Ormond Street. Mr Musgrove told me later that he had first diagnosed my condition as meningitis but on further examination he had realised that I had an infected mastoid. He added that I had a very watchful guardian angel; three more days and it would have been too late – I would have been in the mortuary.

The morning after my incarceration I opened my eyes and wondered where I was. It wasn't the first time I'd awakened in a strange bed, but that's another story. It was all made clear when a nurse came in with a thermometer and a tray of various hospital geegaws. Only then did the nightmare of the last week relive itself in my mind. When she had gone, I lay back on my pillows to take stock. Then I shocked myself into a sitting position at the realisation that had Peter Brough not rung me at that precise time I might now be in the obituary columns. The realisation of my close brush with my maker hit me like a force-ten gale. For most of the day after that I vacillated between elation at my narrow escape and depression at having my wonderful life curtailed in my prime.

That evening all my thoughts were on hold when I donned the earphones to listen to the radio. I learned that the weather was fine, except in Scotland where rain could be expected. The forecast was followed by a half hour on how to grow vegetables, and I dickered idly with the thought that I might get myself an allotment when I was on my feet again. I was about to put the earphones aside and join the fairies when a burst of bright music vibrated through them. It heralded a comedy show, fast, furious, but above all, funny – really, really funny. I wasn't well enough to laugh, but my insides enjoyed it. I listened eagerly to the closing credits, and a cut-glass, wine-soaked voice announced, 'That was *Crazy People*, script by Spike Milligan and Larry Stephens.'

I couldn't wait to ring my bell and almost before I'd taken my finger off it a nurse rushed in, fearing the worst. When I asked for a pen and paper, she smiled with relief – after all, I was a writer. My letter to Spike Milligan and Larry Stephens was glowing and effusive; indeed, I thought *Crazy People* was the best programme I'd heard on radio since *The Brains Trust*. As I stuffed the letter into an envelope, of one thing I was certain: if this show was anything to go by, the country was in for an uplifting winter's listening.

The following day a nurse came in to shave one side of my head and at six in the evening I was wheeled to the operating theatre. Watching the overhead lights in the corridor float by, I enjoyed the ride and felt better than I had for ages. I joked with the porter pushing me along, and was proud of myself and my bravura, little knowing that the pre-op jab of Pentothal had given me Dutch courage – one might say it was the medical equivalent of Pernod.

Opening my bleary eyes much later, I found that I was back in bed. The room was dark, lit only by a shaded lamp. I was half propped up by pillows and I felt warm and cosy. I was about to drift off again when I made out Mr Musgrove sitting by the bed and peering intently at my face, with two nurses leaning over his shoulder. Apparently I murmured, 'Am I dead?' and immediately fell into a dress rehearsal.

When I woke again, it was full daylight and this time a nurse was easing me into a sitting position against several pillows. My door was wide open and other nurses hurried in and out, busy with this or that but completely ignoring me. Why hadn't they let me sleep on, instead of propping me up to admire them at work? I was still woozy and the whole of my head was turbaned with bandages. I felt like a rajah who'd fallen on bad times. It was only then that I noticed two white faces peering in at me, one above the other, the lower being only three feet from the floor – he was either a pygmy or he was kneeling. I'd no idea who those faces belonged to. Then I remembered that the one kneeling was Spike Milligan. I'd met him once before in a pub called the Grafton Arms and he had impressed me then as a man with comic ideas exploding from his mind like an inexhaustible Roman candle. I'd no idea who the other white face belonged to. Spike, trying to speak softly, was hauled to his feet by Matron, and bustled down the corridor and out into the street. For Matron I had nothing but admiration, although I would have liked to have known what Spike said. Two days later my curiosity was assuaged when I received a letter from Spike and Larry apologising for gatecrashing but they had wanted to thank me personally for my praise, especially coming from me. I felt like the trainer of an athlete who's just won gold.

A few more days and I had completed the writing of *Educating Archie* for the week, and on the Thursday Roy Speer, Peter Brough, Tony Hancock, Hattie and Max trooped into my room to sit round the bed on chairs Matron had organised; and when they were all settled, I read out my script. Occasionally Matron would pop her head into the room to keep an eye on things, and eventually she opened the door and announced that time was up. 'Five more minutes,' I pleaded. She hesitated, and then capitulated, and I was able to finish my rendering. More to the point, I got the thumbs up for it.

When they had disappeared, I settled down on my pillows in a fit of exhaustion. After a few minutes of nothing, I began to reminisce. It was twenty-eight years since I had been introduced to the world and life had treated me extremely well, as far as I could see with very little effort on my part; one good thing seemed to follow another as if it had been ordained.

That was the plus side. Now for the bad bits: the way I spent my free time in between triumphs, footloose and fancy free, the West End if not the world my oyster, pubs and long lunches during the day and dark dives until the small hours. It was all too over-indulgent and shallow. I was a ship without an anchor. What a way to spend one's leisure time! There must be a better way than pubs, getting home in the birdsong of daybreak. My career was going up but I was going down; the merry-go-round was whirling ever faster and I didn't seem to have the will to get off.

As I was dwelling on this unfortunate flaw in my character, an extraordinary thing happened. My inner vision went into fast reverse and in my mind I heard the voice of the old Welsh fortune teller in Swansea telling me that my poor dead mother, Harriet, was watching over me and asking if I ever felt a hand on my shoulder. I had said yes, but in truth if I ever felt a hand on my shoulder it would have been the police, and at this stage I didn't take the old witch's words too seriously. After a moment or two my mind switched to fast forward and reviewed the happenings of the last few days, beginning with Peter Brough's timely phone call, when he had never called me before – apparently I had replied to him in a ramble of gobbledegook, which had alerted him to set events in train. Had Peter not done so, after three days I would have been lying on a cold slab, according to Mr Musgrove. Could this be a miracle? If that was the case, the fortune teller had been uncannily correct. Was it possible? Then again I could never recollect a hand on my shoulder. But wait a minute – there had been times when I'd felt a shudder, better described as someone walking over my grave. Perhaps that was my mother's hand, and the more I thought of it the more I became convinced, especially as these shivers down my spine had usually been the prelude to my writing something above my usual standard. We shall see.

Every week the cast of *Educating Archie* gathered round the bed to hear my latest efforts, and here it is worth noting that we recorded the show every Sunday, to be broadcast the following week, so I wasn't able to hear the reaction of the audience; but every Sunday night after the show, Max Bygraves came to the hospital to tell me how it had all gone. I really appreciated the kind thoughtfulness that prompted Max to do this.

Lying in bed all day is conducive to writing. Good ideas were flowing from my pen, and also good intentions, and on a day when I was well on the way to recovery I wrote home. In my letter I told my father and mother that I was in hospital, that the operation had been a great success, and not to worry as everything was coming up roses and I was now on the mend. Two days later at about eleven o'clock in the morning, a nurse ushered them into my room, just in time for coffee. It was a wonderful, wonderful surprise. I had never expected to see them; after all, for them going to

Manchester, only eight miles by tram, was a frightening step into the unknown. So what a courageous effort it must have been to travel two hundred miles to see me – what an ordeal! Even when they left Euston station, they had to make their way, unprotected, through the mass of hurrying humanity, fearful of asking for directions to the hospital when even the English spoken was a foreign language; cockney was incomprehensible to Dad and when he said 'Thank you' to someone it was incomprehensible to them. I never got round to asking how they managed to find the hospital, but now thankfully here they were by the side of my bed. My feelings for them bloomed as never before. We didn't kiss or embrace – in fact we never had; our feelings for each other were taken for granted. I filled in the silences with amusing tales of hospital life, and, still too shy to speak in case a nurse came in or, God forbid, Matron, Dad smiled and nodded, and Mother shook her head which meant the same thing. Gradually I broke down their reserve and when Dad leaned towards me to ask where the lavatory was and would it be all right if he went, I gave him directions and it was then that I had such a lump in my throat. I watched him take off his jacket and drape it over the back of his chair, and then he unbuttoned his cardigan and, taking my *Daily Telegraph* under his arm, made his exit, and my heart could have burst with love. I blew my nose to hide my emotion, and at that moment I determined to spend more time in Oldham and repair my neglect of his genuine kindness and care. My father was still only fifty but having spent most of his hard-working life in a cotton mill he was already becoming a frail old man.

John Musgrove popped in to see me some evenings, whenever he had other patients to visit. The first time this happened, he sat on my bed and unhooked the stud fastening his stiff white collar, and when he swivelled his feet onto the bed I was looking at a very tired man. 'Open the cabinet,' he said, pointing to the bedside locker. It normally housed a chamber pot but its sole contents were a bottle of Dimple Haig and one of Booth's gin, both 'get well' gifts from Hattie and Max. How the dickens had John Musgrove become privy to my secret bar? After we clinked glasses, I asked him a question that had puzzled me for days. When I had first opened my eyes after the operation, why were he and a couple of ministering angels craning forward to stare intently at my face? Between gulps of pure malt whisky he explained that it had been a long and serious operation, and there was always the risk of a deterioration known as facial palsy, in which case one side of the face would droop and bring down that side of the mouth. 'Thank God,' he went on, 'it didn't happen in your case.' Amen to that, I thought; there's little future for an actor whose face hangs down one side.

The thought of my debauched life continued to invade my mind. Of one thing I was certain: I had no desire to return to it once I left the hospital. But tantalisingly the question still remained: what would I do with my evenings? Concerts, books perhaps? I could join a church choir, and don't forget the Four Aces. Another bright idea flashed into my mind: there was a rehearsal room in Camden Town where folk dancing was taught, and a smile creased my lips as I visualised myself in white silk stockings and bells on my ankles. But this was no time for hilarity. None of these things appealed to me, but I desperately needed something to keep my feet on the ground, some gravitas, some respectability. I thought of my friends Max Bygraves and his wife Bloss, Denis Norden and Avril, Frank Muir and Polly, Sid Colin and Deena – I was a little boy again, penniless and gazing longingly through the window of the toffee shop. The more I thought about this, the more I was convinced that my only option was to apply to join the Institution of Marriage. After all, I would soon be thirty and if I left it much later, what beautiful creature would want to tie herself to a doddering old man? I made up my mind that the minute I came out of hospital I would cast my net. My imagination wandered pleasantly over various species of fish and the best place to land them. I recalled the ladies of my acquaintance, their faces radiant in the smoky dimness of a nightclub, sadly ravaged by the light of day; they were hardly suitable for a lifelong partnership. Suddenly in a flash all became clear: if you wanted a good suit, you went to Savile Row, a toy for the children Hamley's, an expensive painting Bond Street. Ergo, I wanted a mate, and who better than a nurse – and here I was in hospital, surrounded by likely candidates. Having come to that conclusion, I forgot all about it, but the subconscious is a wily old bird.

There was one nurse I particularly fancied, mainly because she ignored me. She would say, 'How are you today?' and place a thermometer in my mouth so that I couldn't reply. When she took it out, she read it, shook the thing and was gone before I could remember what she had asked me. But one morning a week later as she was leaving, I broke down her defences.

'What part of Canada do you come from?' I said.

She turned towards me with a look of astonishment. 'How did you know I was Canadian?' she asked.

I shrugged. I'd mixed with enough of them during the war, but I could tell she was pleased. I subsequently discovered that she was fairly new to England and more often than not she was mistaken for either American or mostly Irish; so my recognising her accent earned me brownie points. The ice was melting, and the next time she came into my room to minister I was greeted by a smile and my heart lurched. I realised that she was attractive and I wanted her to smile again, but I'd had my ration for the day.

Edith Eleanor Milbrandt, from a small town south of Calgary, became known to me as Edith and I hoped it would be only a matter of time before she became Mrs Sykes. Soon I'd be out of hospital and in the big wide world again. Each morning I would get up and dress, and one day, looking out of the window at the passing traffic, I rolled back the extraordinary occurrences of the last few weeks: in the beginning the incredible phone call from Peter Brough that undoubtedly saved my life, followed by the wonderful success of the operation, my unimpaired ability to carry on writing *Educating Archie* scripts and the answering of my plea to get off the mad carousel with my meeting Edith. They were uncanny, to say the least, and I felt not a hand on my shoulder but a shiver running down my spine. I was certain that, almost unbelievably, there was only one person to thank, my dear, dead mother Harriet . . . But if I may be so presumptuous, could I suggest, dear Mother, that you do not cut it quite so fine next time?

*   *   *

When I was discharged from the Homeopathic Hospital, Edith and I maintained our relationship. We went to the theatre, the cinema, even just for walks; Edith took me to look round Westminster Abbey, and on another day we saw the beefeaters at the Tower of London – a pageant of history on my doorstep that I would never have visited had it not been for her. However, it wasn't all one-sided: the company of *Educating Archie*, organised by Peter Brough, received an invitation to present a Christmas cabaret at Windsor Castle in the presence of Princess Elizabeth and Prince Philip, and on this right royal occasion my escort was Edith. As we had written most of the cabaret, Sid Colin and I were invited too, Sid with his wife Deena.

I particularly remember a remark by Tony Hancock as we were making our way up the stone steps inside the castle. In the corner of a bend in the steps was a suit of armour, and Tony whispered to me, 'I wonder if they sell snuff here?'

After the show we were all ushered into an ante-room to be presented to the royal family. It was quite a formal occasion, a million miles away from Northmoor Council School in Oldham. Princess Margaret was accompanied by Wing Commander Peter Townsend, and for some reason or other they approached Edith and me.

I introduced her as my fiancée, we exchanged pleasantries and then, out of the blue, Peter Townsend said, 'I've admired your writing in the shows. It always appears as if the cast make it up as they go along – it's all so natural.'

I preened myself, thrilled that Edith was present to hear this glowing tribute from such an eminent source. Princess Margaret nodded happily and looked at him as if she already knew what was coming next.

'I'm trying to write a book,' continued the wing commander. 'But I don't seem to be making much headway and, er, well, any advice from you would be of immense help to me.'

'I'm trying to write a book myself,' I replied, 'but I'm afraid I'm coming up against the same problems as you, sir. As a matter of fact, most of my book is screwed up into little balls in my waste-paper basket.' I could see that he was disappointed. 'My great problem seems to stem from my reading,' I continued. 'For instance, if I have just finished a novel by Hammond Innes, I am influenced by his style of writing and instinctively I try to emulate him; but then I read George Bernard Shaw and my next attempt to write a book is a mishmash of Hammond Innes and G.B.S.'

Princess Margaret nodded, as if to say that was exactly Peter's problem too.

'My advice, for what it is worth, sir,' I said, 'is just write it down as if you are relating a tale to another person, not as somebody else but in language that only you would be able to command.'

After a few more exchanges, they excused themselves and I hoped I hadn't sounded too pompous or patronising.

Edith and I married in a registry office in Chelsea. We decided not to have the whole ceremony in white at a church because it would be asking too much of Edith's parents to attend, as her father was a farmer, which made it impossible for them to come. This was not the case with my father and mother, who were less than half a day's travel away from us, and they were witnesses, happy in the knowledge that at last I was settling down. After the nuptials we were obliged to hand over our ration books, along with a small payment, and we were now man and wife. What did people expect at a registry office – a red carpet and a guard of honour from the Household Cavalry? We were united and that's all that mattered to us.

Our reception took place in Tony Hancock's impressive flat at Queen's Gate, just off Kensington High Street. To be more exact, the flat belonged to his beautiful wife Cicely. It was elegant and tasteful, way out of Tony's league, but he was an exemplary host, never without a drink in his hand, although I suspected that Cicely had done most of the organising.

On the following morning, after a night spent in an exotic suite at the Savoy Hotel, a generous wedding present from Peter Brough, we made our way to London airport for a honeymoon in Jersey.

Tony, knowing my love of brass bands, had arranged for one to play us off on the tarmac – a really splendid surprise – but, alas, he had to cancel it. The date was 14 February 1952, a very sombre day for the country as George VI was to be buried, and a brass band playing 'Wish Me Luck as You Wave Me Goodbye' would have been in very poor taste.

Our honeymoon in Jersey was very wet and blustery, but what did we expect in February? In any case, the object of a honeymoon is to get to know one another, and the weather is way down the list of priorities, as long as the digs are warm and comfortable, and the food tolerable, and in our case they were.

Full of eager anticipation, we arrived back at our new address in Holland Villas Road, Bayswater. We had furnished it but not as yet had the pleasure of putting our feet on the table. My box in the sky in Longridge Road had been fine for a degenerate fly-by-night, but now I was a married man with responsibilities and I looked forward to receiving the Husband of the Year Award. The house was owned by Ben Warriss, the straight man in a very amusing double act, Jewel and Warriss. Ben occupied the basement, and Edith and I the ground floor; and above us was the home of Frankie Howerd.

The happy hour was over. I had to provide: there were now two mouths to feed. Fortuitously, the BBC asked me if I was free to write for Frankie Howerd on a tour of military bases in the Middle East. The prospect was hair-raising. I would have to write the scripts for six shows and audition the most likely service men and women to take part in the sketches, which naturally finished with a Howerd solo patter act. A week was allotted to write, rehearse and to perform in each location. The first stop would be Cyprus, followed by Malta, Egypt, Bahrain, Ismailia and the Bitter Lakes. What a very demanding schedule! But it was a challenge I could not refuse. It was extremely unfair to Edith for me to buzz off just a few days after our honeymoon, but we had to eat, and for these journeys into the unknown I was to be paid sixty guineas a week for each show, and I would be given a War Office chequebook on which I could draw twenty-five pounds a week expenses. I must mention here that I had no sight of the aforesaid War Office chequebook nor the expenses, and I suspect it ended up in the back pocket of some cunning conniver who never left England.

On 1 April, a very appropriate date, we flew out from Kensington Air Station: Roy Speer, the producer; Frank; Blanchie Moore; a lady singer and her pianist; Stanley Unwin; our sound engineer and myself. We were bound for Cyprus.

Kormaxa, an airforce base in Nicosia, was our first stop. I interviewed servicemen and women, picking out those I considered the most suitable to take part in the sketches. Only then could I write them the outlines of interviews and of course Frank's patter. I hadn't realised before just how taxing the job would be. As the show was on radio, it was much easier for Frank and his interviewees; they only had to read it. The tough part was writing. However, mainly because of Frank's popularity and his command of an audience, the first show was a success, which raised my spirits. I had now worked out my itinerary, which would have to include my writing sketches and possible interviews on aeroplanes; and, as we would be visiting the navy and the army, it would be necessary for me to acquaint myself with our surroundings before writing Frank's patter.

We were airborne to our second venue and as all our transport was being undertaken by the RAF our flight was spartan, to say the least. In spite of this, everyone relaxed, except for myself. I was pounding away at a typewriter on my knees, making a two-fingered attack on our next show. For refreshment, coffee in plastic cups was served by a flight sergeant. It was a very austere and basic mode of travel, noisy and cold in direct contrast to the intense heat on the ground awaiting us. Travelling on military aircraft became the pattern of our movements and on three occasions we were escorted by jet fighter planes for most of our journey. Some of our landings and take-offs were a bit on the hairy side, but then not all strips were as well organised as our first operational air station base in Cyprus. One landing was on to a dirt strip with a very short runway that ended in a sheer cliff wall. We pulled up just ten yards from it and I was horrified to look out of the window and see the wrecks of other aircraft who hadn't quite made it. I idly wondered who, if there was to be a disaster, would get top billing. It all added to the adventure of the whole project.

Malta was a great experience. Standing on high ground, we witnessed the fleet enter harbour in Valetta, an aircraft-carrier deck full of aeroplanes, propellers a blur and not just for show, as those propellers were essential in order to swing the leviathan into the berth. It was an awesome sight.

Being at a naval base, the show was naturally of matters nautical. The ratings, a petty officer and a presentable girl from the WRENS, had been selected and rehearsed, and the audience were already packing a large warehouse. I had a feeling that this was going to be a good show; in my mind's eye I could almost hear the laughter and applause. In such a state of euphoria I never saw the sucker punch coming . . . Frank, lying prostrate in a little room behind the stage, was in a bad way. Blanchie Moore dabbed his face with a damp towel, where Roy Speer, in a blue tizzy, knelt by the cot, proffering a microphone to Frank and suggesting that he could make the announcement himself. Either Frank didn't hear him or he'd just died. I was blissfully unaware of this drama until Roy approached to acquaint me with the situation. Ushering me towards the wings as he spoke, he expected me to go out on stage to announce that there would be no show tonight as Frank was ill. Roy looked at me pleadingly, but there was no way I was going to face that mob – after all, it wasn't in my contract, and I was too young to be hanged from the nearest yardarm. The sound of the audience out at the front, clapping in time to 'Why are we waiting . . .' was getting louder. There was nothing else for it. My appearance at least brought their chanting to an end, and they listened intently as I broke the news that Frank would not be appearing tonight, etc., etc. This was greeted by a stunned silence. It didn't bother me – I'd faced much the same reaction during my short spell on the music halls – but an old ham can never resist the lure of a packed audience and in that silence I shrugged and said, 'So, as I write the shows, you are lumbered with me.'

Unbeknownst to myself, it seemed that I'd uttered exactly the right words to suit the situation, because they laughed as they applauded. Half an hour later I was still on the stage, talking about this and that – our trip and where we would be next, about the weather in London. I even called out for Blanchie Moore to abandon her Nightingale role and get to the piano, where she would do more good, and this she did, leading with an arpeggio into twenty minutes of community singing – popular songs of the day, including Hitler and his singular affliction, which was the first time I'd heard it. It was a tour de force; if Churchill had been standing in the wings, he would have no doubt acclaimed it as my finest hour.

The moment I walked through the stage door I was surrounded by a mob of admiring fans. This was a novel experience for me. A writer normally lurks in the shadows, leaving the stage door unnoticed, but on this occasion I wasn't just the writer, I was the star of the evening, and for the first time in my life I was signing autograph books. Then they swept me off to a narrow street known to the navy as the Gut, and I found myself guest of honour in one of the drinking houses. I didn't drink much, as I wanted to savour the moment, and so I made a pint of beer last the evening; and when I finally got up to leave, there were at least ten pints untouched in the place where I'd been sitting. Before I left they insisted I visit them aboard their ship the following day, which I promised to do.

True to my word, on the morrow, the sun speckling the waters, I made my way to the ship aboard a local bumboat. To my astonishment, there were many ratings lining the rails, waving their caps as I appeared; what's more, I boarded the ship to a trill of bo'sun's whistles. It was heady stuff, especially when an officer shook my hand and asked if I would like to visit the ward room first or go below to the mess deck. I said I'd pay my respects to the officers' mess later but first I would go below to meet the lads. Again 'the best laid plans o' mice an' men/Gang aft agley'.

A three-badge seaman in charge of the mess led the applause when I entered and took me to a table on which there was a dixie full of rum. Announcing gravely that I was just in time for sippers, he handed me a half-pint glass, full to the brim. I toasted the navy and said 'God bless all who sail in her,' and then I sipped. Good grief! Had I been wearing a cap it would most assuredly have been blown ten feet in the air. It wasn't unpleasant, it was lethal, and I'd done no more than wet my lips. If only all eyes weren't on me I could have disposed of it somehow, but my retreat was cut off when the three-badger informed me that traditionally any visitor to the mess deck had to drink the whole glass of rum in one swallow. There was nothing else for it; if the worst came to the worst, I would be buried at sea. I lifted the glass and began my execution. I only managed half a glass, but it seemed to satisfy them, and now as a result of my initial intake I had courage enough to knock off the rest. What a splendid bunch they were! I began to wonder if I was too old to enlist. The bulkhead appeared to be moving, which left me wondering if we were already at sea. I even proffered my glass for another helping. This was fun – and that's where memory ends. I later found out that I was carried down to the waiting bumboat – a not very dignified exit from Malta. I awoke the following lunchtime with the biggest and fiercest hangover I've ever experienced. I tried to think through it to the events of yesterday, but I couldn't recall anything except the rum and the sippers. It was then with a pang of guilt that my thoughts shot to Frank – was he still with us? I staggered out of bed to the washbasin and splashed cold water over my face. Perhaps he'd been taken to hospital. Feverishly, I began to pull on my trousers. As I did, I glanced out the window, and there was Frank playing tennis.

The situation in Port Said was volatile. We were billeted in a small hotel and advised for our own safety to stay indoors, which wasn't my idea of seeing the world, so when an invitation came to the hotel asking us all to drinks on board one of Her Majesty's ships tied up in dock, I gladly accepted, resolved this time to sidestep another round of sippers. None of the others accepted the invitation, except for Blanchie Moore and the girl singer. The three of us set out for the dockyard. It was only a fifteen-minute walk, completely without incident; there were no people about, but of course there was a curfew. The first signs of life were two khaki-clad Egyptian soldiers, armed with rifles. Their red fezzes reminded me

ABOVE: Frankie Howerd and me wearing a cheap form of head phones.

BELOW: Gilbert Harding receiving his award. Peter had already accepted the award for best comedy half-hour of the year: *Educating Archie*. My first tickle.

ABOVE: The high spot of a parade along the main street of Royton foiled by a tram line and an injudicious lady's shoe.

BELOW: A near miss. Derek Guyler, my best man, Hattie, a maid of honour, and Joan Sims, my intended, in *Sykes and A...*

Tommy Cooper enjoying himself during a break in the filming of *The Plank*.

ABOVE: I wrote all my 'silents' with the camera. Here I am lining up a full stop.

BELOW: On one of our visits to Rhodesia: Jimmy Edwards entertaining Ian Smith and Janet, his better half.

ABOVE: The butler in a western … I can't
believe it either.

BELOW: Partnering Terry-Thomas in
skulduggery in the film *Monte Carlo or Bust*.

ABOVE: *Heavens Above!* Peter Sellers, the vicar, sharing a joke between takes. My wife in the film was Irene Handl. Also Miriam Karlin and Roy Kinnear starred. I always maintain our profession is a small village.

BELOW: Five rounds with Muhammad Ali wasn't enough for Jim and me.

ABOVE: What a time for the hearing aid battery to run out.

BELOW: Johnny Speight (right) and me meeting at Ipswich railway station with Carl Giles, the legendary cartoonist, for a five-hour luncheon at his home.

This is Your Life. The A team.

of Tommy Cooper and I chuckled, biting my laughter back when they glared at me. They were guarding the dock gates. They leaned their rifles against the wall and I wondered anxiously what was coming next. It was only a routine search, and they started to frisk the two ladies, or more truthfully to feel them, with much giggling. I was embarrassed, but what could I do? The last thing I wanted was a clout round the earhole with an Egyptian rifle butt. In any case, the ladies didn't seem to mind; in fact I think they rather enjoyed it. Their duty done, the two guards opened the gate and waved us all through without a second glance at me.

On the deck of the warship the party was in full swing – mainly officers and local dignitaries with their wives. Although we were offered cocktails, they didn't make such a fuss of us as they had done in Malta. I think they were a little disappointed that Frankie Howerd had not accepted their invitation, so why should they put themselves out for the reserves? Twilight began to deepen into the purple of night, which was our signal to offer our thanks and goodbyes before making our way to the dock gates. Blanchie Moore and the girl singer, now full of cocktails, were eager to be off or – I allowed myself a quiet smile – eager to be searched again, more like, but their luck was out, as the gates were unattended. Although they looked around frantically, there wasn't a soul in sight, which made me wonder: were those soldiers really guarding the gates or did they stand there each evening for a cheap thrill?

Ismailia and the Bitter Lakes was another unhealthy spot. We were in army country and the poor squaddies, mainly National Servicemen, had the unenviable task of keeping the peace. According to one of them, a few weeks before a soldier had been shot by a sniper as he stood in a queue to watch an ENSA show, at the same theatre in fact where we would be recording our broadcast. There had been other fatalities in this district and after an army investigation it had been discovered that a muezzin on a minaret near by, ostensibly calling out prayers, was in fact a spotter observing the movement of British troops and relaying information about the size of British Army convoys, which way they were heading, the arrival of street patrols and the number of personnel. I looked up at the minaret but there was no sign of life. It was an ideal position from which to observe the country. I asked the sergeant what had happened to the muezzin. He shrugged, and said laconically, 'Perhaps he's on holiday.'

When the tour was over, I slept all the way back to Blighty, nearly a stone lighter and desperately in need of a change of scene, preferably somewhere miles away from uniforms, sea, sand and unremitting sunshine.

While I had been zooming all over the Middle East like a demented tsetse fly, Edith had very sensibly returned to her occupation as a nurse. It was good to be back with her again in quiet, leafy Holland Villas Road, but before we could settle down to a new beginning the telephone rang. I assumed it was Dad: ever since I'd had a telephone installed in his house he had been apt to call me several times a week in order to get used to it. His only other calls were to the speaking clock and I'll bet any money that when the voice gave the time he would say 'Thank you' before he hung up. Anyway, it wasn't Dad; it was my brother Vernon. It was such a lovely surprise. After we had exchanged enquiries about the health of our wives, he asked if he could drop in to see me some time. I assured him that he would always be welcome.

Half an hour later, the door bell rang and it was Vernon, all smiles as he introduced me to his colleague: 'Eric, this is Geoffrey.' This was said in a way that implied that the flat was his and he'd lent it to me. Lolling back in the settee in between sips from a malt whisky, Vernon explained that they were both trainee Hoover salesmen, down in London on a course. Geoffrey was very keen on the job and took their instruction seriously, eagerly explaining how to get the householder interested in buying a Hoover: compliment her on the house; if there are children, smile and try to win them over; having gained their confidence, produce the Hoover for a demonstration. Vernon, with bored indifference, raised his eyes to the ceiling on hearing such twaddle and I knew that he had no intention of hoicking a Hoover from door to door. His thoughts were more likely in the boardroom and on the changes he would instil in the curriculum when he was chairman. This was the legacy he had inherited from his early years with Great-grandpa Wilson and Grandma Stacey when he had been idolised and treated like the crown prince, his every wish a command. It was wrong, it was an insidious drip of poison; they were doing him no favours because sooner or later he would have to return to his peasant roots. For the rest of his life poor Vernon took with him the attitude of condescension he had been indoctrinated in: it was only a question of time before he would be invited to be Chancellor of the Exchequer, the only drawback being that he had never learned to add up – but on reflection that's never been a problem before in Westminster.

In spite of this, it was a very pleasurable reunion and the time went all too quickly. As I was seeing them off, Vernon took me to one side and peremptorily flapped his arm, dismissing Geoffrey with 'I'll catch you up.' When he was out of earshot, Vernon quietly announced that he was a bit pushed; typically, he went straight for the jugular, adding could I lend him a few quid? My only surprise was that this request had not come earlier.

'Listen, Vernon,' I said. 'You're not going to waste your time selling Hoovers. Why don't you just get a job so that you have money coming in regularly?'

'What kind of job?' he said.

'Anything,' I replied. 'Sweep the streets, deliver coal.'

He stood back in amazement. 'Sweep the streets?' he said, as if I'd suggested robbery with violence. 'I can't sweep the streets. Not in my position.'

'What position?' I said. 'You're unemployed, with no prospects and skint.'

I knew that my remark wouldn't have the slightest chance of reaching the upper never-never world in which he lived. I gave him twenty-five pounds, which he accepted as if I'd owed it to him all the time.

Geoffrey came back to us, looking at his watch.

'By the way,' said Vernon, 'how's Tony?' and before I could reply he turned to Geoffrey and said, 'Do you ever listen to *Hancock's Half Hour*?'

'Sometimes,' said Geoffrey with little enthusiasm.

Then an idea struck me. 'What are you doing tomorrow night?' I said.

'Nothing,' replied Vernon expectantly.

'Good, because Tony is recording one of his shows and I wonder if you'd like to go?'

'It would be good to see Tony again,' said Vernon. He'd never met him before, but I wasn't about to embarrass him.

Geoffrey said he'd love to go but had some studying to do.

Before the show I introduced Vernon to the BBC secretaries, and much to his delight they promised to look after him while I went round the back to leave a message for Tony that I'd be in the pub next door after the show. It was to be a nice surprise for Vernon. I didn't see the show myself – after all, a fireman doesn't go out to watch a fire on his day off.

The two secretaries brought Vernon into the pub and I could see that he'd been a great success with the girls. Completely devoted to his wife Eve, he wasn't a ladies man, but to him the two girls were his audience and, because they were BBC, worthy of his repertoire. He ordered drinks, but when the barman stood patiently waiting for a few coins of the realm, Vernon had his back to him as he continued his conversation with the girls, or more probably his monologue. I paid for the round just as Tony walked in.

'What are you having?' asked Vernon. Quickly I interrupted to introduce Vernon.

'Oh,' said Tony, offering his hand, and as they shook he added, 'a vodka and tonic.'

Vernon turned to the bar, clicked his fingers and ordered. When the drink was served, Vernon was deep in conversation with Tony, so I paid again.

'A good show, Tony,' said Vernon as they clinked glasses. He was effusive with his praise of the show and, noticing that his glass was empty, he asked them all if it was the same again.

'I'll get these,' I said.

Vernon was in full flow. Now it was the post mortem, and I couldn't believe my ears as he suggested to Tony how he could improve his performance. Tony's smile remained, but his eyes were glazed. Behind Vernon's back I gave Tony a wink and he relaxed. Even Vernon began to realise that he was stepping on hallowed ground. 'Time, gentlemen, please' couldn't come quickly enough, and when it did Vernon said, 'What a shame, it was my round too.'

As I made my way home I smiled to myself. Vernon really was a bobby-dazzler. He hadn't put his hand in his pocket once. Then my thoughts changed: he couldn't be short of a few bob as only yesterday I'd lent him twenty-five quid.

The day after I was driving along Shaftesbury Avenue when it struck me that this was Vernon's last night on the course, and as I would be passing close to the hotel where he was staying it would be nice to pop in and wish him 'Bon voyage' for the morrow. I pulled up outside the hotel and as I entered the first two people I saw were the two BBC secretaries from *Hancock's Half Hour*.

'We didn't expect to see you at the party,' one of them said, and before I could utter 'What party?' a roar of laughter erupted from the bar. I turned round and saw Vernon in the middle of an admiring crowd. At that moment he caught sight of me. 'Come in, Eric,' he shouted above the clamour. Bemused, I wandered into a farewell party for the lads on the Hoover course. The host was, as I knew it would be, my brother Vernon, who was throwing this happy shindig with my hard-earned twenty-five quid . . . You can't help admiring him.

ARCHIVE

25 July 1952. Roy Speer acknowledged that Eric was writing most of each script for the third series of *Educating Archie*, and would receive fifty guineas per script.

I hadn't seen Sid Colin for probably a year. As he was writing the first spot for *Educating Archie*, he simply handed it in to Roy Speer and disappeared; whereas I not only read out my offerings to the cast but spent each recording day in the studio, chopping and changing until it was exactly right for broadcasting. It didn't bother the cast as they would be reading from the script anyway.

We looked forward to Sid's contribution; it always gave the show a flying start. So it was with some trepidation that I heard that Sid would no longer be part of *Educating Archie*. Why, I still don't know, but I suspect that for a writer of his experience one spot a week wasn't really in his class. As for me, I knew that I would never be able to attain his standard. I missed Sid and now as I write this I wish I had taken a little time to get to know him better. For instance, it turned out that he was a brilliant jazz guitarist, having been in the Ambrose Band during the late 1930s; and during the war he was with the Squadronaires, during which time he wrote *Friends and Neighbours*, *If I Only Had Wings* and possibly many more. Sid went from *Educating Archie* to other pastures. Because of the voracious appetite of radio and television, once accepted as a reliable writer you were forever swimming, with no time to tread water.

Edith was now heavily pregnant, and while attending a pre-natal exercise class she met another trainee mother, Elizabeth Powell, a very jolly young lady bubbling with anticipation, with a tendency to giggle when the enormity of the ordeal of giving birth drew ever nearer. Her smile was infectious and Edith could not have found a better friend. In direct contrast, her husband, Bernard, was more serious. His career prospects were rosy. He was a portrait painter and had already painted the Whitney Straits, a very old respected American family; he had also committed to canvas the Gabor sisters and he was not yet thirty years old.

On 6 September 1952, Elizabeth produced twin girls, which was great, but all my attention was focused on Edith, who gave birth to a daughter.

In a room adjoining the maternity ward were a group of new fathers, mostly standing with their hands behind their backs in order to hide the bouquets. The atmosphere was too tense for much chatter, but a very presentable young man approached me and introduced himself as Bernard Powell, the husband of Elizabeth.

We exchanged fatherly congratulations, and that was the end of our conversation, as it was interrupted when a nurse opened the door and we all followed her into the ward in a tight-knit bunch, each man finding his mate and, as if in a conjuror's convention, producing a bunch of flowers from behind his back.

To see my little daughter was probably one of the most emotional moments of my life. I couldn't speak, I was so moved. It was stupendous, colossal, top of the hit parade. I glanced across to Bernard, by Elizabeth's bed; he must have been doubly moved, as he had twins.

For the rest of Edith's and Elizabeth's confinement Bernard and I met, by now a little blasé, and one night after we'd eaten all the grapes from the bedsides I took him to the Adelphi Theatre to meet Tony Hancock and Jimmy Edwards. This was a novelty for Bernard, because it was the first time in his life that he'd visited a vaudeville theatre; it was a glimpse of an alien world for him, a planet of laughter. He was so impressed by the quiet humour of Tony and the more rumbustious attack from Jimmy that he was forced to smile; in fact in all the short period I'd known him it was the first time he had dropped his guard. Perhaps to repay me for a very enjoyable evening, he asked me if I would sit for him, if I could spare an hour or two, and the following afternoon I was immortalised in oils. How anyone could paint such an accurate likeness in less than an hour will always remain a mystery to me. The painting still hangs in my office next to an old photo of my mother.

Edith and I took the baby up north to be christened at St Mary's Parish Church in Oldham. She was named Katherine Lee. The vicar went through the motions as if she was just another child – couldn't he see that she was perfect?

After the ceremony came visits to the relatives to show her off. Kathy accepted all the accolades and the superlatives with a dignified silence, but it was all summed up by my aunt Marie's remark, 'She is a little treasure.'

Naturally Edith wanted to show Katherine to her parents, although this meant a long tiring journey to Canada, past Calgary to a little place called East Coolie. I couldn't complain, as I'd had my bite of the cherry, and in a few days I drove them to London airport and watched as they disappeared into the transit lounge.

When they had gone, I was dejected to such an extent that I could not remember ever plumbing such depths. I had a heaviness of spirit; I didn't breathe, I sighed, and this was the trigger to my understanding: I was lonely, and I missed them, and this was only the first day. I was adrift in an open boat. My old nightlife no longer appealed to me and although I had friends I had no confidants – in any case, what had I to confide? I was wallowing in self-pity when the phone rang. It was Bill Lyon Shaw, asking me if I was free to write a comedy show for Harry Secombe. Dear Harriet, your ways are mysterious but bang on the button.

Seated in Bill's office at the BBC I learned that a writer had been hired to write Harry's one-hour comedy, but the script turned in was abysmal. As far as I could see, in the unlikely event of laughs it could last only fifteen minutes, and that is a generous estimate. There was only one thing for it: I would have to rewrite the whole show. As I accepted, ideas were already fermenting in my brain but Bill's next words snatched me back to reality. The show was for Saturday night and it was now Thursday evening. I had Friday to write it, and Saturday to rehearse on camera, to be ready to go live on air at eight o'clock . . . Ah well, there's always death.

By dawn on Friday morning I had the synopsis and on Friday afternoon I was rehearsing the sketches. Harry and I would be appearing – it had to be me, as an actor wouldn't have time to learn it – and I called on my trusty mate, Spike Milligan. Together we rehearsed a mirror routine I had concocted. Spike was enthusiastic because there were no words to learn.

Luck was on our side. We had one of the most important ingredients for a successful show: a good audience. They were a cheerful lot who would've laughed had the commissionaires come round with collecting boxes for the actors or had some idiot shouted 'Fire'. The show was inevitably a huge hit. Harry was funnier than he'd ever been, his song in his powerful bel canto tenor voice was mercifully in tune but to me, and perhaps I'm biased, the highlight was the mirror routine. It was Spike's first credit on television and, incidentally, also mine, although my name was given as Jim Thighs. It was the beginning of a series of noms de plume – Jack Prolong, Arthur Pules, Wilfred Saddlebag and others. I didn't want people to know it was me up there acting the fool; I was perfectly satisfied with my script credits.

ARCHIVE
13 May 1953. Eric was paid ninety guineas for writing *Nuts in May*.

I can remember the title *Nuts in May*, and I obviously wrote it; perhaps I appeared in it as well. But it couldn't have been all that good, because it has mercifully been erased from my mind . . . I rest my case.

Educating Archie was now in its fifth or sixth series and our ratings were blooming. I meet people today, over fifty years on, who can still remember the show even though they haven't a clue what they were doing yesterday. So for me life was just a bowl of cherries – but I was arrogantly overlooking the fact that in every cherry there's a stone.

The last series had been enhanced by the introduction of Beryl Reid, a very funny lady. Her character, Monica, the saucy schoolgirl, was hilarious – little wonder she was a star in her own right. Unfortunately Archie was the central pillar of the show and Beryl could never really face the fact that she might sometimes have to feed Archie a line so that he could get a laugh on his reply; Beryl was of the opinion it should be the other way round. I could see her point of view but the show was essentially a team effort. Tony, Max and Hattie were the backbone of the team and I made sure that they all had equal opportunity to shine. In one particular scene Beryl was standing on top of a very tall building, threatening to jump off, while Tony, Max and Hattie, in the street below, were desperately trying to talk her out of it. After the last rehearsal before the show the cast were looking forward to what promised to be a feast of laughs – that is, all except Beryl.

'Very funny,' I said when she approached me, but she didn't seem to be too happy.

'It could be funny,' she said, 'but all the attention should be on me, and I'm standing ten feet behind the rest of the cast.'

'Yes,' I said, 'and it comes over great. You really sound as if you are on top of a five-storey building.'

She wasn't mollified. 'But the audience can't see me,' she insisted.

Now I understood. All the rest of the cast wore their own clothes, and why not? They were only voices on the radio. But Beryl insisted on appearing in the gymslip and black stockings of an anarchic St Trinian's schoolgirl, which she felt were essential to her role, and so she must be seen.

'Beryl,' I said, 'don't worry about the audience here tonight. There are millions and millions out there listening to a poor, stranded, little girl threatening to jump off a five-storey building.'

I could see that she wasn't convinced. She looked ready to burst into tears, exactly like her Monica character, whose egg had fallen out of her spoon just before the finishing line, but I was tired and had urgent business to attend to – the pubs were open.

The show lived up to all our expectations and the scene with Monica on the roof was a wonderful word picture; I had proved my point. Then Beryl bombarded me with a list of jokes for her, which I could possibly include in the next show.

The following Sunday morning when the cast received their scripts, Beryl's jokes were conspicuously absent and she gave a rather sulky performance, which did not go unnoticed by Peter Brough.

After the show, Peter took me to one side, put his arm round my shoulders and said, 'Beryl isn't happy.'

I sighed.

'Write her a few funny lines,' he cajoled.

I sighed again.

Peter gave me a little friendly shake. 'Why don't you gag it up for her a bit?' and before I could sigh again he went on, 'She's got a repertoire of jokes. Why don't you talk to her and slip a few belly laughs in?'

By now Roy Speer, the producer, had joined us, sensing that this was a little more serious than the cricket scores.

'Peter,' I said, 'in the first place this isn't a joke show. We deal in situations, and funny lines are subservient to the plot. Two years out of the last three we've been voted the Best Comedy Show of the Year and now you want to change the shape because Beryl Reid is not allowed a four-minute solo spot.'

Now it was Peter's turn to sigh. 'Eric, Eric,' he pleaded. 'Just a couple of gags won't do any harm.'

Oh yes they would, I thought. If Beryl's gags, bearing little relation to the on-going situation, got a tremendous reaction the scene itself would be unbalanced. 'I'm sorry for Beryl,' I said, 'but I'm not going to change my style of writing and that's flat.'

Peter and Roy looked at each other in resignation. I wasn't proud of myself, but there was a principle at stake: no one artist was bigger than the show. And with this in mind I fired my heavy artillery: 'Either Beryl goes or I do.'

Why didn't I keep my big mouth shut? I went!

I can't help thinking that it was time I got myself a new petard – I'd been hoisted enough with my old one. But inwardly I wasn't too bothered. Four years and two radio awards for *Educating Archie* was probably enough, and as writers were as rare as berries on a pine tree there would still be meat on the table at Holland Villas Road.

When Edith and Katherine arrived back from Canada, they were obviously exhausted and it was no time to break the news that I was unemployed. Edith put Katherine to bed and then, after a brief account of her travels in the Wild West, she asked me how *Educating Archie* was.

I told her that I had had enough of writing the show and it was time for a change.

Then she asked me what my next assignment was.

Like the chicken that I was, I said vaguely, 'It's all in the air at the moment.'

'What is it called?'

I said I hadn't decided on a title as yet.

Then she said, 'What is it all about?' There was a long pause, but I knew she hadn't finished. 'Who's in it?' she said. She was relentless, but I was already halfway down the drive, thinking up a suitable cast for a show that had never entered my head.

Edith had a very good idea that we should look for a property out in the country, which would be a much better environment in which to bring up Kathy. I rather fancied the vision of a smallholding, with a couple of cows, chickens running all over the kitchen table and vegetables growing in a small plot, and the more I thought of it the more I welcomed the idea. It was a prospect I applauded and which I approached with all the seriousness of Livingstone setting sail for Africa.

Practically every evening for the next few months we toured the hinterland. Some evenings we motored about fifty miles there and fifty miles back to view some property or other – big houses with pocket-sized gardens, tiny houses set in a couple of acres of grassland, houses that would have suited except that they were on main roads, others that took our fancy that were too far from civilisation. Soon we had seen more than half the houses in Surrey, and judging by our lack of success, Kathy would be old enough to drive Edith and me around before we found our much-desired residence.

The day of 2 June 1953 was an historic one for England and it was also memorable for me as well if you read on.

Princess Elizabeth, with Prince Philip by her side, was about to be crowned Queen of England, and already the streets were thronged with crowds of people looking forward eagerly to a view of the golden coach making its way to Westminster Abbey. Bernard Powell had managed to procure two tickets for a place on the route to the Coronation, but as he would have to babysit the twins, he suggested that Edith might avail herself of his ticket so that she could be company for Elizabeth (not the Queen, I hasten to add), his wife. Dad and Mother happened to be staying with us at the time, and they were only too pleased to keep one eye on nine-month-old Kathy and the other eye on the television, scanning the crowds in the hope of seeing Edith and Elizabeth. I was to drive them to their viewing point.

The two wives climbed into the back of my car, scarves round their heads, each carrying a basket holding sustenance. I couldn't help thinking that they looked like a couple of cleaning women being given a lift to work. Mind you, I wasn't one to cast aspersions. It was very early in the morning and I hadn't bothered to get dolled up; I was still in my old dressing gown over my pyjamas – after all, I only had to drop them off and in two shakes I'd be back home in a hot bath. It all sounded so straightforward. One of the stock questions of most interviewers is 'what was the most embarrassing moment in your life?' Well, on reflection this day must be on the shortlist.

Edith and Elizabeth in the back were eagerly anticipating an exciting day. The police were all over the place, waving the cars this way and that according to the colour of the sticker on the wind-screen. This was going to be a doddle – that is, until I was waved on to the Embankment, where I found myself in the middle lane of elegance. In front, behind and on either side, there were limousines with passengers reclining in the back seats adorned in the ermine-trimmed red gowns of the aristocracy. Panic-stricken, I realised that I was boxed in and as we moved inexorably closer to Westminster Abbey there was no way I could escape. If only I'd been in the outside lane – then I could easily have turned off, pretending I was a delivery van. Even the twittering in the backseat had dried up, as Edith and Elizabeth sensed that all was not as it should be. Now Westminster Abbey was within hailing distance and we were funnelled into a single lane, where we made a wide sweep round to the dropping-off zone. The pavements were already jam-packed with crowds and I was crouching lower and lower into my dressing gown as I waited my turn to offload. The police were now beginning to take an interest.

My turn came and I moved forward. Immediately Boy Scouts ran to the car to open the back door, and Edith and Elizabeth stepped out like a couple of Bulgarian refugees. Straight away they were swallowed up by a posse of policemen, and that was the last I saw of them in my rear-view mirror. I learned later that only the fact that Edith was pregnant and not concealing a fifty-pound bomb saved them from being arrested as illegal immigrants. When I arrived back at the flat, my father said, 'Where did you drop them off?' to which I replied, 'How's Kathy?' knowing that my father would have forgotten his own question.

There was a perfectly reasonable explanation for the cock-up. Thanks to some extraordinary ineptitude, Bernard had been sent the wrong tickets and our windscreen sticker had identified us as a large black limousine carrying a peer of the realm. What should have been on my semi-opaque windscreen had directed the aforesaid limousine to a remote, run-down part of the royal route, where it deposited the unfortunate high-born aristocrat in his ermine-trimmed red gown of office, white silk stockings and buckled shoes, making him the target of all the ribaldry of the unwashed, while his colleagues in Westminster Abbey were wondering if he had forgotten the Coronation was today.

From Holland Villas Road it was but a short journey to a green-grocer's shop in Shepherd's Bush, where Spike Milligan and I rented the top floor of that building as our first office. This journey through the sweet-smelling vegetables launched a partnership that lasted nearly half a century. Those were the days, when we both arrived at our fun factory in suit, collar, tie and even shiny shoes. We enjoyed this discipline of going to work every day, although on reflection it can't have been much fun for Edith. Writing scripts to feed the voracious appetite of weekly broadcasts was a full-time job, only we didn't finish at five-thirty; inspirations, ideas, comedy situations spring to mind with no regard to set hours, meal times pass by unnoticed, relaxation is merely a word and nights are spattered with broken sleep.

One day two young hopefuls appeared in our office, Alan Simpson and Ray Galton. They even brought their own typist with them, although to my knowledge they'd not written anything as yet. Spike and I couldn't afford a typist. He bashed away with two fingers on an old machine while I, now established, wrote out my stuff in longhand to be typed later by BBC secretaries.

Being within the vicinity of Lime Grove, Spike and I had many visitors. Irene Handl was one, a real bundle of eccentricity, always with a Pekinese under each arm, Gretzel and Pretzel. It may be that they were chihuahuas – dogs aren't my strong suit, but they weren't Rottweilers, of that I am sure. Irene's visits were always a delight. Another casual was Gilbert Harding, an irascible character known for his use of the Queen's English, which could demolish most of his critics in a single sentence. Unfortunately he was asthmatic, so climbing the five flights of stairs was an ordeal, but he considered it worthwhile for what he termed an hour of verbal therapy. We were flattered to be in his company.

One day an idea that had been lurking around in my subconscious revealed itself as I pushed my way through sacks of potatoes, carrots and crates of apples on my way upstairs. By the time I'd reached our office, the idea had become a reality. It was to form a company, the title of which came on the second flight: Associated London Scripts. Spike, Frankie Howerd and I naturally would be on the board and, in the hope that one day they might write something, Simpson and Galton. The principal aim of ALS was to corner the market in scriptwriters. When I put forward my idea to the others, they were all for it, but their reticence suggested that they were hoping the idea would soon go away.

In spite of their reluctance to become respectable, I persisted and in a few weeks several scripts were coming through the letterbox. I read and replied to them, but it was like fishing without a hook and I began to wonder if ALS had been a good idea in the first place. What had happened to my philosophy that in every dustbin there's a daffodil? All I'd had up to now had been rubbish. But just as I was about to jack it all in I spotted the daffodil. The script that turned up trumps was written by a young man called Johnny

Speight. I only had to read the first page and halfway down the second to realise with absolute certainty that I'd struck gold. He'd even included his address and telephone number, and in five minutes I was speaking to him. He told me that his present occupation was as an insurance salesman. I told him that I'd never met an insurance salesman before and could he get over to my office as soon as possible? Two hours later, Johnny and his wife Connie were sitting in my office. They were ill at ease to begin with, anxious about why I'd asked them to the office.

'I only wish I could write like that,' I said, tapping his script.

Immediately their sigh of relief could be heard in Notting Hill Gate. 'Did you like it?' stuttered Johnny unnecessarily.

'I've only read page one,' I replied, 'but that one page is worth the Writer of the Year Award.'

They blushed with pleasure, and then my mouth spoke without first clearing it with my brain. 'You're a writer, Johnny,' I said. 'Phone up your head office and tell them to find somebody else to sell insurance.'

They looked at each other, Johnny with delight and Connie with deep reluctance.

The following morning Johnny turned up at the office again, on his own this time. He looked like a new man, as if the doctor had told him that there was no need to amputate his leg after all.

'I've packed in my job,' he said, and it was only then that I realised what an impulsive idiot I'd been. At least he'd have been getting a salary if he sold insurance. What could I do for him at the moment, apart from getting him a job selling vegetables? But again I had one of these wonderful twists of fortune that seem to drop into my lap when the night is blackest. The BBC rang to ask me if I would write a radio series for Frankie Howerd. Normally I would have accepted, but I desperately needed breathing space, so I turned it down. They were very disappointed, but there was nothing I could do. It was only when I put the phone down that inspiration parted my hair. I rang them back. 'I've got an idea,' I said, 'with regard to the Frankie Howerd radio series. There are three very good writers in our office who have just finished their last assignment and would be only too pleased to accept.' The BBC were hesitant, but my inspiration was only half used up. 'Perhaps if I edited the programme you would be able to go ahead?'

To this they readily agreed, so Simpson and Galton and the new Johnny Speight were overjoyed to become professional writers. I breathed a sigh of relief – at least they wouldn't starve at the Speights' residence for the next six weeks.

What a funny old world this is! Johnny happened to know a masseur who used to pummel Frankie Howerd's body at the sauna baths, and he had happened to be talking to Frank, who mentioned my name, and when the masseur next met Johnny he had happened to mention the conversation he'd had with Frank – which was how Johnny had come to send his script to me. From that small beginning one of our greatest comedy writers was off the blocks.

On 26 September of that Coronation year our second child, Susan Jane, was born. I now had two daughters, who were as alike as chalk and cheese. Where Kathy was dark and quiet, Susan was the opposite, fair, boisterous and already eager to sample whatever life had to offer. We still occupied the flat in Holland Villas Road, but now as our family had increased the flat became even smaller, so our evenings were once more a trawl of the Surrey countryside in the hope of finding a place called home.

On our earlier tour of Surrey we had begun our recce in St George's Hill, Weybridge, and immediately I had seen the house I wanted. Edith wasn't too sure and said we couldn't just pick the first house we saw, and so we continued our operations until I reckon we had seen more than fifty houses before Edith gave birth to Susan. Now when we went back to St George's Hill we hit the jackpot: the first house we saw we both liked; and, would you believe it, it was only fifty yards away from the original house that Edith hadn't been too sure about. It had been a long haul, but on the bright side I learned more about Surrey than I could ever have gleaned from an atlas.

*   *   *

At Christmas I was again invited to Windsor Castle. This time I was to take part in the cabaret. Edith was unable to come with me because she had the family to look after, and as it turned out I was glad she didn't. Elizabeth was no longer a princess, she was now the Queen, and another change in the programme was that we were to be informally introduced to the royals before the show and not afterwards. As we all stood casually round the same room as we had before, awaiting the arrival of the royal party and chatting in subdued voices, a silver-haired, distinguished man in a dinner jacket came over.

'So you enjoy these dos?' he asked in a friendly tone.

'Oh yes, sir,' I gushed. 'It's an honour, sir.'

I assumed he was an equerry. He asked more questions and I gushed in reply; I wasn't far off touching my forelock. Then, with a final 'I'm sure you'll go down well tonight,' he took his leave and Harry Secombe sauntered up.

'You two seemed to be getting on well together.'

'Yes,' I replied. 'A very interesting man. They all seem to have a way of making you feel at home.'

Harry seemed puzzled. 'Who're you talking about?' he asked.

'The man I was just talking to,' I said. 'He's an equerry, I think.'

Harry burst out laughing and when Harry laughed it was contagious.

'What's so funny?' I chuckled.

Harry was desperately trying to stifle his mirth in a huge handkerchief. 'He's not an equerry, you pillock. That's my pianist, Len Lightowler.'

Saving my embarrassment, the tall doors opened and the royal party entered, followed by their entourage, and here was another surprise. Princess Margaret and Wing Commander Peter Townsend made a beeline across the room towards me.

The first words Princess Margaret uttered were, 'Did you ever get your book written?'

I was at a loss – I had no idea what she was talking about.

'You were going to write a book,' said the wing commander. Then our conversation of the earlier Christmas sprang to mind.

'No, sir,' I replied. 'But perhaps one day.'

'I never wrote my book either,' said the wing commander.

I was flattered and amazed. What prodigious memories they must have had to bring to mind a very short conversation a year or two ago! It was truly remarkable, considering that they listened to hundreds of thousands of people and millions of words in the course of their duties.

The cabaret took place in the same large room as last year, only this time the big attraction was to be Billy Cotton and his band. I'd already appeared in *The Billy Cotton Band Show* once or twice, so we were no strangers to each other – more like a mutual admiration society. I hadn't given my act much thought and standing on the side in my frock coat and army boots, I still had only a glimmering of what I was about to perpetrate on this auspicious occasion. Now the moment of truth was upon me. In a few moments Queen Elizabeth and her retinue would be taking their seats. When Bill asked me did I want any music . . . Good grief, I'd forgotten all about that, which underlines how unprepared I was. Music was the mainstay of the muddle that was to be my act. Hurriedly I asked Bill if the band could busk 'In a Monastery Garden'. He thought for a moment, and then nodded, already chuckling.

'I hope you're not going to sing,' he said.

'I haven't decided yet,' I replied, 'but keep playing, whatever I do.'

The show was ready to begin and in my mind my act was a riot. As a golfer imagines the shape of flight his golf ball will take before he makes a shot, so it was with me and my comedy routine, only in my case I visualised a hole in one. When the time came, I walked on to the stage to the introductory bars of 'In a Monastery Garden', made my way with dignity to the front, holding on to my cuff in the tradition of most tenors, and on cue sang, 'When the daylight's softly fading'. These were all the words I knew, but unlike Swansea and my salute to Strauss I had an exit strategy. After I'd sung the first line, I began to whistle, chirruping like a bird *à la* Ronnie Ronalde, a brilliant siffleur who whistled his way through this very number. Imitating birdsong here was the comedy that I'd imagined would bring the place down. In the background the band continued with the melody of 'In a Monastery Garden' and I was now on my fifth or sixth impression of a bird noise. I'd done a thrush, a blackbird and a robin, but most likely a bicycle that hadn't been oiled – this didn't get a titter, but I knew that I would get them with my next impression. It was my favourite, the crow. Slapping the back of my neck, I cawed loudly as a crow will inevitably do when you are standing over a putt; and I hopped across the stage, flapping up my coat tails to simulate flight. By this time mandatory cold sweat was trickling from my armpits. I was up to my waist and sinking rapidly in a swamp of indifference. I was dying a death – oh yes, there were stifled sniggers and hiccups, but these were from behind me. The audience, being the staff of Windsor Castle standing behind the seated royal party, were a frozen tableau, and the less reaction I got the more outrageous became my impressions. The band, always the first to smell blood, were now in no fit state to take any further interest in the monastery garden; even Bill had packed in his conducting and was leaning over the grand piano in hysterics. But from the audience there was nothing but a perplexed silence. At the end of my disgrace I whistled myself off with my final impression of a peacock with a bad leg. To their credit, Bill and the band applauded, but there was nothing from the front . . .

Afterwards I was told that Queen Elizabeth had remarked, 'He doesn't sing very well, does he?' Where have I heard that before? It was once the talk of Swansea. Needless to say, I have never been invited back to Windsor Castle.

Back at the office in Shepherd's Bush, the pressure of writing *The Goon Show* single-handed was having its effect on Spike. The sheer momentum of the weekly turnout became a burden too far and he asked me if I'd co-write it with him. As I had abdicated my responsibilities for *Educating Archie*, I wasn't too busy at the time; also it was clear to me that Spike was rushing downhill with no brakes. So I agreed.

It was great for the first twelve weeks; our combination was harmonious. Then the train hit the buffers. It was ludicrous, silly and should have died for lack of nourishment, but it flared up. The cause was trivial: whether it should be 'the' or 'and', or 'in' or 'out' – I can't remember what the actual word was, or whatever it was. By now our voices had increased in volume as if we were conversing with each other across the River Thames . . . Suddenly Spike picked up a heavy paperweight and threw it at me. Had I dodged, ducked or taken evasive action it would probably have killed me. As it was, I stood rooted to the spot with shock and it missed me by a mile, crashing through the window and hurtling down on to the pavement five floors below.

For a moment we stared at each other in amazement. Then I went down to the street and brought back the guided missile, which I plonked on Spike's desk, saying in a calm voice, 'Remember what day this is.' Pathetic and juvenile. Spike stared at me as if I'd just recited 'Humpty Dumpty', his eyes darting all over the place as if he was trying to remember where he was. His shirt was open at the neck and I noticed red spots on his chest which hadn't been there before. It was my first introduction to his manic depression, an illness that was never more than an arm's length away throughout the rest of his life.

After a couple of glasses of wine in Bertorelli's, we decided that we would write alternate weeks and this would give Spike plenty of leeway. This arrangement went along smoothly and perhaps I might have been writing *The Goon Show* with him to this day. However, my latent paranoia began to rear its ugly head and I felt that now that Spike was fully recovered and back on top form there was a slight resentment about my fortnightly offerings. Unfortunately I hadn't imagined it, and the whole situation boiled to a head one Sunday morning at rehearsal. I arrived just after the first read-through and with a sinking heart I surveyed their glum expressions. Then Peter Eton, the producer, shaking his head and obviously uncomfortable with the situation, said, 'It's not very funny, Eric.'

Spike, Harry Secombe and Peter Sellers were unable to meet my eyes and it was my turn for red spots on the chest.

'Perhaps if you put your heart and soul into it the lines will come alive,' I rasped.

My suspicions that I had outstayed my welcome as a writer were now confirmed. So what? It had never been my intention to write regularly for *The Goon Show* anyway. I had a pond full of my own fish to fry and the sooner I could get back to normal I would stay young, but I had never envisaged that my departure would be polluted by acrimony and ill feeling, so I merely told them that they had the script and unless there was a national electricity failure they had no option but to do it. As I turned to go, I fired my parting shot: 'I will never set foot in a *Goon Show* studio again.'

For the rest of the day I mooched around, not quite knowing whether to be relieved or feel hard done by, and at about seven o'clock in the evening I found myself in the Edgware Road.

It had always been the custom after each show for the cast to dine at the Czech restaurant in the Edgware Road. It was normally a hilarious get-together, at which a post mortem of the show was conducted. That night I dined alone at the Czech restaurant, early enough to be finished and homeward bound before the cast arrived. So far so good, but as I walked out into the street to hail a taxi, one pulled up in front of me. Before I'd had a chance to stop it the door swung open and Peter Sellers sprang out and made a beeline for me throwing his arms round me, just as Stanley might have done on seeing Livingstone; he was actually crying.

'Eric,' he said, 'that was the funniest show we've ever done.'

Immediately a great weight fell off my shoulders. What a generous gesture it had been for Peter to make this admission. There were now tears in my eyes but, being a Lancashire man, I had a ludicrous stubborn streak, and I reminded him of what I had said in rehearsal – that I would never walk into a *Goon Show* studio again. And I never did.

In June 1954 the BBC lost its monopoly and a new commercial station called ITV was born. I was asked to wet the baby's head by writing the first six Saturday-night shows. I felt like an artist presented with a brand-new canvas.

Harry Secombe was to star in the shows, supported by Norman

Vaughan and myself. Serious, twitchy and scared to death of the dark, Norman made me laugh just to look at him. I knew we were going to have fun. For each show I wrote an opening and two comedy sketches. However, one day I was driving to rehearsal and listening to the car radio while a military band was playing a march, and as the tune progressed I visualised Harry, Norman and me dressed in First World War khaki uniforms doing a marching display with rifles. By the time the military band came to an end, I was in no condition to drive. I had to pull on to the side of the road to dry my eyes, I was laughing so much. I jotted down the name of the march and half an hour later I was drilling Harry, Norman and myself, armed with broom handles, in a travesty of a military tattoo. This was the first of my 'silents'. It was simple and effective, and sadly it wasn't long before the routine was being pirated. It continued to be so on numerous summer-season shows for years and still no one had the courtesy to ask my permission – that is, until Ronnie Corbett phoned to ask if I had any objection to him including it in his coming summer season. I thanked him for enquiring and the next day he was in my office while I rehearsed him in the finer points of the routine. I declined payment, even though he insisted, and shooed him out of the office, wishing him luck. Two days later I received a box of my favourite cigars. I don't know how your marching routine went, but for your old-world courtesy, Ronnie, you will always have my admiration.

Each week we did a different 'silent' take-off. For instance, in those days there was a very popular, well-dressed act of three well-built men, attired immaculately in white tights, tabards and silvery wigs, and a fourth member of the group, a slight acrobatic girl, whom they gracefully flung from one side of the stage to the other; they just seemed to fling her this way and that and catch her with effortless ease and dead-pan faces. All accomplished with a serene dignity and backed by the gentle music of a Boccherini minuet, the act was called the Ganjou Brothers and Juanita. They were an obvious target for our next burlesque. We called ourselves the Cando Brothers and Youcaneater, played by an extremely balletic girl too light to cause any of us a hernia. Harry Norman and myself were in the white tights, tabards and silver wigs of the Ganjou Brothers, and there the resemblance ended; we could hardly be described as sophisticated and elegant.

Sadly there are no records of shows in those days – they have disappeared without trace – but all in all, as Val Parnell said, 'ITV couldn't have had a better send off.'

Recalling my disappointment at being rejected for flying duties in the RAF during the war, I began to wonder idly if, had I passed the medical, I would have been made of the right stuff to be a fighter pilot. There was only one way to find out. I applied to Fairoaks airfield in Chobham to take flying lessons.

Sitting in the rear cockpit of a Tiger Moth, I felt comfortable, as if I belonged. Granted, it wasn't a Spitfire, but most of the fighter pilots of the Second World War began their education in a Tiger Moth, or something like it. The instructor in the front cockpit put up his thumbs and we were off, lurching and bumping down the field like an old lady hurrying after a bus. Turning into the wind, we waited a second, and then the engine increased in volume and slowly we began the take-off. The little plane seemed eager to be done with the ground, and with a sigh of relief it became airborne. At 1,000 feet we levelled off, and over the side of the cockpit I saw fields, a small copse and doll's houses dotted haphazardly below me, and a long shining road all for the benefit of a solitary Dinky Toy motor car.

I'd flown many times before on commercial and military aircraft, but in all those trips my vision had been restricted to a small perspex window. Now, with my head sticking up into the sky, I could crane round all the points of the compass. The drone of the engine was comforting, and the wind on my face made me feel that I wanted this flight to go on for ever. We banked easily and turned on to what I was later to understand was the base leg and after a few more minutes we banked again and began our descent. The instructor switched off the engine and the propeller jiggled to a stop. It was uncanny: the only sound now was the keening of the wind in the wires and struts of the wings. I was gripped with a feeling of euphoria; without the laborious plodding of the engine, gliding down was even better. Ahead of me, the airfield was getting larger and larger, and when we were about twenty feet off the ground I had a sudden surge of panic as I wondered whether the instructor had fallen asleep; then we levelled out, with a shattering roar the engine came to life again and we began to climb slowly to start a second circuit of the airfield, until finally the instructor guided the plane down as gently as a butterfly with bad feet.

On climbing out of the cockpit, I was more exhilarated than I can ever remember. I was hooked.

After a few weeks I was doing most of the flying and I'm sure my instructor in the front cockpit was grateful for his half hour away from the office. Once I had mastered the take-offs and landings we were into a more advanced stage, and this really sent my blood racing. The spiralling down to earth in a spin, finally pushing the stick forward and gently pulling it back in a gut-wrenching swoop to bring us into clear air again – I soon became proficient in this manoeuvre. In fact when I took off I was eager to pull up the nose and kick over the rudder bar, but the instructor advised patience and I was now experienced enough to know that a spin at thirty feet was not advisable.

Two of my mates, Gabe Bryce and Eddie MacNamara, came over to my house and presented me with a Sidcot overall, a one-piece flying suit with a fur collar, on the back of which was written 'L. A. C. Sykes'. I was terribly proud of this gift, as Gabe Bryce was chief test pilot at Vickers Armstrong Siddeley in Weybridge, and Eddie one of the senior test pilots; both of them had been flying bombers during the war and Gabe, being a regular RAF pilot before the outbreak of war, was flying Blenheims until 1941. When I talked to him on the telephone a few weeks ago and he gave me that information, I said, 'Blenheims? They were death traps.' And he replied jauntily, 'Well, *I'm* still here . . .' It is hard for the young ones of today to visualise a lumbering Blenheim with the might and speed of the Messerschmitts of the all-powerful German Luftwaffe on its tail.

I now looked like a pilot. As well as my Sidcot, I possessed a leather flying helmet and goggles, and all that was lacking was a pair of flying boots. Frustratingly this footwear seemed to have disappeared off the face of the earth; no army and navy store, no ex-service shop, not even pawn shops possessed ex-RAF flying boots. There was only one thing for it. Later, during one of my *Sykes and A . . .* shows with Hattie Jacques and Richard Wattis, I wrote a dream sequence in which I was a fighter pilot, and wardrobe as usual came up trumps, and found a pair of genuine flying boots. I can't remember if the show went well but when it was over I furtively left the studio with a large suitcase. Wardrobe came to collect my gear and by the time they realised that they were two boots short I was halfway home, fully equipped for a life in the clouds.

On my next visit to Fairoaks, with helmet and goggles in my hand and flying boots on my feet, I purposefully strode over to my Tiger Moth like the lads at Biggin Hill in 1940. Somebody shouted my name – it was my old mucker Dick Emery, a comic who'd appeared many times in my shows on radio and television. He proudly took me over to examine his own aircraft. It was a monoplane, and to be quite frank I doubted whether it would ever get off the ground; and when he told me he'd bought it for just seventy pounds I only wondered where he'd got the money from. However, I knew that Dick had plenty of flying hours, as he'd had his pilot's licence for quite some time; in fact it was his suggestion that we should do a fly-past over Guildford, finishing with a mock dog fight. I didn't tell the instructor about the mock dog fight in case he had some objections; I told him only about our fly-past, and he chuckled. 'You are the pilot,' he said, and settled down for something a little different.

At 2,000 feet Dick and I flew alongside each other, banking gently above the spire of Guildford Cathedral in a geriatric impression of the Red Arrows. I imagined the traffic snarled up in Guildford High Street, pedestrians all craning up to stare at us with open admiration – that was all in my mind, but as I looked down I could see that we hadn't made the slightest difference to their stodgy lives. But now this was our 'finest hour'. I dropped behind Dick and although he twisted and turned he was still in my sights. Had I been a First World War pilot in a Sopwith Camel on the tail of a Red Baron, in two short bursts he would have been the dead Red Baron and I would now be in the history books.

From the ground it would have seemed as if we were hurtling through the air, but speed is all relative, and should you fly alongside another plane at the same speed you are in effect standing still; and if some enemy pilot was on your tail your chances of drawing an old-age pension would have been nil. For the first time, I blessed my little cotton socks that I had not left the ground during the war. As our dog fight continued, Dick's monoplane soared gracefully up into a loop, but I wasn't about to follow him. That kind of manoeuvre was beyond my competence, but I did have one trick up my sleeve: I went into a spin. There was, however, a slight difficulty. On a previous occasion when I'd spun the plane there had been an empty sky and fields below, but this time I was directly above the spire of Guildford Cathedral, which was spinning slowly around in my vision, growing ever bigger, and I was mesmerised. The instructor must have read the signs, as he kicked the rudder bar in the opposite direction and eased the stick forward. We were out of the spin, with barely a cigarette paper between us and the roof of the cathedral; and we swooped up into the sky. When we arrived back at Fairoaks, after climbing down from our Tiger Moth the instructor said, 'That's why you haven't been allowed to fly solo,' adding, 'These planes cost money.' But I had proved my point: I was capable of being a fighter pilot. Almost in the same breath, though, I had to admit that had I been I would now be a name on a cenotaph.

On 30 October 1954, my brother John and Irene became a family with a beautiful baby daughter they christened Janet. She was my first niece; a new branch was beginning to emerge on the family tree. By the time I got round to paying them a visit, she was already walking – how time flies! I accept that we have a tendency to use the word beautiful when there is a new baby, but in Janet's case it was well merited: she was going to be Miss Royton at least.

Career-wise apples continued to fall off the tree and the latest one was a real Cox's pippin: I was invited to write the comedy sketches for the pantomime *Mother Goose* at the London Palladium. This was promotion indeed, and another exciting project in a life which up to now had had more highlights than the aurora borealis.

Max Bygraves played Sammy, Richard Hearne (Mr Pastry) his mother and Peter Sellers the squire. Writing comedy sketches for television is merely a blueprint; the stage is the finished article. It is three-dimensional, and each comedy prop must be visible to two or three thousand people in the auditorium. My imagination joyfully accepted the challenge. For instance, in one sketch props provided an outsized washing machine, into which Sammy's mother falls head over heels and lands amongst items of clothing. Two jets of water are squirted in and everything begins to rotate, with Mr Pastry somersaulting, tossing and turning, wide-eyed with panic-stricken resignation, all to the accompaniment of music from the orchestra. The scene ended to a thunderclap of laughter and applause. Peter Sellers was suitably padded and bore a remarkable resemblance to Major Dennis Bloodnok of *The Goon Show*. Despite dire warnings from the management, he gave a performance that was never the same two nights running, and all the funnier for that.

Masterminding the whole production was Charlie Henry, the best comedy stage director in the business.

One of my proudest moment was when in rehearsal he said to me, 'You wrote this, didn't you?'

I nodded.

'Well, then,' he continued, 'just see they do it as you envisaged it.'

I stared at him with the look of an eight-year-old being asked to explain the theory of relativity.

'Direct it,' said Charlie, as he pushed me into the aisle. I couldn't believe it. I was a private who had been made up to sergeant major by the CO. What an opportunity for a lad from the cotton mills to direct a cast of top artists in the country at the number-one venue in theatreland. I walked down the aisle to the orchestra rail and clapped my hands for attention. They all stared at me and I began directing . . . By jingo, power is addictive.

As a matter of fact I was rather sorry when the show was ready for the public.

Making a house into a home takes time-consuming and back-breaking work. For some people it is a lifelong occupation, but for me I wanted it by the weekend. This was a very optimistic goal as it had taken us nearly a month to strip the wallpaper in the lounge. Working on the house was in a way moonlighting, and every morning I had a long-haul drive up to the office in London to get down on paper ideas that had made my night's sleep a 'stop-go' affair. Sadly most of my ideas conceived during my sleeping hours, hilarious at the time, did not bear scrutiny in the light of day. It was a punishing schedule, but every day we were one step nearer to the ideal home.

Edith and I were by now heartily sick of the lounge wall. Scrape, scrape, scrape, and then step down off my chair – Edith had the stepladder – wade knee deep through the debris of torn brown sickly wallpaper for a soothing cup of cocoa at the end of the day – and this was only the interior. Every house by law had at least one acre of land, most of which would be lawn, and every time I looked out of the window at ours the grass seemed to be longer; it was about two feet high and spring had yet to come. Sending the children out to play would be a hazard – we could possibly lose one of them. I began to wonder if an ordinary lawn mower could be had at the local auction rooms. For a moment I contemplated a scythe and my blood ran cold as I visualised myself making a determined sweep and cutting both legs off below the knee. There was a small swimming pool, only ten feet square, and full of cracked and chipped blue tiles; and an even smaller lily pond. A hedge dividing our property from the other half of the house was still to be planted . . .

There was only one drawback to our idyllic domesticity: our comfortable double bed wasn't king-sized but it was too big for the staircase. So Edith and I manhandled it into the lounge, where we slept amongst the scrapings of the nineteenth-century brown wallpaper. This was probably just as well, because after an evening's scraping we were both too tired to walk up the stairs anyway. However, I was determined to get that bed into its rightful place, and in an attempt to accomplish this I sawed down the banisters and half the newel post, but it still malevolently refused to make the trip. I was at that moment very close to being committed to a mental home. Thankfully Edith solved the problem by telephoning the experts, who simply took out the bedroom window and hauled up the stupid, stubborn piece of furniture before repairing the ruins of the staircase.

A few months later things were definitely on the up and up. The lawn outside, while not being exactly Wimbledon, didn't move in the wind. The hedge was waist high and the swimming pool clean but still unfit for water.

Into what was to be our dining room a new fireplace had been built with Plymouth stone. It was an attractive part of the room, and the walls were covered in knotty Canadian white pine. I was proud of my knotty white pine but I remember my father coming down from Oldham, surveying the dining-room walls and nodding approvingly before saying, 'Very nice, Eric. What colour wallpaper are you going to have?'

I was now fully domesticated, happy in the knowledge that I was providing Edith, Kathy and Susan with a delightful, much-desired residence in which to grow up. My career was steadily ascending and the future was inviting. I didn't really have the time to be complacent.

Edith and I attended a wedding reception in a pub off a narrow side street just before Westminster Bridge and behind Scotland Yard. As Big Ben boomed out twelve noon, I parked my Ford Fairlane. The first person I saw when I entered the pub was Bill

Kerr. We embraced as though he'd just come in from the outback, although we'd laughed all the way through yesterday afternoon in my office. The wine flowed freely and my glass was rarely empty . . . Net result: legless! Bill, who moved around on sturdy Australian legs, offered to take Edith and me home in his own car, a gesture she gladly accepted on my behalf.

At about seven in the evening I returned to earth, surprised and delighted to see Bill and his wife in my home. Edith handed me a cup of tea with a 'Wait until they've gone' look. I bitterly regretted my over-indulgence and the trouble I'd put Bill through, so I suggested we visit the local cinema. This was near by in the high street, but as the route was tricky and the roads now in a wintry condition I drove Bill's car. Weybridge at seven o'clock on a Saturday night was deserted and not a soul was to be seen; the only bright spot was the well-lit front of the cinema. We had the place to ourselves and the manager was glad to see us – being alone made him nervous. But the film wasn't up to much and I suspect the manager had edited it himself because of lack of interest. In any case, we left before the end to avoid the embarrassment of having to stand for the National Anthem. It was when we stepped into the street that the troubles began.

A young constable, notebook in hand, was standing by the car.

'Is this your car, sir?' were his first words, not 'What was the film like?' or 'Good evening.'

I didn't want to land Bill in anything, and so I said, 'It's not my car, but I was driving.'

'Can I see your licence, sir?' he said.

I took out my driving licence. The night air was raw and we were all frozen. It was a ludicrous situation. There was only our car parked in front of the cinema – in fact it was the only car in Weybridge at the time, and the cinema was the only well-lit area. He took down my name and address and Bill's name and address, and I added my date of birth in case he'd missed anything. He snapped his notebook shut and instructed me to report to the police station at ten o'clock on Monday morning.

When I reported first thing on Monday morning, a sergeant was sitting behind a desk with the busy policeman standing at his elbow.

'Right, now,' said the sergeant, looking sideways at the constable, who placed a sheet of paper before him.

'Mr Sykes was parked outside the cinema.'

'Yes,' interrupted the sergeant testily. 'That isn't a crime, is it?'

'No,' replied the constable. 'But on the insurance form here it says,' and he quoted, '"Any person possessing a driving licence is legally entitled to drive the car."'

'Well, then,' interrupted the sergeant once again. 'What's the problem?'

'Ah,' spouted the constable triumphantly, 'If we read on, it says, "providing they are Mr Bill Kerr and his wife Margaret Kerr".'

The sergeant sighed and shook his head. Then he covered the second bit with his hand. 'Now read it,' he ordered.

The young copper began, 'Any person with a current driving licence can legally drive this car.' He couldn't read the rest of it because it was hidden under the sergeant's enormous hand.

'Yes, but . . .' rallied the constable.

'Never mind the "buts". Mr Sykes here possesses a current driving licence, I presume.'

I nodded.

'Case solved,' said the sergeant, dismissing the constable with a peremptory wave of his hand before turning to me. 'I hear you're off to Africa later this week with your old mate Harry Secombe.'

'Yes,' I said.

'I wish I was coming with you,' he said. 'I could do with a few laughs.'

That's the way things were done in those halcyon days – all that fuss and red tape over my parking. To make the event even more trivial, when I returned home there was a telephone call from my office to the effect that Scotland Yard had phoned to ask if Mr Sykes would come and shift his Ford Fairlane as the squad cars couldn't get out.

*   *   *

Harry Secombe and I had been invited to entertain British troops in Kenya during the dreadful days of the Mau Mau. Although I'd been to North Africa to entertain troops when I was writing for Frankie Howerd, for me Kenya, Uganda, and Rhodesia were the real Africa, with the jungles and the animals, from the skittish impala to the arrogant lions and the dignified elephant herds.

Why we accepted the invitation in the first place I will never know – perhaps it was for the same reason that people climb Everest. After a short domestic flight from London to Rome, we transferred to a South African Airways long-haul flight on the first leg of our journey to Nairobi. Picking up speed on a runway prior to take-off still exhilarated me. The gentle rise as we took to the air, followed by the clunk of the wheels retracting . . . It was amazing. How the dickens did such a heavy load of metal, passengers and baggage manage to get off the ground at all and continue to be hauled up to 30,000 feet by four puny propellers? It was beyond my comprehension. After all, I was a child of gas lamps and trams, and motor cars were a novelty.

As I looked out of my window at the faraway land below, something caught my eye: the outer port propeller, now visible, had stopped. I looked away – it wasn't my pigeon – but when I looked back a tongue of flame spurted out. Now that was odd. It had never struck me that I could be part of a tragedy; nevertheless I stood up quickly and looked over the seat in front of me so that I could tell one of the air hostesses, but they all seemed to have disappeared. Passengers from the opposite side of the aisle were coming across to have a look at the now flaming engine. Then a harassed hostess pushed her way through them, bearing a glass of something or other, which she took through the door to the flight deck, and when I looked out of the window again there was no sign of fire, which left me wondering what could possibly have been in the glass. Then a voice through the tannoy ordered us to return to our seats and to fasten our safety belts, and an Australian voice announced that this was the captain, there was a slight problem and we would be returning to Rome airport, but there was no cause for alarm.

Harry was staring straight ahead, white-faced. I nudged him and said, 'Don't worry – if the worst comes to the worst, you'll get top billing.'

This broke the ice, but what I saw when I looked out of the window sent a rush of panic through me. We were now banking in large concentric circles and streams of white vapour were shooting out of the engines. Instantly I guessed that this was high-octane fuel being jettisoned to lessen the danger of fire on landing. All the cabin crew were strapped into their seats and there was an ominous calm as we made our final approach. Below us a couple of fire tenders and ambulances were racing along the runway. I also noticed two nuns – good grief, they'd thought of everything. But after a slight bump we were back where we belonged, on the ground.

Later in a hotel in Rome our flight crew walked in to the reception area, recognised Harry and came over to speak to us. The Aussie captain, a short sturdy man, mopped his forehead and said, 'That was a pretty close shave.'

'Well, you made a great landing,' said Harry.

The captain shook his head. 'I didn't land it,' he replied. 'I left that to my second dicky.' The tall pilot by his side was embarrassed, but brightened when the captain added, 'I'm too old for this lark.'

Harry and I looked at each other, wondering if he was serious. Then I asked about the stewardess hurrying up the aisle with a glass.

The captain said, 'That was brandy for me. I needed it to pull myself together.'

I was aghast until a stewardess whispered into my ear, 'Coca-Cola.'

The engine that had caught fire was a write-off and had to be sent to South Africa for a replacement. We had three days of sightseeing in Rome, thanks to the hospitality of South African Airways. When we finally took off again, it was quite boring. I could have used another three days in Rome, when we eventually arrived at Nairobi airport. We were met by a portly, elderly, grey-haired lady, who sternly informed us that we were three days behind schedule, hurrying us through the reception area to another runway and giving us no chance to reply. Outside, a man in a leather flying jacket was standing under the wing of a light aircraft, and here was another problem: he flatly refused to fly, as the weather forecast was decidedly 'iffy'. 'Rubbish,' said our martinet, thrusting our suitcases aboard. The pilot tried to reason with her, but he might as well have saved his breath. She helped us both into the back seat and insisted on fastening our seat belts herself, but when she turned away I loosened mine in order to breathe. Through the open door we saw the pilot, still on the tarmac, hair streaming out behind him and then blowing forward as he turned this way and that for somebody to appeal to. The stern lady shouted 'Oi!' so loudly that the little plane shivered. 'Are you going to take this thing up or shall I?' Reluctantly the pilot climbed aboard, hoping to reason with her, but it was a lost cause. Furiously he fastened his seat belt, preparing the plane for flight with bad grace. A handful of hailstones rattled against the windscreen and he stared severely at her as if she was responsible. She didn't appear to have noticed anything amiss as she applied her lipstick, looking at her reflection in her powder compact.

The pilot jabbed a button and the propeller jerked spasmodically, but stopped after one coughing circuit. Then he pressed again, and this time with a puff of smoke, instantly whisked away by the wind, the propeller began to rotate into a blur. A man in oilskins forced his way to the plane to remove the chocks and immediately we were committed. The pilot released the brake and all systems were go. Buffeted and chivvied by the unruly gusts, we travelled down the runway and turned into the wind in preparation for take-off. Up to then the plane had been in capricious mood as it had hopped skipped and skidded downwind to this point, but now the skylarks were over and battle was joined as the gutsy little aircraft bustled its way into the gale, surging forward gratefully when the wind dropped and picking up speed until the next head-on wind attack – how long was this runway, for God's sake? Harry and I unfastened our seat belts so that we could crane forward. Four heads lined up together as we tried to increase speed, eight eyes desperately squinting through the windscreen, fearfully anticipating the last goodbye, but we still couldn't get airborne. In fact we travelled so far that

I almost relaxed into thinking that we were going all the way by road. Suddenly Harry and I were jerked back into our seats as the doughty little plane shot up into the air on the back of a force-ten gust. Although we were airborne, it seemed to me that we were flying slowly, but this was only my fevered imagination. Thank goodness we'd strapped ourselves in again.

I can honestly say that I have never been so frightened in all my life. The tops of the jungle were below us, and then Harry crushed me into a corner as the plane banked and the jungle filled our window. Then it was my turn to crush into Harry as the plane banked the other way and for a brief moment I could have sworn that we were flying upside down. How the pilot managed to keep control is beyond me. I'd given up; I knew with certainty that we would be tomorrow's headlines. Then in a flash, as if we'd turned a corner, all was tranquil. The wind had tired itself out and, apart from the steady drone of the engines, all was calm. Were we dead? It had all been so sudden. The pilot, on seeing a long flat strip of grass between the trees, was only too glad to get the darn thing down. When the plane finally came to a stop, the iron maiden alighted as if she'd just had a trip round the bay. The pilot got down, Harry jumped down and I was about to follow him when he lurched forward to kiss the ground. This small gesture moved me, and I was about to put my arm round his shoulders in a token of respect when he turned to me, cursing. He hadn't been kissing the grass at all – he'd tripped on the root of a tree.

We were still twenty minutes from our destination, but after a quick call on the radio the pilot turned to us to say, 'They're sending out a car for you.'

Half an hour later we were on our way to an army camp. The pilot cramped himself in with us and I asked him, 'What about your aeroplane?'

'Sod that,' he replied. 'According to the radio message, we are right in the middle of bandit country and the Mau Mau wouldn't pass up a chance of learning to fly.'

Eventually we reached the army camp, to be greeted by a captain ruefully shaking his head and saying, 'You've had a wasted journey.'

Harry and I looked at each other. We'd survived a near-tragedy in Rome, a horrendous flight in a small aeroplane and possibly even death by Mau Mau – it was all too much. The captain went on to explain that had we been here two days ago we would have had troops to entertain, but as it was they were all on red alert and moving into a part of the country where Harry had tripped over a tree root. In other words, our adventures had all been for naught. After a riotous night in an empty officers' mess, we were taken to the airport and thence back to England, arriving whiter than we had been when we had left it, which in the circumstances was not too surprising.

Our pantomime *Mother Goose*, at the London Palladium, had been more successful than we had at first envisaged, and Max Bygraves was asked to appear on the *Ed Sullivan Show* in New York and re-enact a scene with the Goose, played by Harry Cranley. I was also invited so that I could concoct a short excerpt for television. The pantomime must have impressed whoever it was because we were booked for not just one appearance but also another, to be televised on two consecutive Sundays.

We were totally unprepared for the hot summer that was baking New York, when we arrived. The steamy, humid atmosphere lay like an electric blanket over Broadway and I wondered how New Yorkers managed to put up with it. The simple answer is they didn't; when summer approached, they found relief somewhere else. Walking fifty yards was enough before you had to seek the refuge of an air-conditioned bar or a shop, but this was tantamount to walking into a refrigerator, and so one was left with a choice between hypothermia or heat prostration. So, following the example of indigenous New Yorkers, Max, Harry and I booked ourselves into a holiday camp in the Catskill Mountains, where there was good food and swimming pools, and most importantly it was several degrees cooler.

The *Ed Sullivan Show* was one of the most popular television offerings in America and our scene from the pantomime was a novelty. Ed's researchers constantly trawled the world for acts such as ours.

Underneath the stage at the Palace Theatre was a large square, flanked on all sides by the dressing rooms, and it was here that most of the acts to appear on the show that night gathered, as all theatricals tend to do in order to swap anecdotes. Max and I stood on the fringe, spellbound, as Bing Crosby and the Mills Brothers, along with known faces and unremembered names, topped each other for laughs. It was during one of these hilarious moments that Harry Cranley chose to emerge from his room. Just as if the fire bell had clanged, the laughter was cut off as everybody turned to look at him. He was wearing a knee-length paisley dressing gown, below which were two thin white-stockinged legs that terminated in two enormous webbed goose feet. The body of his goose outfit was upstairs in the wings so that he could slip it over his head and waddle on to the stage, but the distinguished cast staring at him couldn't make head or tail of this ashen-faced apparition and especially his king-sized feet. Was he an eccentric tap dancer or had he escaped from somewhere? Quick as a flash, Harry shot back into his room, slamming the door behind him, and the spell was broken as the opening bars of the show boomed out through the tannoy and the dumbfounded group of celebrities dispersed to their rooms to prepare for their entrances. Max's scene with the Goose wasn't exactly a riot, but it wasn't a flop either. It was just that the theatre-going New Yorkers seemed bemused by an intelligent young man chatting amiably to an overweight goose. They were unaware that they were witnessing the most celebrated goose in English panto-mime – in fact it was a role handed down to him by his father, who trained him diligently before handing over his feathers.

On the Monday morning following the television show, Max and I were taking a leisurely stroll around the pool at the holiday camp, and were slightly surprised by the friendliness shown to us by the other inmates, their smiles and the 'Hi fellas' as we passed by. All was revealed when two blokes stopped and said, 'You were great last night,' and it suddenly dawned on us that most of the camp had been watching *The Ed Sullivan Show*. That brought happy smiles to our faces as we accepted the plaudits from an ever-growing crowd; but we were soon brought down to earth when one of them, admiration shining out of his bulging eyes, said, 'Gee, which one of you two guys is the duck?' And that wasn't the end of it. Gathered about one of the sunbathers lying on recliners round the pool was quite a sizeable crowd, mostly girls. Max and I looked at each other with the same thought in mind and we were right. Sprawling indolently like a Caesar of Ancient Rome was the thin, white, emaciated body of Harry Cranley in a too-big pair of faded blue swimming trunks, signing autographs. Probably for the first time in his life, he was the hit, the heartthrob; his northern accent was most likely being interpreted as aristocratic.

'Harry,' I said, bending over him, 'why don't you put on your goose legs and stroll round the pool?'

And for a moment his eyes lit up, until he realised that I was taking the mickey, but he was definitely the king of the holiday camp – so much so that on his next Sunday's appearance on Ed's show he attempted a cocky jig as he entered, and in doing so tripped himself up. Max had to lift him to his feet, almost pulling off the goose head from Harry's shoulders. Oh, how the mighty had fallen! Luckily the audience took it as part of the show. He even got a round of applause when he laid his enormous egg.

While in America, I received a telegram from England. The sender was Jack Hylton, one of our foremost band leaders, and it read, 'Can you write for Tony Hancock?' How's that for brevity? If I cabled back 'Yes' I'd be committed to whatever Jack had in mind for me. After some thought, I replied, 'Your telegram too vague. Returning next week.'

On my arrival in England I contacted him and he asked me if I would write a series of six shows, starring Tony Hancock, for Rediffusion Television. I said yes and once again I was embroiled in the machinery of production. I first recruited June Whitfield, a real all-weather trouper, solid and dependable; and, like Hattie Jacques, she could take a mundane word such as 'Well' and imbue it with a dozen different nuances. In fact with her experience she was the ideal foil to Tony and would be able to look after him in his debut into the turbulent waters of television. After all, it was a quantum leap from radio, where you had the protection of a script which you read into a microphone and the listening audience made up their own minds as to the substance behind the voice; in television there is no escape. Luckily Tony, with his pomposity and his hesitant delivery, conceived and honed in *Educating Archie*, was received joyously by the viewing public, and after six weeks we all felt that it had been a job well done and Tony had begun a new chapter in his career.

Before the applause from Tony's last show had died down, I had been scripting another edition of the *Howerd Crowd* and taking a day off to appear on a panel game, *What's My Line?* Up to now it had been a hectic year in which I hadn't had much time to smell the coffee or enjoy an uninterrupted night's sleep; but I was about to change all that. I had nothing in the pipeline with regards to work, so until the next offer came I was on a fence-mending mission of being Daddy.

Once again my optimistic forecasts were blown out of the water. Will I never learn? Complacency is not an asset and once again I stuck my chin out, with the inevitable conclusion: wallop. At dinner one night I sat down to eat, assessing the joys and stability of family life – an attractive wife, two beautiful daughters and, added to that we had a very intelligent Yugoslavian au pair girl, a black Labrador and a Welsh collie. I believe we had two cats but as they are not my favourite animals I didn't bother them and in return they had nothing to do with me. I counted my blessings between mouthfuls with a feeling of content, when suddenly a wave of nausea passed through me. It was so unexpected and I couldn't face the rest of my egg and chips. Edith took one look at me and led me to a mirror. I was appalled: my face was the colour of an over-ripe lemon. She quickly sent for the medicine man.

Dr Scurlock, whom I had never met, took one look at me and ordered me to bed before he'd even opened his bag of tricks. When I was propped up by my pillows he entered the room and Edith brought a chair for him to sit on, while she stood behind it like the trained nurse she used to be. As he began to examine me, I studied his face. His eyes appeared to be constantly startled, as if he had only just discovered that he had the ability to cure people. After a long meticulous examination, he delivered his verdict: I had infectious hepatitis.

The following morning he visited me again, with a long list of foods that were to be avoided at all costs. They were set down in alphabetical order, starting off with avocado pear. Straight away I was intrigued, as it was the first time in my life that I'd even heard of it, and I was determined that as soon as I was ambulant again an avocado pear and I would say hello. My spirits nosedived at the Bs: butter was next on the list. My first ambition, to have my own overcoat, had evaporated when it disappeared after only fifteen minutes' wear, and now my second, to eat as much butter as I wanted, was to be snatched from my grasp. My world was crumbling. No fats, no eggs, no alcohol – good grief, I was a comedy writer, not a marathon runner; and what's more, these substances were banned for the next ten months. But on the bright side, it couldn't have happened at a better time, as I was unemployed or, as we say in our profession 'resting'; and if lying in bed for twenty-four hours a day is not resting, I don't know what is.

My one great disappointment was that Kathy and Susan were forbidden to enter my bedroom. I might just as well have been working on a series. Then I thought, Hang on. Had I been overdoing it, had I been rushing through when the lights were at red? I began to realise that this hepatitis wasn't just an accident, it had been ordained, and for the first time I relaxed. It was one of the mysterious ways in which my mother worked, and I knew that when I was fit for duty once again she'd let me know. As if she was listening to my thoughts, the phone rang.

'Is that you, Eric?'

Thank goodness, it was a man's voice; otherwise I might have thought that my mother had found another way of getting in touch. I paused, wondering whether to answer as a butler or a foreign national.

'Ronnie Waldman here.'

I was flattered. Ronnie was the Head of Light Entertainment on television, a man I greatly admired – a real pro.

'Ronnie,' I said. I was curious. We'd met before, but only on the usual BBC junket circuit. 'What can I do for you?' I asked, and like the man he was he came straight to the point.

'How would you like to write a pantomime?' he asked. 'One hour, cast who you like and don't worry about the cost.'

My brain went immediately into overdrive, but I was somewhat wary, so I said, 'Can I think it over first? I am in bed, you see.'

'It's nearly lunchtime,' he chuckled. 'It's all right for some.' And before I could explain about my infirmity, he went on, 'Take all the time you want and I'll wait for your call.' And that was that.

About ten days later, I returned his call. 'I'll do it,' I said.

'Good man,' said Ronnie. He was canny and read the situation correctly. He knew in that ten days I'd have written most of the pantomime. He was almost right: I'd written all of it.

In a bout of meditation, I recalled how Peter Brough's chauffeur had driven me off to Harley Street, where I was hospitalised for six weeks; and now here I was in bed again. What mysterious ways my mother employs to chart my career. When my circuit is in danger of overheating, she simply switches it off. Bless you, Harriet.

ARCHIVE

December 1955. Eric is to be paid £400 for *Pantomania*.

Ernest Maxin would be producing the show, which was to be called *Pantomania*, and he sent me a list of suggestions for cast members. They included Kenneth Horne, Peter Sellers, Gilbert Harding, Sir Mortimer Wheeler, Jack Payne, Mrs Dale and either the Grove family or the Lyon family. These ideas from Ernest were certainly acceptable, but I headed my list with Sylvia Peters, Mary Malcolm, and especially Hattie Jacques.

After several more weeks I was declared fit for duty, I was back in a rehearsal room, although still wobbly on my pins, fat free and non-alcoholic. I began to knock things into shape, and eventually the final rehearsal was moving along smoothly. In fact it was going too well; according to stage superstition, a good dress rehearsal is usually a bad omen for the opening night. I needed something to happen. And it did.

ARCHIVE

December 1955. During a rehearsal of *Pantomania* Eric burnt his wrist as he attempted to extinguish Hattie Jacques' inflamed dress.

This archive is inaccurate in that I did not attempt to put the flames out; I succeeded. And it wasn't my wrist; both my hands were burnt, and the BBC should have been thankful that I wasn't the pianist.

Hat, in the role of Fairy Godmother, a vision in white, with a glistening wand in her hand and a sparkling tiara, glided on from the wings, her entrance made more spectacular by a flash that coincided with her appearance. Unfortunately she glided a little too close to the flash and immediately the net at the bottom of her dress caught fire. Luckily I was only a yard away when it happened, and so I was able to beat out the flames and this is when my admiration for her went up into the premier league. During all the time I was beating out the flames like a demented washerwoman, she didn't panic; she stood perfectly still until the flames were just wisps of smoke. Then she smiled and, looking down at me, she giggled and said, 'How's that for an entrance?' What a lady!

At lunchtime it was amusing to watch the distinguished cast in the BBC canteen, all wearing paper hats, standing in line, plates in hand, as they edged forward to receive their dollop of good cheer and, incongruously, a cracker. Trust the BBC to think of everything.

In those early pioneering days of pictures in the home we didn't have the luxury of recording the show in October for transmission on Christmas Day. On the one time of the year when it is important for a Daddy to be at home, I would again be missing. Susan wouldn't mind, as she was too young, but Edith and Kathy might have had something to say about it.

The show went better than I had envisaged, and the whole of the cast shared an enormous smile when it was over. Ronnie Waldman threw an after-the-show party, from which I excused myself, as alcohol was still on my banned list. In any case, I was already high on adrenalin and I couldn't wait to get home.

At the bottom of our garden was a four-foot hedge separating our property from the third hole of St George's Hill Golf Club. It was a short hole and many a member standing on the tee would strike the ball so erratically that it landed in our garden. Like any loyal subject, I'd throw the ball on to the fairway or hand it back to the member as he or she approached the hedge. Most members thanked me, but others took me for the gardener and gave me a perfunctory nod. After a few months of this unpaid ball spotting, I had a bright idea. Instead of returning the golf balls, I'd place them in a bucket and when I'd reached the grand total of fifty I would take up the game, which was beginning to appeal to me. It was a good summer and my bucket was already half full, by which time the golfers were starting to look over the hedge suspiciously. Frustratingly, in many cases they could see the little ball on our land but no one about to return it. Only when they had moved on to the next hole did I put down my binoculars, rush madly down the garden to the homeless golf ball and dash madly back to drop it in the bucket. When I counted my haul during the autumn I had enough balls to play at least three rounds. All I needed now were the golf clubs.

In Lower Regent Street there was a Railway Lost Property office and from there I bought a leather golf bag, complete with a full set of clubs, for seventeen pounds ten shillings. It turned out to be the best investment of my life, apart from my marriage licence.

I went to Bill Cox, the professional at Fulwell Golf Club, and as I'd now made several appearances on television Bill greeted me like an old friend, asking what he could do for me. I told him that I wanted to take up golf, and so we made our way to the practice ground, where he asked me to swing my driver. I swung the club three or four times before Bill stopped me to ask how long I'd been playing. I replied that I hadn't played as yet; this was my first day.

'Yes,' he said. 'But you played as a boy, didn't you?'

I told him I didn't, and he looked astounded. 'Wait here.' And with that he hurried off, returning with three of his young assistants.

'Watch this man swing,' he said and I duly obliged. The assistants were looking at me with wide eyes. 'A professional swing', said Bill, 'with twenty-four-handicap hands.' Then he placed a ball on a tee and said, 'Hit that.'

I addressed the ball and with my professional swing I missed it altogether. Two more misbegotten swings, without coming even close to frightening the ball, and Bill said, 'That'll be enough for today,' and the meeting broke up.

Now fifty years later the professional at Fulwell is Nigel Turner and when we play together I still have the remnants of a professional swing, but to add to my problems I now have a twenty-four-handicap leg. Nevertheless I take pride in my consistency: after every game I always manage to leave myself plenty of room for improvement.

This was my introduction to a game which can be played by most people, where age doesn't necessarily become a liability – it only means that your handicap goes up and your hopes go down. It is a healthy pastime out in the fresh air, walking being one of the best forms of exercise. If golf was made compulsory, I maintain that we would be a much healthier nation.

My golfing experiences would fill a book, but I leave that to others better qualified: Peter Alliss, Brian Barnes, Tommy Horton or even Johnny Miller, Nick Price, Sevvy Ballesteros, Dave Thomas – I've played with them all . . . What did I tell you? I've written one page already.

ARCHIVE

5 June 1956. Eric appears on the Billy Cotton Band Show. He does so again on 23 October (both editions produced from the King's Theatre, Hammersmith).

I always looked forward with eager anticipation to being on with Billy Cotton and his band. It would inevitably end up with Bill, the band and in many cases myself laughing too much to carry on. Bill was a larger-than-life character, a red-cheeked jovial man, solid as a pill box. If I was being attacked by a howling mob, Billy would be the man I'd like to have by my side or better still in front of me. I would go on the show for nothing to be with him – indeed the BBC fee I was getting was such that it wouldn't have been much of a hardship.

Our friendship with Bernard and Elizabeth Powell blossomed and our two families took a holiday together in St Mawes, a beautiful little spot in Cornwall. Our daughters, Kathy and Susan, and Helen and Deborah Powell were ideal companions and I spent some time watching their antics through the lens of my movie camera.

Bernard, however, worried me a little. He was white and drawn, and although he enjoyed the shenanigans of the kiddies and chatted amusingly across the dinner table, I had a feeling that something was wrong. I noticed that he was taking aspirins as if they were Smarties, which set the alarm bells ringing. I asked him if he was all right. 'Oh, just a little pain in my knee,' he said and changed the subject.

My fears were confirmed when in an unguarded moment I caught Elizabeth eyeing him with grave concern. This was obviously more than a slight pain in the knee.

Ronnie Waldman, still eulogising about *Pantomania*, decided it was time for another extravaganza, and from the tranquillity of St Mawes and the worry over Bernard I was thrust into a maelstrom of comedy sketches, ludicrous situations and fun.

The show was to be one hour long and would come from the Earls Court Exhibition Hall. I had written the show to illustrate the pitfalls and disasters of the last get-together before the opening night; ergo I called it *Dress Rehearsal*. In addition to the usual top-liners of the BBC, I'd written myself in as an inept, interfering director, a part I felt well equipped to do as I was now back on the sauce.

The show exceeded all my expectations: it was the hit of that Saturday night. This was not too surprising, as the only opposition was the potter's wheel and the epilogue, and as neither of these got many laughs we walked it.

A few minutes after the closing credits, Ronnie dashed round to my dressing room, his face alight like a child waking up on his birthday. Congratulating me, he said, 'When's the next one?' I looked at him blankly and he said, 'Well, this was *Dress Rehearsal* and they'll be waiting for the *Opening Night*,' and I knew my ship had come in.

A few days later I called Bernard Powell to invite him and Elizabeth to dinner. It was Elizabeth who answered the phone, and the way she said hello filled me with a sense of foreboding. 'What's the matter?' I asked, and she told me that Bernard had cancer. I was shocked, but not entirely surprised. I asked what hospital he was in but Elizabeth said he was at home, and when I asked if I could speak to him she said, 'Sadly he's in bed and I'm afraid . . .' She broke off, unable to speak. I put down the phone and in ten minutes I was on my way to London. As the films of our holiday had been developed, I put my projector in the car, thinking that perhaps he would enjoy half an hour or so of respite.

Elizabeth let me in the front door and I could see from her red eyes that events were now critical. She told me to prepare myself for a shock as he was heavily drugged and he might not recognise me. I put down my projector and the roll of film – I knew that was now out of the question. When I walked into Bernard's bedroom, my nostrils were assailed by a ghastly smell, not the sweet cloying stench of putrefaction pervading Normandy during the war, but the more pungent smell of the insidious evil of malignancy. Only Bernard's head was visible on the pillow, but it wasn't the Bernard that I knew: it was almost a skull. This rotten, decomposing body was an obscenity. I felt my hackles rising, angry at the medical profession for allowing such suffering. Poor Bernard had ceased being human; he was an experiment. When I returned home, Edith asked me how he was and I replied, 'He won't last the week.' Mercifully I was right. He passed away two days later.

What a travesty of justice! He was only thirty years old, on the brink of an illustrious career as a world-famous painter. He had never tasted alcohol in his life, nor had he smoked. As I write this I am looking at my portrait which he painted, remembering his ready wit and more importantly his zest for life.

Every year at Sunningdale Golf Club they hosted the Bowmaker Tournament. This was a two-day event, where actors and comedians would partner a professional golfer. It was a very cherished date in my golf calendar, and I'll just relate one incident that happened to me on the fifth hole.

John Jacobs, one of our Ryder Cup heroes, was my partner that day. I should point out that on the fifth hole, about sixty yards from the green, there is a very small round pond, and I was there, gazing down at my ball, shimmering back at me from under the water, which was only about twelve inches deep. As I stared at it morosely, John, at my elbow, suggested I lift it out and take a penalty drop, forgetting that I am a Lancashire lad and they don't come more stubborn than that. I took a sand wedge from my caddie and John was horrified. I was wearing a pair of new yellow slacks and he pointed out to me that it would be stupid to get them all splashed with water; why didn't I simply lift it out? Seeing that I was determined to go ahead, he moved out of range of the calamity he was expecting. It was like a dream come true: the blade of my sand wedge cut through the water with scarcely a ripple and the ball flew gracefully out, up into the air, and landed on the green; the water had hardly moved. John, of course, was so astounded that he was speechless. We finished the hole and walked over to the sixth tee, to be met by Peter Alliss and Guy Wolstenholme, two of our finest golfers, who, having had to wait, had walked over from the adjoining fairway to have a chat. John couldn't wait to tell them of the miracle shot he had just seen and I felt ten foot tall. I teed up and with a beautiful swing I launched the ball straight as a die – unfortunately straight as a die all along the ground into the deep rough only fifteen yards away. John turned to Peter and Guy and said, 'Of course, he's no good on dry land.'

A few weeks later, still at the Earls Court Exhibition Hall, I was halfway through the final rehearsal of *Opening Night*, when I had a sudden vision of Ronnie rushing into the dressing room and saying, '*Dress Rehearsal, Opening Night*, they'll all be waiting for it – *Closing Night*' and I was already wishing I hadn't started all this.

At the end of the dress rehearsal Ronnie came round to my dressing room with a stranger in his wake whom he introduced as Tom Sloan, his assistant, and then he complimented me on the run-through, citing this and that for special mention, which I accepted with a stony face.

'What's the matter?' he said.

'It runs only fifty minutes,' I replied.

'So?' queried Ronnie.

'You're paying me for an hour and I am ten minutes short.'

Ronnie was relieved – he must have thought that one of my relatives had just died.

'Eric,' he said, 'keep it exactly as it is. Whatever you do, don't pad it. It is a perfect fifty minutes.' He went on, 'I'll put something in that ten minutes to fill in the hour.'

I felt as if a weight had been lifted off my shoulders and Ronnie and his colleague took their leave. Seconds later the door opened again and Tom Sloan popped his head into the room. 'You're over-indulged,' he said, and he closed the door before I could react. What a thing to say to an artist ten minutes before he is due to walk on the stage!

I needn't have worried. The fifty minutes were stretched into one hour by the volume of laughs, and the wonderful performances of the cast. They were the same newsreaders and presenters as in *Dress*

Rehearsal, but on this occasion all their stiffness was gone. They were now accustomed to hearing laughs, which is a rare commodity when you are a newsreader, and they revelled in letting their hair down. Once again we rang the bell and I was vindicated.

For the record, Tom Sloan followed Ronnie Waldman some time later as Head of Light Entertainment, and from then on the great ship of comedy settled in the water.

All work and no play makes Jack a dull boy, but as I'm not Jack it doesn't really concern me.

I was invited one day to take part in a charity cricket match that would take place in a couple of weeks on a Sunday. I said, 'I suppose so,' casually, as if I was doing them a favour, but in reality only death would have prevented me from walking out on to the cricket field. I hadn't played the game since I was a boy at school, when I even played in the first eleven. It sounds grand, but we played on coconut matting and had only one pad to guard the legs of the whole team. I really fancied myself as a wicket keeper, although my gloves had belonged to Auntie Emmy and were stuffed with cotton wool – not a brilliant CV.

I can't remember what ground it was, but when I entered the dressing room in my brand-new whites the first thing I saw was a pair of wicket keeper's gloves lying on a bench. What an omen! On finding out that we were to field first, I sat on them and proceeded to strap on a pair of pads lying in a corner. One for each leg – what a luxury!

The rest of our team arrived straight from the nearest pub and it was like old home week – Harry Secombe, Tony Hancock, Sid James, Terry-Thomas and Trevor Howard, all proud to be taking the field in each other's company. No one queried me sitting there like a real wicket keeper, so I relaxed. When the bell went, we took the field and the applause was gratifying. The sun was shining from a blue background – a perfect day for cricket.

When the other side's opening partnership strode up to the wicket, I recognised one of them, a young Brian Close, a genuine professional cricketer. I took off my glove in order to shake hands, but he stared down at it as if I was asking him for an entrance fee. Then he took guard and gazed round the field, as if this game was for real. Sid James, in the slips, whispered to me, 'Have you ever seen him bowl?' He was referring to Tony Hancock, who was our opening bowler.

I shook my head.

'He's slow,' he said. 'Not a spin bowler, but a slow bowler.'

Tony's idea of a run-up was a leisurely amble and his first ball surprised the batsman. It bounced twice before it reached him and it was so wide that he ignored it. Behind the wicket, where I'd been standing back, I had to walk forward to pick it up. The crowd rustled, assuming it was just a warm-up. For the next ball I stood up to the wicket. This delivery was a better length and Brian Close could have belted it easily for six. Instead he lifted his bat to let it go through, which surprised me, and the ball belted me, bang in my 'no-go area'. So green was I to cricket at this level that to me a box was something to hold chocolates or where our betters supped champagne as they watched the match; a wicket keeper's box strapped round his loins to protect his wherewithals was some piece of equipment I'd never even heard of. I went down in agony, clutching myself as gently as I could. They took off my pads and I was helped off the field. What an ignominious beginning! It was the end of my debut. Even worse, Harry Secombe phoned Edith to tell her that I was all right.

Over the subsequent years I kept wicket – fully protected by a wicket keeper's box – against other cricketers of eminence, my favourite being Freddie Trueman. One time we played on the same side and I took his first over like a professional.

It must be added that I was standing well back; in fact I wasn't far from standing in the crowd, so I edged forward to be level with the slips. But unfortunately in his second over he broke my finger. The moment I took the ball I realised that I was lucky to get away with a broken finger – it could have taken my arm off. The top of my middle digit was leaning tiredly to one side and the lads crowded round me sympathetically.

Freddie ambled up and said, 'What's the matter with thee?' I showed him the finger.

'What's up with it?' he said.

'It's bent,' I replied with some asperity.

'All actors are bent,' he said and strolled away. It was the second time I had had to make an ignominious retreat. I still wasn't used to playing with a hard ball.

A couple of years later, Freddie was being interviewed on radio and when asked, 'Who was the bravest wicket keeper you bowled to?' without hesitation he shot back, 'Eric Sykes.' There was a stunned pause from the interviewer, and then Fred went on, 'He stopped every ball with his chest.' What a bowler, and what a joy to be in his company!

Another friend of mine, Brian Johnston, also an ardent keeper, would invariably ask me on meeting if I was still behind the timbers. In fact whenever we chanced to be on the same side we tossed a coin to decide who donned the gloves. In one particular match I won the toss and it wasn't long before I wished I hadn't, and here's why. Keith Miller, an Australian who oozed talent and charisma, was one of the greatest all-rounders the game has ever known. I'd seen him bat, but his spin bowling was still a mystery to me. He ambled three paces up to the wicket and bowled at such a slow pace that the batsman raised his bat to let it go through and even I had no difficulty in stopping it. What was slightly disconcerting was that the slip cordon, all professionals, were standing twenty yards behind me, but I wasn't left in the dark for too long. Again Keith ambled up to the stumps and from the moment his arm was at its height the action was all a blur. The short ball zoomed off the track like a guided missile, the batsman ducked, I ducked and the fielder on the boundary didn't even bother to unfold his arms as the ball sailed over his head into the crowd.

Keith's drinking partner was our own Denis Compton, who not only played football for Arsenal but was one of our finest batsmen in the days before they introduced helmets, which was fortunate for Dennis because he made money from Brylcreem adverts, and when he introduced me to Keith after the match we paid homage to a few watering holes. It was the one and only time I enjoyed the company of Keith Miller, but ever after that day when Denis and I met we invariably toasted Keith's health.

In 1957 Val Parnell and Lew Grade asked me if I was prepared to write a one-hour Saturday night show billed as *Val Parnell's Saturday Spectacular presented by Eric Sykes*.

'When do you want it?' I asked, but Val put his hand up.

'The second *Spectacular* will be a fortnight later.'

'So you want two one-hour shows?' I asked.

Val again shook his head. 'That's only number two. Number three will be three weeks after that, and so on and so on.'

By now I was beginning to get cold feet. I knew instinctively that I was standing on the edge of a minefield.

'To put it bluntly, Eric,' said Val: 'twenty-six one-hour shows – one a fortnight.'

I did a quick mental sum in my head and I was appalled. 'That schedule is a whole year, Val,' I gasped, and I got up, ready to leave. I knew of easier ways to commit suicide.

'Sit down, Eric,' said Val, smiling in an avuncular way. 'You haven't heard the best bit . . .' He nodded at Lew Grade, who carried on, 'We'll guarantee that the star of each show will have inter-national stature – Jack Benny, Bob Hope, George Burns and Gracie Allen, Bing Crosby.'

He didn't need to go on. Mentioning Bing Crosby was like saying to an alcoholic, 'They're open.' I could see myself singing a duet with Bing, a soft-shoe shuffle with George Burns, a feed for Jack Benny – I couldn't wait to start work. Naturally every show would have to be constructed round the star, but until I knew who it was I couldn't begin. However, as a back-up for each show I naturally cast Hattie Jacques; she was dependable and adaptable, and over the years we had built up a rapport with the public. I was fortunate also that Jack Parnell would be in charge of our regular orchestra. Jack was Val's nephew, but I didn't let that put me off; he was an extremely talented musician, having taught himself to play an acceptable Bach on the piano and probably other things as well. He was better known as the celebrated drummer in Ted Heath's band. Jack was now conducting the band on my shows and also appearing in sketches – tall and lugubrious, he was a ready-made foil.

Our first guest was the internationally famous American Mel Tormé, which wasn't a bad way to get off the mark. He was a singer, a composer, a musician, and, what delighted me most of all, one of the great jazz drummers of the time, which gave me my first idea. I modestly confessed that I too could do a bit with the sticks and on two occasions in the past Jack and I had performed together on drums, and this time there would be three of us. On the Monday Mel arrived in the rehearsal room, where I had arranged for nine tom-toms to be placed in line, three in front of Jack, three in front of Mel and three in front of me.

'What do you suggest, man?' said Mel. I lifted my sticks to go into my routine, expecting Jack to join me, but he didn't – he was looking out of the window, completely disinterested. When I'd finished, Mel stared at me like an athlete watching a one-legged man making his way upstairs. Then he looked at Jack and said, 'How about this?' and he began a steady drum beat which entailed throwing up a stick and catching it; then he moved easily into a more complicated routine until both of his sticks were just a blur. As he introduced his two other tom-toms, it was smooth, capturing me completely – such a beautiful exposition, tailored like a dinner jacket cut in Savile Row. It was my turn to look at him as if he'd just stepped on my hamster.

'See you later, folks,' said Mel and he disappeared.

When he'd gone, I turned to Jack. 'What was all that about?' I said.

Jack was unperturbed, 'It's an old routine and it always works,' he said.

Casually picking up his sticks, he began pounding the drums, doing exactly the same routine as Mel had done ten minutes ago, even throwing up his stick and catching it.

There was nothing else for it: I'd gone to the well and it was up to me to bring back a bucket of water. Jack sympathised with my innocence and took me through the routine bar by bar until his eyes were glazed, but he appreciated my limitations. We went through it again, and again, until my eyes were glazed as well and the porter was waiting to lock up the rehearsal room. But it was worth it.

Mel, having his own singing act, would only be appearing with Jack and me for the drum routine, so from that Monday we hadn't seen him until ten minutes before the show on Saturday night. With Mel in the middle, Jack and I on each side of him, we began a synchronised drumming act. Mel was pleasantly surprised. He and Jack could go through this in their sleep, but I had to concentrate like mad, only relaxing when Mel said, 'You're counting, man.' And I certainly was, eight bars of this and sixteen bars of that, and when we'd finished the applause brought me out of my trance – it was tumultuous. We all took several bows and Mel went on to his own singing act to finish the show. Afterwards he came up to me with a rueful grin on his face, saying that the drum routine had been a hard act to follow. I shrugged and replied, 'You've only got yourself to blame – how's that for being cool, man?'

The phone rang with the news that my next international star was to be Edmund Hockridge, another singer, and, bless him, he would be the last to describe himself as international, although he was big in this country. As it turned out, not only were his songs a success; he was a tremendous asset in our comedy sketches. In fact, to be perfectly honest, he got more laughs than me, and with the help of Hattie and a couple more stalwarts this show was actually a better one than Mel's debut. Hey ho, only twenty-four more shows to do.

Show number three, another singer. My heart sank. This was supposed to be a comedy show, not a musical. But at least it was Joan Regan, one of my particular favourites. She had great warmth in her singing voice and, more importantly to the show, a wonderful sense of humour, which made it easier for me to write the comedy sketches around her. Joan's infectious laugh caused Hattie to giggle, making the audience laugh even more, which had little to do with my writing, but a comedy show without laughs is like fried fish without chips, and so like a good trouper I joined in the laughter myself, making a mental note that I could always use the sketches in a later show.

Sadly Joan Regan was the last drip from the well of world-famous stars, and I was left dangling at the end of my bungy jump. Whatever happened to Jack Benny, George Burns, Bing Crosby, et al? I rang up my old mate Peter Sellers, one facet of his enormous talent being his inability to sing. I told him that Jack Benny had broken his leg and was unable to appear, and would he help me out of a hole? He not only helped me out of it; he brushed me down. It was one of our most hilarious shows to date, so much so that the following fortnight he was asked back by popular demand – at least that's what I told him. I still had over twenty more shows to write, but looking on the bright side I saw I had a choice: I could either carry on or jump off Beachy Head, and as I wasn't afraid of heights it was an inviting prospect. Wearily, I was still adrift in an open boat with no sign of a beach.

Val Parnell and Lew Grade had disappeared over the horizon and I was hung out to dry. My stars for future Saturday nights included Tommy Steele, Lonnie Donegan and Dickie Valentine; then that line of seasoned entertainers petered out, and I was left with my own colleagues: Hattie Jacques; the following two weeks Deryck Guyler; two unknowns whom I introduced as being my own discovery, one of whom played the spoons rather well; and another one of my mates; Spike Milligan, who starred in two of the shows. By this time I was ten years older and failing rapidly. I would have starred anyone who fancied it; I even contemplated walking up and down Oxford Street with a sandwich board asking for volunteers. Secretly I still held a very faint flicker of hope that either Val or Lew would walk through the door and introduce me to Bing Crosby, but as I had only four more shows left the flicker began to dim.

Sitting in my armchair at home, I looked at Taffy, my very clever Welsh collie, who was giving me the once-over with a 'What shall we do next?' look in his eyes, and a wild crazy thought sprang to mind – why not? It hadn't done Lassie's career any harm. It was a forlorn hope. Once I mentioned the show he slunk from the room with his tail between his legs; he was a working dog, not a freak. Incidentally Lassie was the star of many American films, a barking success, but typically of Americans they tend to climb on the band-wagon and overload it – as in *One Hundred and One Dalmatians*, for instance. How I survived the twenty-six shows with all my faculties intact is beyond me, and here I must thank all my friends who rallied round to save me from the knacker's yard.

As for my home life, it had been another year of 'When did you last see your father?'

ARCHIVE

3 September 1957. Eric appears again on the *Billy Cotton Band Show* from Earls Court.

With regard to this latest archive it would have been easier for all of us if Bill had put me under contract himself.

In the new year, 1958, I was determined to spend as much time as I could with my family and establish my rightful place in the pecking order as Dad.

However, the best-laid plans etc. . . . I answered the phone and after a few minutes' conversation my hopes of regaining the head of the table were dashed again. I was offered a part in a big extrava-ganza at the London Palladium, entitled *Large as Life*, starring Harry Secombe, second top Terry-Thomas, third on the bill yours truly and Hattie fourth, backed by a top-of-the-market supporting cast. The old timers G. H. Elliott, Hettie King and Dickie Henderson Senior were to close the first half, and there were also a couple of speciality acts, singers and of course dancers. Once again I found myself trying to find a humble way of breaking the news to Edith.

After three or four weeks' rehearsal, we were ready to face the public, all of us on high octane. The success of the show depended largely on the comedy and, as I'd written all the sketches, I would have to take my share of the responsibility should we close in two weeks. I need not have worried. The show was a hit from the first night, promising the prospect of a very long run. All very well, but I still had to break the news to Edith; there is more to marriage than providing a home to live in. As my evenings would be occupied for the foreseeable future, Edith said it would be a good time to take another trip to Canada with the two kiddies and on this occasion to show off our second child, Susan. I did wonder, though, in an idle moment, if Edith was going to Canada every time we had a child, whether I could afford to have any more.

As is always the case, once they had gone I missed them, and wandered through the deserted house, tidying up teddy bears and dolls in the girls' bedroom, already totting up the weeks before I'd see them again.

The schedule of appearances at the London Palladium was punishing and when the show finally came off after eight months I was well into middle age. It amazes me now when I look back how we managed it: thirteen shows a week, twice nightly and three times on Saturdays; no time off for holidays, injury was frowned upon and illness unforgivable, unless you could manage to be ill in your own time. For instance, one evening during the second house a gentleman went into Harry's dressing room – very mysterious, and the plot thickened when I popped in to see Harry after the show for our usual relaxing glass of something or other: his dresser told me that he'd already gone off to hospital to have his haemorrhoids seen to. I was astonished: Harry had never mentioned this before, he was extremely active on stage and he hadn't been walking stiffly with a white face.

'I didn't know Harry had piles,' I said.

'Neither did Harry,' replied his dresser, 'until that specialist came to see him tonight.'

Amazingly, as if nothing had happened, Harry was on stage the following night. Had I dreamt it all? He'd been through a painful operation – or had he? When I asked Harry about it, he just said in a joky voice, 'The show must go on, folks.'

Can you imagine the same scenario in the present day? Someone in Harry's position would be convalescing for at least a week or two and when he did return he would be performing with a slight limp.

Some weeks later it was my turn to have an accident. I was in my garden using a pickaxe to tear out some roots, I missed one swing completely and the half of the axe caught me in the ribs. It was agony; every breath was an intense stab of pain. I knew for certain that I'd broken at least three or four ribs. Bent double, I lurched towards the house like Quasimodo just finishing the marathon. As I was the only one in residence, I phoned for an ambulance. Naturally, as each word was uttered painfully, they must have thought I had only seconds to live, so the response was quite quick. When the ambulance men jumped from their cab, eager to deal with an emergency, they stopped dead in their tracks when they saw me, disappointed not to see any blood. However, as they had to go back to the hospital anyway, they agreed to take me with them and I was diagnosed as having two cracked ribs. I would have breathed a sigh of relief if I could. With my chest strapped tightly and a bottleful of painkillers, I, like Harry, was on stage that same night.

Fortunately we were the only casualties, which is remarkable in a way, considering the number of people concerned. It was a healthy bunch who crowded through the stage door on their way home every night in their street clothes, reminding me of when the cotton mills closed for the day and the workers streamed out through the gates.

My evenings were occupied by the theatre; only the days were a problem . . . As in the past, my downward slide into self-pity was abruptly halted, this time by a brainwave: I would decorate a small room on the ground floor of our new home. It was indeed small, no more than ten or twelve feet square, lit by one window looking across the patio.

I painted one whole wall a brilliant red and built bookshelves with a large opening in the middle to house a television set. All the shelves I painted a gleaming white, and against the red background they were stunningly attractive; it seemed a shame to spoil the effect with books. My next inspiration was to paste a coloured map of the world on one side. It covered the whole wall beautifully, right down to the skirting board, but my pièce de résistance was the ceiling. I went down to the grocer's and asked for their eggboxes, papier-mâché squares that held eggs like miniature tank traps. These I painted alternately black and white and stuck them on the ceiling, resembling a giant chessboard. Not only was it pleasing to the eye but it added to the acoustics. Finally I filled the shelves with my *Encyclopaedia Britannica*, a full set of the Dialogues of Plato, which up to this present day I have yet to venture reading. Steinbeck, Joseph Conrad, Hemingway and my favourite of all books, *The Fountainhead* by Ayn Rand, helped to fill the rest of my shelves. I even installed a television set in the space that I had prepared. I was really chuffed by my handiwork. I had never before considered myself a practical man and this interior design of mine was a one-off – a flash in the old fryer. I couldn't wait to see Kathy's and Susan's faces when they saw it.

The great day of my family's return finally arrived. I drove them home in my Ford Fairlane, a long blue American car with whitewall tyres, Kathy and Susan in the back seat and Edith next to me in the front. I thought my luxury transport would make a good impression, but nobody said anything. I'd overlooked the fact that cars like this one were ten a penny on Canadian roads. I wasn't despondent as I had another surprise up my sleeve – my newly decorated room at home. I can't tell you how gratified I was when Kathy and Susan gazed round with big eyes as if they had stepped into a fairy grotto. Edith also gave the place the once-over with, I thought, mild appreciation until she noticed the eggboxes on the ceiling. Then she looked at me enquiringly, and on the spur of the moment I said they helped the acoustics, but I overstated my case by saying, 'As they have in theatres.' Almost as the words left my mouth, I realised what a load of cobblers I'd just imparted and Edith left the room trying to recall if she had ever seen a theatre with eggboxes on the ceiling.

Still, it was good to have them back and, leaving them to unpack and settle themselves, I made my nightly trip to the London Palladium, which we were now accepting as a way of life.

About this time we took on a new au pair, our fourth from Europe, and again we landed on our feet. She was a treasure, young, hard-working, diligent and speaking better English than I did, but the most important ingredient was that Kathy and Susan immediately took a shine to her. On 2 July 1958 our third daughter, Julie Louise, was born. It was a hard birth for Edith, so much so she and Julie were hospitalised for six weeks. During this period our au pair girl became indispensable, as I was at the Palladium each evening and most of Saturday. It was a great relief to know that my children, Kathy and Susan, were being well looked after while Edith was in hospital with Julie.

When the show finally closed, after eight months, I was left with mixed memories. The discipline backstage was strict – in fact I maintain that the Palladium was the only concentration camp where the inmates were allowed out during the day – but in spite of this I benefited greatly from the experience.

Again my plans for regaining my throne at home went spiralling up the flue. The week after *Large as Life* closed at the Palladium, we opened with the same show at the Opera House Manchester. This meant living in a hotel, but after the last show every Saturday night Harry, Hattie and I caught the night train to London, arriving in the still, dark hours of Sunday. When I reached Weybridge, it took me all my willpower to haul myself upstairs to bed, trying not to wake Edith, and by the time I surfaced it was almost bedtime for Kathy and Susan, so it is understandable that they both regarded me as some kind of distant relative. Julie was concerned only with appeasing her hunger and sleeping. My work was keeping me away, but at least it removed the worry of financing a further walkabout of Canada with Julie.

After eight weeks, the run of the Opera House Manchester was done and I looked forward to getting to know my children better, not just standing around gazing at them all as if they were the Crown jewels. Of one thing I was certain: my family was big enough and Julie would be my youngest. I was adamant – no more.

So much for being adamant . . . Soon Edith was pregnant again – doesn't anybody ever listen to me? – and on 2 June 1959 David Kurt was born to us. Glory be, what a turn-up for the book – a boy at last! But at what cost – again it was a painful birth for Edith. Two dangerous births were warning enough and David was definitely to be the last of the tribe.

When Edith brought him home, my mind wandered into the realms of parenthood. In a few years I would be able to talk to my son and he would understand. Even as the thought passed through my mind, it fell over a stumbling block. – When Julie was about two years old, she adopted David and incredibly took on her little shoulders the responsibility for bringing him up. There must be a place for me somewhere, I thought.

ARCHIVE

February 1959. Eric Maschwitz wrote to Eric Sykes to explain why the BBC had vetoed an impersonation of Lord Montgomery that Eric had included in a script for the forthcoming *Gala Opening*.

I had written *Gala Opening* for television and in the show a well-known personage was to open a fete and say a few words to the assembly. I had not only written the part of this honoured guest for Lord Montgomery but sent him a copy of the script, after which I received a telephone call from the noble lord asking me various questions about the role. I explained to him that it was chiefly a comedy, to which he replied that he didn't think that it was very funny, and it was at this stage the conversation began to crumble. I can't recall who took the part, but it certainly was not an impersonation of Lord Montgomery, as the only value to the show would have been his presence. Without his name the show was received moderately. You can't win 'em all.

Beryl Taylor, my cousin – daughter of Aunt Marie and Uncle Stan – whom I hadn't seen since she was a toddler before the war, was now a comely lass of twenty-two and, more to the point, Edith, Kathy and Susan and I rumbled up north to attend her wedding. How they shoot up when you're not looking! Kathy and Susan were to be bridesmaids, old enough to be excited and fastidious in their appearance. Beryl now had a younger brother, Brian, whose function was to usher friends and neighbours into their pews. He was extremely shy, which was not so surprising as it was one of his dad's most endearing qualities.

Aunt Marie, covered in confetti, cried and Uncle Stan, similarly confettied, blew his nose when the happy couple drove off in a clatter of tin cans. I took Aunt Marie for a drive in my shiny new car round the leafy lanes of New Longton as a special treat, and in no time at all she was back to her old smiling self in case any of her neighbours were watching.

Leslie Grade, the younger brother of Lew Grade and Bernard Delfont, telephoned and asked me if I'd write a one-off comedy television show for Jane Russell. Immediately I was on my guard, as I was still limping from the twenty-six one-hour shows starring Bing Crosby, Frank Sinatra and Jack Benny who never materialised. On this occasion I'd first make sure that it was the same Jane Russell I had in mind and not some transvestite from the north of England whom the Grade agency was representing.

Leslie assured me that it was the real American Jane Russell who had leapt through the screen courtesy of a film called *The Outlaw*. Nonetheless I wasn't fully convinced that I could write for her until we'd had a chance to talk to each other, which we did at Heathrow on her arrival. 'She was charming, attractive and with a glorious sense of humour – we were now Jane and Eric, and she was the genuine article. Speaking to Leslie when I returned home, I agreed to write the show. And when was the transmission date? There was quite a silence before he said, 'Next Saturday night.' Here was the five-card trick again; I'd agreed to something that wasn't what it seemed – one day in which to write the show, followed by five days of rehearsal, culminating in a live show on Saturday night peak time. I was scribbling away through Saturday night and most of Sunday. At ten thirty on Monday morning I handed Jane the script, which she read, punctuating the lines with roars of hearty laughter

. . . Bingo! We were into rehearsal and by that first evening we were dog tired but happy. We were both on the same wavelength, altering and smoothing the words I'd put down on paper and changing our reaction to them in the process from chuckles to hysterical laughter, probably brought on by sheer exhaustion. Even the lady companion who had arrived with Jane agreed it was a real humdinger. On the Tuesday we actually enjoyed the rehearsal, still chopping and changing, cementing the good bits and improving the mediocre.

After the rehearsal I had a phone call from Leslie Grade.

'Eric,' he said, without a suitable preamble, 'will you take a cut?'

I was flabbergasted. Perhaps I had misinterpreted. 'What's the problem, Leslie?' I said.

'This woman is asking so much money, bringing a companion over with her and everything.'

'I'm sorry,' I replied, 'but didn't you ascertain all this when you made the deal with her?'

'Will you take a cut in your salary?'

'No,' I said firmly.

'Do me a favour, Eric.'

'I've already done you a favour, Leslie, by writing the show, rehearsing it and all in a few days.'

There was a long pause before he broke the silence. 'So you won't take a cut?'

'No,' I said. 'And that's final.'

But Leslie had the last word. 'OK,' he said, 'but you'll never work again.'

Frightening words to an actor or comedian, but to a writer it was just empty rhetoric. A writer will always put words to paper, and if those words are good enough he will be an on-going commodity, so I wasn't worried at all by Leslie's threat. With the advent of television comedy, writers were emerging like weeds through a crack in the pavement.

The good side of it was that Jane was so happy with the success of the show that Saturday that she bought me an exquisite gold cigarette lighter.

*　　*　　*

Harry Secombe and I were once again bound for Africa, not to entertain the troops but to accept an invitation from the commanding officer of the King's African Rifles in Uganda to spend a week with him at his headquarters in Jinja.

Our first evening was an experience I will never forget. After dinner, the CO, Harry and I were seated on the veranda sipping our chotapegs – known in English as pure malt whisky – while we stared in awe at an African thunderstorm of gigantic proportions; we had front-row seats in an opera that would have made Wagner at his most ferocious seem more like Handel in a gentle mood. The pitch black was lit intermittently by flashes of lightning, followed by crashes of thunder that threatened our eardrums. It wasn't the sullen, cold rain of England; this was a merciless, straight-down-no-messing rain.

No more than fifty yards across the dirt parade ground was a jungle. As a clear fork of pure light flashed down there was a gout of flame as a tree was stricken, and then soon extinguished by the sheer wall of water. The CO stood up and bade us goodnight – he'd seen it all before. Harry and I were mesmerised; it was like a re-run of our war experiences. But after our long journey we eventually decided that enough was enough – the bottle was empty anyway – and we made our way to our various rooms. No doubt there would be a storm like this another night.

Two officers had been detailed to chaperone us during our stay, and when we mentioned the storm, one of them said coolly, 'Oh, was it raining?'

This exchange was made in a jolting jeep as we were taken out to visit a tribe of Karamojongs, a hostile lot by all accounts. On arrival we were greeted by a very tall man brandishing a spear in one hand and carrying a three-legged stool in the other; and to complete our astonishment, he was wearing not a stitch of clothing . . . Welcome to Karamoja. I didn't like the way he was jabbing his spear in my direction, but one of the officers waved him away and he backed off. It turned out that this wasn't just a mystery tour for our benefit; the two officers were looking round for likely lads – it was the custom to recruit from the Karamojongs to the King's

African Rifles for six months' National Service. Once they'd been selected, the most difficult obstacle to overcome was getting them to don uniform, as they'd never been accustomed to wearing anything at all. Khaki shorts on heads, legs through armholes of their battledress tunics and socks being beyond their comprehension had long since ceased to raise a smile from the clothing department. The King's African Rifles had more serious problems on their hands regarding their National Servicemen of Karamoja: when they finally ended their National Service and returned to their tribe, they were dying, as if struck down by an epidemic. The cause of this catastrophe was a mystery until the reason became clear: while serving in the King's African Rifles they drank clean pure water, but on returning to Karamoja they resumed their old way of life and drank from the streams and rivers, which were heavily polluted with all kinds of bugs and killer germs. While we were with the Karamojongs, Harry took out his camera and was about to take a picture when a spear thudded into the ground beside him and the officers decided it was time to leave.

The following day, in the velvet blackness before dawn, the four of us left for the wilderness. Our jeep was festooned with water bags and we also carried food packs, an emergency precaution, I hoped – I assumed we would be back before nightfall. The object was to observe some of the wildlife, and in less than an hour in the half-light of dawn I could make out the vague shapes and horns of wildebeest. A few more miles and the morning sun lit the vast plains. About fifty yards to our right, a pack of hyenas lolloped past, taking no notice of our jeep, intent on some far-off assignation. Jeff, one of the officers, told us that hyenas normally worked in pairs; a pack was unusual and as we were going in the same direction we might see some action.

Far ahead was a little dot. As we approached, it took on the shape of an African wrapped in a blanket, carrying only a wooden staff. We stopped by him and exchanged *jambo*s. It was weird – where had he come from and where was he bound? This wild endless plain was a hunting ground for beasts and here was this man strolling along as if he was going to the pictures. The officer spoke to him in Swahili and I recognised the word '*simba*', meaning lion. The man immediately turned and pointed in the direction taken by the hyena pack, and with a nod of his head he continued on his way. To where and why was beyond my comprehension. I watched him go, and the vast plain stretching before him was endless.

Sometime later, we saw the first signs of action. A few large blackbirds were circling in the sky, trying to work up an appetite for whatever was on offer. Ahead of us, a herd of wildebeest were nervously cropping the stark grass, knowing that they were the breakfast. We stopped but kept the engine running; we were the only false note in a normal routine. Suddenly to our right two young lions burst out of the undergrowth and from the opposite direction two more streaked forward. The wildebeest stirred in panic – all except one that had been selected. The kill was almost clinical, and as the lions struggled to drag the dead beast into a clump of bushes the herd calmly carried on munching the grass; it was as if they knew that they were not now on the menu. The hyenas furtively edged towards the corpse after the lions had had their fill; they were next in the pecking order, then the vultures, followed by the insects. There would be nothing left by the next day.

This protocol amongst the wild was a daily feature, every creature knowing their place in the scale of things. And what of the African walking blithely along with only a staff to protect himself? We who are supposed to be civilised were as much out of our depth in these surroundings as he would have been in Tesco – it is such a small world and yet we are so far apart.

On our last day in Jinja, the CO suggested that I might take the morning parade. Before I could laugh it off, he nodded towards the soldiers of the King's African Rifles, who were formed up and standing at ease. Why not? For all they knew, I could be the Prime Minister. As I walked from the CO's hut, a command rang out: 'Parade! Parade! SHUN!' There were several explosions of dust as two ranks of boots came to attention. The sergeant major, a massive fellow well over six feet, followed me along the ranks with drawn sword. I think I made a pretty professional job of it, having been in the forces myself during the war; I even walked with my hands behind my back like royalty. When I finished my inspection, I addressed the sergeant major. 'A very good turnout indeed,' and, carried away by my own deception, I added, 'You may dismiss the parade.' A flicker of uncertainty passed over his wooden expression, but he'd had his orders and as I turned to go he dismissed the men. When I returned to the bungalow, straight backed, head high, I was brought down to earth when the colonel, smiling said, 'You were out of order there, old boy. You shouldn't have dismissed them – they'll be off for the whole day now.' It was then that the reason for the puzzlement on the sergeant major's face became obvious.

'He's a good man,' were the colonel's parting words. 'We could do with more soldiers like Sergeant Major Idi Amin.'

This enormous sergeant major was later promoted to lieutenant, then to captain, and from there took an amazing leap to the super-heights of general, his last appointment being dictator of all Uganda. While in these heady realms of power, he ruled with a malignancy and a vileness that shocked the world until he was finally deposed and inexplicably placed under house arrest in exile, allowed to live out his life in luxury.

Had I revisited Uganda in the days of his prime, I might have ended a promising career as a snack for the crocodiles.

Tom Sloan, being the Head of Light Entertainment, was allocated two offices on the fourth floor of the newly built Television Centre, one for his secretary and the adjoining one with a window over-looking the inner circle of BBC television, at the centre of which was an enormous stone statue of a naked man. I don't think it is significant, but Tom's window faced his backside. It was here that a meeting was to take place. Tom was flanked by two of his producers. One of them sported a little goatee beard, and also smoked a pipe – the trappings of an intellectual or a prat.

Tom opened the meeting, announcing 'the reason I've called you all together'.

We glanced at each other. We were only three sitting opposite the tribunal: Denis Norden, Frank Muir and myself.

'We've got to find new writers,' Sloan went on.

The one with the pipe nodded sagely. My mind went back to the abortive meeting with the heads of drama who couldn't quite get to grips with Frankie Howerd's comedy play and I knew instinctively that Tom and his companions were cut from the same cloth.

As there was no answer to this banal statement of the obvious, he posed a direct question. 'What do you think of the idea that we institute a school for young writers?'

Inwardly I groaned. It wasn't a new idea; it had been tried and discarded in America years ago. If this scheme went ahead, I could imagine the types granted entry to this College of Humour – close friends, relatives and toadies. On completing a course in this school for comedy writers, they would doubtless be promoted immediately to comedy producers, and in a year or two would be convening meetings to discuss the dearth of comedy scriptwriters – and the heavy wheels of bureaucracy would sink even deeper into the mire.

'When BBC television is up and running,' I said, 'you won't have the impossible task of looking for new writers. Budding writers will find you – you'll be inundated with comedy scripts.'

The one with the goatee beard glanced at Tom Sloan, and as Tom appeared to be impressed, he nodded as well. It seemed as if I'd hit the nail on the head. Their pond was unruffled; all they had to do was sit and wait for the deluge.

But I hadn't finished. 'The only difficulty,' I went on, 'is finding somebody competent, with enough experience of comedy writing, to decide which of these scripts should be accepted and developed and which should be destined for the waste-paper basket.'

Tom Sloan leaned forward with a triumphant proclamation, 'Who better than you three?'

So this was the purpose of the meeting. I had spread my two kings on the table, which he trumped with a royal flush. I immediately ruled myself out, as I was desperately hoping to find new writers for Associated London Scripts and this, I declared, would be a conflict of interests. This left Denis and Frank, who, after some persuasion, agreed to a part-time occupation as Consultants and Advisors on Comedy to the BBC – and thank Harriet, my guardian angel, for that, as future events will illustrate, although cynics will doubtless put it down to another example of coincidence.

At home an idea was beginning to take shape in my mind. I would take the family off for a holiday in Alassio, Italy. I knew the place well, having spent a few weeks there when Max Bygraves was making a programme entitled *Roman Holiday*. I'd written the script, but as the show was mainly a musical my contribution was minimal, and I was able to enjoy the delights of Alassio with Edith. Why shouldn't we visit Alassio again, this time for a complete rest? After all, it was high time we had a family holiday, away from the disruptions of my work. Edith and the children were over the moon and my stock was high . . . for the moment.

Alassio was a children's paradise. David, still too young to walk, learned to manage a few wobbly steps on the soft sands before falling down on all fours to crawl madly into the sea. Luckily Italian mamas adore children and there were never fewer than four of these black-frocked angels watching David as if he was one of their own. There was always one of them stalking David to lift him out of the surf and haul him back to the start line; and then the whole procedure would begin again. If for some reason or other the Italians had other things to do, either Edith or I took over the rescuing of our youngest from the mighty ocean.

In the evenings Edith and I were free to go out for dinner, as we had one of our au pair girls to attend to the littl'uns. On one of these occasions we visited the roof gardens of the Café Roma, where we enjoyed the food and the wine under the black Italian sky, speckled with active, twinkling stars, a reminder that the skies over Britain were once like this. This idyllic moment was rudely interrupted when the compère of what was to be a cabaret whispered into the microphone words that escaped me and then in a loud voice announced 'Eric Sykes'. The other diners applauded. I stood and acknowledged their reception, but as I sat down again they were still applauding and the compère was beckoning me to the stand. I took the microphone, and after a handful of gags and a few chuckles

I returned to my table, where Edith had already gathered up her handbag – a sure sign that my time was up. I paid the bill and we left before the cabaret.

A few evenings later, we decided that we would eat again at the roof garden of the Café Roma; after all, the food had been good and the night sky enchanting. So when we'd seen the children off to bed, we made tracks. We had just finished our meal with a coffee and sambuca, when someone leaned over my shoulder. It was the compère, and this time he whispered in my ear, would it be OK to announce me again? I shook my head and told him that I had come here to eat, not to entertain; and after settling the bill, Edith and I took the lift down to the foyer. But before we reached the exit, a well-dressed man introduced himself as one of the Berini brothers, who owned the Café Roma. He asked me if I'd enjoyed the meal, and I said it was delicious. He looked at me steadily for a moment; then, as if the thought had just occurred to him, he made me an offer. I knew immediately that this wasn't just a casual enquiry; I realised then that inviting me to the microphone had been a clumsy audition and obviously I'd passed. The deal was to do the cabaret on Saturday night, for which I would receive 10 per cent of the takings. It was tempting. My brain was racing like a one-legged tortoise. What the heck, it was only for one night, and to be quite mercenary, 10 per cent of the takings would go a long way to providing for my entourage of six at the best hotel in Alassio. I held out my hand and he shook it. My Saturday evening was catered for.

As Edith and I walked back to the hotel, I explained what had transpired. She was silent throughout, and when I'd finished, my enthusiasm evaporated. If only I'd talked to her before rushing in, falling over myself to accept . . . It was too late now: I'd shaken hands, and in those days that was as good as a written contract. One thing that had escaped me, and a very important thing at that, was that I hadn't got an act, and as this was Thursday I had only two days to get one together. Back to the old routine: I had to cut myself off from my family in order to concentrate and within two days I was completely stripped of my rank and back in the kennel.

Saturday dawned as usual, and as we stepped out of the hotel on that bright sunlit morning there were enough of us to look as if we were a small delegation: Edith, me, Kathy and Susan and the au pair girl, Julie struggling to trundle David along in his pushchair, and the au pair girl. It was Susan who spotted something, pointing down the street. We all stopped in shocked surprise. Every ten yards or so banners were stretched across the road, proclaiming that Eric Sykes was appearing for one night only at the Café Roma. Edith, the four children and the au pair stopped dead in their tracks, staring at me accusingly. Had nobody explained to them that it was what I did for a living? Worse was to follow. As we meandered to our favourite spot on the beach, a low-flying aircraft dispatched hundreds of leaflets on to the heads of the sunbathers, reiterating what the banners had already told them – that I would be appearing that night at the Café Roma. Edith handed one to me as if it was my divorce papers. And if the banners and pamphlets weren't enough, I discovered later that the Berini brothers were also bringing in coachloads of English tourists from neighbouring resorts. I stared out to sea and the thought of swimming back to England crossed my mind. It was all too much. I'd been expecting a nice quiet evening, a few titters and a few quid in my back pocket. I was known as a scriptwriter but as for my being a cabaret artist – Noël Coward had nothing to fear.

Anyway, half an hour before the show, the place was jampacked. The tables were crowded together and on each one there was a complimentary bottle of champagne. A three-piece group on the stage were already playing popular tunes and would later become part of my act, as I had rehearsed them. My mind was blank. I couldn't remember who they were. However, all the over-the-top publicity had convinced the punters that I must be something special and the ovation I received gave me just the encouragement I needed. Had there been only a smattering of applause, three quick steps and I would have been over the parapet, hurtling to the street five storeys below – such an escape had passed fleetingly across my mind. As it was, though, I said, 'Good evening, everybody' and that got a big laugh, causing me to turn round to see if the band were up to something. To say that I went well was an understatement: the evening was a really momentous one-off.

The morning after, I called into the office on the ground floor of the Café Roma to collect my dosh, only to be taken severely aback when they handed me a very fat roll of lire. Returning to the hotel, I sat on the bed and counted my 10 per cent. I was flabbergasted. My pay would cover not only the cost of the suite and three other rooms at the Hotel Mediterranée for our three weeks' stay but also the cost of the air fare and the train journey – in fact all our expenses were paid, and there was a sizeable wad left over. I couldn't wait to break the news to Edith and reclaim my stripes. As I anticipated, she was impressed and I glowed – a sure precursor to impending disaster.

I'm not, and never have been, a sunbather, but after the strain of Saturday night I felt I deserved a tan, so I stretched out on my towel, praying that I would not be swamped by hordes of autograph hunters. Sure enough, in fewer than three minutes a shadow fell over me; and a chuckly voice said, 'Eric.' I shielded my eyes and looked up. It was Norman Vaughan. I stood up, delighted and surprised to meet him here in Alassio. The last time we'd appeared together was with Harry Secombe for the debut of ITV. Norman introduced me to his wife. They had just arrived that day and after exchanges, reminiscences and a few laughs, a sudden thought occurred to me.

'Hey, Norman,' I said, 'how would you like to earn a few quid to pay for your holiday?' He brightened, rubbing his hands together, and I told him about the Café Roma. Naturally he was all for it. 'Leave it to me,' I said, as if I was in charge of the entertainment of Italy.

The Berini brothers were not altogether enthusiastic. 'Is he famous?' one of them asked me.

I snorted. 'In England he's the flavour of the month. As a matter of fact he hosts *Beat the Clock* at the London Palladium, and apart from the Queen's Christmas speech you can't get a much bigger audience than that.'

This little snippet convinced them and they agreed the same deal that I'd negotiated for myself. All was set for Thursday night. Norman was delighted. Everything in the garden seemed weedless. But at about nine o'clock on Thursday morning I was startled out of my boiled egg by a frantic hammering on the door. It was Mrs Vaughan and before I could ask her in she blurted out, 'Can you come and see Norman? He's in the hospital.'

Immediately I remembered that Norman was of a very nervous disposition, and what I thought had happened was confirmed when Mrs Vaughan explained apologetically that on leaving their hotel that morning the sight of all the banners saying 'Norman Vaughan tonight' was too much for him, and he had collapsed in the street. The hospital was run by an order of nuns. I was ushered into a little whitewashed room where Norman was in bed. His ashen face was the only bit of him visible.

'Don't let them operate,' he whined.

The rosy-cheeked nun by his bedside smiled and shook her head.

Norman spoke up again. 'I'm sorry, Eric, I can't do the show tonight.'

'Obviously,' I replied. 'Just get better – that's all. I'll explain to the Berini brothers. Don't worry.'

Hardly surprisingly, the Berini brothers weren't too pleased. They berated each other in rapid, heated Italian, which to my ears was gobbledegook; my knowledge of the language was restricted to *grazie* and *prego*.

One of them turned to me and said in English, 'You will have to do it.'

'That's not possible,' I replied, taking a step back. 'The banners are all out advertising Norman Vaughan.'

'Don't worry about that,' he snapped. 'We'll attend to it.'

He was as good as his word. In another hour fresh banners were hung across the road, this time proclaiming 'Eric Sykes' farewell appearance' – but in their haste they'd spelt 'farewell' 'fairwell'. A small aeroplane was already dropping leaflets. Why, oh why, did we have to dine at the Café Roma in the first place? My dream of a cosy holiday had been blown to smithereens.

*　　*　　*

Frank Muir and Denis Norden were directly responsible for what turned out to be one of the most important steps in my career. A pilot script featuring Hattie Jacques and myself and written by Johnny Speight was submitted to the BBC – that is, Frank and Denis. They were exhilarated and impressed by Johnny's script, and to them the pairing of Hattie and me seemed inspirational.

Here is the situation. Hattie was to be my wife, and our next-door neighbour was to be an upper-class twit played by Richard Wattis, an experienced film actor specialising in Foreign Office underlings and passport officials – in fact any low-grade position in the Civil Service was his meat. The drift of the comedy would be the 'haves' and the 'have nots', and your guess as to who were to be the have nots is correct. It was to be the running battle of Sebastopol Terrace, where unfortunately we were to live. There was only one objection I had to make and that was the casting of Hattie and me as a married couple. I explained to Johnny that in being husband and wife we would be restricted.

'What's the alternative?' he said.

'We're brother and sister,' I replied. 'The relationship between siblings is usually much warmer than that of married couples, leaving us more scope. Hat could have a boyfriend, I could have a girlfriend – perfectly acceptable.' I was looking to the future. For me this wasn't just a pilot: I visualised it as show number one in a long-running series. Then another idea struck me. 'Better still,' I continued, 'we're not just brother and sister, we're twins,' and while he was still chuckling, I added, 'Identical twins.'

We recorded the show *Sykes and A . . .* and from the studio audience reaction we were convinced it would lead to a series. Frank and Denis were also delighted with the result. Tom Sloan rang them, having watched the show on the television set in his office, sounding excited and happy with the half hour. 'Congratulations,' he said, 'we have discovered a new star of television,' and before Denis could modestly accept the plaudits Tom went on to say, 'Richard Wattis.'

They thought he was joking. 'What about Eric?' Denis asked.

Tom was dismissive. 'Richard Wattis,' he said 'is acting Sykes off the screen.'

Denis couldn't believe his ears. 'But they're not supposed to be acting, Tom,' he said reasonably. 'They are supposed to be real people, and Eric's bumbling, gauche approach to life is in direct contrast to Richard's snide, smooth superiority. They complement each other.'

There was a very long pause before Tom replied. 'All right,' he said peevishly, and with a political correctness that had yet to be invented he added, 'Be it on your own heads.'

Well, Mr Sloan, it was still on Frank's and Denis's heads twenty years later when the show was still running.

Meantime Johnny's script for that first successful show was also his last. Unused to the rush and scramble of situation half hours, he was as yet learning his trade and felt that he could not possibly satisfy the voracious appetite of television at this stage. So I wrote show number two, Spike wrote number three, Frank and Dennis wrote number four, and I wrote the last two. From then on for the next twenty years I was responsible for the scripting of the shows.

A bad, bad day, an occurrence that still haunts me and will do so forever till the day I myself become a memory.

A tranquil, normal, domestic morning, all the family at home engaged in various activities, myself at the typewriter, the two dogs sunning themselves in the warm sunshine – it was a scene that might have been written by Barbara Cartland in her prime, when suddenly Edith screamed 'David!' Her scream was like nothing I had ever heard from Edith before. I was on my feet in a flash, and looked out of the window in time to see little David tottering inexorably towards the lily pond. I was out of the door, racing across the patio. By now David had disappeared. I jumped down on to the lawn, running frantically to the pool. My right leg went into the pond, wide of where I thought he must be. At the same time I felt down, thankfully touching the back of his jersey. At the first attempt I lifted him out and swung him on to the grass, face down, by which time Edith and the other children had arrived.

Being a trained nurse, Edith, thank God, managed to bring David back to us, so much so that David's expression asked the question, 'What's all the fuss about?'

My imagination has tortured me ever since with variations on 'What if . . . ?' The water in the lily pond was only two feet deep but black enough to make David invisible. What if I'd stepped on him when I put my foot in the water? What if he hadn't happened to be exactly where I plunged my hand in? Even more terrifying, what would have happened if Edith hadn't spotted him toddling unsteadily towards the pond? I cannot even bear to write what the consequences might have been. Needless to say, the same day I drained the lily pond, and it became a sandpit. To this day I cannot recollect either David or Julie ever playing in it.

ARCHIVE

30 September 1960. Bush Bailey, Assistant Head of Artists' Bookings, wrote to the booking manager complaining about Richard Wattis's agent, who, after noting Wattis's fee for the second series of *Sykes and A . . .*, was asking for a raise in Richard's fee for the next series. While this would probably be just about tolerable, grumbled Bailey, any subsequent increase would most certainly not be accepted. As Hattie Jacques was considered indispensable, Bailey hoped that Eric could be persuaded to write Wattis out, and either do without a next-door neighbour or create a new one who could be played by a cheaper actor.

ARCHIVE

2 October 1960. Tom Sloan wrote to Bailey saying that he had spoken to Eric about the basic problem (without going into any detail), and that Eric had been 'disappointed' but 'understanding'.

I understood all right: the accountants were gnawing at the woodwork. We already had a new member of the cast, Deryck Guyler, who played Constable Turnbull. He had appeared in one or two episodes to begin with, but his popularity with the public grew more quickly than weeds on a bombsite and he became a regular member of the team – and another expense. But it is my firm belief that you can't buy talent on the cheap, so my cast remained unchanged, and I made sure that Richard was with us until the day he died many years later.

One bright morning in 1961 I awoke, which was no hardship, but what occurred next proved to be one of the most crucial days of my life. I swung my legs out of bed, knowing that the rest of me would follow, but something was different: the room was gently tilting, a common occurrence when crossing the Bay of Biscay in a rust bucket of a ship but unusual in a sturdy well-built house in Weybridge. Worse was to follow when I tried to stand: I fell across the bed. Panic began to take over. Within twenty minutes the redoubtable Dr Scurlock had arrived. He didn't waste time making all the arrangements. My left ear was playing up. I was sure that Mr Musgrove would sort it out, but in this case he couldn't as he was in New York and whatever was ailing me would not wait for him to return. I was an emergency and another ENT specialist received me, Mr John Ballantyne, and without being disloyal to Mr Musgrove I would like to stress that my meeting John Ballantyne was to be the most propitious in my life.

During the war John had been the senior medical officer in the Royal Scots, and when he was stationed in Gibraltar he met a very attractive WREN also based on the Rock, a girl called Barbara, whom he married. To this day, nearly fifty years later, John and Barbara are two of my closest friends. It wasn't long after our first meeting that I realised that John was a man of great compassion, to whom a patient was never a case but a human being. His vocation was to better people's lives and from the poorest to the most affluent he gave his utmost care and attention.

The operation on my left ear was hazardous and not without pitfalls, as I found when I came round from the anaesthetic: I was deaf – not just hard of hearing, but stone deaf. But at least my room wasn't moving. Perhaps I was still woozy, for I didn't seem to be aware of the seriousness of my impairment. I'd been rushed into hospital on a Friday, two days before I was due to appear in a Royal Command Performance at the Palladium. Now on Sunday evening I was thinking of all the artists who would be on the stage that night, nervous, anxious, excited, as I should have been.

As a surprise, the matron had arranged for a large television set to be brought into my room and placed at the foot of my bed. It was only then that my deafness came home to me. I crawled towards the set. The picture was clear, but there was no sound. I put my ear to the glass and although I could feel the vibration I could not hear even a whisper. A cold hand of fear gripped my innards. Out of the corner of my eye I saw my door burst open and two irate gentlemen in dressing gowns gesticulating at me. I stared at them blankly, knowing they were angry from the redness of their faces but having no idea why they should be so upset. Luckily the matron appeared between them and ushered them away, giving me a beautiful smile before she closed the door. Two minutes later she returned and with sign language and gestures she explained that the two men were complaining about the extreme loudness of the television set. She leaned across and switched it off. I crawled up the bed and got under the sheets. Then she plumped up the pillows and, putting her left forefinger into the air, she crossed the top of it with the right forefinger. I understood that she was asking me if I would like a cup of tea. I was going to have to get used to this conversing by sign language.

On the Monday morning I was sitting up in bed, reading the nurses' lips as they mouthed, 'Good morning' and 'How are you?' to which I gave them a thumbs up. Perhaps I could get accustomed to living in a cotton-wool world.

I hadn't seen John Ballantyne since before the operation, but then I wasn't in any pain; nor did it seem that I had any complications, and I was not on the danger list, so why should he visit me? Then I noticed the door opening slowly and I said confidently, 'Come in, John,' assuming it was John Ballantyne. The door opened wider and a young fellow came in. He was smiling, and it was that smile that identified him: it was John Williams. It's not every patient who gets a visit from the number one classical guitarist in the world.

341

I'd met John once before when we were guests on *The Billy Cotton Band Show*, an unlikely booking for someone of John's eminence, but that was the secret of Billy Cotton's success – he would probably have asked Nureyev to be one of his guests if he could dance a ballet to 'I've Got a Lovely Bunch of Coconuts'. On that occasion from the moment he sat down to play his guitar I was mesmerised. He began with a fugue by Bach, in which every note was pure and demanding, and followed it with such an extremely fast exposition of sheer brilliance that had I been listening to it on the radio I would have sworn that he had at least three dozen fingers.

Now here he was by my bedside. It was only when he pulled up a chair that I noticed that he was carrying his guitar case, and only then did I realise what was about to take place. He took out his guitar and from the way he was tightening and loosening the strings he was obviously tuning it. How could I tell him that I was as deaf as a post? The situation had now gone too far and I did not want to embarrass him, so I smiled, he mouthed something, I nodded eagerly, and he smiled and began to play. I was again captivated by the speed of his fingers, but I couldn't hear a thing. Nevertheless, when he finally leaned back to get my reaction, I said, 'Great, John. Oh, that was beautiful.'

And before I could make further eulogies he was well into part two of my private concert. What a ludicrous situation – the maestro of maestros playing to a man who couldn't hear a five-hundred-pounder had it exploded in the next room! Suddenly I had the answer. I pretended to doze off – after all, I was a patient in hospital. It worked. After five minutes, when I glanced through my eyelashes, the room was empty and he'd gone. It was hard to believe that I had done this to the young, gentle man of whom Segovia had remarked, 'God has kissed this boy's brow'. John's outstanding mastery of the guitar was not confined to the Carnegie, Wigmore or Albert Halls; he entertained anyone who wished to hear, or in my case those who couldn't. In the world of medicine, John Ballantyne was blessed with the same generosity of spirit: he was not concerned solely with his Harley Street practice and also spent a lot of time in the poor quarters in the East End of London; his time and expertise was a gift for anyone needing treatment.

Over subsequent years the two Johns have been my role models. Parties hosted by John Williams and his lovely wife Kathy at which they entertained guests including Paco Peña, and once a private supper with the great maestro, Segovia, and dinners and lunches with John Ballantyne and Barbara have enriched my life – which reminds me that I am long overdue to host our next get-together.

However, that night as I lay in my hospital bed staring up at the dark ceiling remembering my private concert, resigned to the fact that I was deaf – never again would I hear the voices of my children or the birds' song as they chirruped in the new day – I was melancholy. Before my melancholy could degenerate into self-pity, I turned on my side to await the merciful oblivion of sleep. Then an extraordinary thing happened. When I closed my eyes, I remembered something I hadn't done since I was a child and I prayed. It wasn't much of a prayer; it was more a statement. I didn't ask to be cured – I'd accepted that that was out of the question and I would have to learn to live again in a new environment. All I asked in my prayer was to be given the courage and the strength to live with my disability – not a lot to ask. And in some extraordinary way I felt comforted, and I slept.

When I woke, the morning was miserable, rain was pounding the window and it was barely light when the door opened and a cheerful nurse mouthed, 'Good morning.'

I said, 'It's not so good out there.'

'Yes,' she said in a normal voice. 'And it's been like that all night.' I shook my head in sympathy for the poor devils on their way to work in this weather.

The nurse had turned to leave when she stopped and did the biggest double take I'd ever seen in my life. 'You can hear,' she yelped; then, lost for words, she turned around and rushed out of the room.

At first I didn't gather what was happening. For the moment I had forgotten that I was deaf, and then, with a sudden surge of exhilaration, I realised that my hearing had returned. 'I can hear,'

I whispered, and I actually heard myself whispering, but I was wary too . . . In a panic, I slowly sat up in bed, trying to keep my head perfectly still in case any slight movement brought back my deafness, and it was in this position that John Ballantyne found me when he entered the room, accompanied by a fellow ENT surgeon.

'The nurse says you can hear,' said John.

'Yes,' I replied stupidly.

John looked at his colleague in bafflement. Then they examined my ear as if it was a new species. This went on for some time, each taking turns to peer into the otoscope, and after a time the two colleagues retired to a corner for a quiet conference. Then John came to the side of the bed, shaking his head in disbelief.

'There is no medical reason whatsoever why you should have regained your hearing,' he said.

But I knew the reason and it had nothing to do with medicine. It was a miracle and not something I could discuss even with John. This was strictly a matter between me and Harriet.

I was not yet out of the wood. Edith was sitting by the bed on one of her visits when my left arm suddenly became paralysed. I couldn't move it at all; my hand was claw-like and I couldn't feel my fingers. Edith left the room to go for help, and I must confess that I really thought I was about to cash in my chips. A nurse entered and struggled to unclench my fist, but my fingers were immovable. All the time I was explaining to her how the sensation had crept upon me; I believed it was imperative for her to pass on this knowledge to any other suffering unfortunate. John Ballantyne, having been alerted, hurried in to give me an injection and with a great sigh of relief I went to sleep, and I woke up later as good as new. John explained to me that it had all been caused by anxiety, so from that day I've tried desperately to avoid being anxious . . . where the dickens did Edith get to?

Before I left hospital, I was fitted for a hearing aid – a mixed blessing, as it turned out. Sounds are magnified, but not always to one's advantage. For instance, I am able to hear a conversation a few yards behind me while the person I am facing is inaudible and if I turn my back to listen to what my conversant is saying it could be misconstrued. It was during *Sykes and A . . .* that I encountered my worst moments. The deaf aid enabled me to hear what Hattie was saying, which wasn't a problem, but that machiavellian piece of plastic in my ear also picked up the producer's instructions to his camera crew and it wasn't easy to fillet my exchanges with Hattie accompanied by 'Pan in number two'. Hattie, unperturbed, would deliver her next line and before I could reply into my ear came the producer's voice with 'Crab left number three' – interference which I found disconcerting, to say the least.

It was only during a dress rehearsal that the producer became aware of this when, through my hearing aid, I heard him say, 'What's the silly bastard doing now?' I walked up to the boom mike and said, 'The silly bastard is listening to every word you say.' There was a stunned silence, followed by laughter from the crew, but the producer walked on eggshells for the rest of the series. It was a very hazardous period and had it not been for John Ballantyne the show would have been beyond my capabilities. Half an hour before each transmission John came down to my dressing room to clean out my ear and my deaf aid in order to prepare me for another edition of *Sykes and A . . .* I am now eighty-two years old and I am still waiting for the bill.

Although I'd made brief appearances in three films, my first big break in the fantasy world of cinema came in a movie called *Village of Daughters*, a very funny sequence of events in which an inept salesman finds himself in a small Italian village, where most of the families possess a beautiful daughter – hence the title. My role was a gift, the lead in fact, and I became the inept salesman. It was a brilliant script and I enjoyed playing the part immensely.

Village of Daughters was premiered in Edinburgh and naturally I went along to see the first night. It was awful. Everybody round me in the film seemed to know what they were doing and I was the odd man out. I left the cinema before the film was finished. The reviews were not even lukewarm.

It's a sad fact of life that if you start at the top there's only one way to go and that's down. Mercifully the film was taken off before it could leave a permanent scar. Of course some people actually enjoyed it, but by now they are either dead or in a mental home.

We had moved from the dear, semi-detached Woodhaven East to a much more salubrious residence just a par five up the hill: White Knights, a beautiful house in two and a quarter acres of land.

I now employed a gardener, Mr Mannering, and his wife, who lived on the premises in a comfortable little flat above the garage. With an au pair girl from Sweden sunning herself on the patio, a Welsh collie and a black Labrador protecting us from evil and two cats loftily accepting whatever is put before them – otherwise they are useless – I think the only thing missing was a partridge in a pear tree.

Financially I could see no reason to be pessimistic about my future and with this in mind I made a recce from Gibraltar up the coast of Spain, looking for a suitable site on which to build a villa. When I arrived at Marbella I knew that this was where I would put down my Spanish roots. At that time the area was completely rural, and from Marbella to San Pedro there was no road, just a dirt track. I put down a deposit on a plot of land. How I came to be in touch with a Scottish architect domiciled in Andalusia is still a mystery. When we first met to discuss my project, his unfocused eyes should have been a warning sign; however, we shook hands and I returned to England. I was pleasantly surprised when, a month later, I received the plans for my proposed villa, my future bolthole in the sun; they were impressive and professionally drawn up. I made a flying visit to Spain, and he and I discussed the site, how much the villa would cost and when the builders would be able to start work. He said they were all ready to go and I gave him the thumbs up. Some months later, I returned to Andalusia. The villa was nearing completion but there was one huge, insurmountable snag: the villa was back to front. The large patio where I had dreamed pleasantly of reclining in a chair in the cool of the evening sipping a Rioja while I gazed at the mountains, behind which the setting sun dipped into night, was instead overlooking a collection of huts and shanties and the detritus only an age-old camp like this could accumulate.

The architects blamed the builders, who in turn blamed their starvation wages, and I blamed myself for embarking on such a crackpot scheme. It was too much to digest, but my troubles were only just beginning. I still had to organise an electricity supply, which was a novelty in the area. Lamps and candles may satisfy the needs of indigenous campers, but they don't energise a washing machine, or provide constant hot water. A telephone doesn't operate without being connected to something. But a more pressing problem presented itself when I turned on a tap and nothing happened. We could not survive without water; a well would have to be dug, but where? After making enquiries, I contacted a professional water diviner. I was at my wit's end as I watched him with his overcoat draped over his shoulder wandering back and forth across the hill holding a bent twig, but after a short *paseo* he stopped suddenly. The twig was twitching in his hands, and he pointed at the ground, whereupon two workmen who had been following him with their shovels began to dig. I felt like an alien from Mars.

Back in England I received constant reports on the well. They were down to two metres – still dry; a week later, four metres, until, praise be, they struck a damp patch about fifteen metres below ground and the bricklayers moved in.

A year later Edith and I made a trip to Spain in order to buy beds, chairs, tables and all the essentials to make the villa habitable. We now had water – not a lot, but more than enough for a cup of tea; and the electricity was erratic. Before long we took the family to Spain for a few weeks' holiday. This wasn't a disaster, or it wasn't until one day when, while David and Julie were enjoying the beach, Kathy and Susan, being older, were at a riding school. Susan, poor darling, fell off her uneducated mount and suffered a dislocated shoulder. She was in great pain and we took her to the local doctor in San Pedro. When she emerged, I could scarcely believe my eyes: there was enough plaster of Paris on her shoulder and her arm to have built another *Venus de Milo*. This was not very pleasant in itself, but the discomfiture of bearing all that archaic plasterwork in the hot sun must have been purgatory.

We cut short our holiday and our first port of call was the local doctor. He was appalled when he saw Susan for the first time and angry at this barbaric piece of doctoring. In half an hour she walked out with her arm in a sling.

From out of the blue I was chosen to be in a celebrity football team to play a match at Brentford's ground. I couldn't wait to accept. The game would be played in the evening under floodlights against a local team. It wouldn't be too taxing, as each half would only be fifteen minutes, after which the professional match would follow. It seemed like a good idea when it was first mooted.

Our dressing room at the football ground was warm, the air heavy with cigarette smoke and most of us were enjoying gin from the cups meant for hot sweet tea. We all looked the genuine article: striped shirts – numbers on the back were unheard of in those days, and in any case no one knew which position we'd been allotted and we had each chosen our football strip from a sackful of assorted shirts; shorts; shin pads; even football boots, although such had been the rush that my right one was slightly bigger than the left. Only Jimmy Edwards knew his position: long trousers tucked into his boots, a polo-necked sweater and a cap, so he was obviously our goal keeper. Jack Hawkins, one of our leading film heart-throbs, was also in the team and I made a mental note to be close to him if the photographers happened to be around; also he supplied the gin. We were a jolly lot and laughter was continuous, brought to an end when an official popped his head round the door to inform us it was time. As we left the dressing room, the cold of the passage hit us like the inside of an ice-cream factory and all the bonhomie evaporated as we rubbed our hands together, exuding clouds of gin-sodden breath. 'Off you go,' said the same official, showing his disapproval of our turning the beautiful game into a circus. Well, to coin a phrase, the best was yet to come. Another official came in the tunnel from outside, covered in white as if he'd been painting the ceiling, and with a shock we realised it was beginning to sleet. 'What are you waiting for?' he said and waved us out.

As we ran on to the pitch we must have made a brave spectacle dashing through the racing flakes, but for me running out bravely was my first mistake. By the time I'd reached the pitch I was blown and gasping for breath. Gin and cigarettes aren't the wisest preparation for a footballer's life. In order to recover, I knelt down and pretended to re-tie the laces in my boots. I was still fiddling with my bootlaces when the whistle went and they kicked off, and before I could get to my feet the ball passed me, most of the players chasing after it, and, judging by the roar from the crowd, somebody scored.

My most embarrassing moment came when the ball rolled to my feet. I had a quick look round, but most of the players seemed to be in a huddle, arguing with each other in the corner of the field, so, as there was nothing else for it, I set off on an epic run towards goal. I swerved round three of the opposition but the sleet was heavier now and they probably hadn't seen me. I only hoped I was going in the right direction. Then the bill for my burst of energy was presented as I reached the opposition penalty area. I had only the goal keeper to beat and he was standing with his hands on his hips. He could see that I hadn't the strength to lift my leg, let alone shoot. I tried and the ball trickled to him. He picked it up and kicked it down field; then as he passed me, he said kindly. 'Can you find your way back?' I limped down the touchline, wondering if I'd got my boots on the right feet. Oh yes, it was very easy to stand on the terraces blowing raspberries, but in those days the ball was encased in heavy leather and a mild header could lead to permanent brain damage – all very well for footballers of the stature of Stanley Matthews, who could take a corner with such accuracy that the lace would be facing the goal mouth as the centre forward headed it in, or such was the legend, but not for the likes of me.

There was only one thing for it. Jimmy Edwards in goal was having a busy time picking the ball out of the net, but at least he wouldn't have to run. I muttered to Jim that my hamstring had gone, and he understood at once that I was volunteering to take over the goal. He accepted, although he refused to hand over his polo-necked jersey: he explained to me that underneath it, braces were keeping his trousers up and he didn't want the public to see him in his underwear. He didn't even lend me his cap, making the excuse that it was his milking cap and if the cows picked up the scent of a stranger it would affect the yield. We changed over, I went in goal and he strolled out reluctantly into the night. Then a sudden thought struck me.

'In the dressing room,' I yelled, 'you told us your brother Alan milked the cows.'

'Yes,' he replied. 'This is his cap.'

I gave up. In any case, while we'd been arguing they'd scored again, and I'd never even seen it go past me.

Jack Hawkins gave our team some clout and after the match he came off looking as well groomed as he had when he began, which is hardly surprising: when I come to think of it, he hadn't moved one inch in any direction, although he did a lot of pointing, like a French traffic policeman during the rush hour, indicating where others should be running into position; and if my memory serves me right, he walked off slowly waving to the crowd. I doubt if he kicked the ball once, but this might have had something to do with his contract with the film studio.

A young footballer with a chin out of all proportion to the rest of his face, playing for Fulham, refereed the match. He's still with us, still a mate and still called Jimmy Hill.

Rumours spread like a malevolent flu bug, and by this I am not intimating that my performance under the floodlights of a wintry Brentford had anything at all to do with it, but shortly afterwards I was invited by the directors of Oldham Athletic Football Club to join the board. I agreed hesitantly, as if I'd have to check my diary, although secretly I wouldn't have turned it down for a gold clock, and on the next Saturday I drove up to Oldham to attend a match in my official capacity. A propos of nothing, capacity is not the make of a car. However, owing to pressures of business and the cost of petrol, it was the only match I ever witnessed from the directors' box. Then the bubble burst. A year or two later, I received a warm, cheery letter from the board, enquiring after my health and wondering if I could see my way clear to donating £3,000 as the club was in financial difficulties. Unfortunately it was at a time when I was also in financial difficulties and I took the easy way out: I resigned.

ARCHIVE

24 August 1962. Tom Sloan wrote to Eric to congratulate him on winning third prize – for *Sykes and a Bath* – at the Alexandria Film Festival in Egypt. According to Donald Baverstock, the episode made its two Hollywood rivals look 'stale and processed' by comparison, and the other television executives present had been astonished by the speed at which Eric and his team had made such shows while maintaining such a high quality of performance and production. Baverstock also noted that *Sykes and a Bath* only missed out on the gold prize by two votes.

ARCHIVE

December 1962. It was proposed that Eric be given a £100 rise for his next [sixth] series of *Sykes and A . . .*

On the tenth tee at Sudbroke Park I hit a moderate drive. I think my opponent was Garfield Morgan. Garfield outdrove me by about thirty yards. I doubt if Garfield remembers this incident, because in all probability it wasn't him, but we played many, many rounds of golf together over the years and now we are both in the twilight zone. It is still a great pleasure to meet him and enjoy his laconic wit. He is one of the most underrated actors in our profession and for that alone he deserves a mention. We were about to walk off the tee when a man in a sports jacket and flannels, accompanied by a beautiful blonde, came towards me. I recognised the man but I couldn't bring his name to mind.

'Sean Connery,' he said, 'and this is Diane.'

We'd never met before but I'd seen him in a film called *The Hill*, and what an impact he made – his screen presence was such that he eclipsed all the other actors. So when he asked if they could walk a few holes with us, I replied, 'Be my guest.'

The blonde turned out to be his wife Diane Cilento. I was flattered by their presence and although I was four down to Garfield the day seemed much brighter. With a seven iron I hit a glorious shot high and handsome on to the centre of the green. Diane clapped her hands together and Sean said, 'I wish I could play golf like that.'

'So do I,' I replied. 'If the rest of my game was like that I'd have no need to work for a living.'

Perhaps that one shot inspired Sean to take up golf. What neither of us realised at the time was that it was the beginning of a warm friendship, and scores of golf games later it is still as strong as ever.

As scriptwriters were now acceptable appendages to television, ALS had moved to a more salubrious address in Cumberland House, Kensington High Street, so Irene Handl with Pretzel and Gretzel under each arm no longer had to crawl over sacks of potatoes before attempting the five flights up to our office. Very much upmarket, we were now a force to be reckoned with. We took over the ground floor in Cumberland House, and from my window was Kensington Gardens and slightly to the left a large bomb site, being cleared by yellow-helmeted workers, which would eventually be the Royal Garden Hotel. Our work's canteen was just along the road, called Fu Tong's, and such was our fame that I had my own chopsticks with my name on them.

One day a long procession headed by Trevor Huddleston and Michael Foot passed the window. They had walked all the way from Aldermaston and were beginning to show signs of fatigue. Spike ran out across the road and joined them for their last lap to Trafalgar Square. Nuclear disarmament was just one of his causes.

A lot of my friendships have matured on the golf course. One was with Noel Murphy, a jovial, six-foot-four Irishman, softly spoken with a scholarly stoop that owed nothing to education – it was merely on account of his height; he was a folk singer by trade and a golfer in his leisure hours. On the first day of his membership to the Stage Golfing Society, he asked me if I fancied a game, and as

I had been bewitched listening to his Irish anecdotes, I was all for it. From his drive on the first tee, I was given a masterclass in how to play golf. With the prodigious length and accuracy of his drives, and the delicacy of his short game, he completed the round in level par. Only then did he tell me that he was a four handicap golfer. Since then he has improved, and now has a handicap of plus one, which as any golfer will know is a pretty hot potato.

But there was more to him than golf. When his wife Sue, also an athlete, presented him with a baby girl, Siobhan, they decided that a flat overlooking Twickenham High Street, with its daily stream of rumbling, heavy traffic belching out exhaust emissions and polluting the air was no fit setting in which to bring up a child. Noel and Sue made a brave decision: they upped sticks and moved to a little cottage in a tiny village by the sea in Cornwall – a tremendous sacrifice, as Noel was just beginning to make a name in the bright lights. This enormous gamble appears to have paid dividends: they are still a very happy family and Siobhan, now sixteen years old, is a low handicap golfer and shows promise of playing for the county, which proves that genes play an enormous part in one's development. This brings me to the question of what genes I have inherited from Dad, bless him. I wasn't up to much in the cotton mill, and I didn't fancy bell-ringing, but on deep reflection the only thing he seems to have handed down is how to look good in overalls. This is what is known as a digression.

Once in an idle chat with Noel just before I lined up my fifth putt, he mentioned that Rick Wakeman was an ardent fan of mine. 'Really,' I said, concentrating on putt number six. Noel went on to say that Rick recorded everyone of my television shows. I was thunderstruck. I'd admired Rick for years, never realising that besides having a prodigious talent at the piano he was also a man of impeccable taste.

Now, before we pass on, a tale of avarice, temptation and redemption. Another good mate, in spite of the money he has taken off me at golf, is Norman Angel, and I should point out here that golf is a game wide open to cheats, hastily adding that this doesn't apply to any of my friends, nor myself – but there are exceptional cases. On one of our games on the west course at Wentworth, I was in a bunker by the green on the sixteenth hole. I splashed out competently, but Norman asked if I had hit the ball twice, and all too quickly I replied no. I won the hole, the match and a fiver. As we walked towards the seventeenth tee, I re-ran the bunker shot in my mind, and doubt crept in. By the time we had reached the eighteenth, I was convinced that I had indeed struck the ball twice, but I said nothing – it was much too late to confess now. After that day of ignominy we played many times, but I was never fully at ease, although Norman was always his cheerful enthusiastic self.

Weeks went by and there was never a day when I did not feel a sense of guilt. I couldn't bear it any longer and one day as we walked on to the first tee, I said, 'Do you remember when we played a match about six months ago and you asked me if I'd hit my bunker shot twice?' There was a pause, and I finished abjectly, 'Well, I did.'

Laughing his head off, he put his arm round my shoulders and replied, 'I thought you did,' and he pushed away the fiver I was offering him. Having owned up, I felt as if a great burden had been lifted from my shoulders.

And that's a lesson I won't forget in a hurry. I got six months hard for nicking a fiver.

ARCHIVE
11 April 1963. Bush Bailey noted in a memo the intention to negotiate an exclusive long-term contract for Eric.

In 1963 Julie begins her education at Heath House Junior School and naturally her protégé, little brother David, attends the same institution. I sincerely hope that David doesn't expect Julie to do his homework. It is an emotional day for Edith and me as we hand over the last of our children to be educated by professionals.

One night, in the company of Sean Connery, Bruce Forsyth and a very young Jimmy Tarbuck, I watched Henry Cooper take on

Cassius Clay for the heavyweight championship of the world. We were only four rows from the ringside, close enough to see a small patch on the back of the referee's trousers. Cassius Clay was the flavour of the month and clearly the favourite, but he was not having it all his own way: Henry was stalking him, and in the fifth round he unleashed a killer punch, a left hook known as 'Enry's 'ammer. Cassius Clay went down as if he'd suddenly decided to sit this one out, and Henry backed off, allowing us a full frontal of Cassius's eyes staring vacantly as if he was wondering what he was doing sitting peacefully in the middle of the Milky Way. The referee stepped in belatedly and started to count, but after fifteen seconds he'd only got to five and the bell went for the end of the round. Cassius, still in fairyland, was helped to his feet and brought back to life in his corner. Everybody in the hall knew that Henry had won by a knockout but after being revived Cassius managed to survive the rest of the bout and was declared the winner on points.

Over the years Henry and I have become great buddies. I consider him the most gentle gentleman, richly deserving his knighthood, and with his lovely wife Albina they are the perfect role model for any young married couple. In my eyes he is still champion of the world.

I have a very clear picture imprinted on my mind of Kathy and Susan as they are about to leave for Lady Eleanor Hollis School, scrubbed and polished, their school uniforms pressed and pristine. Both of them are smiling, which is mandatory whenever anyone takes a picture, although in this case the camera is my memory.

Lady Eleanor Hollis was and is a prestigious establishment for young ladies, and on one parents' day I happened to come across Richard Attenborough and his wife Sheila. If they had a daughter being educated there, I knew for certain that Kathy and Susan were in the right place.

Opposite our old house, Woodhaven East, was a larger house, rented by an American family, but when they finally returned to the land of the free, the residents who took their place spoke English or a version of it – Liverpudlian to be exact. They were John Lennon and family. I met him when we happened to arrive home one evening at the same time. The last fifty yards of our journey was a narrow lane to our respective houses, and we spent two or three minutes in 'After you . . . no, after you,' which ended in him inviting me in for a cup of tea.

Now that we had upped sticks to a much grander dwelling we were still within catapult distance of the Lennon ménage. A few months after moving in to our new home, it was Christmas Day and a dark figure crossed our lawn, leaving deep footprints in an otherwise virgin carpet of snow. It was John Lennon, bearing a bottle of wine, and we had a convivial hour together, with lots of giggles from my girls, Kathy and Susan, as they tried to eavesdrop on our festive conversation.

One year later on Christmas Day, at midday I telephoned John and we exchanged the season's greetings, after which I mentioned hesitantly that every Christmas it had been his habit to cross the lawn with a bottle of wine, at which he laughed. I went on, 'I hate to bring it up, but we were rather counting on it as guests will soon be arriving.' We both laughed and I thought that was the end of it for another year, but within five minutes his lonely figure was crossing the lawn again and he said, 'I'm sorry, but I thought it was your turn this year.' Once more we shared the bottle, and this time Julie and David were old enough to eavesdrop along with Kathy and Susan.

Some months later I was post synching at Twickenham studios and the Beatles were in the process of making their film debut, *A Hard Day's Night*. Naturally Kathy and Susan were thrilled to bits and asked me to get their autographs, which they duly signed on two pages of paper. To this day, Kathy, now an established film producer, still has their signatures, more precious now with memories of having wished John Lennon on two occasions a merry Christmas.

*　　*　　*

The year 1964 was one of pleasant surprises, dominated and eclipsed by a near-tragedy.

Having spent a glorious three weeks' holiday at our villa in Spain, we ate our usual pre-flight lunch in Fuengirola before going on to the airport. It was a ritual at which we all enjoyed garlic prawns in an earthenware dish called *pil-pil*, the idea being that each exhalation of garlic breath after the meal was lethal. On arriving at the airport, we would hoist our suitcases on to the bench in the customs shed, where we would be asked the usual question: 'Anything to declare?' Leaning towards him, I'd reply in a breathy voice, 'Pardon?' whereupon the official would rock back on his heels and make a chalk cross on our suitcase quickly in order to see the back of us.

It had always been fun in the past, but on this occasion David and Julie didn't eat. This was rather odd at the time, because *pil-pil* was one of their favourite dishes. Edith was worried and even I felt a qualm of unease; the flush on their faces had nothing to do with the Spanish *sol* and their listless eyes set the alarm bells ringing. On the flight home it became obvious that both the children were suffering. In fact by the time we arrived at London airport, David was barely conscious. From the airport Edith telephoned Dr Scurlock, and we arrived home to meet him on the doorstep. Once again, he rose to the occasion and within an hour of landing the two little mites were in an isolation ward at St Mary's Hospital in Chertsey, where to our shocked horror they were diagnosed as having typhoid.

Every day Edith and I visited the hospital. Frustratingly, but understandably, we were not allowed to enter their rooms, but could stare at them through a glass partition as if they were specimens at the zoo. They were in the hands of the doctors and nurses, who fought this pernicious disease; sadly it is only at times like these that we fully appreciate the skill, care and lavish attention of such people. David and Julie were in adjoining rooms, separated from each other by a glass wall, which was heartening, because being able to see each other was of great benefit to both of them. David was only five years old and the most serious case; fortunately Julie was a little less worrying. I say fortunately because Julie had always taken it upon herself to look after David and in this case he had never needed her more. However, as Julie improved, David seemed to worsen. His little body became so emaciated that I was reminded of the skeletal, degraded inmates that I had seen in Belsen, his little bones threatening to break the skin of his face, and looking much older than his age.

David lying still in a semi-conscious state, Julie keeping a silent vigil through the separating glass – tantalisingly, Edith and I could only stand and watch, drawing comfort from the optimism of the doctors and the nursing staff. Then blessedly David, with the resilience of children, was able to stare back at Julie and acknowledge our presence. When we visited again the following day, he was sitting up in bed.

Once again, we'd all been on the edge of catastrophe concerning David – first the lily pond, which I'd drained to make a sandpit, and now this insidious disease, contracted in Spain . . . I sold the villa. I can never thank enough Dr Scurlock, the nursing staff and doctors, for their dedication in bringing back our two little toddlers from the brink.

ARCHIVE

26 February 1964. Kenneth Adam [BBC I Controller] sent Eric a telegram congratulating him on the previous evening's show, saying it 'reduced the entire Adam family to a state of complete helplessness. Please do not be quite so funny again or permanent harm may be done.'

ARCHIVE

9 November 1964. Tom Sloan asked that a congratulatory telegram be sent to Eric to mark the recording of his fiftieth situation comedy show for BBC TV on 12 November. After the recording, a party was thrown, and Eric was presented with a cigarette case.

ARCHIVE

August 1965. Eric began discussing his hopes for his next series with the new controller of BBC1, Michael Peacock. He suggested

RIGHT: One of Vera's most popular songs was 'We'll Meet Again'… and we did.

LEFT: John Williams with his tutor.

RIGHT: Honorary doctorate. Lancaster University.

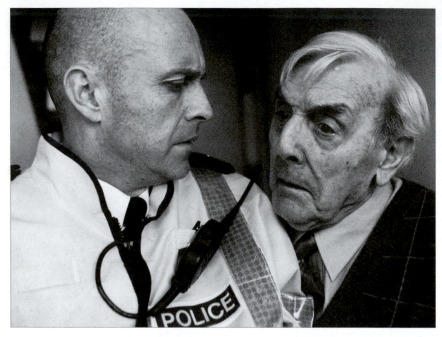

ABOVE: Face to face with Paul Usher in *The Bill*.

BELOW: One of the perks in *Stan the Man*.

ABOVE: *Three Sisters.* The other one couldn't come.

BELOW: No wonder we never saw Alan Bennett.

ABOVE: Peter Bowles and Carmen Silvera, with apologies to Mol.

BELOW: Talking Heads: Peter Hall asking me out to lunch.

ABOVE: A visit from the Doctor. A novelty these days, even when it's Christopher Timothy.

BELOW: Fionnula Flanagan, Elaine Cassidy and me admiring the performance of Nicole Kidman.

ABOVE: Spike Milligan interrupting the play, *The Nineteenth Hole*, to present me with a Lifetime Achievement Award. The audience were delighted with an extra interval.

BELOW: Sean has the happy knack of turning up when least expected. A pleasant surprise for all my friends at my last book launch.

ABOVE: Bill Kenwright's office: day.
Bill: Eric, I have a feeling we are being
watched.

BELOW: A scene from *As You Like It*: not the
first time I've died on stage.

Investiture of my CBE: daughter Kathy, grandson Thomas and wife Edith.

either Tuesday or Thursday at 8.00 p.m., or, failing that 7.25 on Sundays. Peacock said he would schedule it at 7.30 on Tuesdays.

When I was about two years old, some of the Ashton family emigrated to Australia. Whether they did so because of Britain's unemployment problems, the cost of living or the weather, I've no idea, but of one thing I am certain: I refuse to accept responsibility for their mass exodus. After a few years, letters from Australia began to arrive, extolling the beauties and advantages in this land at the other side of the world. I was too young to understand the mysteries of joined-up writing and nobody bothered to explain what the letters were about, but I was able to admire the small sepia snapshots that came with the writing, of a little smiling group all donned in whites against a background of a rose-covered cottage. What intrigued me most was that one or two of them were holding tennis racquets.

In England only the rich and well-to-do played tennis, and in Oldham we became aware of the game only because there was a tennis court in Westwood Park just off Featherstall Road. It was a desolate, run-down, grassed area, surrounded by a very high wire enclosure; I can't even remember seeing a net – I suspect ardent tennis players had to bring their own – and I never actually saw anyone playing. But here on these photos our smiling relatives looked as if they played the game as keenly as I had played Ducky Funny Whip. I was glad that they'd fallen on their feet, but envious as well. These grainy snaps sowed in me a seed of longing that was later to develop into a burning obsession to see Australia for myself.

And now forty years later I was invited to a cocktail party at Australia House in London, a junket primarily to pay tribute to the Beatles. I normally do my best to be somewhere else, thus avoiding this kind of get-together, but the word 'Australia' was enough for me to accept; and here I was in the midst of the chattering classes, wondering what on earth had possessed me to accept in the first place, when a very smartly frocked lady approached and introduced herself as the Australian ambassador's wife. She seemed genuinely pleased to meet me – so effusive, in fact, that I wondered if she hadn't mistaken me for one of the Beatles. She rattled on about her husband, who apparently was one of my greatest fans – so much so that if my programme was on television he would cancel all meetings in order to watch me. My ego was being polished, and who was I to break off the conversation, or perhaps eulogy is a better word. She put her hand on my arm and said, 'Don't move – I'll go and get him,' and she charged into the crowd.

I just had time for a quick gulp of what was now becoming tolerable when a man emerged from the press of people, beaming like a Turner sunrise. 'Hello, Eric,' he said. 'I'm the Australian High Commissioner,' and he began to regurgitate most of what his wife had been saying a moment ago; but now he was begging me to visit Australia, where, he assured me, I would be greeted by a ticker-tape welcome from the airport through the streets of Sydney. Jocularly I told him that I was already working on a ten-pound assisted passage.

Being serious for a moment, he said he would give me ten pounds out of his own pocket if I'd promise to visit his beloved country. Returning his genuine admiration, I explained that it had always been an ambition of mine to visit Australia, but only when I had something to show the audiences out there. In effect, I would need to do an act or appear in a play, and although a ticker-tape welcome was tempting, there is no such thing as a free lunch. I mentioned to him that his words had strengthened my resolve to put Australia at the top of my agenda.

David came home from school in a flurry of excitement. For the first time he'd been playing in goal for his school. He flung his little satchel down and, eyes gleaming, he told Edith they'd won two nil. Then, as if I hadn't heard it, he told me exactly the same: they'd won two nil. He skipped into another room, whooping and cheering, to tell his sisters they'd won two nil, and breathlessly he even told our Welsh collie. Only then did he calm down, his expression now thoughtful. Tugging my trouser leg, he said, 'Dad,' in a small plaintive voice, 'what's nil?' Exclamations like this from children add to every parent's treasured memories.

In 1962 ALS folded its tents in Cumberland House to travel upmarket again to Orme Court in Bayswater. A run-down, derelict shell of a once-elegant house with only two advantages to fuel my enthusiasm: it was the only house in the row with permission to conduct business affairs – essential in those days – and more importantly it was freehold. Spike was no problem; as long as he had his typewriter and a stout door to keep out the unwanted he was content. Simpson and Galton weren't too sure, but as the price split four ways was reasonable they finally capitulated, and after a couple of months with the house barely habitable other writers began to fill up the rooms. As ALS was a non-profit organisation, rents for some of these writers were as little as four pounds a week; also, because we had little knowledge of commerce, we paid for all their phone calls, heating and lighting. Even so, it was my ambition that one day every room would be taken by an eager writer. Now over forty years later it is an investment I have never regretted. Although all the offices are occupied I am the only resident script writer, but the building is resonant still with comedy ideas pervading every nook and cranny.

I played in a charity golf match in Scotland – I can't remember which course, and now, as I shuffle my brains, I'm not even sure it was in Scotland. In those days pro-celebrity golf was an innovation, and the match attracted large galleries of those who loved the game and many more to see their favourites of the stage, television and films in glorious Technicolor, live and more importantly within touching distance. They lined the course and for the more eminent, stands had been erected around the eighteenth green.

In those days my golf handicap was nine, and I was really enjoying my game. My second shot to the eighteenth was well struck but not too well aimed, and it thunked down into a deep bunker at the back of the green. Walking up the fairway, I heard the commentator, John Jacobs, one of our Ryder Cup heroes, on the tannoy informing the crowds that Gary Player might have difficulty in getting the ball out of the bunker; and as I surveyed my Dunlop 65, half buried in the sand, I was inclined to agree. A good score could be ruined by my next stroke. I swung at the ball and in one of those shots of a lifetime I not only splashed out on to the green six feet from the pin but completed my moment of glory by holing the putt. The applause ran over me like a warm shower and I acknowledged it in the traditional way by touching the neb of my cap. However, the highlight of my day was yet to come. As we made our way off the green, a man, vaguely familiar, sitting at the end of the front row, pipe in mouth, legs splayed out before him, stopped me, took his pipe out and said, 'By jingo, you're a cool one.' I thanked him and moved on. Only when I was in the locker room did recognition illuminate my mind. The fact that his legs were splayed out before him was the key: he hadn't any. Those were the artificial limbs of Douglas Bader, one of the most celebrated fighter pilots of the Second World War, a real hero, and he'd actually spoken to me – could life get any sweeter? It could. That first meeting was the beginning of a firm acquaintance – at that stage he was too exalted for me to claim as a friend.

We played in many other charity golf days and private matches, which he invariably won as he was a four-handicap golfer, an amazing man who marched stiffly around the golf course on his artificial legs. I remember well how, during a match in the bitter cold of a Scottish summer, all of us wrapped up like extras in *Scott of the Antarctic*, incredibly Douglas, puffing on his pipe, was in short sleeves. It was unbelievable: it must have been below zero. Only afterwards did he explain that as he had no legs his blood had not so far to travel to warm his torso. What an extraordinary man! I tried to emulate his courage, his determination and most of all his golf. He was the master and I the pupil.

Then one day our relationship changed dramatically, entirely because of a film called *Those Magnificent Men in their Flying Machines*, directed by Ken Annakin and written by Jack Davies –

what a team! The film had a simple premise, based on historical fact.

At the beginning of the twentieth century, the *Daily Express* offered a prize of £10,000 for the first man to fly an aeroplane from London to Paris. One must bear in mind that in that age of clean air flying was strictly for the birds, but ragbags of new-fangled contraptions were being assembled, mainly of canvas, string, glue and, of course, a propeller. The lure of £10,000, plus the kudos of being the first man to fly from London to Paris, attracted budding aviators from all over the world. For the purposes of the film, these included a hero from America, a German (very Teutonic), a proud Italian who kissed all his children before climbing into his cockpit, the inscrutable Japanese and of course competitors from Great Britain.

Long before the film was put to bed, we had the feeling that it was going to be a smash hit, and it was. The comedy was refreshing, and the love interest healthy and innocent, but the real magnificence of the film was the aeroplanes. At one point Ken Annakin had about a dozen of those flying death traps in the air at the same time – an incredible feat. Obviously they were flown not by actors but by a faceless group of professional pilots. One of these was a woman because all the planes in the film as near as no matter were exact replicas of the originals and the French aeroplane was a Demoiselle, purpose-built for a very light French pilot, and in testing the male pilots couldn't get the Demoiselle off the ground but a woman pilot could just about manage. Believe me, some of the stunts she carried out were hair-raising and she made three attempts at one manoeuvre before she was satisfied. What a pleasure it was to take part in that classic comedy film! I had a role that suited me down to the ground: I was the abject, cringing, manservant chauffeur and doormat to Terry-Thomas, a vile, despicable upper-class twit who was determined to win by fair means or foul.

Some weeks later, after the picture had made its triumphal march from cinema to cinema, I happened to meet Douglas Bader again at a charity golf day. I heard him call my name as he stumped across the fairway to shake me by the hand. 'That flying film,' he said, 'a masterpiece,' and he shook me by the hand again. You'd have thought I'd not only written and directed the film but flown all the planes myself. The boot was now on the other foot (an unfortunate choice of words, considering his disability, but I think they might amuse him were he still among us).

As the weeks progressed, his enthusiasm for the film grew, and a few months later we met again in a golf club locker room, where I was changing my shoes. His face lit up as he reiterated his whole-hearted admiration for the film. 'Seven times I've seen it,' he told me, 'and it gets better.' I couldn't see how a film could get better – it was only celluloid – but now our acquaintance had blossomed into a warm friendship.

ARCHIVE

1 December 1964. Eric wrote a long letter to BBC1 Controller Kenneth Adam, detailing his frustrations during the last series of *Sykes*. He was particularly angry about the way the show had been used as a ratings weapon, and scheduled on Friday evenings when so many people were out. 'The *Sykes* shows are just a half hour in a long viewing week to the BBC, but to me it has been my career, and it is horrifying to feel it is being jeopardised in the battle of the ratings.'

ARCHIVE

10 December 1964. Donald Baverstock wrote to Kenneth Adam, advising him to make Eric fully aware of how much the BBC still appreciated his talents. Adam did just that later the same day, assuring Eric that he was 'no less important an element in our programmes than you ever were', and remained 'a pillar of strength in light entertainment at its best'.

ARCHIVE

14 December 1964. Eric wrote to assure Adam that it was all 'water under the bridge'.

My secretary buzzed me to say that there was a telephone call from Royton. At first I assumed it was my father, as my father and mother had left Oldham to live in Royton and I said, 'Hello, Dad,' and was embarrassed when the call turned out to be from Royton Town Hall inviting Hattie and me to be guests of honour in a local parade. I was flattered, although being an Oldham lad we had always looked upon Royton as a poor relation; nevertheless on Hattie's behalf I accepted the invitation. It was an exciting prospect, and Hattie and I arrived at Royton Town Hall to a warm welcome. When one of the civic dignitaries asked Hattie what she would have to drink, she thanked them and asked for a whiskette, and the ice was broken in both senses.

Outside in the street, the parade was assembling, with large floats each depicting a scene. For instance, the local hospital had a bed surrounded by goose-pimpled nurses; a recruiting lorry for the Territorial Army was followed by a gaily coloured wagon carrying three blacked-up banjo players representing the era of jazz. Interspersed amongst this pageantry of colour were a Boy Scout band, the Salvation Army and the Territorials. It was a dull, leaden sky, but fortunately there was no wind. I thought it was breathtaking. What a marvellous turnout! We could neither see the beginning nor the end of the procession as we were bang in the middle in an elegant sports car, the hood down so that the public could get a good view of us, oh heady stuff. Immediately we were settled in the back seat, the parade began, with a roll of drums from a band too far ahead to see. We revelled in it, waving and smiling at the onlookers. I didn't hear any cheers to mark our progress but saw plenty of happy faces, and parents lifting up their offspring, who were totally unimpressed and regarded us with suspicion. There was one little lad, waving a small paper Union Jack on a stick, who shouted, 'Hooray,' only to receive a smart clout from his mother. I pretended I hadn't seen it.

Directly ahead of us was a brass band, which I assumed was that of the Salvation Army – it couldn't have been the Boys' Brigade because in the middle of the back row was a girl playing trumpet. At the end of Shaw Road we stopped, as we had done once or twice before, except that this time the part of the procession immediately in front of the Salvation Army band was disappearing gently round the bend. Fortuitously, we were right opposite the house where Mother and Dad lived, and there they were standing on their doorstep, waving. I waved back and pointed them out to Hattie, who also waved. The band in front were still marking time, while the stretch of road in front of them was deserted. By now Hattie, on the near side, was chatting to the bystanders lining the route. She signed an autograph book, which she passed over to me to sign, while she put her signature on somebody's handkerchief (unused, thank God), which she also passed over to me. Then a little girl held out her bare arm, which Hattie signed, but before she could pass her over to me the driver turned round to us and said, 'About time too.' Craning forward, I saw the reason for the hold-up: the poor girl trumpeter in the band before us had unfortunately managed to wedge the heel of her shoe in the tram line and some of the bystanders had been helping to extricate it, which they had finally managed, although when the band set off again she marched with a limp, as the heel of her shoe was in her pocket. This was when more trouble began. Our high-powered vehicle, ill-suited to standing idle with its engine running, became overheated and when the driver pressed the accelerator it stalled. It was our turn to block the parade while the Salvation Army band limped round the corner at the top of the road, and the driver lifted the bonnet, reeling as a cloud of hot steam engulfed him.

As if nothing had happened, Hattie was in deep conversation with the crowd, and I wished I had something to read. Some of the young bucks amongst the onlookers craned into the machinery, offering advice on something they knew nothing about as a car like this was a novelty to them. Behind us the procession was becoming impatient, and a clown on stilts strolled forward and ordered us to get the thing off the road. One or two young men got behind the car and pushed it into Shaw Road, the bonnet still up to allow the engine to cool, and the parade continued without us. We were still seated in the back of the car when the tail of the procession passed, hurrying now to catch up with the others, and not even looking in our direction. Our driver went into a call box across the road to ring for a taxi, but before it arrived it started to rain and they couldn't get the hood of the car up, so Hat and I hustled out of the car and stood in a shop doorway. Then we ran across the road and had tea with Mother and Dad, so it wasn't a bad day after all. I must have forgotten the old maxim 'pride goes before a fall'.

ARCHIVE

16 November 1965. Eric held a press conference to announce that he would not write another series for any channel until the television ratings war ended.

Big Bad Mouse was a comedy play in two acts. Its first try-out starred Dave King and Charlie Chester, an extremely strong piece of casting – with this pair it should still be running, but sadly it didn't last long enough to merit a review. It didn't even make enough to pay the usherettes, and so it was withdrawn before it could cause irreparable damage.

The authors were undaunted. Their next leading men were Terry Scott and Hugh Lloyd, a redoubtable duo – in fact they were the ideal couple to breathe some life into this Dead Sea scroll. Sadly the short tour of this *Big Bad Mouse* was as catastrophic as its first outing with Dave King. At this juncture any decent author would have shredded the play and applied for a day job, but where there's life there's . . .

. . . Michael Codron, one of our foremost entrepreneurs. He asked me if I would like to work with Jimmy Edwards. Would I? If I had to list my top ten funniest comedians, Jim's name would be near the top. The important thing was how did he feel about working with me, and I can't tell you how flattered I was to hear that Jim would be over the moon if I agreed. Neither Jim nor I cared what the vehicle was – had it been *The Cherry Orchard*, *Waiting for Godot* or even *Hamlet on Ice* it would have made little difference; the prospect of working together was enough.

The play didn't leap out at us; it cringed between its covers. It was a one-set play, the offices of Chunkibix Ltd, a biscuit factory. Jim's character was Mr Price Hargreaves and I was his cowering underling, Mr Bloom. The plot was as follows: I was wrongly accused of chasing a girl across Wandsworth Common but instead of ostracising me all the girls decided that I was Jack the Lad and the frog was a prince. Rehearsals were onerous in the stifling heat of a small room at the height of an exceptionally hot summer. On the first day, when the lunch break came, poor Jim, heavy with sweat in his braces, addressed the director, asserting that it was too hot to rehearse. The director unsympathetically retorted that it was the same for everyone and he would see Jim back at two o'clock sharp. This was too much for Jim, who replied that he was buggering off and would return on the morrow, and with that he picked up his jacket and swept out. I was appalled, and told the director that there was no point going through the play time and time again in this sweatbox. He was adamant, and so was I, telling him in no uncertain terms that I'd had enough as well. As I walked along the corridor on my way out, I turned the corner and there was Jim, flattened against the wall. Having heard my conversation with the director, he breathed a sigh of relief, saying, 'If you hadn't walked out, I don't know what I would have done' – already we were a team.

A week before the play opened, we were confronted by a real spirit crusher when the authors threatened us with court action should we alter a word of the original script. Although we didn't know it at the time, we were being lured into the same trap as Dave King, Charlie Chester, Terry Scott and Hugh Lloyd had been.

On the opening night, the theatre was packed; it was the rest of the week that let us down, but at least it gave us five extra days' rehearsal . . . We stuck religiously to the lines written, but there would have been more laughs in a graveyard.

Bad news travels fast in the world of theatre and the next date on our tour apart from the Monday was a repetition of our opening. Whether the audience enjoyed our performance we had no idea; it is always difficult to assess the success of a comedy when it is greeted with stony silence. Every week was lacklustre. Both Jim and I were saying all the right lines in the right order, but we were getting a bit fed up with playing to the manager and the night watchman.

The original deal had been for a six-week tour of the provinces followed by a run in the West End, but as we approached the last week of our tour the glitter of the bright lights was gradually diminishing.

Our date for the last week of the tour was at one of my favourite venues, the Palace Theatre Manchester. Jim and I were looking forward to it, hoping for better things as a drowning man watches the lifeboat approaching. Sadly, however, in our case the lifeboat was heading in the wrong direction.

We opened to a very sparse house, affording us the same as the last five weeks. It could hardly be described as a triumphant tour. We'd done our best – at least we'd done our best to ruin whatever past reputations we had so happily put together over the years.

Before the show on the Tuesday night, Jim walked morosely into my dressing room and, refilling his glass from my bottle of Glenfiddich, he said glumly, 'Well, it's obvious we won't be going into the West End, so I'm going to have a bit of fun.'

'If you're going to have a bit of fun, so am I,' I replied and we clinked glasses.

The first opening salvo came from Jim. In the play it was the firm's Christmas party and Jim was sipping cold tea, smoking a cheap cheroot. He went forward, leaned against the proscenium and addressed the audience. 'Cold tea,' he grimaced. 'You'd think on the last week they'd have given me the real thing.' Then he held up his cheroot. 'And a real cigar.'

I turned to the audience and said, 'I wished they'd given me a real actor.'

It was the first laugh we'd heard in six weeks, and it was the trigger – not just to a pistol shot, but to a twenty-one gun salute. When the curtain finally fell, the audience were still applauding. Jim and I stepped forward and our curtain speech was longer than the second half. And here's an odd thing. Frankie Howerd was in the audience and he came round the back to see us. 'That's the funniest thing I've ever seen,' he said, which was foreign to Frank's nature; in other similar circumstances he would simply have said,

'Very good,' so from Frank this utterance was praise indeed, until he added, 'I would have liked to have seen the play, though.'

For the rest of the week the original script receded to make way for our ad libs. The audiences improved and by Saturday night second house the theatre was packed to capacity and the box office said they'd had to turn a thousand people away. Perhaps this should be taken with a pinch of snuff, but outside the theatre the mounted police were desperately trying to disperse the crowds, and that is a fact. Michael Codron, the producer, had travelled up to Manchester in order to have a few drinks with us as a consolation prize. Unfortunately because of the disappointed throng Michael was unable to get within fifty yards of the theatre, let alone see the show, which incidentally overran by forty-five minutes.

When we were having drinks with Michael Codron, after he'd finally made it through the stage door, Jim said, 'Well, Michael, if you take the show off now you'll want your head testing.' Michael was no slouch and although he hadn't watched the play he'd seen the upheaval caused by disappointed punters unable to get tickets, and a week later we opened at the Shaftesbury Theatre in London's West End.

Variety Club lunches are held up and down the country. They are always well organised and well patronised, and, most importantly, through them millions of pounds have been raised for the benefit of less fortunate children.

It was at one of these functions that I found myself seated next to Douglas Fairbanks Junior. He was an amiable fellow, and although he obviously didn't know me from a knife and fork we conversed as equals. I told him it was quite warm for the time of year and he said, 'Really?' I was just about to ask him if he knew Errol Flynn when the toastmaster banged his gavel and I was spared my drivel. The grace was short and humorous and I can't remember the food – it was the usual fare, passable – but the highlight of the show for me was one of the guest speakers, my old mate Tommy Cooper. As he rose to begin his speech, wearing his obligatory fez, his reception was fantastic; the warmth of the welcome affected the whole room – even the waiters applauded. How could he possibly follow that? But he did. To open, he raised a hunting horn to his lips and blew a feeble squeak, following it with, 'It may not sound much but in five minutes this place'll be full of Vikings.' The dining room erupted. Only Tom could have got away with an inanity like that, but that was his secret.

After the lunch we reminisced about times past.

'Do you remember,' I said, 'when I carried your suitcase down to the Bag of Nails?'

'I'll never forget it,' he replied with a chuckle, and I knew there was more to come. He smiled ruefully as he described his first and last disastrous appearance at that venue. Apparently the clientele of that club weren't exactly from *Who's Who* and were more likely to appear in police records – villains, hard men and hoodlums out on a night's bender. Tom made his entrance, smartly dressed in dinner jacket and fez, to be greeted by hoots, whistles, raspberries and a shower of bread rolls as they tried to knock his fez off before he had even said, 'Good evening, everybody.' The stage now looked as if a bakery had taken a direct hit from a marauding bomber. Tommy's patience snapped. 'Stop that,' he shouted and the whole place fell silent.

Tom was petrified by a man in the front row, his face scarred from years inside, his nose red in celebration of his release, who said belligerently. 'Why shouldn't I throw bread rolls at your fez?'

In a panic Tom replied, 'Because I haven't got an ad lib for people throwing bread rolls at my hat.'

There was a moment's pause. Then the whole audience laughed and he was able to continue his act. Had he made the wrong reply he might well have ended up in concrete supporting the flyover into Chiswick and we would never have known the funniest man in the world.

In every prospective comedian's career there is a Bag of Nails, perhaps more than one, and if, like Tommy Cooper, you can overcome such hazards you will eventually, with luck, be at the top; and it will be almost a cert that having these experiences behind you you'll stay there.

After a few weeks at the Shaftesbury Theatre, *Big Bad Mouse* was established with the prospect of a long run. The audiences were royally entertained, not only in the theatre but across the road in the pub just before curtain up where Jim and I used to meet frequently for a tot before going to work. On one occasion the crowd standing at the bar began looking at their watches, restless, until Jim said, 'It's no good looking at the time. They can't start till we get there.' So saying, we all crossed the road in a body and a good time was had by all.

3 November 1966: I make particular note of the date because at ten past eleven that night, after a lifetime of smoking like a rusty old tramp steamer, I stubbed out my last cigarette. It is quite remarkable that when a heavy cigarettist gives up the habit he very rarely forgets the date – talk about conversion on the road to Damascus.

The trouble began during the first house of the evening. My voice began to croak, until every word was an effort; and by the curtain call I couldn't raise a thank-you. The emergency bells were rung and five minutes before the beginning of the second house the marines had landed in the form of John Ballantyne. After a quick examination of my throat, he declared me unfit for battle. Half an hour later in John's home we were sipping a malt whisky, the room heavy with tobacco smoke; his wife Barbara joined us in a glass but, not being a smoker, she was passive on that score. I stood up to leave and John delivered his verdict: I was to give up cigarettes and whisky for four days. I mulled over this for a few moments, after which I lobbed back over the net with, 'I'll give up cigarettes for four days but I cannot guarantee the whisky.' He agreed, telling me that he hadn't expected agreement on both counts and was quite prepared to accept a compromise. Miracle of miracles, not only did I give up cigarettes for four days but I haven't bought a packet since. That was almost forty years ago and I must admit that the craving has almost disappeared. As Jim didn't smoke, my abstinence was a blessing to him, but the malt whisky was never far from our elbows.

The show itself kept us in peak condition, until one night when Jim unfortunately had a birthday and it showed from the front so much that I told the audience we had an arrangement that one of us would be sober on stage each night and at the last stocktaking Jim owed me ninety-seven turns.

It was a sublime existence – golf during the day and the Shaftesbury at night – but it had to be put on hold when the opportunity came to write comedy sketches for a new stage show featuring Frankie Howerd and Cilla Black. How could I refuse, especially as the venue was to be the Prince of Wales Theatre in London's Piccadilly? Simpson and Galton were taken on board to contribute a couple of sketches, which took some of the weight off me. I wrote my contributions during the day and every evening left the office for *Big Bad Mouse* – long days but in our profession too much was infinitely better than nothing. However, problems, like many other aspects of everyday life, tend to grow, and in any case at times one is unable to see problems ahead until they barricade the road.

Having completed the writing of the comedy sketches and received Frank's approval, I could now settle down to my day job of writing the next series of shows for me and Hattie. There was no rush – I had a few months in hand before the amber began flashing – so if the days were sunny I would be on the golf course preparing myself for the evening show at the Shaftesbury, and a huge horse would be tethered outside some pub or other where Jim was also warming up. I never seem to anticipate the sucker punch; I should be streetwise enough by now to recognise the signs – when everything in the garden looks rosy there is inevitably a freak snowstorm. I was inveigled into directing the comedy of the show at the Prince of Wales. I can never resist an exciting challenge and to direct at the Prince of Wales would be not just a step up the ladder but a Cape Canaveral send-off.

At ten thirty each morning I was at the Prince of Wales Theatre, putting life into the words of the sketches; at one o'clock lunch break; back into the theatre until six before going over to the

Shaftesbury – it was wearying; had I been a camel I would have refused to carry straw. In all this time I had not yet discussed my fee for directing, but a meeting had been arranged to hammer out a settlement with Bernard Delfont. I'm not quite sure whether he owned the Prince of Wales Theatre, but he most certainly ran it as if he did.

After the curtain had come down on *Big Bad Mouse*, I drove myself across town to the Prince of Wales. Bernard Delfont was sitting in the empty stalls in the fifth row, but I didn't join him; I sat in the front row immediately ahead. I was tired to a point beyond sleep. We didn't exchange greetings or how are yous; it was business from the kick-off. I was no match for Delfont, who was an extremely clever negotiator. It was a ludicrous situation – me in the front row talking to an empty stage and Bernard five rows behind talking to the back of my head. It was after midnight when he suggested forty pounds and I assumed that the fee would be weekly for the length of the run. It was not a fee that would cause tremors on the Stock Market – it was well below the wage for an usherette – but I was prepared to accept it and make for home. What a gullible idiot I was! Bernard's offer of forty pounds was to be the one and overall payment for all my hard work. I was shocked into full consciousness. Forty pounds for directing, three weeks' rehearsal – I hadn't the energy to get up and leave. In fact I can't remember what we finally agreed upon – one thing is certain, we agreed on nothing – but I will never forget Bernard Delfont's last words, 'You'll never work again.'

The way I felt it would be a happy release. He was repeating his brother Leslie Grade's mantra. The only Grade who had yet to deliver this *coup de grâce* was Lew. He was the eldest and realised that banging your head against a brick wall is not a healthy pastime.

Big Bad Mouse wasn't work, it was fun, but after my mauling at the Prince of Wales I decided to exercise my get-out clause in the contract. Michael Codron fully understood and accepted my decision to quit. In fact he did more than that: he presented me with a beautiful rosewood humidor, full of very expensive cigars. Inside the lid was a gold plaque thanking me for all I had done to make the play a success. It was a wonderful gesture, one which I will never forget. The only snag was that I had given up cigarettes for the last six months; now I was about to become hooked on cigars. Roy Castle took my place in the cast, and without a break the play continued as if I'd never been; such is the world of theatre. Apart from my charity work at the Prince of Wales Theatre, I had finished writing my next series of *Sykes and A . . .* with Hattie Jacques, and we started rehearsing it to follow on my leaving *Big Bad Mouse*. It was a welcome change of direction; doing my television shows would be like a holiday and after a series on television I would be ready to make another career change – perhaps a film, or who knows even a book. My modus operandi could best be described as that of a farmer who rotates his crops; the only way we differ is that I don't seem to have a field to lie fallow.

After twelve months at the Shaftesbury Theatre *Big Bad Mouse* retired with honour. Over the last year Roy Castle had worked wonders with my part in the play and Jim, finally exhausted yet triumphant, decided to call it a day. The play had been merely a peg on which Jim and I had hung our overcoats; the original *Big Bad Mouse* had been in fact whittled down to pamphlet size and we had not altered a word of that, so there was no fear of litigation and it was now a closed book – or so some thought.

Comedy is an acquired taste and one man's laughter is another man's perplexity. But to me a visual laugh is worth three pages of dialogue; two visual laughs and you're well on the way to fame and fortune.

Peter Sellers once said to me that we were on the same wavelength regarding comedy. Laurel and Hardy were the greatest exponents of the kind of laughter that appealed to us both – no camera tricks for them, no whip hands, no zooming in and out, no tight close-ups, just two very funny gentlemen saying little, without doubt visually the best double act to hit the cinema.

Having lunch with Peter one day, I told him my ideas for a silent movie I had in mind, which I had christened *The Plank*. I explained some of the visual jokes and it was obvious that he was seeing the same word pictures as I described them. Two inept workmen at war with a plank of wood with a malevolent sense of humour – half an hour later we still hadn't finished our hors d'oeuvres and quite a bit of that had been spluttered over the table as Peter laughed. Even as I spoke to him, I was having more ideas and developing them on the hoof.

We never got to the fish and chips because Peter was so excited that he desperately wanted to play one of the hopeless workmen. I left the restaurant in high spirits. With Peter starring in the film I knew I would have no difficulty in raising the money. Even this chore was taken out of my hands as unbeknownst to me Peter was already seated in Bernard Delfont's office in Soho explaining the adventures of the machiavellian plank. Bernard mentally had his wallet out; he knew he'd been dealt a royal flush, as with Peter Sellers starring he would recoup his outlay before one frame had been shot. Peter didn't mention this meeting to me as like most of us he was superstitious and wasn't going to count his chickens.

In less than a week a film crew was being assembled: lighting, cameraman, producer, props, wardrobe, chuck wagon, honey wagon (and for those of you leading normal lives a honey wagon is not a vehicle crammed with the bees' delight, it is actually toilets) and, to complete the transport, two Winnie Bagos in which the actors could change. Even the first location for the opening shots on a building site had been organised. The juggernaut was now well and truly rolling and unstoppable. While all this was going on behind my back, I was still wondering who best to approach, cap in hand, with regard to raising the money – whether to approach Lew Grade or Michael Codron. It was only when Peter rang to inform me that shooting would begin in three weeks' time that I became aware that the film was already into production . . . It was utterly incredible. If there was any grass about, it certainly didn't grow under the feet of Peter Sellers. On reflection I decided that a building site was the obvious place to start.

Peter was getting more excited by the day at the thought of having fun in a silent movie which offered him plenty of opportunity to improvise. As far as I was concerned, funny situations were already chasing each other round my brain and everything in the garden was rosy, but alas it is a well-known fact that if you go outside without an umbrella it is bound to rain, and it did – a cloudburst. A blockbuster in Hollywood was about to go into production and Peter was asked if he would play the leading role. The script was brilliant and the director of the very first water. It was an offer Peter could not refuse. I was shattered. How could I postpone the shooting? Peter would be working in Hollywood for the next six months at least and Bernard Delfont would not keep the pot boiling until Peter's return. Here was a glimmer of hope: I knew that Bernard would not drop the project at this stage, as he had already invested money in it and he wasn't about to lose it lightly.

Nevertheless I was in the doldrums on a sailboat. Who could possibly replace Peter Sellers? But again I metaphorically lifted the dustbin lid and there was the yellow gleam of a daffodil. A name flashed in front of my mind, and two days later Tommy Cooper reported for duty. He was to take over from Peter and what an inspirational choice it was.

Forgive me for not having detected at first the unmistakable hand of my mother behind this brilliant strategy of using Peter to raise the money and then supplanting him with Tommy Cooper. From that moment I knew that *The Plank* was going to be a success. Thank you, Harriet.

Tommy jumped at the chance of being in a film where he didn't have to speak. No words to learn and only one costume – what a great start on his glittering path to Hollywood! And the more I thought about him the more I could hardly believe my luck.

On the first day of shooting I turned up at the location. It was still dark. A chuck wagon, lit by a paraffin lamp, was wreathed in steam from the coffee urn; I could see the white-coated back of the cook busy frying bacon, eggs and sausages; other dark shapes were flitting here and there with lamps; work was already in progress to make sure that everything was ready when it was light enough. It was bitterly cold and one of the crew came up and handed me a hot mug of steaming coffee. As I sipped it, deep in thought, I was aware that he was looking me over. I turned to him and he introduced himself as my first assistant. We shook hands and then he said, 'I hope you've done your homework, guv'nor'. I pondered the use of the word 'guv'nor', realising that I was now responsible for the whole of this circus. It was an awesome thought, but even as it was crossing my mind inspiration elbowed it aside. I'd just worked out my first three shots of the film. Elation exploded inside me and I couldn't wait for the light of day.

Tom arrived, dressed in blue overalls, jacket and cap, a larger version of my own costume – the uniform of the working classes that Tom and I would wear until the end of the picture. In fact when the day's work was finished we both went to our homes in our costumes so as to be ready for the next day's shoot. Our meeting was emotional, to say the least. This wasn't the timid, nervous Tommy Cooper who had disappeared through the forbidding door of the Bag of Nails years before; he was now a colossus astride the world of comedy. It was as if we'd both been adrift for days on a makeshift raft and had just sighted land.

I explained to him what we would be doing for the first three set-ups. Already he was chuckling and by the time we'd finished the morning's work, so were the crew. I had one great advantage over many other film directors: as there was nothing on paper, nobody could form their own ideas about how things should be done, so there was no argument, no dissention. Only Arthur Wooster, the lighting cameraman, was privy to the next three shots, and what a gold-plated asset he turned out to be! When he had lined up the shot through the viewfinder I explained to him what would be happening, and we worked together in great harmony and at a cracking rate. To put it simply, I was writing the script with the camera.

I didn't deliberately decide not to put a word on paper; it was certainly not arrogance. The truth is I couldn't. How does one write a script without words? One cannot commit to paper a purely visual scenario; it is the product of one person's imagination. A writer scripts a normal dialogue scenario to mean one thing, and then the director shoots it in his own particular way, after which it is cut by an editor, who may have other ideas; and by the time the film is finished it may have little bearing on the dialogue in the original script. And on this, m'lud, may I suggest the court recess.

Tommy and I had some hilarious moments when we were not actually working on the film. For instance, one day we had a rather eminent cast, with Joan Young, Jimmy Edwards, Wilfred Hyde White and Henry Cooper on the call sheet, and I arranged for us all to have lunch at a nearby tavern. A notice saying 'private' was tacked on to the door of a room above the bar. I invited Arthur Wooster and with Tom and me we would be twelve in all.

At one o'clock we wrapped and they made their way to the pub. Tom was about to join the others when I called him back; I wanted to explain to him the set-up after lunch. So we were a little late in arriving. Just as we were about to mount the stairs, an officious barman rushed in front of us and said, 'You can't go up there – it's a private party.' 'Yes,' I said, 'they are my guests,' but as we were still in overalls he was not convinced, and before we knew it Tom and I found ourselves out in the street. Fortunately for us Tom's anxious face at the window was recognised by the landlord, who hurried forward to let us in.

I was at the head of the table, while Tom sat on my right; the conversation was happy and relaxed, punctuated by laughs and the clatter of knives and forks. However, in spite of this atmosphere, throughout the meal I noticed that the guests were all glancing at Tom, expecting a private cabaret. He must have spotted this as well, because after a time he put down his knife and fork and lay flat out on the floor. Everyone craned to have a look at him. He just lay there for a few minutes, and then he got up and sat down again to continue his meal. 'What was all that about?' I asked him, and he replied, 'I just thought I'd do something visual.' After a moment's puzzlement, the rest of the table burst into laughter. This little scene demonstrates the mood of the picture: although we were only halfway through the schedule, there was already a warm smell of success amongst the crew and the distinguished cast. Is it any wonder that the show was indeed a success and Tom became the flavour of the month, an acquired taste to most people's liking?

Dear old Tom so enjoyed the experience of being a film star that he wanted to make another picture before the mood wore off, which led to another silent entitled *It's Your Move*. Richard Briers and the gorgeous Sylvia Simms were a honeymoon couple arriving at their empty home; Jimmy Edwards recreated his role in *The Plank* as the bumbling bobby; and of course Tom and I were the accident-prone removal men delivering the furniture. This was made for Thames Television and once again we hit the jackpot.

En passant, whenever Tom was free from the strictures of his agent we worked together, learning from each other and both agreeing that one visual gag is worth ten pages of dialogue. The most important element of comedy is timing, which is why editing my silent movies has given me more pleasure than the excitement of directing. Once the film is in the can, the heat is off and I can put in the finishing touches, like an author who, having finished writing a book, has the time to invent a title. I say that, but in fact the title *The Plank* came first in my mind and the film sprang from that small beginning.

In 1968, following Kathy and Susan, Julie is enrolled at Lady Eleanor Hollies School. I should think Edith and I have more than played our part in supplying pupils for that illustrious place of education. David will be exempt from joining Julie as it is an all-girl's school; in any case he has to stand alone sometime.

Gloom blackened the day for Associated London Scripts when Robert Stigwood, a high-flying entrepreneur, made a bid for it. It is important to stress that ALS never at any time employed writers; it was my idea to encourage young aspirants and even to offer them office space at a very low rent. Negotiations for this transfer to the Stigwood Organisation had been carried out in great secrecy, so much so that Spike Milligan and I were unaware of what was going on. This was not unusual; had a landmine exploded in the next street we would probably have answered absentmindedly 'Come in'. Metaphorically a bomb was already on its way down. The deal being negotiated was for Stigwood to take over ALS which presumably included Spike and me, a scheme in which we would abandon our present workplace and skip happily uptown to do our writing in the offices of the Stigwood Organisation.

Much to my surprise, I was approached by Simpson and Galton, who asked me to move over with them. This was the first I'd heard of the deal. In fact the sellout had already been negotiated and agreed upon; it was a fait accompli. I found it hard to take in the audacity of such shenanigans being carried on without my knowledge; after all, Associated London Scripts was the brainchild of Spike and me. In no uncertain manner I told them that I was not about to leave ALS and I was sure that Spike would be of the same mind. Here I must confess that these were not my exact words, but you get the gist. Unable to resist the lure of share incentives, and the thought of working in Argyle Street, Simpson and Galton upped sticks to join the Stigwood Organisation, leaving the better half of ALS behind them. This was the decimation of all my hopes for ALS. Granted, I had had only one big success, which was Johnny Speight, but if I could find a few more writers even half as good as Johnny I would feel that my dreams had been fulfilled.

Spike didn't appear to let this defection affect him, and why should it? He was under the protection of Norma Farnes. I use the word protection in its true sense. Norma, an attractive Yorkshire lass and a ray of sunshine, was Spike's mentor, his bodyguard, his accountant – in fact I would go so far as to say that without Norma, Spike would have got off the bus long before the terminus. The shabbiness of the whole transaction affected me more than I realised, and desperation and blackness slowly drove me to the very gates of a nervous breakdown. Again, like the ingrate I was, I'd forgotten all about Harriet. Thankfully she had not forgotten me; the sun was about to clear the horizon.

Still in the depths of despair, which had robbed me of a night's sleep, I took myself off to my only place of solace, the golf course. Before I left home, I had phoned Sean Connery and in half an hour we were standing on the first tee. As always, we both looked forward to these days, but on this particular occasion I was spraying shots right left and very rarely centre, bleak thoughts making my bad play worse. I was just about to wrap a four iron around an innocent tree when Sean said, 'How would you like a trip to South America?' I stared at him, wondering what that had got to do with my lost ball. Then he went on, 'I'm making a film there and there's a part in it for you if you want it.' I hadn't said a word to anyone about the break up of ALS – it was too personal – but the way I was behaving had alerted Sean to the fact that something was seriously wrong, and his offer of a film part came like somebody switching on the light in a dark room.

The film script for *Shalako* arrived the following morning and I sat up in bed to read it. As I did, my heart sank. My character was a mortally wounded Victorian soldier, carried on a stretcher, who moaned and groaned his way through several pages, only to die just before the credits. Sadly I had to admit to myself it wasn't me. Thousands of out-of-work actors would gladly have sold their wives and children simply to appear in a film with Sean Connery, especially in this part – with no words to learn, only moans and groans, and not only that to be carried everywhere, it was a peach of a part; but I must admit that it was beyond my limited acting capabilities. After all, I was a humorist and I wanted laughter, not tears. I'd had enough of those from various theatre managers.

With great reluctance I rang the producer to tell him that the role of the wounded officer was not for me. There was a pause and I heard the rustle of the script. Then he came back on the line to tell me that I'd been reading the wrong part; the role recommended to me was that of the butler, the only light relief in the picture. With a great sigh of pleasure I accepted the part. My spirits soared from the cold damp cellar to the penthouse suite; or, as in my philosophy, this was the daffodil in the dustbin. I lay back on the pillow, my thoughts scattered like a hen's breakfast. When I had been playing golf yesterday I doubt whether the thought of me playing a part in *Shalako* had even crossed Sean's mind, but he'd hit on the perfect remedy.

We didn't go to South America, as it turned out. The film was shot in Almeria, Spain. I didn't care – it wouldn't have mattered to me if we had made the whole thing in Newport Pagnell in the pouring rain. Playing the role of the butler in that international cast alongside Brigitte Bardot, Honor Blackman, Jack Hawkins, Stephen Boyd and Peter van Eyck, a German star, was completely therapeutic. *Shalako* was just what the doctor ordered and soon the memory of Associated London Scripts was as cold as yesterday's rice pudding.

The director was the American Eddie Dmytryk, a much respected man of the cinema. I was fascinated by his methods of direction and the quiet way he dominated the set. The person who impressed me most of all was Bob Simmons, the stunt man who coached Sean in all his hairy activities. Bob was also responsible for selecting and schooling ninety Arab horses to be used in the film and with the help of his colleague Ken Buckle he taught me how to ride. For starters they seated me on an elderly grey mare. Riding on either side of me, they took me through the rudiments of posting, cantering and, if the old mare could manage it, a gallop. It was a seasoned old nag and moved only when either Bob or Ken were present; otherwise I would sit on it, juggling up and down, desperately trying to get it to shift while the old beast slept beneath my legs.

In a couple of weeks Bob decided the time had come to upgrade me to a thoroughbred. A few more days and I was a competent enough horseman to look forward to our weekends. After Sunday breakfast Sean, Bob, Ken and I mounted our horses and galloped off like real buckaroos. The valleys and hills of Almeria were a duplication of the wilds of Texas – a barren, lonely wasteland with arid rock formations and cactus plants, and not a soul or a habitation to be seen. Then suddenly as we cantered up the side of a hill we looked down and a golden panorama lay below us. On closer inspection it was an orange orchard – with a 'whoops' we galloped down amongst the trees, and plucked oranges, which were a welcome thirst quencher; we didn't even have to dismount. Satisfied, we galloped into the open. I had no idea where we were heading but suddenly they all stopped and Bob pointed ahead. In the shimmering distance we saw a lonely hacienda, which turned out to be a café, where we were to have our lunch. As we moved in line abreast, Bob yelled, 'Chaaaaaarge,' and off we raced towards the distant estaminet as if we were in a dress rehearsal for the *Charge of the Light Brigade*.

On a four-day break from filming, Sean and I decided to spend some time in my old stamping ground, Marbella. Transport was no problem: being the star of the show, Sean had a huge limousine at his disposal and a uniformed chauffeur. It would be a four- or five-hour journey, so for the first hundred kilometres or so Sean and I reminisced – a bit of politics, a few laughs – and then a silence as we dozed, lulled by the singing tyres of the car on the hot dusty road through the monotonous landscape.

We both woke at the same time as the driver pulled up and pointed to a broken-down old shack with a big sign in front saying 'BAR', a lonely old ruin situated about ten yards from the road. In two minutes we were standing at a counter, behind which were bottles. It was dark, cool and empty until a little old man rose from nowhere, surprised to see us; as there were no other buildings in the vicinity, customers were a rare breed. '*Buenos días*', he said in a voice obviously unused to speaking. Sean asked him for whisky but the man stared, uncomprehending, shook his head and said, 'No wikki.'

Sean leaned over and said slightly louder, '*Dos* whiskies.'

Not understanding, the man gestured to the bottles of doubtful wine behind him. I pretended to play the bagpipes and danced a smatter of a highland reel, saying, '*Dos* whiskies.'

'*Momento*,' he said and disappeared under the bar again. After a few moments' fumbling he rose and showed us a dusty bottle of Johnny Walker's Black Label. We could not believe our eyes, and nodded eagerly, rubbing our hands in anticipation. The man set two tumblers on the counter and filled each one to the brim. I knew enough Spanish to gasp, '*Agua por favor*.'

This he understood, and we took our glasses and a large jug of blessed water to a table. After two refills of the water jug and an hour later we rose not too brightly. To put it mildly, I was under the influence and Sean wasn't too far behind because he offered to pay. I asked, 'How much?' and the old man looked blankly, so I rubbed my finger and thumb together in the international sign language of money. Nodding, he pulled a dirty paper from his top pocket and wrote out the bill: seventeen pesetas. I stared at it incredulously – I wasn't that far gone. In real money seventeen pesetas was about five pence. Five pennies for a whole bottle of Johnny Walker Black Label! Sean immediately sobered up and asked him if he'd got any more bottles but sadly we found that that was the only one; he had had it for years and was only too glad to palm it off on to two innocent *ingleses*. I paid for it next morning with a monumental hangover but I put it down to the water.

After the break, we returned to Almeria to resume the filming of *Shalako*. A day later, I received a very unexpected visitor in the shape of Michael Mills, one of Tom Sloan's deputies and Head of Comedy. A fly had crawled into my apple crumble. His mission was to present me with a script for the lead in a new situation comedy entitled *Oh Brother*. The following morning being a day off, I sat on the floor of the veranda, my back against the wall of the hotel, and began to read. A shadow fell across my reading, and Sean sat down beside me to do a little revision of his *Shalako* script. We nodded at each other and then turned back to immerse ourselves in our separate problems. My script was all about an order of monks and the only thing to be said for it was that I would be wearing a monk's habit, which would hide the fact that underneath I'd be dressed for a quick getaway at the end of the show. Sean read through five or six pages of his script, his face clouding over, and then casually tore the pages out, screwed them into a ball and threw them over the veranda rail, which is what is known as editing.

'What's yours like?'

'So, so,' I replied.

'Is it funnier than your own show with Hattie Jacques?'

The realisation hit me suddenly like a runaway tractor. *Sykes and*

A . . . was still one of the top-rated programmes on the BBC, so why had Michael Mills come all this way to entice me to do something else? Had he been talking to Tom Sloan? I rose to my feet, went into the hotel and handed the script back to Michael, who was sipping a rosé at the bar. It was as if he had anticipated my reaction, because it didn't seem to bother him that I'd turned his offer down. It must have been a slack period at the BBC, as he stayed there for another three days, all expenses paid; or, who knows, he may have stayed on to offer the part to Jack Hawkins.

My BBC television situation comedy show with Hattie must have been in its tenth year, and was still attracting very high ratings. Tom Sloan was still refusing to recognise our success – in fact I believe that when our series was on television Tom decided it was a good time to go out to dinner.

Standing at the BBC bar one evening, I noticed him at the other end. Seeing me, he sidled over and with a smile that must have hurt him he asked me what I would like to drink. Before I could get over the shock, he went on, 'How's it going?'

Out of sync, I replied, 'I'll have a large whisky.'

Having had enough of this idle chat, he dived straight in with, 'It's time we offered you a five-year contract.' I felt that every word he spoke was an effort.

'Thanks for the offer, Tom,' I said, 'but I'll have to turn you down.'

He was flabbergasted 'Why?' he asked.

I told him that the thought of having to write one more series scared the daylights out of me and to be hooked for the next five years would be an ocean too wide.

He hadn't thought it necessary to mention the salary. Now, exasperated, he blustered, 'How much money do you want?'

'It is not a question of money,' I said. 'Money is irrelevant, but five years is an eternity.'

He stood back apace, as if I'd said, 'God is a transvestite.' 'What do you mean, money is irrelevant?' he challenged.

'Let me put it this way, Tom,' I said. 'If you were to offer me a million pounds, tax free, with the proviso that I would no longer write, act, appear on stage, in television or films, I would have to turn you down.' He was astounded, so I tried to make it simple. 'In short, Tom,' I explained patiently, 'for a million pounds you would have bought my life and no amount of money is worth that.'

He backed away, horrified, as if I had just broken out in boils. 'You're mad,' he croaked. How anyone could turn down a million pounds was beyond his comprehension, even if it did cost his life.

A week later I was summoned to Tom's office. I wondered if his mind was going and he was going to offer me a five-year contract. I heard him say 'Come in' to my knock, which was almost the end of our conversation.

'About the Montreux Festival,' said Tom, and I hadn't yet closed the door behind me. The Montreux Festival was the shop window of all the choice shows on television from anywhere in Europe.

'What about Montreux?' I said neutrally.

'How would you like to write something special for the BBC so that we could enter it in the Golden Rose?'

'Tom,' I said, 'I write something special every week in my show with Hattie Jacques. Why don't you submit one of them?'

He looked at me, puzzled, which consolidated my belief that had it not been for Frank Muir and Denis Norden my show would have been stillborn. At that moment, his secretary stuck her head into the room. Before she could utter a word, he said, 'I'm coming,' and left the room, leaving me to stare out of his window at the backside of the large statue.

It was only then that an intriguing thought occurred to me. It was not long since the big chiefs of BBC television's Light Entertainment had complimented me warmly on coming close to winning the prestigious Golden Palm award at the Alexandria Film Festival with my *Sykes and a Bath* and, even more mystifyingly, praised me on keeping up the standard in all my subsequent shows. Even more mystifyingly, according to the archives, did not Tom write me a letter, also complimenting me on this very subject? So the question still to be answered is why did not Tom Sloan submit any of my shows as I asked, and why was he so keen on me writing something special? Perhaps I am being unduly paranoid to think that should I have written something special and it had carried off a trophy Tom would have claimed the kudos. On the other hand, if what I wrote was a resounding flop, it would have proved him right and that I was indeed a flash in the pan.

I didn't write anything special and Tom never submitted any one of our shows, so the score remained nil nil at halftime.

Since the runaway success of the *Arthur Haynes Show* in 1957, Johnny Speight had fast-forwarded himself to the top of the writers' league, so when he wrote a show for Spike Milligan and me, we couldn't wait to start rehearsals, even though we hadn't yet seen the script.

The action took place in a small factory, whose main product was cheap rubbish. The firm conducted its low-grade business under the name of Lillycrap, and the workforce spent more time arguing the pros and cons of politics, racism and West Ham football club than working. I was the foreman in charge of this polyglot workforce played by Kenny Lynch, Norman Rossington, Geoffrey Hughes and Sam Kydd – what a cast!

In the first scene I was sitting at a bench, on which was a slowly moving belt. As each red nose with a small moustache underneath stopped in front of me, I tried the nose on in the mirror before me and if this monstrosity was unflawed I pressed a treadle, the belt moved on to the next red nose and so on. Then the same performance with a number of naughty fidos, followed by the big ear section. I was in the process of trying one of these on when Spike made his first entrance as a Pakistani. Insisting he was Irish and that his eyes were blue to prove it, he was applying to me for a job and I was assuring him that we already had our quota of foreigners. All through this back and forth I was wearing the big ear.

The show was entitled *Curry and Chips*, and so convinced were we of its chances of success that Norma registered a company under the name of Lillycrap Ltd and Johnny, Spike and I produced the

whole shebang. The first six shows were received just as we anticipated: the audiences were unanimous in giving us a thumbs up.
We were now not only performers but also businessmen; possibly
we were on the first rung of a new career.

However, there's usually a black cloud that spoils the picnic. The
powers in charge of Independent Television, although admitting
that the show was very amusing, ran scared at the prospect of
Johnny Speight on political satire, and as they were the guv'nors
our life as directors of Lillycrap Ltd was hilarious but short. It is a
strange fact that those who proclaim loudly against the introduction
of censorship banned such a beautiful Johnny Speight production
as *Curry and Chips*.

In 1970 an exciting event took place at Gleneagles Golf Club. This
is not another golfing story; it has little to do with the game but
everything about people.

Bing Crosby and the rest of his team, fifteen international American actors, came over from the USA to take on Sean Connery's
team from the UK. What a fabulous way to raise money for charity!
There were only four matches, but although the crowds wouldn't
see much golf Bing Crosby and Sean alone would be worth the
price of admission. My partner for the day was Val Doonican, a
genial Irishman who captured millions of hearts crooning ballads
from a rocking chair. Our opponents were Steve Forrest and George
C. Scott, a formidable character in his screen roles, which he carried
over to the golf course. Our conversation for the whole match was
parsimonious. I said, 'Good morning,' and George C. Scott nodded,
and I think that was it. The golf was quite forgettable – so much so
that I can't remember any of it.

The dinner in the evening is the main thrust of this narrative. It
was both magical and illuminating. The cocktail party preceding
the banquet was a noisy crowded affair. I was spellbound – so many
familiar faces I'd only ever seen from a seat in the cinema. I couldn't
help thinking that if a bomb were to drop on this assembly the
world would be a much poorer place. I'd met Bing Crosby once

before at Coombe Hill Golf Club, but when he came over to shake my hand I was surprised and delighted that he even remembered my name. We exchanged pleasantries and I was just about to mention how I used to impersonate him in a bucket when he introduced me to Phil Harris, a man I had idolised over the years for his memorable renderings of 'Dark Town Poker Club' and 'Woodman, Spare that Tree', which I had not only listened to hundreds of times but even memorised. He seemed genuinely pleased when I told him. 'Did you hear that, Alice?' he said. It was then that I noticed his wife. It couldn't be, but it was: my very first heart-throb Alice Faye. Many's the time I'd seen her on the screen supporting Betty Grable, and many's the time I had declared to myself that it should have been the other way round. Now in some extraordinary way she was still the girl of my dreams, age seeming to have had little effect on her. Fortunately the toast master announced that dinner was served, sparing me just in time from revealing my adolescent fantasies.

George C. Scott, who had not been present for cocktails, blew into the dining room with an icy blast of no good; he looked as if he'd just received his income tax demand. He'd obviously drunk more than his ration, but from the way he plonked a bottle of vodka on the table before him it was clear that he hadn't even started. By the time the sweet arrived, the vodka bottle was empty, and the atmosphere in that room presaged a cold front approaching. George C. Scott placed his hands on the table, while his angry red eyes lit on me, which is when I decided that the best place for me was somewhere else. With this in mind I made myself scarce. The rest of this sorry saga is anecdotal. Apparently George C. Scott roared into his suite, smashed up the furniture and hurled the table lamps against the wall, Burt Lancaster scurrying behind him and endeavouring to pick up the pieces. George fended him off and ripped the telephone lines from their wall sockets. This was a mistake, as without a telephone he had no means of calling a car to take him to the airport. At three o'clock in the morning he stormed out the front door of the hotel, closely followed by a porter yelling that he'd forgotten his golf bag. George turned and screamed back to throw the lot in the Liffey, from which I gathered that his geography was suspect.

After listening to this tragic narrative I felt nothing but pity for the man. If this is the price of fame, why do so many people fight tooth and nail to achieve it?

I frolic about in my make-believe house in Sebastopol Terrace under the watchful eye of my twin sister Hattie, but in the real world outside my head my eldest daughter Kathy has left school, having attained three A-levels in English, economic history and economics. Quite obviously she hasn't followed in my footsteps, since I spent a great deal of my education gazing out of the classroom windows at the busy dogs enjoying the Mucky Broos and each other. Kathy has now moved on to higher education, and has enrolled at Exeter University. There is only one drawback to this: she will be unable to commute, and as for most parents it is an emotional day when the first one flies the coop.

Monte Carlo or *Bust* can only be described as a sequel to *Magnificent Men*. With the same successful pairing of director Ken Annakin and writer Jack Davies, it was *Magnificent Men in their Flying Machines* on wheels. Terry-Thomas recreated his character of an autocratic rotter rogue in an international car race across France, with a will to win at all costs, even blackmailing his cringing pathetic doormat personal manservant, who was portrayed by me – a gift of a part. Gert Frobe, the Prussian bag of wind in *Magnificent Men in their Flying Machines*, was also an entrant. Blue chips in the world of entertainment, Peter Cook and Dudley Moore joined the cast. With all these ingredients it promised to be a banquet of fun. Most of the film was shot at the de Laurentis studios in Rome, where we spent eleven joyous weeks. Terry-Thomas and I were able to fly home to England every weekend, meeting at Heathrow airport on Sunday for our return flight, and here is an insight into the fun of being with Terry: even on the bread-and-butter flights of Al

Italia, he would hand over a small hamper to the stewardesses, who accepted it with due humility – for all they knew, he could have been the managing director of the airline, but more likely they recognised him for what he was, an international film star. Later I felt a small qualm as the other passengers picked at their plastic airline food with little enthusiasm while Terry and I helped ourselves to delicate home-made chicken sandwiches washed down with a Chablis of excellent vintage.

After a day's shooting, Jack Davies, his wife Dorothy and I spent many a happy evening in the pavement cafés in the Via Veneto, sipping a stream of sambucas as we watched the world stroll by.

Tony Curtis was leading man, an American actor of light and shade. There were days when his mood was full of energy and vibrancy, but on other days he would be down – the extraordinary change illustrating his Dr Jekyll and Mr Hyde personality. The first time he spoke to me was on one of his Dr Jekyll days. I was puffing contentedly on one of my Havanas when he came over, saying what a beautiful aroma, alluding to my cigar, and explaining that Cuban cigars were difficult to get in America. I wondered if I should offer him one, but as soon as the thought crossed my mind I gave it an early bath. The reason for his friendly manner became obvious when he asked me if I could bring him back a box of Havanas next time I went home, as I did most weekends. Havana cigars were not easy to find, but in my third tobacconist I was successful. Back in the studios on Monday I made my way to his dressing room. When I entered, he just scowled at me and I knew it was one of his bad days.

'One box of Havana cigars,' I said jauntily, putting them down by his elbow.

He didn't look interested and after a moment he turned to me and said, 'Well?'

'I managed to get you a box of Havanas,' I replied, adding, 'Eighty pounds.'

That seemed to hit a nerve. His face said it all: in his mind he hadn't expected to pay; I should have been honoured to present him with a gift. He turned his head. 'How would you like it?' he said sarcastically. 'Dollars or lire?' I was about to pick the cigars up and walk out but the only thing that held me back was that I couldn't afford to buy myself top-quality cigars at this price – it wasn't Christmas and it wasn't even my birthday. 'Sterling, if that doesn't inconvenience you.'

'I'll mention it to my accountant,' he said, turning back to the mirror. I was dismissed.

After a week of reminders I received my eighty pounds, delivered by a low menial of the crew.

Have the words 'thank you' been deleted from the American dictionary?

Notwithstanding, the whole trip was a hilarious romp which I wouldn't have missed for the world.

January 1971. The day Edith and I took David to boarding school wasn't a day to celebrate – it was too full of emotion. I felt as if my world was gradually disintegrating; from the moment we loaded his little wooden trunk into the boot of the car I couldn't trust myself to speak. Good grief, the school was only a few miles away in Epsom – it was not as if we were waving him aboard a convict ship bound for Botany Bay. The worst moment was our final embrace in the school yard. Neither Edith nor I spoke on the drive back home. However desperately I tried to look on the bright side, there didn't seem to be one, but on reflection I decided that it was all part of life's rich pageant.

Rhubarb, rhubarb – two words traditionally repeated ad infinitum by extras in a crowd scene to create a hubbub. *Rhubarb, Rhubarb* was the title of a 'silent' picture of mine. The word 'silent' is misleading in this case, as all the characters in the film spoke aloud, although 'rhubarb' was the only word uttered. For instance, 'I think your ball is in the rough behind the green' became 'Rhubarb rhubarb rhubarb, rhubarb, rhubarb, rhubarb.' I don't think I can explain it better than that. Hattie Jacques played the part of a nanny rocking a pram absentmindedly while sitting on a bench totally immersed in a book, and a close-up over her shoulder revealed that the only words in her library book were 'Rhubarb rhubarb etc.' I think this takes care of the title of the film.

As usual, most of my repertory company of humorists appeared in this 'silent', primarily because they had always made me laugh, funny people who would be the last to recognise themselves. For me the cherry on the cake of *Rhubarb, Rhubarb* was Bill Fraser as an inebriated club secretary. At long, long last I was able to repay him in some small way for his tremendous help in giving my career a kick-start and more importantly for saving me from perdition on a foggy night on the Embankment.

Charlie Drake was also my first choice for any part as long as it didn't require him to be over six feet. In my mind he is one of our foremost hilarious exponents of visual comedy, as shown in his classic series called *The Worker*, in which he bounced off another favourite of mine, Henry McGee. For some time now Charlie has been fighting ill health, so I write this in the hope that it will brighten his day to know that he's not forgotten.

Rhubarb, Rhubarb was a very enjoyable film to make, which we did on the tranquillity of a golf course. I'd love to shoot a re-make of this film, but sadly there aren't many of us left and possibly my gentle style of humour would be out of sync with the brash 'no holds barred' of today's confrontational comedy.

After another series of *Sykes and A . . .*, Paul Elliott rang to ask me how I felt about exhuming *Big Bad Mouse*. Naturally I was enthusiastic about the prospect, but Jim was the key factor, so I agreed, but only on the proviso that Jim would agree. Paul said there was no problem: Jim had already accepted on the proviso that I was included. It was the beginning of holidays with pay and laughs all the way, a prelude to future appearances in Singapore, Hong Kong, Australia, America, Canada, Rhodesia (now Zimbabwe). The world was definitely our oyster and Jim and I were the squeezed lemon and red pepper to go with it.

*   *   *

When I felt that *Sykes and A . . .* was coming to the point of overstaying its welcome, I re-wrote one of the episodes as a stage play so that we could travel to exotic spots in the world for a working holiday. This, I felt, would be a splendid thank-you for twenty years of success. However, Richard Wattis declined the offer, simply because he was afraid of flying. Desperately I tried to allay his fears by describing the luxury of first-class travel on a 747. He wasn't moved. 'Good grief,' he said fearfully, 'you won't get me in one of those. I have to take a Librium to cross the road.' Poor Richard – it was the last time I saw him. I was appearing in *Big Bad Mouse* in Florida when the news came that he had died in a restaurant, which was a nice way to go. I only hoped it happened before he paid the bill.

I was still determined to write my stage play, but in the meantime Jim and I were in the air en route to the Antipodes. Melbourne was to be my introduction to Australia and *Big Bad Mouse* my ticket. I was about to fulfil a long-felt yearning to set foot in the land of sunshine, rose-covered cottages and tennis rackets. Jim had been a regular visitor to Australia; indeed he'd once been up before the beak on a charge of using obscene language during his act in a night club. The magistrate had asked Jim if he would promise not to use words like that in future, to which Jim replied, 'I can't promise that, your honour.' Exasperated, the magistrate came back with, 'Well, do your best,' and dismissed the case.

From the moment I entered my room at the Chateau Commodore Hotel in Melbourne, I was hooked. Before I left England Max Bygraves had marked my card, suggesting I made contact with Viv Billings, an old golf pro now managing a golf shop. This was my first port of call. When I entered, he was speaking to somebody on the phone, and turning to welcome a prospective customer, he recognised me immediately. I guessed this because he dropped the phone, leaving it dangling on its chord but still squawking. His face lit up like Christmas Eve in Regent Street and he came round the counter to pump my hand up and down in a handshake that left my fingers white. Calling it a day, Viv closed his shop and took me home to introduce me to his wife Betty, who embraced me as if I was her long-lost son. Viv's second introduction was to George Norman and his wife Ada, close friends of theirs, and I was inaugurated into the tribe, although my feet had yet to touch the ground.

George, a one-armed man who could whip a tie round his neck and execute a Windsor knot single-handed quicker than I could with two, always had a smile on his face and Ada followed suit. They lived in a house on Greenacres Golf Club and when he left in the mornings to go to his office he put the front-door key under the mat so that Jim and I could let ourselves in and mix ourselves a drink before enjoying a round of golf. George sometimes joined us and his golf far out-classed mine – we called him the one-armed bandit. The best was yet to come. Jim and I were appearing at the Comedy Theatre in Exhibition Road, not far from a small music hall. Its significance was incredible: to my utter astonishment and joy above all things it was run by Vic Gordon no less, or Gordon Horsewell as I knew him in *Three Bags Full* in Schleswig-Holstein, the same Vic who'd later put me in touch with Frankie Howerd. I didn't even know he'd emigrated, and now to meet him again in Melbourne . . . Call it coincidence if you will, but I have inside knowledge, and I know for certain who was pulling the strings. Needless to say, Viv, George and Ada made a fuss of Vic and our tribe was in danger of becoming a movement.

Since that memorable baptism in Melbourne I have revisited the country many times; as a matter of fact, I think I've seen more of the country than most Australians. But not all my visits to the Antipodes were connected to my theatre work.

Besides hurtling round the Formula One track like a maniac, James Hunt, the world champion racing driver, found his relaxation on the golf course. So it was no surprise when he and I received invitations to play in a Pro-Am golf match preceding the Australian Open, all expenses, first-class, paid. It was a long way to travel for a game of golf but the offer was one I could not refuse, especially as it had been tendered by my new old friend Viv Billings.

James and I met for the first time in the front section of a British Airways 747. It was a long-haul flight: apart from a short refuelling stop in Bombay, we were in the air for twenty-six hours, quite long enough for us to get to know each other. I have always had problems with sleep and James produced a bottle of Night Nurse. I took a swallow just to keep him happy, knowing that it would have little effect on me. Wallop. I missed two meals and James shook me awake just in time to fasten my seatbelt for landing.

In the airport we were greeted by press photographers, microphones were thrust at us and a television camera pointed its implacable eye towards us as if we were the Prime Minister and the Foreign Secretary. I was still under the influence of the Night Nurse, so I can't recall too much of what happened. All I remember is that it was the last I was to see of James.

Outside in the hot sunshine I was given a rapturous welcome by Viv Billings, who took me under his wing and swept me off to another press conference, where I was asked all the same questions that I had answered at the airport. This lasted half an hour, but I didn't mind, as in a few more minutes I would be curled up in a sumptuous bed in a nice cool suite in one of the best hotels somewhere downtown. Viv, however, had other ideas. I was whisked off for a visit to a golf clothing shop, where I tried on a couple of pairs of golf slacks, which were to be worn during my match on the morrow. By this time my tanks were running dry, but it wasn't over yet. We called in at the club house for a quick lunch before a television interview on the town hall steps. From there we were driven back to the golf course, where a television camera beamed me all over Australia driving a ball from the tee. By this time my eyelids were beginning to droop and I was looking like Robert Mitchum after a thick night out. At six o'clock I was driven back to the hotel, where, filled with pleasant visions of that nice little room, I wondered idly if I could manage to undress before I fell into bed. On the other hand Viv was still bright as a sparkler. Then he lobbed in a hand grenade. When he said he would see me at seven o'clock, I replied that it was a wee bit early in the morning. Viv laughed as if I'd made a funny and chuckled that he was referring to seven o'clock this evening – less than one hour away. I felt like a beggar having his last crust snatched from him. He went on to explain that everyone would be there for the big gala dinner. My brain had superseded me and was fast asleep, so I couldn't think of an excuse; in any case, while I was struggling to remain upright Viv had disappeared. I tried not to look at the bed as I walked into the cold shower, and at seven o'clock I was sipping a glass of wine in an ante-room amidst a cacophony of conversation that receded and crescendoed as I pulled myself back to full consciousness.

The dinner was an effort and I was a very poor ha'p'orth as a conversationalist. Just as the pudding was being served, Viv came across and in order to be heard above the babble of conversation he shouted in my ear. 'Don't do more than half an hour,' he said, patting me encouragingly on the shoulder before disappearing into the cigarette smoke of his own table. Adrenalin surged through me as I frantically tried to cobble together some semblance of a humorous speech, but my tired old brain couldn't get past 'There were two peanuts walking down Piccadilly and one was assaulted.' There were three speakers before me and when I mounted the podium it had already gone midnight. I was desperately trying to look as if I was enjoying it, failing miserably in the attempt. As one of the guests said to me the following day, 'You'd had a few last night, sport' in a real heavy Australian accent.

My only happy memory of the evening was Peter Thompson coming up to my table and saying, 'I liked your swing on television this afternoon.' Not bad, coming from the great Australian golfer, a five times winner of the British Open.

Incidentally the Australian Open championship that year was won by Ian Baker Finch. I know because on the eighteenth green I had the honour of presenting him with the trophy. A few years later this remarkable man won the British Open, and if that isn't enough he married Viv Billing's daughter.

And here's another incidental from that trip: a couple of years later James Hunt and I met again in South Africa. I was appearing at the Civic Theatre, Johannesburg in *A Hatful of Sykes* and James was racing Formula One at the Kylami circuit. I was unaware of this until he rang me to ask if I would join him for breakfast on the following day, after which he would drive me to the racetrack, where I would be able to watch a few practice laps. I was standing eagerly in the hotel lobby when James drove up to take me to breakfast. What a thrilling day it turned out to be! I have vivid memories of the scream of the high-powered engines, the oily smells of hot metal, the unbelievable speed of the cars as they passed in front of me, infinitely more quickly than it looks on television and much more dangerous. James would do two laps then go back into the pit for a few heated words with his mechanics before he was off again on another suicidal circuit. Everyone seemed to be much too busy to chat, and I was too enthralled to ask questions. It was then that it was brought home to me just how near the limit this game of speed was. I was only sorry that I would be unable to see the actual race, as Sunday was our travel day. Unfortunately James didn't win or else I would have had two happy endings to my tale, which had begun on a British Airways 747 to Australia almost two years before.

Now to put all her education to the test Kathy, with a BA to her name, was about to take on all comers. She applied to the BBC for a secretarial position, and I rode up on my white steed with an offer to help: I knew one or two people at the BBC and I only had to pick up a telephone. But Kathy was horrified. She thanked me, at the same time making it clear that she wanted to chart her course in her own way. However, I need not have worried. The BBC had no vacancies, but, unruffled, she worked at Trident Television for a year as an executive secretary, which was the starting gun to the real world.

I heard the sad news that Tom Sloan had passed away, and although we had often crossed swords I missed him. The king is dead, long

live Michael Mills, who was still Head of Comedy, and the battle
began again.

An idea had been wandering aimlessly around in my head for a
series of six weekly shows with Hattie Jacques, Ian Wallace to sing
the ballads and myself for light refreshment. This was to be our
first venture under the patronage of Michael Mills, who introduced
me to one of his protégés, a young producer who shall be nameless
– suffice it to say that he was only six months out of BBC training
college. Sadly it is one of the well-known facts of life that a new
broom invariably wants to sweep clean, and this latest discovery of
Michael's was no exception. His opening salvo was to sweep away
all our hard endeavours of the last twenty years: he wanted to direct
and alter the script – which he did, and I had to spend precious
hours taking out all the rubbish he had inserted.

I discovered all this burning uneducated zeal on our first morning. Together Hattie and I were sitting in a coach, waiting to be
called to the location. All the action that was required was for Hattie
and me to board a bus, which would then move off. End of action.
We sat in the coach from nine o'clock until half past eleven, by
which time I was beginning to fume and Hattie to pacify and
counsel patience. At eleven thirty a boy came over to inform us
that we were wanted on set. We walked round to where the scene
was being shot. The budding Spielberg gushed over to us, proudly
explaining that he had already shot twenty-five set-ups. Hat
squeezed my arm and puffs of steam shot out from both my ears.
In fact he had recreated a mini play of his own. He had written
dialogue for the driver and conductor which not only would in
itself have made a passable soap opera but had little to do with
Hattie and me getting on a bus. It had been Michael Mills' promise
to me that all the direction of our outside filming would be my
domain, so I exercised my option. Sighting the camera on the
corner of the street, I called, 'Action.' The bus approached the stop
and pulled up. 'Cut,' I said. Moving the camera to a position
opposite, I called, 'Action.' Hattie and I came round the corner,

climbed aboard and the bus drove off. In two shots and five minutes I had accomplished what he had taken three hours to mess up.

In the studio he was just as well meaning but incompetent. Exhilarated by the power he felt he was wielding, he completely ruined two sketches, both concerning Alfred Marks and myself. As Alfred uttered the tag line, he cut incomprehensibly to a close-up of the back of my head. When I challenged him about this complete shambles, he was unflummoxed and replied coolly that the shot he had chosen to finish off the sketch was more dramatic. It was the last straw. I had to take matters into my own hands and I gave him what is politely known in the business as the bum's rush. Michael Mills was furious and he refused to accept the enormous gaffes his protégé had committed.

I was in no mood for an argument and decided to give him a face saver. I said, 'As far as comedy is concerned, we are incompatible.'

'He knows his technology,' said Mills urbanely. 'I think you should give him more time.'

I was appalled. 'Are you suggesting,' I said acidly, 'that I leave myself entirely in this man's hands?'

And to my horror he said, 'That's exactly what I'm suggesting.'

I had to leave before I hit him with the typewriter.

Dennis Main Wilson, who had done so many of my shows before, took over and we were back amongst the laughs again. When the series finally ended, we were all flushed and exhilarated, having won back our stripes. I was summoned to the office of Michael Mills. Foolishly I expected a pat on the back, and who knows, perhaps a large Glenfiddich, but one look at his face and I knew I would be back on the wagon that very night. With his eyes shining like a religious zealot's, he said, 'I want you to know that I've had the whole series wiped.' This I couldn't believe, as some of the visual scenes I could modestly claim as my best. 'You've destroyed them?' I blurted. And as I stared at him with incredulity, he finished with, 'That will show you who's boss.' I left the room before my Neanderthal instincts took over.

It was obvious that Michael Mills had never forgiven me for turning down the lead role in *Oh Brother*, a part that was eventually taken by Derek Nimmo. Incidentally the series turned out to be very successful.

In 1975 my little Rottweiler Kathy is installed as senior secretary to the Head of Drama Plays, at BBC television, all this achieved by her own efforts. I can only stand and admire her tenacity. Oh, if only Kathy had been there when I'd read the play I'd written for Frankie Howerd in the middle fifties.

Big Bad Mouse, apart from being a money earner for Jimmy Edwards and me, was becoming therapy, or as a normal person would put it a holiday. One of our overseas venues was Salisbury, the capital of Rhodesia, where we both stayed at the magnificent Monomatapa Hotel. Referred to as 'the ton of tomatoes', it was an extremely impressive building, with swimming pool, lawns and an excellent cuisine. Jim and I were allocated suites on the top floor, each suite decorated to suit a different nationality. For instance, quite understandably, the walls of Jim's suite were decorated with paintings of hunting scenes – in fact, the whole place was a shrine to a tally-ho England – while mine for some unaccountable reason was Spanish baroque, sombre and slightly menacing, and far removed from Lancashire. What did I expect? A wall full of cotton mills?

We were appearing at the Seven Arts Theatre, a warm friendly place with only one drawback: it had a corrugated iron roof, which meant that during the hot summer months the artists baked and in the monsoons the most stentorian thespians were rendered inarticulate. In fact the thunderous tattoo of heavy rain eclipsed even the booming declamations of Jimmy, and as he did the vocals and I did the visuals he wasn't best pleased. So for any future shows there, avoid the rainy season, unless of course you are in a ballet.

A most unforgettable occasion on this visit was when Jim and I were introduced to Ian Smith, the premier during the turbulent sixties. He was a tall, handsome man, bearing facial scars of a devastating crash in his Spitfire defending Britain in the Second

World War. Mrs Smith, a strikingly beautiful lady, quiet and unassuming, insisted we call her Janet, but behind her smile lurked a constant worry for the strain her husband was undergoing. Ian Smith was engaged in a more complicated war than the Battle of Britain, his opponent being Harold Wilson, our Prime Minister, a man I didn't entirely trust – his verbal footwork was usually obscured by a thick pall of smoke from his pipe. The stakes were high: Britain was determined to take Rhodesia from the premiership of Ian Smith and Ian was just as determined not to let go.

In a grand publicity coup Harold Wilson arranged to have talks with Ian Smith aboard a British warship, a neutral venue ha ha: a British warship with a crew of British sailors against one Rhodesian could hardly be called neutral. Nevertheless, Ian boarded the ship. During the first night at sea he was invited below to take drinks in the petty officers' mess. He was extremely surprised, but he accepted the invitation with more than a little trepidation. On entering the POs' mess, he received surprise number two: he was greeted by a round of applause. He was still bemused when the Chief Petty Officer handed him a glass of grog. For a moment Ian must have thought he had boarded the wrong ship, but there was no mistake, for they raised their glasses to drink his health. It was hardly the reception that Ian had envisaged. As he sipped his Nelson's blood, he confided to the Chief Petty Officer that on coming aboard he'd expected at best antipathy but realistically antagonism, so the warm welcome in the mess was doubly appreciated. The Chief Petty Officer spoke seriously when he addressed Ian. 'Sir,' he said, 'there are three hundred and twenty-six crew on this ship. Three hundred and twenty-five are on your side and only one against.' He took a sip before adding, 'And he fell overboard last night.'

Ian recounted this anecdote with obvious relish. If the views expressed on board that ship were anything to go by, HM's government wouldn't be having it all their own way.

When *Big Bad Mouse* finally ended its run in Rhodesia, Jim went home to England but as prearranged I stayed on for a holiday with

Edith, and Julie and David, now in their early teens. I knew that they would enjoy the wonders of this magnificent land.

From Salisbury we travelled up country by plane to Victoria Falls. What an incredible start to a sightseeing tour! We walked from the hotel where we'd stopped for tea through partial jungle, and still some distance from the falls we could hear the roar of millions of gallons of water cascading over the edge of a cliff. Getting closer, we saw the sun-glinted spray high above the treetops; and when we stepped into the open, we watched, spellbound, the awesome beauty and majesty of it all. A few years ago I had visited Niagara Falls, but what a contrast it was, to my eyes tacky, weary and over-commercialised, every day gazed upon by millions of gawpers; it was no comparison to the scene before us. Apart from the roar of the water, all was tranquil and one felt humbled and in a strange way cleansed. In a flash of vision I imagined what David Livingstone's reaction must have been on first encountering this wonder. It is not surprising that he named it Victoria. David and Julie gazed at it, unable to find words – there was nothing like this in Weybridge.

We were staying in little chalets which hung over the edge of a hill. Large windows afforded us a view of a small pool far below, where towards evening we could observe the wildlife congregating for a cooling drink – no different from our locals in fact. One morning the game warden, a huge Dutchman who spoke fluent, pedantic English, invited me to help him place salt blocks round the pool down below. These blocks enticed many different species of animal to the pool at eventide. This chore completed, I looked up to the chalets and waved, hoping that Julie and David would be watching – it's no good being intrepid without an audience. I climbed back into the jeep and the Dutchman, before switching on the engine, asked me if I'd like to see an elephant. Taking my questioning look for a yes, he drove off into the jungle. We were surrounded by trees and I began to wonder if I hadn't been a little too rash – after all I had the family to think of. As quietly as he could, he stopped the jeep, took his rifle from the back and then, stepping down, took a salt cellar from his top pocket and poured a stream of salt on to the ground. Instinctively I knew that this was to test the strength and direction of the wind. He beckoned me to follow and then strolled warily into the trees. I followed, all the time looking back over my shoulder at our transport in case of emergency.

Suddenly the Dutchman stopped and I almost walked into his back. He put his finger to his lips and pointed and there, not ten paces ahead, was the backside of a huge elephant, jutting out from the cover of some trees. It was enormous. We were close enough to see scars on its haunches. It was either dead or asleep and oddly enough the game warden's rifle was still lolling indolently in the crook of his arm. I was ready to go. I didn't want to see the rest of it – the hind quarters were enough for me and I could imagine the rest; it was too close. Suddenly the Dutchman cupped his hands to his mouth and shouted, 'Hup!' I jumped and before I came back to earth the elephant had disappeared into the undergrowth with a tiny squeal, tail in the air.

'What would have happened if he'd run at us?' I stuttered.

'I would have shot him,' he said.

I didn't believe him. His gun still lolled in the crook of his arm and at the speed with which Jumbo took off we would have been flattened while he was still trying to raise his gun.

'You've just destroyed a myth,' I said. 'I'd been taught that a bull elephant was one of the most dangerous of all animals.'

'Not this one,' he replied.

My admiration for him increased. If he could recognise one of them after only seeing the back half, he was truly a man to respect.

Later that evening we climbed aboard a truck. Edith sat in the front with the driver and Julie, David and I stood on the back, elbows on the roof of the cab. From there we went to the landing strip. The night was warm and black above us, with more bright stars than I'd ever seen in my life. A slight breeze sprang up as we began to roll up at the airstrip. This was our destination, a favourite place to see some wildlife. In second gear, we began to roll slowly up the strip ahead of us. A grazing herd of impala didn't seem too perturbed by our intrusion; they were probably used to it – in fact some of them were leaping over the beams of our headlamps as if it were a game . . . Something in my peripheral vision moved and I discerned a young lion stalking the impala. Ignoring the truck, it didn't even give us a glance, intent only on its supper. Then Julie pointed out another shape on the other side. It was another lion. Both David and Julie weren't too bothered – in fact had the truck stopped I felt they would have jumped down to stroke them. Thankfully the impala, getting wind of the cats, took off and the young lions leapt after them into the blackness of the night. The entertainment was over. We turned round and, suddenly remembering the load of fresh meat on the back of the truck, I was frantic to get home in case the lions were given the slip. It was with great relief that we arrived back and jumped down. The children were flushed with excitement but Edith, taking one look at my white face, asked me if it had been cold on the back of the truck and had I noticed the lions?

I suspected that the young'uns would not be particularly enamoured by a visit to the grave of Cecil Rhodes, remembering that on a previous tour of Rhodesia I'd driven up to see it in Bulawayo. It had been a scary experience for me, the hot cloying air somnolent, silent with a feeling of malevolence – a feeling engendered by the barrenness of the surrounding landscape: there was not a tree or a hut, the only living creatures a plague of lizards skittering over the black stone, under which lay the remains of the father of Rhodesia . . . So that was out. Instead Edith and I decided that once we'd landed in Bulawayo we'd take them to a game park.

We left Victoria Falls in a little Cessna, taking off up the same strip that had afforded us last night's adventure. It wasn't a long flight. The panoramic views as we flew over the Kariba dam were breathtaking, and I think we spotted a herd of elephants; in any event the journey was all too short. When we finally landed in Bulawayo, we were met by the assistant game warden, who took us under his wing. The game park was not the usual kind but a place where members of the public brought animals which they had domesticated as cuddly little pets and had now grown up to be unmanageable, if not downright dangerous. There was also a warthog that had been brought up to be a dog. Dogs are prone to chase passing cars and this warthog was no exception.

The assistant game warden took us to a wooden amphitheatre about fifteen feet in diameter and eight feet high, not unlike a toy bull ring, the difference being that this was a racetrack on which four piglets would race round and round. Each lap was no more than twenty yards, and their jockeys were monkeys, no bigger than a child's doll, in various racing blouses and caps, standing quietly in the starting gates as they awaited the off. We were the only spectators – that is, until another two dozen tourists wandered in and the place became packed.

A bell clanged and we all leaned forward with eager anticipation. Then we gasped as the gate shot up and the piglets raced round and round at an alarming rate. Five laps was enough, and on the sixth, without checking their pace, they all veered off into a tunnel in the stand and it was over; not one of the spectators was aware that the race had finished until they had all disappeared. What amazed me most of all was that although the tiny jockeys rode bareback, not one of them fell off; they crouched over their piglets as if their backsides were superglued.

I mentioned this to the deputy warden, but he assured me that this was not the case. The whole spectacle had evolved by a curious accident of nature. The piglets and the monkeys shared the pigpen. It was hot and humid during the day but the nights were cold and the monkeys snuggled up to the backs of the sleeping piglets for warmth, so forging relationships which had led to the piglets' gold cup that we had all enjoyed. He explained all this as we strolled along a fifteen-feet-high wire fence. Our day had hardly begun. While Julie and David couldn't stop talking about the short, sweet pig race, the warden unlocked a gate in the fence and ushered us inside the enclosure. As he took us up a grass hillock, I was a tad uneasy – shades of the lorry on our night's trek up the airstrip at Victoria Falls. At the top of the slight rise, we halted and there, about thirty feet in front of us, were two cheetahs lying out in the afternoon sun. Behind them was a small knot of spectators staring through the wire netting at our family staring at the cheetahs. I glanced at the warden but he smiled and quietly mentioned that the cheetah on the left had a broken foreleg and that its mate, having run full pelt into a stump of a tree in the long grass, was deaf in one ear. Join the club, I thought, but I was uneasy – a deaf cheetah could still have the better of us in one bound. I was partly mollified when the warden whispered that they were both heavily sedated. The deaf one opened his mouth wide in a yawn, but on the other hand being hard of hearing he might have thought he'd roared. Casually we strolled back to the gate, but I noticed that the warden had positioned himself where he could keep a wary eye on his patients. Ushering Julie, David and Edith out, he restrained me and asked if I'd like to see a hyena, locking the gate while he asked me – talk about a captive audience. Without waiting for a reply, he put two fingers in his mouth and let out a piercing whistle, and a hyena almost as big as a small donkey lolloped over the crest of a hill, making straight for us. There was nothing hostile in its approach but I would have been happier to have been on the other side of the wire fence with the spectators.

'Take a picture if you want,' said the warden. I lifted my movie camera up and strangely the brute didn't look half as fearsome through the eyepiece, even though it was now so close that if I'd dropped the camera it would have raised a lump on its head. At the time I was wearing shorts and I was just about to stop the camera when I felt something licking my leg. In fact licking is too mild a word – it was more like a wet iron file being rasped across my bare flesh. As I had the hyena in a close-up I realised with cold horror that another hyena had taken a fancy to me. I took the camera from my face very slowly and smiled uncertainly at the new arrival, and just as suddenly they took off and clumsily disappeared back over the hill. The warden looked at the silly grin fixed rigidly on my face. 'You were lucky,' he said. 'You shouldn't have shown them your teeth.'

While Edith took David and Julie to see more of the attractions, the deputy warden and I supped a cold beer, sitting on a bench under a tree. He asked me if I'd ever assisted in an operating theatre. Of course I hadn't; the theatres in my profession were of an entirely different operation. 'Come on,' he said, rising, and before I could ask where we were going we were back in the large enclosure and he was locking the gate behind him.

In front of us was a table and stretched out on the table was a comatose cheetah. We were quite close to the wire netting surrounding the enclosure in order to give the spectators outside a ringside view as a veterinary surgeon set its broken leg. One of the assistants was holding on to the sound foreleg while the deputy warden and I took a rear leg apiece. It is important to point out here that the cheetah was only sedated and not spark out – a full anaesthetic would not have done it much good. The surgeon took hold of the broken member and immediately the cheetah squeaked and twitched; in fact the back leg I had hold of jerked so much that I nearly joined it on the table and I realised that my task wasn't going to be as easy as I'd imagined. Holding on to the hind leg became hard and hair-raising work, and when the surgeon slapped wet plaster of Paris on, everybody holding the cheetah down was jerked about like a crazy team of folk dancers. I couldn't let go, but my imagination was running riot: if it managed to free its leg from my sweaty grasp those claws would probably take my arm off. After about twenty minutes I'd had enough and when the veterinary surgeon said we could all relax I could have kissed her, even though she was built like an overweight rhinoceros. I couldn't wait to take the family home and stand under a cold shower. It was only then that emotions other than fear, panic and rank cowardice were replaced by a small glimmering of pride. After all, there aren't many men in the history of the wild who can claim the distinction of hanging on to the hind leg of a live cheetah for half an hour and living to tell the tale.

On the whole I think Edith and the children enjoyed their vacation, and without a doubt the piglet Derby won the day.

It was not uncommon for me to be writing my scripts for the forthcoming series of *Sykes and A . . .* during the day while appearing on stage eight times a week in some play or other. It wasn't as onerous as it sounds: writing is a sedentary occupation, but romping about the stage could be described as occupational therapy. However, I may be forgiven for breathing an immense sigh of relief when all my scripts were accepted and the final curtain had fallen on whatever play it happened to be. Footloose and fancy-free, I looked forward to starting rehearsals for the series on television in the warm company of Hattie, Deryck and Richard. Like a conscientious farmer, I was leaving two fields fallow in order to plant a fresh crop.

Continuing my countryside analogy, another field was films for the cinema, to be perfectly frank my favourite medium. *Theatre of Blood* was the title of my next foray into acting for the approval of an implacable camera. Vincent Price as a lunatic Shakespearian thespian, whose daughter, Diana Rigg, was as much up the wall as her daddy, were the stars and the cast were straight out of the front pages of *Spotlight*: Ian Hendry, Harry Andrews, Coral Browne, Robert Coote, Jack Hawkins, Michael Hordern, Arthur Lowe, Robert Morley, Dennis Price, Diana Dors, Milo O'Shea and myself.

Ian Hendry was a friend of mine; Robert Morley and I had hit it off in the film *Those Magnificent Men in their Flying Machines*; Arthur Lowe was a nodding acquaintance; and Jack Hawkins and I had appeared together alongside Sean Connery and Brigitte Bardot in *Shalako* – we'd also played football together on a horrendous freezing night under floodlights at Brentford. So the cast were a family reunited.

A few months later, after the picture had been cut and printed and was showing in the cinemas, a car drove up to my house and the chauffeur announced that Mr Vincent Price, who happened to be making another film in Shepperton Studios, would be delighted if I would join him for lunch, the studios being a hop and a spit from Weybridge. I gladly climbed into the car.

When I met Vincent, I had quite a shock. His character in this film was Dr Death, a scary hombre in black frock coat full of muck and cobwebs, but the most chilling aspect was his face: the make-up was spot on and he looked like someone who had died several weeks ago. What I thought was a welcoming smile wasn't: the teeth had been painted on his upper lip. In spite of all this, there was no doubt about the warmth of his greeting.

I'm not one for practical jokes, but during lunch an unbidden one was taking shape in my mind.

Edith had invited two guests to lunch, a husband and wife I vaguely remembered as being slightly pompous, and the vision of them sitting on my patio sipping champagne as if they were at Royal Ascot had inspired my Machiavellian scheme. I outlined it to Vincent and his enthusiasm rubberstamped my schoolboy skylark. After lunch Vincent and I drove back to my house and sure enough the scene was exactly as I'd visualised it. Giving Vincent his props, I walked on to the patio to sit down at the table with Edith's unsuspecting guests. After a few perfunctory exchanges, I called out, 'Dr Death' and Vincent made his entrance, progressing to the table carrying a silver tray on which was a bottle of champagne in a bucket of ice. The sight of this long-dead manservant was enough for me, but to be brutally honest, our prank backfired with an almighty bang. For a start, the guests didn't recognise Vincent Price, which was my first mistake – I'd visualised them knowing who he was and being impressed by such an international star. The guests sat there frozen faced, and I'd let Edith down. As retreat was my only possible option, I went back to Shepperton with Vincent, leaving my poor wife to pick up the pieces. You can't win 'em all.

Needless to say, I have not seen either of the guests since. Sad really, considering that that day Vincent gave the best performance of his illustrious career.

Jimmy Edwards and I were back again in Rhodesia, with *Big Bad Mouse* as our excuse. I was beginning to love the country – in fact I was a born-again Rhodesian. My main interests in the country lay in travelling during the day, exploring the intricacies of Salisbury and, mainly, enjoying the golf course. Jim's recreations were more convivial: drinks with old friends and acquaintances, gargantuan lunches followed by a couple of hours' shut-eye at the Monomatapa Hotel surrounded by murals of red coats, horses, hounds and stirrup cups. One day, however, we received an invite to lunch at an army mess in Bulawayo. Jim accepted for both of us – he never turned down a good free meal and provided the wine was tolerable he would be home, if not dry.

The Rhodesian Army were very hospitable; the food was excellent, the wines good and the world seemed a much happier place as we took our coffee out on to the veranda. Immediately I perked up. On the lawn before us the regimental band was assembling. This was promising; the grey clouds in my head evaporated. Here I must admit that if I have a weakness it is for brass bands, be they Salvation Army, Bickershaw Colliery, Black Dyke Mills or Foden Motor Works. Military bands of all the services set my pulses throbbing with something akin to patriotism, but I have a special place in my heart for the drums and the evocative skirl of the pipes of any Scots regiment. Now to complete a perfect day here was the Rhodesian Army band, laughing as they tuned their instruments, sun glinting on the brass, kettle drums rattling. I pulled back my shoulders as they crashed into their first offering: it was magnificent, and the music uplifted my very soul. I could have marched behind that band, carried along by the solid beat of the big drummer, resplendent in leopard-skin apron and banging his drum as if it had misbehaved. The next number was a slow march, and there was even a waltz somewhere, but the best was yet to come. The highlight of the afternoon's entertainment was a rendering of the regimental march 'Sweet Banana'.

The day that had started as bleak mid-winter was coming to a close in a beautiful African twilight. But there is no such thing as a free lunch, a cliché I would normally avoid, but in this case it is applicable, as the cap fits – there you are, another cliché, proving that they are contagious. Two days after our wonderful visit to the mess in Bulawayo, Jim and I were asked if we would entertain the troops. Naturally we were only too pleased to repay their wonderful hospitality. It is always daunting to walk on to a stage armed only with your wits, but on this occasion the soldiers were what we would call a pie audience: some were white, most were black but more importantly they all laughed with equal gusto in the same places. It turned out to be a very good impromptu concert. Jim and I, flushed with success and a little whisky, were sitting ducks for the sucker punch.

Unbeknown to us, the show had been televised, and on the following morning I had a telephone call at the Monomatapa, from a newspaper reporter at the *Daily Telegraph* who informed me that excerpts from our concert to the troops had been shown by the BBC in England. Immediately my stomach was full of sirens, flashing red lights and alarm bells frantically bouncing up and down on the scrambled egg I'd had for breakfast. The word 'excerpt' hit me hardest. Jim and I had made no secret of where our sympathies lay and a few references about Harold Wilson had been less than complimentary. It was likely that these were the 'excerpts' which would have been lumped together in an edited version of our show. When the reporter asked me for an interview, I was wary; I could answer his questions for half an hour, but again only 'excerpts' of my answers would be printed. I had a brainwave. 'How about if I write the column myself? It'll save time.' He agreed readily and I suspect he was relieved not to have to go through the tedious business of conducting an interview.

With the dawn the *Daily Telegraph* was pushed under my door and I read my piece. It wasn't bad at all; in fact I wondered for a second or two if there wasn't a latent journalist in me. As the days went by, there were no repercussions – perhaps not many people had read it and it had gone by unnoticed. After all, it had not been on the front page but was in the section that people normally leave at the newsagents. As far as I was concerned, that was the end of the matter. How could I possibly be so naïve? I relaxed, and while my guard was down, sucker punch number two was on its way.

A week later, the run of our play having ended, we returned to England. Much as I enjoyed Rhodesia, it was always good to be home. Putting down my suitcase, I was about to utter a husky 'Hello' to Edith when the phone rang. It was the BBC, inviting me on to a chat show to be interviewed by Eamonn Andrews. When I asked what the subject would be, the spokesperson replied, 'Your concert in Rhodesia.' Good grief, I thought that was dead and buried – it was almost a fortnight ago. We must have ruffled a few high-profile feathers. The programme had obviously been cobbled together in haste to fan the embers of our Rhodesia troop concert into flame. This being the case, Eamonn, always highly strung, was already perspiring. It was an interview that would have to be handled like runny gelignite, especially as he and I were good friends.

He bowled me a few short balls, eliciting from me my love of Rhodesia and support for Ian Smith, but when he turned to my opposite number, hostilities began. I can't remember his name – the brain tends to lock away the memory of most unpleasant incidents only to release them to put the mockers on a happy moment. The discussion ended in a bitter slanging match, throughout which Eamonn was ignored, until a hurried 'Well, I'm afraid that's all we have time for.'

Now could we please put the unhappiness of our Rhodesia concert to rest? Not an unreasonable request . . . There was one more spark in this everyday story of theatrical life. *Big Bad Mouse* was touring again, our first date the Coventry Hippodrome. On opening night, I walked from my hotel to the theatre, and when I arrived there was what at first I took to be a queue at the box office, the dream of every performer. In fact it was a demonstration, the whole theatre was being encircled by students holding up placards reading 'BAN SYKES AND EDWARDS. RACISTS'. They were ambling slowly round and round, white-faced and dead-looking. It was a pretty cold night and I assumed that the heating had failed in their university and that this protest was as good a way as any to ward off hypothermia. I pushed through the line and somebody handed me a pamphlet. Luckily I was muffled up against the cold and thus unrecognisable. Another surprise lay in wait. As I walked through the stage door, two burly constables were standing just inside. I don't know what it is about policemen, but when they are indoors wearing greatcoats, gloves and helmets they fill a medium-sized room. 'This is him,' said one of them. I nodded and proceeded to my dressing room, only to find that they were still with me. 'Just to see you don't come to any harm,' said the spokesman as they followed me in, taking off their helmets as if my dressing room was a holy place. I motioned them to sit down. Not a word passed between us while I changed into my costume, but before I went out I pointed to a bottle of Queen Anne whisky. 'Help yourselves to a nip,' I said and I made my way to the stage. When I returned at the interval they were still sitting, implacable as two garden gnomes, just as I had left them except for one thing: the whisky bottle was now half empty.

At the end of the show, sweaty and breathing hard, I returned to my dressing room, and yes, you've guessed it, the bottle was empty. So I quickly nipped next door to Jim's room to nick some of his. When I came back with half a glass, the two policemen rose to their feet, and put on their helmets, and one of them said very politely, 'You'll be all right now, sir,' and they left, leaving no sign of them having been except for the empty bottle of Queen Anne. It is so comforting to be under police protection.

Paul Elliott, who had taken over the production of *Big Bad Mouse*, now took up the reins of *A Hatful of Sykes*, my stage show. We toured the provinces for a few weeks in order to knock it into shape enough for it to be able to say hello to the world.

Our first venue was the Seven Arts Theatre, Rhodesia, where I still had what was turning out to be my permanent suite on the top floor of the Monomatapa Hotel. This was the beginning of a holiday. It was so good to see Hattie sitting by the pool beneath an umbrella, smiling as she watched two white bathing caps keeping the sun off the heads of Deryck Guyler and his wife Paddy as they swam in synchronised breaststroke back and forward – in fact they had a morning routine of five lengths before they had their coffee.

I sat under the umbrella next to Hattie. Peace, tranquillity and warmth. This, however, was only the Band Aid on a festering sore. As I looked away from the pool and down on to a street running away from the Monomatapa, something didn't quite fit. Almost immediately I knew the answer: the street, usually full, alive with pedestrians and traffic, was deserted and completely static – that is except for what looked like a rather large rucksack parked by the kerb. Other guests of the hotel became curious; drinks about to be drunk were suspended. At that moment two British soldiers rounded the corner at the top of the street and approached the mysterious baggage, over which they crouched. After a few moments, they walked smartly away, disappearing round the corner, and about ten seconds later there was a loud crack and a gout of flame, and smoke erupted from whatever it was. Everyone remembered the drink in their hand and as if it had been rehearsed they lifted the glasses to mouths already agape and took a hearty swig. It was just another incident in a trouble-torn Rhodesia.

Rhodesia was our first port of call in a very colourful itinerary: Hobart in Tasmania, and then Ottawa, Hamilton, Halifax, Nova Scotia, Johannesburg and Cape Town. Not a bad little package tour with weekly salaries thrown in, and all we had to do in return was to entertain our hosts.

As usual in all my association with Hattie, she was the life and soul of the party. Taking over the stewardship of our happy band of rogues and vagabonds, she was our counsellor, nurse and barbecue cook, a make-believe sister to be proud of.

Unbeknown to me at the time, that wonderful magical tour was to be the last time Hattie and I would work together.

I went to see my father, who was in an old people's home just a short walk from where he lived, which was fortunate because Mother visited him every day. Dad seemed in high spirits and appeared to be quite normal until he said to me, 'Our Eric is coming to visit.'

I took his hands and said softly, 'I am Eric,' but he didn't appear to have heard; he was too excited by the prospect of my visit. I stayed to have a cup of tea with him while he rambled on disjointedly about people I had never even heard of, understanding only when he referred to me as being late and wondered if I'd been held up in traffic that this wasn't Dad: this was some stranger wearing his body.

I never saw him again, and Mother wasn't too long in following him to a better life.

About a month later, Jimmy Edwards and I were finishing our run of *Big Bad Mouse* at the O'Keefe Centre in Toronto. We were due to fly out on the Sunday for our next venue, Chicago, which as everyone knows is in America and only cigar smokers are aware that you cannot get Havanas in the land of plenty. I called in at the cigar shop in the arcade of the Royal York Hotel in Toronto and asked for six boxes of my favourite cigars. The lady behind the counter said, 'If you're going to America they'll only allow you two boxes.' I thought for a moment and decided to take a chance. If the Americans got stroppy, Jim could claim that two boxes were his and at least I would have cut my losses but there is a saying about crossing that bridge when you come to it. So with my hand luggage bulging, I took a cab to the airport, and went through passport control and customs completely relaxed. This side of the border was a doddle. When I zipped open my hand luggage for inspection, the official said, 'Jeeze, you smoke a lot,' and zipping up my bag again he wished me, 'Bon voyage.'

It was an anxious flight for me, which I mentioned to Jim. He obviously put it down to a fear of flying. Chicago wasn't a very long haul but as we neared our destination my uneasiness increased. I took down my bag from the overhead compartment and shrugged into my overcoat. Jim said, 'You've got half an hour yet.' I didn't answer him. I was becoming furtive. I took four boxes of cigars out of the bag. Two of them I placed together and shoved up inside my overcoat. I had to ask Jim to help, as they had to be pushed up my back. He now tumbled to my stratagem and began to chuckle. The other two boxes I put inside my coat under my arms and when we landed between banks of snow Jim could hardly contain himself. Inside the airport, I had to bend forward to keep secure the two boxes up my back and the boxes under each arm, with a heavy suitcase in one hand and a light bag in the other. Jim was now beyond control, tears streaming down his face as he leaned against the wall to get his breath back. The passengers from the plane gave us a wide berth, which was hardly surprising – a beefy one with a huge handlebar moustache having hysterics against the wall while his companion, a bony cripple with an oblong hunch on his back, struggled to calm his laughing companion. It was a very long walk through the airport and I was exhausted when we finally passed through the exit doors. Then it came to me: we were outside in the bitter frost of a Chicago winter. 'Where's the customs?' I said. Jim had another paroxysm of laughter; he couldn't speak, and when he did, it was with difficulty, but he managed to enlighten me. 'The customs,' he said, pausing for another gulp of mirth, 'the customs were the ones you came through in Toronto.'

After allowing the penny to drop, I joined in Jim's merriment. Welcome to Chicago. On the Monday morning I was still chuckling as I visualised what a ludicrous specimen I must have seemed as I limped through the airport festooned with boxes of cigars. Whenever I flew to distant lands I always seemed to leave my brains at Heathrow.

A Chicago winter is no place for the unwary. The cold is bearable; it is the chill factor that is the killer. The malevolent winds blowing in off Lake Michigan have no difficulty in picking out visitors from the unsuitability of their clothing. Jim, being built like a wartime bunker, was impervious to the onslaught, but I was a different kettle of halibut. The mad wind hounded me so much that on one particular blow I took a cab merely to get to the other side of the road. The driver refused payment as there was nothing on his clock for a U-turn.

The Studebaker Theater on Michigan Avenue was to be our introduction to America. It wasn't a huge place, but big enough for comfort. From the stalls, I took in the empty stage. The set had not yet been erected. There were hanging ropes, gantries looking down on to the stage from about twelve feet, and a feeling of age and dust. It could have been a replica of a poop deck on one of Admiral Nelson's flagships. This would all be changed when the stage hands erected the set of Chunkybix, our office in the play.

On the morning of our opening performance, Jim telephoned

my room to suggest that a walk through Chicago would be a good advert for our show. I understood exactly what he meant.

Jim breezed into town like a strong gust of wind off Lake Eerie in his British, warm, knee-length brown overcoat to match his bowler hat, shining red cheeks behind his imposing white moustache – a walking Union Jack. Passers-by stared with open-mouthed curiosity. They must have thought that Father Christmas and his chief carpenter were doing a recce before Christmas. Jim decided that a bracer wouldn't do any harm and as there appeared to be a large bar next door to the theatre he began to smack his lips at the prospect of what we were about to see. The place was enormous: all along the wall was a bar fifty feet long, behind which were five or six barmen preparing themselves for their regulars. As we were the only customers bearing down on them, they gaped in wonder at Jim; an aircraft carrier to my mine sweeper, striding towards them, he looked formidable. We made our way to the centre of the long bar and commanded their whole attention when he ordered two pink gins.

'Pardon, sir,' said the barman. 'We have Booth's gin, Beefeaters, Gordon's – we have every gin there is except pink.'

'Bring me a glass,' said Jim, in a voice that brooked no argument. The other barmen eased up inquisitively towards their unfortunate colleague.

'Do you have angostura bitters?' said Jim in a mellifluous English accent.

'Yes, sir,' replied the barman. 'We have every drink in the world.'

'Except pink gin,' replied Jim acidly.

The barman looked round to his mates for support. He produced the angostura bitters and waited for Jim's next command.

'Shake a few drops into the glass.'

The barman did so.

'Now, swill it round the glass,' said Jim, twirling his finger to demonstrate.

Again the barman did so, and then he stood back to await the pay-off. By this time all the barmen were together in a small bunch, goggle-eyed at this mystery man from another clime.

'Throw it away,' said Jim.

'Throw it away,' echoed the barman, looking at the others as if he suspected it was going to be a practical joke, but he emptied the angostura into his sink somewhere under the bar.

'Now fill the glass with Beefeaters.' Jim took the glass, sipped it and exhaled. 'Ah, that is what I call a pink gin.'

The barman, only too pleased at his newly found skill, mixed one for me. It was the first in my life, or better still my last. A glass of paraffin would have been preferable. I'd never seen Jim partake of a pink gin before, but Jim was as cunning as an alcoholic fox: his demonstration was a very clever subterfuge to attract publicity for our opening night. The bartenders would talk to their customers, eager to describe the portly aristocratic actor from England, and he would become the talk of Chicago, exactly as Jim had envisaged. It succeeded well beyond his expectations, for in the evening edition of the local paper there was a whole column devoted to Jim and his pink gin and the theatre was packed. What was more, they were a wonderful lot, exuding whiffs of pink gin every time they laughed.

When Jim made his first entrance, the applause was fair but not ecstatic, and when it died down Jim, as was his usual practice, glared at them and in the waspish tones of a dyspeptic housemaster declared, 'I would scarcely describe *that* as an ovation.' Whereupon he clapped his bowler hat on his head and made a smart exit upstage, appearing again immediately to a tumultuous welcome. It never failed. Shortly afterwards came my first appearance. At this Jim normally strode to the side of the stage and addressed the audience: 'Eric will be on any second now. Whatever you do, don't applaud. He doesn't like it – it brings him out in a rash.' Naturally when I entered the applause was generous, but on this particular opening in Chicago my entrance round was tumultuous. I accepted the applause with modest bows and made ineffectual attempts to put an end to it. Jim had a look of complete astonishment on his face. I'd never before been welcomed with such an ovation. Eventually I turned towards the wings, drawing my forefinger swiftly across my throat, and the applause was cut off. It was a recording of some great artist's appearance and it did the trick. The audience were laughing and I hadn't opened my mouth. Then I said, 'I'm no fool, I brought my own,' and from that moment we couldn't go wrong; the laughter and the ad libs throughout the show made us overrun by twenty minutes. After the curtain came down, the cast applauded us too. They'd never actually seen either of us as Jim and I had not attended rehearsal. The cast had been taken through their paces by the company manager, and the stage hands had been leaning on the fly rail looking down on the proceedings, bored out of their minds by what they took to be an English play. How it had managed to travel to the US of A was beyond them. However, when the final curtain came down they hurried on to the stage in order to shake our hands, and one of them said, 'Gee, this is vaudeville.' He will never know that he had awarded us the highest accolade.

On the Tuesday morning the reviews in the *Chicago Tribune* were flattering and effusive. Jim's ploy with the pink gins had proved to be worth a hundred sandwich boards and the Tuesday night's audience confirmed it. We had arrived not with a whimper but a nuclear explosion; the gates were open.

News of success, especially in the American theatre, travels quicker than *Apollo II*. Reviews in the newspaper of any new show are avidly devoured even before a quick flip through the obituary column, which is why Jim and I were astonished and delighted to receive an invite from the legendary Peggy Lee, who was appearing in cabaret at the Empire Room in the Parma House; it was an open invitation to one of her performances any evening after our own curtain had come down. I couldn't wait to accept: Peggy Lee had been one of my idols ever since I could afford a gramophone. As for Jim, he was excited at the prospect of drinking a glass of champagne with her – in fact he was excited at the prospect of drinking a glass of champagne with anybody as long as it was on the house.

When we arrived we were escorted to a table by the cabaret floor and almost before we were seated two glasses and an ice bucket containing a bottle of champagne were placed before us. Jim's evening was made even before it had begun.

A door opened and Peggy walked out, looking more beautiful than I had ever imagined. The applause was rapturous, and from that moment she took hold of the audience. She even found space to introduce Jim and me to the audience, who applauded us in spite of the fact that she announced us as Eric Edwards and Jimmy Sykes. We didn't know whether to stand or change places.

After her show a minion came over to our table to escort us to Peggy's inner sanctum. The door from the cabaret floor led into her dressing room and when we entered she was lying on an enormous bed, holding an oxygen mask to her face. As far as I could see, the bed was the only furniture in the room, apart from a fairly middle-class chair, which Jim, being the elder, took. This left me standing, but only for a moment. She patted the bed beside her. It was a natural friendly gesture, but it was also ludicrous: if I sat on the bed, I'd have my back to her. So, taking the bull by the proverbials, I stretched out beside her on the bed, tipping my newly bought but as yet never worn Stetson over my face and in passable American drawling, 'Thankee kindly, ma'am.' Having the hat over my eyes, I couldn't judge her reaction, but the shaking of the bed gave me the OK – she was chuckling. Jim and I did most of the talking, as talking would have been difficult for Peggy while holding a mask to her face but from the way her eyes were dancing it was obvious that she was enjoying listening.

About ten minutes before Peggy's second performance, there was a knock on the door. Jim answered it, standing aside as an elderly lady dressed in black came in. She wasn't too pleased to see me lying on the bed with my hat on, and the bed began to shake again as Peggy enjoyed her discomfiture. She sat primly on the edge of the chair and Peggy spoke for the first time. Lifting her mask, she introduced us. The old lady was Ginger Rogers. Before we could recover our composure, there was another knock on the door. We turned eagerly towards it, expecting Fred Astaire, but it was only one of the staff to tell Miss Peggy five minutes please. She slipped off the bed to touch up her make-up and we thanked her profusely and made our exits, giving Ginger the opportunity to say, 'Who did you say they were?'

Our show at the Studebaker improved with every performance and fortune was smiling on us. One night while I was offstage, a huge cockroach was making its laborious way across the stage. Jim pointed to it and followed it quietly. The audience were standing in order to see it better, and when Jim felt the time was right he lifted his great size-twelve boot and squashed it flat. A gasp went up from the audience and as they sat down again Jim said, 'I shouldn't have done that. Eric will be on in a minute and he's against blood sports.' Another roar of laughter. Then he took a sheet of foolscap and wrote on it the word 'DEAD' and placed it over the cockroach. In my dressing room I heard all this laughter and I knew instinctively that something out of the ordinary had happened, so before I went on I asked the stage manager what was going on and he told me the whole story. When I made my entrance, I could see the sheet of foolscap, but I deliberately ignored it, walking up and down and stepping over the piece of paper. Jim's eyebrows were going up and down in a frantic signal; he was thinking I hadn't noticed, and even the audience were wondering if I'd missed it. Eventually I stopped, lifted the paper and turned to Jim accusingly. 'Thank you very much,' I said. 'I was training that one,' which brought a round of applause.

But that was only the prologue. Two nights later a small group of Americans came round the back to congratulate us on one of the funniest evenings they'd ever spent. It was so gratifying, even more so on foreign soil.

They were recounting some of our antics when one of them said, 'We saw the show two nights ago and it was funnier tonight. The only thing is, what happened to the cockroach?'

I said, 'Jim killed it.'

'I know,' replied the man, 'but you've got more than one, haven't you?'

It was amazing. I said, 'The British customs are very strict and they only allow us to take one out of the country at a time.'

The man was unfazed. 'I can bring you hundreds of cockroaches,' he said eagerly. Jim laughed until I thought he would have a seizure, especially when the man went on. 'No, I'm serious,' he said. 'I'm on vacation at the moment but when I get back to Milwaukee I'll send you a crate.'

I thanked him very much. It made Jim and me laugh for the rest of the evening.

We were beginning to enjoy ourselves as kings of the heap, but I will never learn. The bookings were better than they had ever been since records had been kept, Broadway was just around the corner and, if that wasn't enough, we were looking forward to a crateful of cockroaches from Milwaukee. It is at times like these that one has to be careful: disillusionment is usually just around the corner.

On Wednesday Jim and I made our triumphal way to the theatre for a matinee. We were both looking forward to repeating the euphoria of the first two nights. As we neared the Studebaker, my heart beat joyously as I noticed the milling crowds outside. But something was not quite right: the surging crowds were not clamouring to go in but coming out of the theatre to hang about on the pavement – very odd. We pushed our way through the puzzled mob and on entering the theatre we noticed policemen herding the last few of our audience up the aisles towards the exits. In my dressing room a plain-clothes man introduced himself as Lootenant whatever – I didn't get his name; I knew he was a detective, though, because he wore a dirty mac and didn't take off his fedora. He explained that the theatre was being closed down. He was sorry, but he had his orders. We were the innocents picking buttercups in a minefield. Apparently Mayor Daly was up for re-election and his principal objective was to clean up the city. Because of an overspill of porn movies he had closed all the cinemas – a draconian step, but Mayor Daly was a tough cookie. There were howls of dissent from the cinemas, who fired back, 'You've closed us down, but what about the theatres?' 'Close them as well,' was his no-nonsense reply, and that's why the police had declared the Studebaker Theater a no-go area.

I pleaded with the Lootenant. Our show was squeaky clean – not a harsh word, not a double entendre or even a single one; nobody swore; nor did any of the cast strip off. But the surrogate Colombo was adamant. It was ridiculous, really, to close all the theatres in Chicago when in actual fact we were the only one open. When I explained this to the Lootenant, he spread his arms and said, 'In seven weeks we're expecting Henry Fonda,' and then, appealing to my better nature, he added, 'And you wouldn't want us to close on Henry, would you?' I couldn't make the connection, but as we left the theatre the crowds were still milling, so Jim and I gave them half-an-hour's ad lib performance, Jim on trombone and me with two waste-paper bins for bongos, at the end of which they applauded, and the most enthusiastic was the Lootenant.

As news of our undignified bum's rush reached Paul Elliott in London he very generously arranged for us to spend a few days in Fort Lauderdale, Florida, before we opened at the National Theater in Washington, DC. Golf is my first passion but a close second is deep-sea fishing, and as I didn't have any golf clubs with me and there were fishing boats tied up I spent the next few days at sea after the big ones. These unfortunately avoided me like the plague, but I did see a few. The warm sun put a little bit of colour back into our cheeks and when we finally made our way to Washington, our tanks had been replenished.

Our hotel in Washington was palatial, possessing an annexe consisting of several self-contained flats. Most things in America tend to be exaggerated and this was no exception, the place was so enormous that when the bell boy deposited my suitcase in my flat, it took me half an hour to find where he'd dumped it, and while I was looking for it I discovered a grand piano in the corner of one of the rooms. There were more surprises in the pipeline. Jim came in with the paper, from which he had found out that Peter Cook and Dudley Moore were appearing at the National Theater in *Beyond the Fridge*. Immediately we booked seats. It would not only be a treat to see them both again but would give us the chance to see what the stage was like from the audience's point of view. The theatre was packed and the laughter was continuous – it made us proud to be British and slightly apprehensive about how we would follow that level of entertainment. When the show was over, Jim went off to some party or other and I went back stage. The magnificent two were surprised and delighted to see me, and before they could ask me what I was doing in America I cut them short, telling them that

Jim and I would be following them in next week, and with tongue in cheek I thanked them for a most generous warm-up.

On the Sunday prior to our opening I was watching an American football game on a television set so big that the players were taller than me. Answering a ring at the door bell, I opened the door to the manageress, a smart middle-aged lady called Rose – her surname was on a tag pinned to the front of her blouse, but to stare in that direction for any length of time would show a lack of breeding. She asked me if I would like to visit Muhammad Ali, as he was occupying the flat below. I was thunderstruck and hastily replied that I'd like to very much and asked if she would kindly contact Jim so that we could go together. By jingo, an audience with Muhammad Ali! Prudently I thought I mustn't remind him that I was at the ringside when Henry Cooper belted him a left hook that despatched the then Cassius Clay into another dimension. Ten minutes later we were in the flat below. I had estimated that we would call, introduce ourselves, shake hands, end of story, but it didn't turn out like that. It was incredible. The moment we walked in, he invited us to sit down on the settee with him and he kicked off with a funny anecdote and after a funnier one in return from Jim in no time at all we were chatting together as if it was a family reunion. I can't help thinking that Rose must have given us a tremendous build-up.

We explained to him how we ad-libbed on the stage and he countered with how he had sometimes ad-libbed during his fights. Sometimes it works, he told us, but when it doesn't you are in the realms of astrology. He was really loose and a couple of other fellows in the room were laughing with us. I told him how we sometimes had guests walk into our office on stage and we'd take it from there. The most recent case was Henny Youngman, an American comedian who played a violin badly. The only difficulty was that once he had got a laugh we couldn't get him off, and when he eventually went we'd both forgotten where we were in the play. Muhammad Ali suddenly became serious. 'Tell you what,' he said, and he told us that the following evening he had to fulfil a speaking engagement, which he estimated wouldn't take more than twenty minutes, and after it he could make his way to the theatre and be the surprise guest of the evening. It was just what the doctor had ordered – what a send-off for our opening night!

Jim and I rose to take our leave and Muhammad surprised us again by saying that one of the guys in the room was a photographer and why didn't we have a picture taken together? So we sat down again. Two flashes and we took our leave. What a lovely way to spend an afternoon! Unfortunately, he never joined us on stage. According to our landlady, Rose, his speech, which should have taken no longer than twenty minutes, turned out to be over three hours, finishing an hour after our final curtain. She passed on a message from him to say how disappointed he was to have missed us. It was then that I remembered the photographs. She said not to worry, she'd see we got them. The good lady did more than that: she collected the prints. Muhammad Ali, passing through on the following Sunday, popped into the hotel to collect his photos and to sign mine, and here is the most intriguing message he wrote on the photo: 'To Eric Sykes. A man's wealth is in his head not in the bank. If it's in the bank, it belongs to somebody else.' And he signed it Muhammad Ali.

While we were at the National Theater in Washington in *Big Bad Mouse*, Woody Herman and his orchestra were to appear at a tea room, a venue only a couple of blocks away. To us it was a magnet.

Jim and I washed, polished and, a credit to our profession, arrived early in order to secure a good place in the queue. Much to our astonishment, there wasn't one. It was Jim who had broken the news of the event to me, and I began to wonder if this was the wrong place or, even worse, we had arrived on the wrong day. However, Jim, cupping his hand round his eyes to look in through the window, gave me a beaming smile, as he always did when proved right.

We sat at a table only two yards from a very large orchestra engaged in their tuning up routine and wallop 'Woodcutter's Ball' had us reeling in our chairs. No other customers entered the café, so Jim and I were treated to a right royal performance. When we finally left for our own show, Woody Herman bowed to us and my hand automatically went in to my pocket, where it stayed as I realised just in time that a five-dollar tip might be an insult. For four more days on the trot we occupied our usual table, but now we were three as Woody had joined us. How could such a wonderful, world-famous swing band perform in a very ordinary tea room and be ignored? I still insist on calling it a tea room, but it was perhaps something in between a café and a night club.

On another occasion just outside Washington I came across the Ink Spots. As far as I was concerned, my number one in the close harmony business was the Mills Brothers, but as a consolation prize, and as they were live, the Ink Spots would do. Of the four, three of them were replacements, but the deep one who spoke in a low melodious voice – 'Honey lamb, honey chile' – was one of the originals. Once again audiences were so sparse that it was noticeable, to the extent that after a few performances the old man came over and asked if I had any requests. 'The "Java Jive",' I replied without hesitation, and on my subsequent visits they all smiled as I took my seat to 'Java Jive'.

When we were in Chicago I had been making my way to the theatre through a street of very old houses, hobbling against the snow, and had stopped in amazement when I saw a cheaply painted notice over a door down steps to the basement, simply reading 'Count Basie's Orchestra'. After a few moments I came to the conclusion that Count Basie must have several orchestras and this was probably one of the not so good. Satisfied with my solution, I completely forgot about it until descending in the lift (which is a contradiction in terms) I discovered with delight that I was sharing my ride with Count Basie himself. By the time we reached ground level, we were a mutual admiration society. We even struggled through the drifts together, me to the theatre and Count Basie to his broken-down basement, where I left him after promising that I would most certainly attend his late performance. In turn he smilingly agreed to come to our matinée.

Woody Herman, the Ink Spots and Count Basie – three internationally known acts, every one of which could have easily filled the Albert Hall or the Palladium, whereas in their own country they were virtually ignored, appearing in venues well below their weight.

Could it be that Americans, who have a surfeit of most things, tend to overlook what is under their noses?

It's now 1976 and Julie is attending the Chelsea School of Human Movement in Eastbourne, part of East Sussex University, being trained to become a PE teacher and achieving a Certificate of Education. I have no idea what is implied by 'Human Movement', but I'm sure it's legal and whatever it turns out to be I know that my Julie will be hovering somewhere about top of the class.

The Bob Hope Classic was a golf tournament over four days, traditionally opening with a cabaret. One year I was asked if I would do a spot in the show, which was to be held at the Grosvenor House, Park Lane. I was about to reply automatically that unfortunately I'd be in Manchester on that evening with a bad leg and would be unable to accept, but this 'get-out clause' was a non-starter, as I was appearing every night at the Aldwych Theatre, a short cab ride from the Grosvenor House, and as the cabaret didn't start until eleven o'clock every exit was blocked . . . Then a brainwave knocked me sideways: John Williams.

In almost every one of my spectaculars for Thames Television I arranged to have two spots reserved for John Williams. The first number was a guitar duet, featuring John and myself, purely for comedy and the second was for John on his own to play anything of his choice. He was never required for rehearsal and would arrive at the studio about fifteen minutes before the 'off', when I would explain what I had in mind, which usually took no more than five minutes. I'm proud to admit it was always one of the highlights of the shows.

Now I rang John up to ask if he was free on that date. He was, and my problem was solved. At five minutes to eleven he arrived at the Grosvenor with his guitar, dressed in jeans etc. as I knew he would. In fact in all the years I've known him I've yet to see him wear a tie or even a jacket, but when you are the finest guitarist in the world you could walk on stage in a top hat and baggy shorts and no one would notice. As always, these cabarets were sparkling affairs, the men in tuxedos and the ladies with enough wealth around their necks and hanging from their ears to finance the national debt, and that's not counting their fingers.

The audience were mostly Americans, and I was politely received when I walked on to the stage with my guitar. They didn't quite know what to expect. After a few minutes of banter, I introduced my most promising pupil, John Williams. They were even more perplexed, but from the moment we sat down to play, the fun began as we repeated one of our television slots, and when John hit the final chord they would have given us a standing ovation except that quite a few of them couldn't.

To say that we were successful would be modest. Even while I was packing up in the dressing room, a man from the BBC came in to invite me on his chat show. I might have agreed, until he said that he hadn't realised I could be so funny. Doesn't anybody at the BBC watch my shows?

The organisers had arranged for me to stay the night at the same hotel as the American celebrities, and the following morning, as I stepped out of the lift, Telly Savalas and James Garner were approaching. Their faces lit up when they saw me and they took turns to pump my hand.

'Hey,' said James Garner, 'that cabaret, your act was the funniest I've ever seen. We were still talking about you.'

I humbly accepted the accolades.

Then Telly Savalas put in his four pence. 'It was great,' he said. 'How long have you two guys been working together?'

I shall say no more.

Meanwhile my brother John is still working in a local office in Oldham while Irene manages their shop in Turf Lane, which is also their home – in fact the shop is their front room. It is a treasure trove of almost everything – toffees, chocolate bars, vegetables, wines, spirits and, although they aren't registered as a Post Office, stamps.

Now to refill their cup of happiness their daughter Janet is to marry Steve Harling. Good grief, I thought she was still at school! Events are racing past me at an alarming rate and I wonder if I'll ever catch up. Now Janet will be building her own household with Steve. What used to be her bedroom is now where I lay my weary head every time I visit. It still remains as it was during her occupation, with dolls and teddies that stare inquisitively at me as I prepare for bed. I usually sleep well in this tranquil orderly atmosphere of goodwill, which reminds me that there is a better world outside the bright lights of London. John and I play a round of golf on the Royton and Crompton Golf Course and in the evenings there is always the snooker table. I am closer to John than anyone else in our family.

Janet and Steve have two sons, Ian born in 1980 and David in 1984. By jingo, they are sprouting up all over the place.

Off to Kenya on another golfing junket, organised once again by the Variety Club of Great Britain, with our usual team, Stanley Baker, Sean Connery, Henry Cooper, Dickie Henderson and one or two old golf professionals from England and America; and my day was made special when I was marked down to partner Sam Snead. Not all our party, however, were golfers. Edith had not yet taken up the game but she accompanied me to enjoy the African sun. Gwyneth, Dickie Henderson's wife, made sure that Edith was looked after. The most prestigious of all our party were John Mills and his wife Mary, whose presence alone added glitter and sparkle to an already impressive roll call. We all enjoyed our golf matches, although nobody actually won except the charity for which these events were organised, and our holiday was just beginning.

First we were bussed round the game park to let the wild animals have a look at us. We saw lions, an old bull elephant and a rhinoceros, but not one of them looked in our direction, although in their defence I must admit that in the heat of the afternoon it was siesta time in the game park. I began to look forward to a cold shower and a hot dinner at the hotel, but this was not to be. When the buses finally stopped, we were not in the streets of Nairobi but in a large clearing in the jungle, in the middle of which was a long trestle table piled high with a cold collation. African staff were guarding it from the pilfering fingers of a colony of monkeys in a large tree whose branches reached out over our supper.

After eating, we were issued with storm lanterns already lit, and not before time: there is no such thing as a leisurely twilight in Africa – it's light one minute and the next before you can strike a match it is dark. We were all housed in small tents. I lay on a cot on one side and Edith on the other, with the lantern on the grass between us. Luckily we decided not to put it out, because no sooner had I relaxed and closed my eyes, something I always did before sleep, my stomach awoke. Snatching up the lantern, I made my way, stiff legged, towards the canvas-shrouded latrine. As I did so, a dark shape passed me, going in the other direction. It subsequently turned out to be Mary Mills, suffering the same discomfort as myself. In fact as I made my groggy way back from the latrine Mary passed me, going in the opposite direction with a great sense of urgency. This lantern gavotte was the pattern for the rest of the night. It was dawn when I finally collapsed, a spent man, but before I could groan the tent flap was pushed aside and Mary ducked inside. 'How do you feel?' she asked, and before I could reply she handed me a medicine bottle. 'Try some of this,' she said. 'It's cured me.' I took a swig and gave the bottle back. I wasn't convinced, but inside half an hour I was hungry for my breakfast. It was miraculous. Mary never told me what the bottle contained, but it was too powerful to be legal.

Later that morning we were all taken to a Masai village, a small collection of dreary round huts. The interpreter asked us not to take photographs, explaining that the tribe would not venture from their huts during one of these sightseeings. He went on to inform us that all the huts were made of cow dung. I couldn't resist it. 'I wish you'd told me this yesterday,' I said. 'I could have built them a town hall,' and Mary chipped in with, 'I could have built them a high-rise block.' That was my first meeting with the Mills family, but certainly not the last.

Incidentally, our pro-am golf match was the prelude to the Kenya

Open, played by such stalwarts as Ballesteros, Tommy Horton and Bernard Gallagher, who, if my memory serves me right, I'm almost sure was the winner that year.

A great man I was proud to call a friend was John Junor, whose weekly newspaper column invariably left scars on the politically inept. When he was editor of the *Sunday Express*, I became a regular reader. Had he written a column in *The Ringing World* I would have bought that as well. Many a happy day we spent on the Walton Heath golf course, and on occasions the third member of our golfing round was Denis Thatcher, and although we never managed to burn up the course his conversation singed it. John was a member of the Royal and Ancient Golf Club and, appreciating my keenness for the game, he proposed me for membership in 1974. The seconder was Douglas Bader. With that top-of-the-tree support, one would have thought it would be a walkover. Far from it – I still had to pass stringent rules of acceptance. John would invariably ring me to ask if there was any news, and when I replied that I had had no communication from the R. & A., he'd reply, 'That's good.' In fact I received no news from them until 1978, almost four years to the day since I had been proposed for membership; and this was the occasion of a very remarkable coincidence.

I arrived in Australia to begin a season of *Big Bad Mouse* with Jimmy Edwards and at the reception desk in the Hotel Parmelia a handful of mail was passed across to me. Flipping through the envelopes, I stopped in mid-flip. One envelope had the back of my neck twitching and my mouth was suddenly dry. It was from the R. & A. 'Dear Mr Sykes,' it began and went on to congratulate me on the good news that I was now a member of the Royal and Ancient Golf Club. My legs turned to rubber and I sat down suddenly weak. For years the thought of this day had lain dormant at the back of my mind and now to receive the news in Australia, the other end of the world from St Andrews!

It being Sunday, the dining room was closed and lunch would be a buffet affair on the first floor. I loaded my plate with bits of this and that, hardly noticing what kind of cold collation I was piling on to it, before I made my way to an empty table. En route I felt a tug at the back of my jacket – not my favourite method of approach. I turned and it was Douglas Bader. I nearly dropped the whole mess in his lap. It was incredible: four years ago Douglas had seconded my application to join the R. & A. and here he was on the very same day I was accepted for membership. Now that is what I call a coincidence, wouldn't you agree?

In 1979 Kathy spends a year at the sharp end, being an assistant floor manager – not a job for the fainthearted. For Kathy it is just a staging post; she has her eye on bigger game. Inexorably she is on her way up.

Meanwhile back in academia Julie is forging ahead with a following wind. She is now head of the PE department at Heathfield School, Ascot, no less. How's that for a back flip and two cartwheels? To say I am impressed is an understatement. Heathfield School is extraordinarily selective in its choice of pupils, so it follows that the powers that be must be even more choosy in their appointment of staff. Although I have nothing to do with any of it, I know they have chosen well with Julie. I'm sure every proud father would agree with my sentiments.

My son David has been reluctant to appear in these pages. As he puts it, unlike his sisters, his achievements in college 'do not warrant the oxygen of publicity' – exactly what I would have said in another era, when my headmaster wrote in my school leaving report: 'Inclined to be scatterbrained'. On looking back over my life, I am truly amazed at the accuracy of his diagnosis. However my one great advantage over David was that I had a war in which to think things out.

In his turn David decides to go backpacking around Asia – a very dicey project in this uncertain world, especially as he is travelling alone and is still a teenager. This is his war.

At the time I was appearing in Australia when a telephone call came through to the hotel where I was staying and it was David.

'Hello, David,' I said. 'Where are you, in Thailand?'

'No,' he replied. 'Downstairs in reception.'

After the first pleasant shock I didn't know whether to be happy or sad at the thought that he had left some of his youth behind. The experiences of his travels had made an indelible mark on him and he was at a crossroads. When he finally ended his globetrot and hung up his rucksack, he amazed everyone by displaying an extraordinary gift for wood carving. In his work his love for cats, both wild and domestic, was evident. His carvings were imaginative and lifelike – for example, a lioness transporting her cub by the scruff of its neck, a cheetah in the heat of the chase, a water buffalo staring inquisitively at nothing and a tabby cat about to pounce. Each one of his collection was a thing of beauty at which one could only marvel; to run one's hands over the finished product was an exquisite experience. Where and when had he discovered this enormous talent? Tales of David's carvings soon spread like poppies in Picardy.

Aside from staging pantomimes and other productions, for relaxation Paul Elliott part-owned a racehorse called Perian, trained by Geoff Lewis. So captivated was Paul by David's carvings that he commissioned him to create a likeness in wood of the horse. David produced from a photograph a small replica of Perian, so absolutely lifelike that it still dominates a shelf in Paul's home. Word spread like a bush fire to America too and it wasn't long before David received a telephone call from Giorgio Armani requesting him to carve an ordinary domestic cat. Of course David did. Giorgio was so impressed that when he opened a branch of menswear in London he put his showroom at David's disposal to mount an exhibition of his carvings. It was an outstanding evening. All the family were there, as well as Max Bygraves and Jack Ashley, now Lord Ashley, who made a very fine speech, as all the proceeds were to be donated to the Royal National Institute for the Deaf.

It was a speech I should have made, had I been there. Unfortunately I was appearing at the Swan Theatre, High Wycombe. It sounds pathetic and with hindsight it was.

*   *   *

'You can't go to London like that,' said Edith one day.

This should have rung the alarm bells. I often went to London dressed casually. I had a meeting with Paul Elliott, who was managing my affairs at that time, and Philip Jones, Head of Light Entertainment at Thames Television.

'Why don't you wear a suit?' Edith went on.

Edith had never before concerned herself with my appearance. I thought for a moment that perhaps they wanted to take me out to dinner to discuss a new project, but I was already changed before another thought troubled me: our meeting was scheduled for three o'clock – too late for lunch and much too early for dinner.

I met Paul in London and we walked round Piccadilly, up Shaftesbury Avenue and up Dean Street, turning left and eventually finding ourselves back in Piccadilly. His conversation was more of a monologue – his favourite dream of running out on to the pitch at Wembley as captain of the England team, how many pantomimes he was organising for next year. He even pointed out the theatre where his wife was appearing. I'd never heard Paul trot out such inanities and I was just about to suggest he visit a doctor when I spotted Philip Jones approaching. Gone was the languid stroll; we were now marching purposefully. We stopped outside the front of the New London Theatre and Paul asked me if I'd got a comb.

'What's going on?' I asked.

'It's just a press interview,' said Paul.

I still couldn't understand all the secrecy surrounding something that everybody seemed to know about except me. I was soon to be enlightened. As they pushed me through the door, I was greeted by Eamonn Andrews, holding a large red book. 'Eric Sykes, this is your life.'

The theatre was packed and applauding and I was in what is known as a quandary. I had warned the producer, Jacko, an old friend of mine, that if he ever tricked me into being the subject for the show I'd walk off, leaving a dozen new laid on his face.

I had to think quickly, but nothing upstairs was working; I was in several minds. I half turned, but Paul and Philip, standing shoulder to shoulder, cut off that escape route. Then I thought of all the people – family and friends – round the back who had taken the trouble to come and support me. Eamonn was getting nervous, having seen the indecision on my face. Accepting defeat, I walked down the aisle and up on to the stage, and as soon as I was seated Eamonn proclaimed, 'And here is your wife, Edith.'

She made an entrance and we embraced. She was trembling slightly, unused to being in the limelight. Then Eamonn introduced the rest of my family – Kathy, Susan, Julie and David – and they all trooped on, Edith trying not to look at me – oh, the devious ways of women! But as they sat by me, I was so proud of them all: the girls were stunning and David, a broth of a lad, and had the show ended there I would have been satisfied. But there was more to come: Bill Fraser, Tommy Cooper with a plank over his shoulder, Frankie Howerd with a chip on his, Max Bygraves, Spike Milligan, Johnny Speight, Harry Secombe, good grief, surely our half-hour was up. Then Zsa Zsa Gabor from Las Vegas dropped in to say nice things about me. A heart-warming surprise came as Bobby Hall was introduced, a pal from Oldham I hadn't seen since before the war. At last my darling television sister Hattie was there – in fact my *Life* wouldn't have been the same without her. What a fitting way to end the programme. But there was more. Dear old Terry-Thomas, pushed on in a wheelchair, had taken the trouble to make my day, although he was a very sick man. There was enough talent on the stage to supply three Royal Command Performances. To steady the ship my elder brother Vernon and his wife Eve were introduced followed by my younger brother John and his wife Irene. The show had been running almost an hour and still they came: Peter Brough and Archie Andrews, Johnny Speight and, to my delight, Douglas Bader. Talk about my cup overflowing, next on was Tony Jacklin, the British and US Open golf champion in the same year, and my extra special guitarist John Williams. Jimmy Edwards filled an already overcrowded stage and to close the bill, the icing on the cake, my old mate Sean Connery, having flown in from somewhere or other, made a short speech describing me as a character I am still endeavouring to live up to.

All in all, I had to admit it was a very emotional day and I thanked Paul Elliott and Phillip Jones for one of the most exciting and yet in a strange way humbling experiences of my life.

Not long after the programme was put to bed, Eamonn Andrews and Terry-Thomas died, but worst of all, the tragedy that hit me most, dear old Hattie Jacques passed away. For over thirty years she had been my television sister and there was a bond between us that will never be replaced. From her example I learned how to relax and enjoy myself, to accept the good things with modesty and to hide the hardships behind a smile. It turned out that she had not been well for some time, but any whimpering on her part was done in the privacy of her own home.

God bless you, darling Hat.

Susan's career as a nurse is to be short lived. She has met the right fella. His name is Chris. He is a Rhodesian by birth, British by choice.

On a bright sunny day Edith, I and the rest of the family attend the wedding ceremony. It is a day of mixed emotions, as happiness is streaked with sighs at the thought of another one leaving the family home.

Jim Nelson was my bookkeeper. That was his official title, but he was more than that. Whenever he popped downstairs to my office and hoppity hopped through the door – long ago he had suffered a bout of polio – his optimistic view of life was a tonic. His bright outlook never failed to lift me out of any depression I was in. As long as he hoppity hopped into my room, all was well with the world.

Once again when one blithely takes things for granted ... The sky exploded when about half a mile from the office Jim was killed in a car crash. I was shattered. He was part of the fittings, indestructible. It was several days before my mind accepted the fact that he was no longer with us. It must have been a couple of weeks before I began to take stock of Jim's absence. I had to find a replacement.

The solution was obvious. She was occupying the office below mine: Norma Farnes, who had shepherded Spike Milligan through the sunshine and thunderstorms of his career, a doughty Yorkshire lass, and they don't come much doughtier than that. After all, after twenty years under the same roof we were a family. I approached her with fingers crossed. I needn't have worried: she readily took me on, adding me to her portfolio of one.

Typically, she rolled up her sleeves and went into Jim's office for my accounts. After a time, she came into my office, slightly dishevelled, unlike her usually well-groomed self.

'Bad news,' she said.

'Jim's been fiddling the books?' I suggested humorously.

'No, no, no, of course not,' she said. 'Jim couldn't have fiddled the books. There aren't any.'

This news almost had me in a head lock. 'But surely,' I spluttered, 'he must have kept records?'

'He did,' Norma said, 'in a carrier bag.'

All my bills, outgoings, incomes, transactions, salaries, all this data in a carrier bag.

Had Norma been in two minds about whether to take me under her wing, now was the time for her to go to Manchester with a bad leg. How I underestimated her! After a lifetime of Spike, this problem of mine must have seemed like a stroll in the park. Nevertheless, it turned out to be a little heavier than that. It took Norma a few more weeks to discover the magnitude of my finances and that's a hollow laugh: I had a six-figure overdraft, and in order to balance the books the bank was about to foreclose on our office building. What a calamity! Jim couldn't have been aware of the looming catastrophe as he blithely continued to give me a piggyback to Carey Street.

Jim would undoubtedly have handed over the deeds with a cheerful smile and a hoppity hop, and when the bowler-hatted gentlemen walked through the front door it would never have crossed my mind that they were bailiffs. But with our Norma the bank now had a fight on its hands; no way was she about to change her lifestyle and sit behind her desk on the pavement.

Having considered the taking over of our building a mere formality, the bank was caught slightly off-balance when Norma entered the arena, but not unduly perturbed, until she took her gloves off and the battle began. A challenge is something that makes her eyes light up. The bank, with all its computers and other peoples' money, was ill-equipped to cross swords. Norma was implacable, coolly persuasive, reasonable and not giving an inch; one might just as well have tried to move Big Ben up to Bishop's Stortford. The bank finally decided that there were easier ways to make money and took its threat away, and we still had a roof over our heads.

Now was the question of the overdraft, or more immediately the £19,000 a year interest I was paying on it – a treadmill to which there is no end. After a very short ponder, the solution hit me like a blast of cold air on opening the fridge door. Sitting in my garage at home was my beloved Aggie, a black drop-head two-door Bentley. She was auctioned at Sotheby's, which brought my overdraft down to manageable proportions. I didn't go to the auction – it was rather like putting one of my children up for sale. In all the years I'd been at the wheel Aggie had never let me down, and I have one consolation: she was sold to a private buyer and not to a dealer, so I know she has a good home.

Despite the fact that Jim Nelson had taken me to within a hair's breadth of making my debut in the dock at the Old Bailey, I missed him and I know that had he lived I would be looking forward to his visits in whatever prison I was in.

Jack Hobbs was a journalist who haunted our office from time to time, encouraging Spike Milligan to write books. As far as I was concerned, apart from perfunctory greetings we hardly ever conversed, until one day we happened to bump into each other at the King Edward pub. Neither of us spilt a drop, but it was an icebreaker, and after a few laughs things became serious when he asked me why didn't I write a novel? The thought had attempted to cross my mind for months, but because my mind was cluttered with more immediate problems the idea of writing a book was at the back of the queue.

Nevertheless, one day when I was relaxing the devil made work for my idle hands and I found myself typing chapter one of my first book, *Sykes of Sebastopol Terrace*, a spin-off from my television series.

I read it and to my astonishment I was quite pleased with the result. Jack Hobbs also read it and laughed out loud – all the more astonishing because he was sober. He knew how to make the next moves and thanks to his experience it was published by Michael Joseph in 1981. In one fell swoop I had become an author and I might be on the library shelves with Charles Dickens, George Bernard Shaw and my favourite author at the time, W. Somerset Maugham. So taken was I by my first attempt at being a writer that I dallied in my daydreams with the idea of changing my name to E. Lancashire Sykes, but thankfully it was only a passing whim and I didn't try to stop it.

About this time Susan and Chris also have an issue: their first-born, Matthew. Too young as yet to appreciate it, he is the advance guard of a new generation. Susan is a mother, the thought of which pulls me up with a jolt; Edith and I are now grandparents . . . *Tempus* doesn't half *fugit*.

Sad news has just reached me: my brother Vernon's wife Eve has passed away. She was never of robust health and was frequently bedridden in her latter years. Vernon lovingly lavished care and attention on making Eve comfortable; he cooked, washed clothes and tidied up their little house. For his devotion, my admiration and my heart go out to him. When Eve slipped quietly into the other world, it must have been a blessed relief for them both.

Paul Elliott enjoyed the soubriquet 'king of pantomime', producing sometimes more than twenty traditional Christmas shows every year, and it was he who cajoled me into appearing in *Dick Whittington* at the Wimbledon Theatre.

A pantomime is for many children a first visit to the theatre and it is the only branch of entertainment that encompasses every facet of our profession, with singing, dancing and acting, as well as a love interest, a plot in which good eventually triumphs over evil, and all this education made palatable by outrageous, hilarious comedy. In the early 1950s I wrote two pantomimes for the Palladium, but that was enough for me. Sadly the traditions of pantomime were being hijacked by young male pop singers who were now playing the princes; the place of actors was being taken by celebrities new to the stage; and for humour near-the-knuckle jokes were destroying the wonder of pantomimes of early days. It is known as progress, but at what cost! Can it be a good thing to take the innocent joy from a child's eyes? Why do we stampede to educate them with the ugliness of the world, when there is so much to admire? As soap boxes have given way to the internet, I'll wrap up, as I'm already out of my depth in the labyrinth of modern technology.

However, Paul Elliott's pantomimes were traditional, in the old school, so I was happy to learn my trade as Alderman Fitzwarren in the company of Roy Kinnear, Brian Murphy, Michael Robbins and Jan Hunt playing the title role. I so enjoyed the experience that I have since appeared in many more pantomimes, even one during the Christmas season in Toronto, Canada, where the grown-ups might have been a little bemused but the children lapped it up, and that's all I ask.

Thank the Lord I was finished with the deaf aid, which was causing many problems in the ear itself. I am now equipped with an ingenious invention which looks like a pair of spectacles but has no lenses because it is primarily a hearing aid. When I wear this aid, the arm of the spectacle frame vibrates against the skull as sound vibrates a healthy eardrum – a process known as bone conduction. As my sight was still as good as ever then, I saw no reason to have the frames decked out with plain glass. I sometimes say to the inquisitive that for years I've been on the stage cracking jokes but unable to hear the laughs, but since I've worn these glasses I've realised that I haven't been getting any.

*   *   *

After her grounding at Heathfield School Julie has now veered towards television, gaining her first foothold as a runner for Thames Television, a position for which she had been admirably trained as a PE teacher. This post will last until 1986, which leaves me on the horns of a dilemma: it must have been quite a run to have lasted four years, but everybody has to start somewhere. From that lowly beginning she is promoted to assistant floor manager. Knowing Julie, she is on her way; it isn't long before she becomes floor manager.

Although Julie and I were now working in television, our paths never converged, except on one memorable occasion. Thames Television were researching a history of the London Palladium and in this respect I was to be interviewed on the stage by Paul Merton, who was not being a stand-up comic on this occasion – in fact he was sitting down. Naturally, this being a divergence from his normal trade, he was nervous and on the verge of sweating. It was contagious, and I began to twitch. With about a minute to recording, the floor manager appeared from behind the camera, still in the dimness outside the lit area, and shouted, 'All right, Dad?' Paul Merton actually jumped, as if an electrical current had passed through the seat of his chair. I was equally surprised, until there was a burst of laughter from the camera crew and Julie stepped into the light, earphones on her head and a smile on her face as big as a slice of melon. It had been a perfect set-up, and was exactly what was required; the ice was broken and the interview a cakewalk.

About a year after Eve's death, Vernon was coping with approaching his old-age pension, a long, bleak passage to eternity, when an extraordinary thing happened. I sometimes forget that my mother was also his. The sun broke through the clouds when he met Matilda Monk, a cheerful, attractive lady, and the violins began from that moment. Matilda became Till and she called Vernon Bill.

I was unable to go to the wedding but when I visited them both my heart sang with joy to see a smile on Vernon's face again. Till was exactly what the doctor ordered, she had transported Vernon from damp cellar to penthouse suite; their love for each other was apparent in every touch and gesture; there was a warmth emanating from Vernon that had not been evident in his past, and suddenly he seemed to be twenty years younger. I thanked Mother on his behalf for the gift in the shape of Till that she had bestowed upon him. His last few years were extremely happy ones, but not many, because my dear brother died in November 1984. If only I could have known him better.

Alan Ayckbourn's play *Time and Time Again* was a pleasant offshoot from my normal routine, somewhere between boisterous vaudeville and Shakespeare, and very enjoyable. Also appearing were Anne Stallybrass, Matthew Kelly and Caroline Goodall, who later played Mrs Schindler in the film *Schindler's List* directed by Steven Spielberg. Perhaps he had seen Caroline in the play, in which case why didn't he ask me to play Mr Schindler? Just a thought. Anne, Matthew and Caroline helped me through the transition into light comedy, but after a few weeks I missed the belly laughs to which I was addicted and like a smoker lighting up in his first week of withdrawal my determination snapped. It happened on our opening night in the Crucible Theatre, Sheffield, the home of snooker.

In my first appearance at the beginning of the play, I looked around and, turning to the audience, said, 'It's the first time I've worked in a billiard hall.' The audience laughed, the cast laughed, but the lady running the theatre apparently didn't and before the end of act one a complaint was already in the post to Paul Elliott. By the way, to prevent anything terminal happening to Mr Ayckbourn, it was my only deviation from his immaculate lines.

Paul's response to the lady running the theatre was to ignore her complaint and inform her that on Friday he would be putting on my understudy so that I could take part in a golf match. In all fairness, it wasn't just an ordinary golf match. It was a prestigious affair hosted by no less a presence than Prince Philip, and I was to join other British stars of stage, screen and labour exchange versus an American team of well-knowns.

This didn't cut any ice with the lady who ran the theatre. She ranted and raved about my contempt for my audiences, my lack of discipline and especially my lack of judgement. All this I found could have applied better to the lady herself. After all, at the same time she was running the theatre next door and her choice of play for the week was *As You Like It* set in the First World War, which attracted the biggest audience of ten patrons. I can only assume that they had wandered into the wrong building and were expecting to see Anne Stallybrass, Matthew Kelly and me. If that isn't the raspberry I don't know what is.

After our eventful week at the Crucible Theatre, our little caravan moved on to open in Poole, and it was there that I received a telephone call from Paul Elliott to ask me whether, when *Time and Time Again* ended its run, I would be interested in taking over from Bernard Cribbins and Richard Briers in the farce *Run for Your Wife*. My partner would be Terry Scott. My eyes lit up. I had not long put down the phone when it rang again with a lucrative offer of a commercial for a holiday firm. It was to be directed by a friend of mine, another golfer, Robert Young. This was good news. Even better, the film was to be shot in Ibiza. How's that for a week's paid holiday with digs and food thrown in? Once again I'd fallen on my feet. By a marvellous coincidence the date of the commercial followed the last week of our *Time and Time Again* tour. Goodbye the provinces and hello Ibiza. It was just the tonic I needed – hours on beaches and in and out of swimming pools. For one set-up we were taken to an island populated only by nudists, so our appearance must have been a novelty. Two young ladies assisting Robert Young completely ignored their jobs as they ogled the naked men, until Robert, exasperated, said to one of them, 'Do you think we could have your assistance once you've finished your window shopping?'

One shot required me to sit in a large cane chair on the beach, dressed in shirt, shorts and bare feet – my only concession to nudity. At each side of the camera a small knot of sightseers gathered, mainly young ladies all completely starkers. Unembarrassed, I had to concentrate hard to carry out the job I was being paid to do.

Between takes I went a few paces forward to cool my feet by standing in the sea, a very stupid thing to do, as the sun still burns through a few inches of water – a fact I learned to my cost. When we finally boarded the motor boat for the mainland, I knew I was in trouble: my feet were angry red and burning as if I'd been scalded. Our hotel overlooked a bull ring and from the balcony in front of my room I spent that last evening with both feet in a bucket of ice watching the macho performance of the matadors. I had to be helped to board the plane home. Every step was agony, as if I was doing a religious stroll over hot coals.

The day after we arrived back in England, I reported for rehearsal of *Run for Your Wife* at the Shaftesbury Theatre. I was still walking like a very old man having trouble with his legs. Ray Cooney, directing his own play, was aghast. It was obvious that I wouldn't be able to carry out any of the moves, and if I did by the time I had made my entrance and walked to the settee it would be just about time to wrap for the day. The difficulties, however, were overcome when Ray suggested I lay on the settee for the rehearsal and spoke my lines from a prone position. The only drawback was that I had to stay there for the whole of the run-through and as my part wasn't very big I inadvertently fell asleep. I woke suddenly when Ray shook my shoulder to tell me that I'd missed my entrance. I rehearsed from that settee long after my feet had healed.

Terry Scott and I hit it off from the start, naturally playing roles slightly different from those of Bernard and Richard. Indeed, so pleased were we with our partnership that we continued to work together in the play at the Criterion, the Aldwych and in a record-breaking season at the Pier Theatre Bournemouth. Terry was a real joy to work with, his only flaw being that he didn't play golf.

The Stage Golfing Society has for many, many years been affiliated to the Richmond Golf Club at Ham Common. As a member of the SGS, I was out on the beautiful parkland course as often as possible and sometimes when not. I only had to tell my secretary that I was off to a script conference for her reply invariably to be, 'If it's an emergency, what golf course will you be on?' In fact I am what one would call a golf nut, and I have entered every competition that my busy schedule allowed. But for all my efforts I only ever won one of these tournaments. The first prize was not a cup, an inscribed tray or a salver but a five-pound voucher for Leichner make-up, which could only be tendered in one shop near Trafalgar Square.

After this triumph, my winning streak seemed to dry up, until my next win many years later, when the BBC were televising a golf half-hour from Scotland, where two world-famous professional golfers, usually from America, partnered different celebrities for a nine-hole Stableford competition. On this occasion the visiting Americans were Lee Trevino and Ben Crenshaw, and for our match I was Lee's partner and Jimmy Tarbuck partnered Ben Crenshaw. I won't bore you with the match, because it bored me and I was glad when I holed out my last putt.

As I left the green, Sean Connery met me, looking very excited. 'You've won.'

I couldn't fathom what he was on about.

'You've scored nineteen points and Tarbuck eighteen. You've won it. Nobody will score more than nineteen points.'

I still couldn't fathom what he was on about. I didn't even know there was a competition for us amateurs, but when it dawned on me I said, 'Hang on a minute, your match is tomorrow and then there's Garfield Sobers – he's no slouch either.'

Sean shook his head. 'Having to wait on every shot until the television camera is in place will be the biggest handicap,' and he was adamant that nobody would beat nineteen points.

The atmosphere in the club house was decidedly gloomy. I was sitting with others round a table, refreshing myself with a pint of draught next to my old pal Peter Alliss. He wasn't in the tournament but he'd accompanied our match all the way round. He shook his head sadly.

'What's the matter, Peter?' I said, fearing a death in his family.

'Poor old Jim,' he muttered, and I knew he was referring to Jimmy Tarbuck. 'Five years Jim's been in this tournament and he'd set his heart on winning.' Then he paused and looked at me strangely before continuing, 'And to be beaten by you . . .' He stressed the word 'you', and it was obvious that he wasn't congratulating me.

I wasn't best pleased. 'That's not very nice, is it, Peter?'

'I'm sorry, Eric. I didn't mean it like that,' adding, 'but you're not a winner, are you?'

That was the only low point. I still didn't know if I had won the tournament – after all, it wasn't over yet. I was flown back to Bournemouth in a little two-seater for my evening show and the following afternoon I received a phone call from Scotland. It was a very excited Lee Trevino, telling me that I'd won the amateur prize, which was a full set of Waterford Crystal.

I was only partly delighted, because the way I'd played I didn't deserve it: I'd played like a man who hadn't fully recovered from intricate brain surgery. Should I hand the prize back? I felt rather like a man who finds a purse stuffed full of money and doesn't hand it in at the nearest police station. However, the value of my latest prize was to provide the next awkward twist to the saga.

Unaccustomed as I was to collecting trophies, I had completely overlooked the fact that amateurs are only allowed to accept prizes of less than one hundred pounds and with my set of Waterford Crystal I was guilty of being five times over the limit. I only became aware of my misdemeanour when I received a telephone call from the Royal and Ancient Golf Club to the effect that a complaint had been received from some anonymous person about my contravention of the rules of golf. This was a serious matter and being a member of the Royal and Ancient I should have known better. 'Don't worry,' I replied, 'Leave it to me.'

Immediately after breaking the connection, I telephoned the head office of Waterford Crystal. When I was eventually put through to the chairman or president, whichever he was, the top man, I explained my predicament, suggesting that if he would let me know the difference between the hundred-pound limit and the value of the exquisite set of Waterford Crystal, a cheque covering it would be on its way that very afternoon.

He appeared to be thinking aloud as he mumbled, 'The difference between one hundred pounds and the Waterford merchandise?' There was a pause, and I imagined him making rapid calculations on a pad by his elbow. Then, just as I was about to ask if he was still there, he said, 'How about a fiver?'

I thought it was a joke. 'As much as that?' I answered with mock incredulity.

'The problem is, Eric,' he said, 'anything over a fiver and I have to call a special board meeting.'

'I understand,' I said. 'So in order to save you unnecessary expense I'll accept your assessment.' And the deal was done.

My cheque for five pounds was in the post when I telephoned the R. & A. with the good news that I had settled the difference by cheque.

'Thank you so much,' said the voice from St Andrews. 'It really is very good of you to get us out of this hole.'

Friendships and charity golf matches have enabled me to play with my golfing gods Peter Alliss, John Jacobs, Dave Thomas, Sevvy Ballesteros, Brian Barnes, Tommy Horton and Tony Fisher. John Jacobs did his best to get me down to an acceptable handicap and as most of the others were prone to give me tips I developed a style that would have baffled a professional contortionist. Bernard Gallagher, another friend, was largely responsible for my honorary membership of Wentworth Golf Club, and my golfing roll of honour would not be complete without the legendary Christie O'Connor, with whom I played many an enjoyable round, especially at the clubhouse bar.

While I was in *Run for Your Wife* at the Royal Alexander Theater in Toronto, the prop man approached me and said he'd read somewhere that I was stationed near Reigate in 1943. I nodded and it turned out that he had been with the Canadian Army and had been billeted quite close by at about the same time. It was rather like a parlour game when he said he'd then landed in Normandy and I came back with 'So did I.' We were probably within mortar range of each other. His name was Buddy Lloyd and with the natural hospitality of the Canadians he invited one or two from our company to go round to his place one night for a drink after the show.

His was a lovely house, not big but comfortable. I didn't see much of it as he led us straight to a basement, in which there was a bar with bottles stacked behind. The rest of the room was a shrine to Vera Lynn, known as the forces' sweetheart. Each wall was plastered with press cuttings, photographs and theatre bills, and while we sipped whiskies he took me on a guided tour, explaining how he'd come by this or that and the day he first heard her sing. He was becoming whisky maudlin and I decided to call it a night.

Some weeks later Buddy strode towards me as I came through the stage door. He was excited. 'Vera Lynn is coming to Toronto,' he blurted, 'to the Royal York Hotel.'

'Will you be going to see her?' I said.

His eyes lit up; then just as quickly the fire went out. 'Fat chance,' he said. 'It'll be for the bigwigs.'

The following morning I made a few phone calls and when I went into the theatre I told Buddy that it was all fixed and I'd arranged seats for us both. On the big day I met Buddy outside the Royal York Hotel and we were shown to our seats. It sounds grand, but the seats were ordinary chairs from the hotel, only about two dozen of them and placed outside in the open air, facing a temporary stage. The dignitaries, councillors and whatever took their seats and the show began. A red carpet led from the hotel entrance to the stage and it was flanked by a guard of honour in red tunics and busbies, who presented arms when Vera emerged and took her place on the stage to ecstatic applause. She was magnificent and I was proud to be British. She talked and sang many of the old wartime favourites – 'We'll Meet Again', 'White Cliffs of Dover', etc. – and when she finally left the stage to a standing ovation, all the dignitaries followed her into the hotel. I had one more pleasant surprise for Buddy. Leading him into the hotel, I took him in the lift to the first floor and we slipped into an enormous ballroom, at the centre of which was a line of dignitaries standing shoulder to shoulder – the Mayor, the City Fathers and hangers-on. At that moment, a far door opened and in walked Vera. She might well have been the Queen as she walked down the line, shaking hands as they bowed their heads, a few words here and a curtsey from the wives. As she got to the end of the line, she turned and glanced at us on the far side of the room.

Suddenly Vera shrieked 'Eric' and rushed over to fling her arms round my neck. I introduced her to Buddy, who was too overcome to speak, and when I explained to him that one of my phone calls had been to Vera herself and the tickets were due to her influence, I was elevated in Buddy's eyes to international stardom.

Vera and I still meet occasionally at charity dinners or lunches and she is still as big-hearted and generous as she was on that day at the Royal York Hotel.

In his final appearance that shocked the nation Tommy Cooper collapsed on the stage in the middle of his act during *Sunday Night at the London Palladium*. I watched it because only that morning he'd phoned to tell me that he had put in a special bit that he knew would amuse me. This was strange in itself because it was the first time he'd ever phoned me at home; more importantly, it was almost unheard of for one comedian to ask another to watch his performance. The bit he wanted me to see was only something between ourselves. One night when I had been watching his cabaret act in a working men's club, he had come out with a bit of business which fell flat as a pancake but I had thought it was hilarious and my laughter seemed louder in its loneliness. This, I guessed, was what Tom had in mind when he phoned me. Sadly he never got that far, as he left us all when he was only halfway through his act.

One thought I find deeply disturbing: did Tom have a premonition that this was to be his last appearance? The question often haunts me. One day I may stumble on the answer, but it will not be in this life.

A few days after Tom's going his son came to me with a fez, 'I know my father would like you to have it,' he said.

Tommy's fez since then has occupied pride of place in my office.

Edith and I now have a granddaughter as well as a grandson, born to Susan and Chris. Her name is to be Eleanor, after Edith's mother.

As they have their hands full bringing up a family and live some distance away, we meet only on special occasions such as birthdays, Christmas and Easter, and each time we have these get-togethers it seems that children are sprouting up all over the place. I must admit I am very proud to be the patriarch. I hope I'm correct with that word. It sounded plausible when I first thought of it.

One of the more attractive aspects of our profession is the unexpected: a telephone call, bumping into someone of influence in a busy street or, most of all, a letter that looks important.

Such a herald of good fortune slipped through my letterbox one rainy morning and by the time I'd finished reading the beautifully typed missive the sun was shining again. It was an invitation to the Montreux Festival. To my astonishment the international panel of European judges were to honour me with an award in recognition of my services to television. I was delighted but for the most part puzzled, as not one of my series with Hattie Jacques had been shown at the festival; nevertheless I wasn't about to look this gift horse in the mouth.

Obviously Bill Cotton, Head of Light Entertainment at the BBC and son of my old mate on whose band shows I had made several appearances, would be present. The morning after my acceptance of the award would be a good moment, I deemed, to present him with the synopses of five different ideas – a perfect opportunity, wouldn't you say, *amigo*? I was chuffed, a sure sign that things were not going to turn out smelling of roses. Will I never learn?

The night was marvellous. I accepted the award with due humility and my speech of acceptance was funny in parts, humble and short enough to be unremembered, and I went to bed happy, looking forward to my masterstroke on the morrow. At about ten o'clock in the morning, I walked along the heavily carpeted corridor to the large imposing double doors, vastly different from the barely carpeted passage on the top floor where my room was situated but then I wasn't the head of anything. I knocked respectfully and entered on the command 'Come in'.

Once in the room I looked around the opulence and for a moment I couldn't see anyone. In a wild thought I assumed that the voice that had said 'Come in' was somehow recorded, but then right in front of me over the back of a settee I spotted the head and shoulders of Bill Cotton. There was another man with him, but as he was also facing the front I couldn't recognise who it was. Both of them must have known I was behind them, but neither turned to smile, say 'Good morning' or 'How's your father?' Anything would have been more acceptable than these two waxworks, arms folded, staring ahead in a synchronised game of don't-look-round … I stood there, hesitantly holding out my sheets of ideas like a doorstep salesman trying to sell a life insurance policy to a deaf ninety-year-old. I cleared my throat to let them know that I was there, which brought no response. 'I've got five ideas on paper,' I said to the back of their heads, 'and I wonder if you could give them the once-over and let me know what you think?'

I leaned slightly towards them, hoping to catch their eyes – even their ears would do. I never expected a warm handshake, a bunch of flowers and a glass of wine, but this cold shoulder was ludicrous. I was beginning to wonder if I hadn't disturbed them in some kind of meditation ritual. Bill finally broke the silence. Addressing the wall in front of him, he said, 'Your day's gone Eric. We're now into alternative comedy.'

I was shattered. Had I heard them incorrectly? I knew that my hearing was faulty, but surely it was not that much out of kilter. How could I have been honoured a few hours ago by an international panel of judges for my services to television to be told the following morning that I was redundant, not wanted on voyage, kaput? Could this be the same BBC who were frantically endeavouring to find writers?

In my opinion Ronnie Waldman was the first and last inspiring Head of Light Entertainment, and those who followed in his footsteps were a disappointing bunch of trainee bureaucrats with a limited knowledge of what makes people laugh.

To my mind there were some producers at the BBC much better qualified for the job of Head of Light Entertainment, but these producers preferred being at the sharp end, turning out successful situation comedies. The best of these in my opinion was Duncan Wood, a man who walked alone and lesser mortals followed. He made wonderful pictures where there was only dialogue. A very quiet unassuming six footer, he exuded confidence and authority. He did eventually become Head of Light Entertainment, but in a much humbler offshoot of the BBC in the north of England. What a waste of a huge talent!

Having got that off my chest, I'll continue with problems of my own. Being thrown on to the scrap heap didn't bother me in the least; in fact I was getting weary of constantly having to battle my corner against superior odds. So it was a relief to get out from under, especially as Thames Television at Teddington was in its ascendancy under the guidance of their Head of Light Entertainment Philip Jones, someone Ronnie Waldman would heartily have endorsed. Philip instinctively understood writers, actors and the essentials of good comedy.

As well as the one-hour spectaculars for Thames Television in which Hattie and I had appeared together in between our series *Sykes and A . . .* on the BBC – consisting of comedy sketches and musical numbers, with a spot for John Williams and myself in a guitar duet, and better suited for commercial television, where the adverts were natural breaks between acts – I had also filmed all my half-hour 'silents' under the auspices of Thames Television. There was never anything on paper for my 'silents'. Philip understood immediately when I explained to him that it was impossible to write a script where there was no dialogue. Had I made them for the BBC I would have had to submit several sheets of blank foolscap, which would have had to be passed on from committee to committee to have had any chance of acceptance. Philip never once asked to see a script; instead all he asked of me was 'When do you want to do it?'

Thames Television, as its name implies, was situated alongside the river Thames. Permanently tied up to the bank was a very old vessel, emasculated when its engines had been removed and destined to spend the rest of its life as a floating restaurant. Philip used it for entertaining and business lunches, as there he could exchange ideas about television events uninterrupted by the clatter of plates, knives and forks of Thames Television's staff canteen. On one of these occasions, Paul Elliott, who was managing me at the time, and I were invited aboard in order to discuss a project Philip had in mind for me. Gin and tonics were the opening salvos – a well-trodden path to ensure a good meeting; we had many laughs, partly because we enjoyed each other's company; also the sun was shining and it was a lovely day to be aboard ship. With the help of the gin and tonics and excellent wines, by the time we came to the coffee and brandy, I was convinced that the ship was halfway across the Bay of Biscay. At about four o'clock, we helped each other down the gangplank. It had been a truly immobile cruise.

The following day, I telephoned Philip to thank him for his hospitality and we exchanged courtesies until I came to the real crux of my telephone call. In a pause between laughs, I said, with assumed casualness, 'By the way, Philip, can you tell me what we finally agreed?' Philip laughed and replied, 'I was just about to ask you that.'

Another meeting was arranged, this time on dry land, but I still can't remember what was discussed.

I was happy to host a golf classic at Gerrards Cross sponsored by 3M, an annual event which was to last over fourteen years.

The staff at Gerrards Cross provided superb meals, which seemed each year better than the last, and the members of the golf club gave up their precious Sundays to be starters or marshals, or take on any other little job that would oil the wheels of yet another splendid turnout. As far as celebrities were concerned, this tournament was the most popular in their golfing diary and like other golf classics it was a chance to renew old acquaintances, rather like Crewe station in the old days of vaudeville when the platforms would be littered by four or five different shows changing trains for various theatre bookings.

Garfield Morgan, Bernard Cribbins, Rick Wakeman and Robert

Powell to my knowledge never missed a year. One time I invited Sean Connery to play and he was delighted to accept. Sadly it was the only time in our long friendship he let me down: he won it.

Paul booked me to appear in one of his pantomimes in Aberdeen. It was a good venue for Christmas treats, as the Scots take them seriously, so I was looking forward to visiting Aberdeen again in a specialised facet of entertainment. Prior to rehearsals, Paul arranged a press photograph of the principals for publicity. The first meeting of the cast of a pantomime is always more akin to a family reunion and our photo call was a huge success. I spent the journey back to London wrapped in a warm glow of anticipation and I couldn't wait for the start of rehearsals. Little did I suspect that when the pantomime opened someone else would be playing my part.

A few days later, blissfully unaware of impending disaster, I was talking to Edith – not a world-shattering conversation; in fact I couldn't even remember what it was about while I was speaking. What was more remarkable was that Edith was not replying but looking at me in a strange way as if I was an alien, and for my own part I felt as if my head was full of space. I carried on with my diatribe, but now the scene had changed and I was lying on a bed in a local hospital, continuing my conversation, only this time with a nurse; and in half an hour I was ambulanced to a hospital in Guildford, still conversing with anybody who would listen, even if I was alone. I was diagnosed as having had a slight stroke.

Paul came to visit me in the hospital and told me not to worry about the pantomime. When I replied 'What pantomime?' he accepted that the diagnosis was bang on the button and he would reluctantly have to find a replacement.

After sessions of therapy, brain scans, hospital diets and above all rest I was declared fit to return to the world. Hospital is a good place for thought ... I'd been hauled out of the very strenuous physical experience that goes with a prestigious pantomime, which could have proved a fairy tale too far. As it was, I left hospital rejuvenated and ready to take on all comers. At the risk of repeating myself, I doff my cap to my mother. It is amazing how she always manages to be on the ball at the right time.

In a train from Esher to London, I glanced at somebody's discarded newspaper, and my left eye seemed to be playing tricks: the newsprint wobbled as if the newspaper was lying at the bottom of a disturbed pond.

The following day Mr Mathalone, an eminent eye specialist, diagnosed my complaint as macular disciform, a common dysfunction in old age and incurable. Good grief, I was only sixty-seven, a mere stripling! After a few more visits to Mr Mathalone we were on a Bruce and Eric footing. I had secretly hoped that the left eye would recover even after his pessimistic forecast; however, I gave up hope when he applied the laser to prevent more deterioration. Even then I wasn't too perturbed. After all, I still had a very inquisitive right eye, I could still read and play golf and I was still able to drive my car in the fast lane; and when I come to think about it, Cyclops managed all right, even though his eye was in the centre of his forehead, which could be an advantage on short putts.

The new year sees the arrival of a new member of the family. Susan and Chris are blessed with a baby boy, who will be christened William, and known to his sister Eleanor as Willum, to Matthew as Will, and to his mother as put that down.

In 1990 I appeared in *Cinderella* at the Theatre Royal Plymouth, with Des O'Connor and Peggy Mount. Working with Des was an advanced lesson in how to do pantomime; his relaxed and easy contact with an audience of all ages was an education. It was also a learning curve for me, as I endeavoured to work with one good eye. I still had sight in the left one, albeit peripheral. I would have been home and dry in *Treasure Island* as Long John Silver with a patch. Not withstanding my one or two difficulties on stage, the drive home presented no problems, but unknown to me at the time Plymouth to Esher was to be my last long drive.

For the next two years I hardly noticed my disability. I was still appearing in *Run for Your Wife* at the Aldwych Theatre, and every evening I would drive my car to the station at Esher, travel up to London by train and walk over Waterloo Bridge to the theatre. After the show a car was waiting for Terry Scott and me at the stage door and we were driven to Waterloo station, where we just had time to have a large whisky each before he boarded his train to Guildford and a few minutes later mine departed for Esher. It was a very enjoyable routine, but the axe was about to fall . . . One evening as I stood on Esher station waiting to see my train come round the bend, I noticed that the railway lines in the distance were wavering, and immediately a cold lump of suet pudding hit my stomach. The right eye had had enough of doing all the work and was about to join the left one in the museum.

In 1991 Bruce Mathalone performed the last rites on my good eye and it was the end of a large part of my life's activities – no reading, no driving and only if I had someone with me would I ever be able to play golf again. I was now a registered blind person, entitled to a parking spot, which was not a big deal as I'd already sold my car – no driving like Michael Schumacher down the A3.

Oddly enough, I do not consider myself to be a blind person to whom all is night. I am able to walk down the street without the aid of a white stick but I must admit I am very nervous about crossing a road. I am comforted by the thought that my guardian angel has probably decided to slow me down, or perhaps there is nothing more for me to see. Whatever it is, I am still optimistic that one day I will regain my sight, although two very eminent eye specialists since Mr Mathalone have examined me and declared that the backs of my eyes are, to put it crudely, a bomb site. Even a bomb site can be built up again and as if to support this theory a young athletic man and his very attractive wife came to see me in my office.

Robert Redfern and his wife Anne, having improved the sight of other unfortunates suffering macular disciform, were determined that I should regain my sight at least in my right eye. The methods they use are greeted with scepticism by some members of the medical profession, but as any mariner will tell you it is any port in a storm and believe me it was raining hard. Their treatment is not invasive: they merely supply me with pills, squirts under the tongue and electrical impulses round my eyes. I religiously do everything they ask, except for giving up bread and potatoes, which I will not do. Although I have still to regain my sight, I say without hesitation that I feel ten times healthier and what sight I have left has not deteriorated in any way. I wait patiently for a miracle, but if not, so be it. Only one person knows the answer to this. The court will recess.

On 14 February 1991 David doesn't send a Valentine card to Laura Tapping. He does much better than that: he marries her. An interesting coincidence as Edith and I were also wedded on Valentine's day, in 1952. From now on we will be able to celebrate our wedding anniversaries at the same time. They will be a glorious opportunity to gather the whole family together for an anniversary lunch.

Here I digress to leap forward to the present in order to refer back to the past and I wish you luck in picking the bones out of that lot.

Today as I write this I have received a letter from a Mr J. J. Taylor, who claims he was on the advanced wireless operating course at Madley with me, and although I cannot recall him I have a photograph on the wall in my office of the 1942 intake, and there he is fifth along the back row. However, in his letter he describes how he and all the others laughed as I entertained them in the hut and I certainly don't remember that. He goes on to say how sorry everybody was when they were posted away without me. Not as sorry as I was, but I appreciate their sentiments. They were transported to South Kensington to a post telegraph course and from there to North Africa. I bring in this anecdote because it verifies my 'marooned in Madley in the ghost camp' . . . I rest my case.

Johnny Speight wrote a television show called *The Nineteenth Hole*, which, as every golfer knows, is the bar of any golf club. It was brilliantly directed by William G. Stewart, whom I'd known from the early days when Hattie and I were doing our series *Sykes and A* . . . – he was the bright young call-boy who knocked on my door and said, 'Five minutes, Mr Sykes' – so *The Nineteenth Hole* was one big happy family. My part was that of the club secretary – flat cap, collar and tie, tweed jacket above voluminous plus fours, officious, incompetent and useless. As always, John's writing was concise, hilarious and, most importantly, bang on target. Each week's episode was a different situation bungled at the hands of the unbelievably inept secretary, me. The first concerned a four-handicap male golfer who had had a sex change. This was not a figment of John's fertile imagination but an actual occurrence in real life at two well-known golf clubs . . . What a well-stocked pond for Johnny to fish in! Such storylines were typical of John's writing and his unerring ability to hit the bull's eye every time. So happy was he with the television series that he decided to write it into a stage play, which for me was like three Christmases in one. There was only one little fly in the Germolene: we needed someone with the clout, the ability and, most of all, enough faith in Johnny and me to stage it.

My first thought, naturally, was of Paul Elliott, but he was already committed to several productions and although he would have been happy to take on *The Nineteenth Hole* it would have to have been at the end of a very long queue. Michael Codron, another producer for whom I have the greatest regard, had his money on other things. Then Norma Farnes suggested Bill Kenwright. I'd heard the name but I'd never met him. It was worth a shot.

Bill Kenwright had a very imposing address in Shaftesbury Avenue. As John and I were ushered into his impressive office, he came round his enormous desk to meet us and, what's more, he had a huge smile across his face, which was a good sign. He asked us what we would like to drink. John opted for a cup of tea, no milk, and so did I, although the sun was well over the yardarm, and while his secretary went out to organise the drinks Bill shepherded us to a settee in the corner of the room. He sat in an armchair opposite, still with a smile on his lips, eyes twinkling as though we had just passed an extremely funny audition.

Then he slapped his hands on his knees and said, 'Well, what can I do for you lads?'

I cleared my throat. 'John's written a play all about a golf club called *The Nineteenth Hole*.'

John put his four pence in with, 'Eric plays the golf secretary.'

And Bill finished the round with, 'And you were wondering if I would produce it?'

We nodded and John proffered him the script, but he ignored it and asked, 'When do you want to do it?'

'Don't you want to read it first?' said Johnny, but Bill's attention was focused on a large calendar.

'How about August?' he said. 'Three weeks for rehearsals and then a short provincial tour.'

I couldn't believe my ears. I looked at John and he couldn't believe it either, and his ears were in much better condition than mine. Was that all there was to it?

'Well, that's settled then,' said Bill, rubbing his hands together and at that moment the secretary entered with a silver tray bearing our drinks as if she'd known it was to be a celebration.

'We'll open in Leatherhead, at the beginning of September,' said Bill.

True to his word, he provided us with an excellent cast and an elaborate set of a golf club bar room. It was magnificent, created by one of the best-known set designers in the West End.

After three weeks' rehearsal, we were ready for the opening night, and that was the only time we'd seen Bill Kenwright since our meeting in his office weeks ago. Is it any wonder that Bill is one of the most respected producers in the theatre? He had complete faith in Johnny's writing and my performance. Thankfully it paid off. From that day I was one of Bill's most ardent devotees. Ours is a friendship that is still warming my heart to this day.

The Big Freeze was the latest of my 'silent' films, starring Bob Hoskins, Sir John Mills, Spike Milligan, Donald Pleasance and, for economy's sake, myself. The whole film was shot in a twenty-below-zero Finland with, naturally, a host of Finnish actors and actresses, language being no barrier as there weren't any words. Finland being the land of suicides, so they tell me, it is hardly surprising that for me it was the most unhappy six weeks of my life. This was due in a large part to the daily battle with my first assistant, who had little faith in my ability to direct and believed he could make a much better job of it, although how he could have accomplished this is beyond me, as like with my other 'silent' films there wasn't a word on paper – I had always written my 'silents' with the camera. After two weeks, the situation was becoming desperate. Something had to be done, so I told him in no uncertain terms that his idea of comedy and mine were worlds apart, to which he replied, 'All right, then, we'll try it your way.' Which will give you some idea of what I was up against.

More trouble seeped through the pipeline when John Mills, who had only agreed to appear in the film because of our friendship, apologetically told me one evening that his agent, Laurence Evans, in London had advised him to cease work on the production as he had not yet received a penny from the producer. John was very perturbed by this turn of events: the last thing he wanted was to hold up the shooting schedule. I understood his dilemma; he had been put in an invidious position. I thanked him for telling me and assured him that I would take it from there. I telephoned Norma in London, who telephoned the producer and was told that John's payment was all in hand, after which she rang John's agent, who was unimpressed by the ambiguity of the producer's response. Norma telephoned me to apprise me of the state of affairs, and I wasn't impressed either. It was now about ten o'clock in the evening and

I still hadn't sat down to dinner – not that I could eat anything with my stomach like a rogue washing machine. Then Norma called me with news that didn't surprise me: she had contacted Joy Jameson, Donald Pleasance's agent, and, would you believe it, she was in the same predicament. I didn't ask Norma about Spike and Bob Hoskins – the last thing I wanted was to add to the suicide rate. The matter was at last resolved and at three o'clock in the morning I returned my borrowed mobile to snatch a couple of hours' sleep before my five-thirty alarm call.

The next day's troubles began when the editor resigned, having spliced only two frames, expostulating that his hands were tied when there was no script on paper. Had he not ascertained that fact when he took on the job? John, Spike and Donald encouraged me by giving 110 per cent, but deep in my heart I accepted that the buck stopped at my desk.

Dear Bob Hoskins and I hit it off from the moment we met. On the first day we were walking up the street when he decided that the weather was too fierce for the kind of reefer coat I was wearing and took off his heavy white fur jacket and put it over my shoulders, insisting that I keep it. God knows how he survived in that frozen land.

It wasn't long before he could see the road blocks the production staff were putting up at every turn and in truth had it not been for his cheerful outlook throughout my ordeal I doubt whether I would have lasted the course. In fact it was largely his brilliance and brightness on and off the screen that saved the film from the cutting-room floor.

The final wrap couldn't come too soon for me. When it did, we took the plane back to England and the production staff passed us in the aisle without acknowledging our presence, which suited me fine. Back in England I edited what I had managed to put together, with the help of André Jacquemin, whose grasp of technology was far beyond my limited capabilities. We managed to create a passable film, the burden was lifted and I had all the time in the world to enjoy a nervous breakdown.

* * *

There was only one bright spot that cheered me during my ordeal in Finland. It was the news that David and Laura now have a son, whom they are going to call Thomas. This wonderful snippet gives me back a sense of proportion; *The Big Freeze* was of little importance against what is happening in Esher.

In 1984 I had written *The Great Crime of Grapplewick*, my second book. It was originally penned as a film, but producers of all shapes and sizes ignored it, so rather than let it rot in the graveyard of my desk drawer I rewrote it as a novel. It must have been a good yarn because now ten years later it was reprinted by Virgin Books.

Nothing daunted, *UFOs are Coming Wednesday* was my second attempt at a screen play. Surprise, surprise, producers of all shapes and sizes ignored it. Ergo my third novel of the above name was published by Virgin Books.

The International Fishing Contest destined for box office success of the year was again ignored by producers etc., but I'd be jiggered if I was going to write this as a novel.

After the success of *The Nineteenth Hole*, Bill Kenwright led me through a masterclass in stage plays, including *Rough Crossing* by Tom Stoppard. A comedy drama, *Two of a Kind*, written by Hugh Janes, with Michael Denison, Dulcie Gray and Carmen Silvera was the play that made me realise for the first time that I may after all have the glimmerings of an actor in me. Apart from the laughs, there were many dramatic scenes that saddened even me when I was doing them, and there was many a tear-stained face in the audience, whereas in the past all the tears had usually been from the management. After *Two of a Kind* I was of a more serious bent. I even grew my hair longer, but before I could decide whether to have my eyebrows trimmed I was in rehearsal for *Fools Rush In* with Dennis Waterman and Gerald Harper. My part suited me down to the ground, in as much as that for most of it I was seated, but the best was yet to come: in the play Dennis served me with a freshly cooked omelette every night, which saved me going out for supper. As one old thespian was heard to declare, 'The money isn't much but there's a practical steak and kidney pudding in the second act.' Fortunately the run of *Fools Rush In* came to an end just before I became addicted to eggs.

One gruelling morning when Dennis had taken me to the cleaners over a very tight golf match, I received a phone call from Peter Hall, inviting me to have lunch with him. I told him that I was appearing in Brighton, to which he replied he knew that when he phoned me. *Touché.*

The day after, I took the train to London and made my way to the restaurant, where I was met by Norma. 'We are the guests of Sir Peter Hall,' she said to a passing waiter, who beamed and pointed to a table. 'He usually sits there,' he said, 'but he's not here yet.' Two Chardonnays later Peter bustled in as if he was only allowed a five-minute lunchbreak. He ordered more wine and guided us through the menu.

Throughout the meal Peter dominated the conversation, extolling the genius of Molière – very entertaining, but I couldn't see where it was leading, until he remarked that Molière loved vaudevillians. At this a lamp went on in my head, not bright but flickering. Peter went on to tell me that he was about to direct *School for Wives* by Molière. I still didn't tumble, until his next words, uttered off-handedly, that there was a part in it that might have been specially written for me.

I shook my head violently, as if I'd been attacked by wasps. 'I'm not . . .,' I started.

But Peter cut me off. Leaning swiftly across the table, he put up his hand as if he was about to cross a busy road and said, 'Don't tell me you can't do it, because I know you can.'

But I wasn't convinced. I shook my head again, not too fiercely this time as I was getting dizzy.

'As you are probably the greatest vaudevillian in this country, Molière must have had you in mind.'

A masterstroke – he'd pressed the right button. I lowered my head modestly to hide my delight. I'm such a sucker for flattery, and from that moment my mind was made up and I was determined not to let either him or Molière down. We shook hands, and Peter looked at his watch and hurried out of the restaurant seconds before the waiter placed the bill before me.

I couldn't wait to get back to Brighton and tell Dennis casually that my next play would be *School for Wives* by Molière. He didn't seem to be unduly impressed, but in the performance that night he not only served me an omelette but brought me a piece of cake as well.

It came as no surprise to me that *School for Wives* was a Bill Kenwright production; he was turning them out like bullets from a water-cooled machine gun and I wouldn't have had it any other way. Molière and Ray Cooney were hardly in the same league, as different as the puffer pulling out of Oldham Central station from the Orient Express, but if Bill and Peter Hall thought I could do it, who was I to quibble?

Peter Bowles was the leading man, ably abetted by Henry McGee, the most underrated actor of our generation. My wife, played by Carmen Silvera, and I were servants to Peter Bowles.

Rehearsing at the Old Vic wasn't all a bed of roses: there were the odd patches of weeds. For instance, on one occasion as we neared the end of the day's work, Peter dismissed the cast, except for Peter Bowles and me, so that he could go over one of our scenes. Peter Bowles wasn't too happy with my portrayal of his servant and I could understand his predicament: he was miffed because he was having to learn and act everything exactly as Molière had intended, whereas Peter Hall had given me carte blanche to play the role as I saw it. This was the result of one of the discussions in which Peter Hall and I had indulged. When he had pointed out that Molière was a devotee of vaudeville, I broke in, 'In which case he could not possibly have written words for vaudevillians, as the veterans of vaudeville were usually the dregs of humanity, the rogues and vaga-bonds, uneducated and illiterate.' Reluctantly he had nodded his head and I pressed on, 'Molière would have used the vaudevillians to spice up his plays'. Peter nodded again. 'I take your point,' he said. 'Let's see what you can come up with.' Game, set and match. Having seen the logic of my argument, Peter Hall had handed over the 'Get out of jail free' card.

Unfortunately Peter Bowles had no knowledge of our conversation and assumed that I had arrogantly elbowed out Molière's work in order to ad lib some of my own drollery, without consulting the director. He angrily proceeded to read me the riot act, throughout which Peter Hall sat impassively in the front row of the stalls, one leg nonchalantly crossed over the other one as if he was listening to a particularly dull portion of the play. Eventually I had had enough. I poured petrol over my boat and got out my matches, yelling, 'I didn't want to do the play in the first place and I object to you telling me how to play my part when I haven't said a word about yours,' and over my shoulder I made my parting shot: 'I've never walked out on a play in my life but on this occasion I make an exception.' And with that I flounced out of the stage door, having resigned from Molière, the classical theatre and the incomprehensibility of straight actors.

Ten minutes later I flounced back into a frozen tableau. The two Peters were both in exactly the same position as when I had left. I approached Peter Bowles and apologised for my behaviour, admitting that I was out of order and suggesting we should carry on rehearsal where we had left off. Peter Hall didn't seem to be bothered one way or another – it was as if my walking out was a common defiant gesture and they knew that I'd be back. But in this case they'd underestimated my febrile obstinacy – a Lancashire trait. In fact what had actually happened was that when I walked out through the stage door I discovered that it was dark – to be more exact pitch black. Had it not been for the lights of the traffic at the end of the street, I would have been completely blind. I made my way to the main thoroughfare to hail a taxi. It was a busy part of London, but unfortunately as vehicles passed me I was unable to distinguish one car from the next; several taxis could have raced along without me recognising them. It was one of the disadvantages of being partially sighted.

Frustrated, I made my way precariously back down the dark street but I couldn't find the stage door. In a panic, I waited for a passer-by to ask for help. Luckily at that moment somebody left the stage door open and suddenly light flooded the pavement. I rushed for it before it closed and I was in blackness again. It was a close-run thing. Had I been sighted, I would have been halfway to my office in a cab by then.

P.S. *School for Wives* opened at the Piccadilly Theatre and in spite of our rehearsal differences Peter Bowles and I worked extremely well together. In fact, so successful was it that at the end of our run at the Piccadilly the play was transferred to the Comedy Theatre, but after a few weeks I was reluctantly forced to jump ship.

During this drama David and Laura have a baby girl called Sophie. They are now what I call a well-balanced family and Thomas has a little sister. I have been promoted as well: what with Susan's three children, I am now a granddad for a fifth time. It may sound a bit banal on paper but I think a little boast is called for on this occasion.

The reason I jumped ship from *School for Wives* was that I was exhausted, abnormally so, which brought Norma to ask me when I last had a check-up. I couldn't remember, apart from being passed A1 when I joined the air force in early 1942, but this wasn't good enough for Norma, and a few days later I was weighed, blood tested, questioned, prodded and stared at – you'd think it was a medical for an astronaut, very professional it was, as it should be with BUPA. I have nothing but admiration for this organisation. Private hospital bills have been settled without delay and in fact were it not for BUPA I couldn't afford to be ill, and this check-up was all part of the service. However, the tests were not quite complete, and I had to present myself at the New Victoria Hospital, Coombe Lane, Kingston, an institution that was to become as familiar to me as my own front room. My appointment was with a Mr Cullings, cardiologist. My first impression when I met him was one of confidence; he struck me as the kind of person who would get out of his car, cross the road and help me change a tyre. As he proceeded to put me through various hoops, I was eager to demonstrate my fitness so that he could return to the sufferers who really needed his attention; I felt a little shamefaced to be wasting his valuable time. I could not have been more mistaken. How idiotic to even think of myself as Mr Universe, pest-free and fire-proof . . . my comeuppance was about to bite me in the backside.

Finally Mr Cullings invited me on to the treadmill, a moving belt on which I was to walk, getting nowhere except out of breath. It was amazing: had I been actually walking I would have covered not more than fifty yards and already I was puffing like Thomas the Tank Engine. Judging by the expression on Mr Cullings' face he would not be entering me for a marathon.

When he told me that I would have to be hospitalised for a heart bypass operation, he did so in such a matter-of-fact tone of voice that I nodded as if he'd advised me to wear a vest during the cold weather. The gravity of the situation never entered my thoughts. On the other hand, had he shaken his head, sadly avoided my eyes and broken the bad news to the wall behind me, I would have been perturbed, if not downright worried. As it was, I felt assured that I was in good hands. I found later that one of Mr Cullings' strengths was his ability to communicate.

At home, awaiting my call from the hospital, I was immersed in a book by John Grisham, a favourite American author of mine. As my days of being able to read were far behind me, I was listening to a talking book, and by some extraordinary coincidence I heard a passage referring to a man lying in a hospital bed awaiting a heart bypass operation. In graphic detail I was led through a pre-op description in which the patient was able to watch a televised operation of the surgeon pushing a long thin rod into his groin. The patient, wet with panic and shock, fainted. Now I was not so sanguine about my own operation and, needing to be consoled, I rang Mr Cullings at his home. His wife said he was at the hospital and could she help? She sounded as if she could, so I plunged in, regaling her with the passage in John Grisham's novel and asking if I would have to go through the same ordeal. When she laughed, I was reassured, and even more so when she explained what the procedure entailed.

Needless to say, John Grisham has been demoted, his place taken by Bernard Cornwell.

A few days later I took my small kit of slippers and pyjamas to St Anthony's Hospital, Cheam, and before I could get the bed warm I was lifted on to a trolley and wheeled away to a dark room. Two nurses stood side by side, hands clasped behind their backs like two sailors waiting for the skipper to arrive. They didn't speak, but their smiles gave me confidence for my wellbeing. Two dark shapes approached, and they both crouched by my feet, eyes glued to a small television set which lit their faces so that I recognised Mr Cullings. It took them no more than three minutes to accomplish what they were at and without a word they disappeared into the darkness. 'Well done,' said one of the nurses and I was transported back to my room.

Was that it? I would take John Grisham's novels with a pinch of salt in future. Following a tap on the door, a tall, cheerful, well-dressed man entered, introducing himself as John Smith. He would be carrying out the heart bypass surgery. For a moment I was nonplussed – I'd innocently assumed that the last few minutes in a darkened room was the operation.

Shortly afterwards I was being wheeled along the corridors to the operating theatre, where I finally received my passport to the land of nod, and from that moment I must obviously speculate. After surgery I was offloaded into the intensive care unit. My body was inert, incapable of feeling, but for the mind it was carnival night: a horror was awaiting for which no one had prepared me. These were the hallucinations brought on by drugs; in fact so heavily was I sedated that I am now convinced that they pumped me with every drug available – everything, that is, except Ecstasy.

As I lay in the intensive care unit, my brain played tricks. It wasn't a dream, it was real. I was in a hospital bed in Australia, recovering from a heart bypass operation, and I couldn't convince the nurses that I was supposed to be in Cheam, England. Showing little regard for me, they were all tarting themselves up for a wagon ride on a float in the Lamumba parade. I begged them to give me a telephone so that I could call home to tell Edith I was in Australia, and all I got in return was 'You're doing fine.' I pleaded for them to put me in touch with Mr Smith, the surgeon who had operated on me, but I was told that he had flown back to England straight after the op, and they smilingly refused to call the Australian police. It was straight out of the book of nightmares. I was crying with frustration, wanting to run from something and unable to move my legs, screaming for help with no sounds coming from my throat. Frightened and exhausted, I appealed to a smiling black nurse who was leaning on the bars of my cot. She had such a warm, splendid face that I knew I'd found an ally, but by this time I was too flaked out to care. 'You're doing fine,' she said, but I'd heard that one before. 'I don't know where you've been, honey, but wherever it was you're back.' It was only then that I realised I was again in hospital in blessed Cheam and the nightmare was over.

I learned later from some of the staff that what I had experienced was a common occurrence. All I can say is that I'd had a glimpse of madness, taking steps on a journey which I have no desire to retrace. It is beyond me how intelligent human beings can inject themselves with drugs purely for recreation. When people ask me now about my illness I tell them that there is no problem with having a heart bypass but all the hassle is in getting planning permission.

Since then I report to the hospital for check-ups by Mr Cullings, only now he is Bill and his wife Eileen. She is a retired ward sister and a practice manager for her husband's consultancy. I've no idea what the job description of practice manager entails; all I know is that when anything medical nags me I speak to Eileen and she dispels my anxieties, which in most cases are merely the result of my tearaway imagination. If Bill and Eileen had charge of the NHS it would be almost a pleasure to be ill.

I have nothing but admiration for all the medicos I have come into contact with during my periodic under-the-weather bouts. I would be abrogating my duties if I did not also mention Dr Mary Clarke of St Anthony's Hospital, Cheam. Even if she only listens while you talk, you leave her surgery having forgotten what you came for in the first place.

I never seem to learn any of my lessons. I wrote another novel, called *Smelling of Roses*. Yes, you've guessed it: I originally wrote this as a screenplay and the same producers, older but no wiser, ignored it. I had innocently thought that Peter Sellers, who was absolutely thrilled after reading the film script, would be my ace in the hole, especially as his oppo was to be Peter O'Toole and the lady love of the piece Sophia Loren. Now of course my two lead roles would be Bob Hoskins and Dennis Waterman, and who knows the lady could be my granddaughter Sophie, but as she is now only seven years old I may not last long enough to see the rushes.

One evening a couple of months after my operation, I began to have pains in my chest – not enough to worry me in the normal course of events, but as I'd just had a heart bypass these small rumblings took on a deeper significance and so Edith sent for the doctor.

Shortly afterwards, a pleasant handsome woman strode into our kitchen as if it was an emergency. It was Dr Kearsey, who was to be my GP. She sat down at the table in order to listen to my complaint. I told her that it wasn't too long since I'd had a heart bypass and I mentioned Mr Cullings. I went on for so long that after I'd finished I'd quite forgotten why she was there and I think she realised that she'd been called out unnecessarily. It was then that I discovered what a good psychologist she was, for she suggested that the best thing I could do would be to have a large whisky and when I asked her if I could have it on the National Health we became buddies. I still had to explain to Edith when she'd gone that I truly had suffered chest pains, to which she replied, 'If you weren't wearing a belt I would suggest you loosen your braces.' Ah, what it is to be in a funny household!

*   *   *

On a day in August 1998, Edith, David and Julie accompanied me as I was driven up the M1 on a grisly errand to pay our last respects to John's wife, Irene. It was the day of her funeral. When we arrived at the house, John and I embraced. Trying to put on a brave face, he was being comforted by his daughter Janet and her husband Steve. Their two sons Ian and David I was meeting for the first time. What impressed me most was their good manners and their respect for the occasion as they took around trays of dry sherry. After the church ceremony, we all made our way for a mandatory ham tea. In a better frame of mind, I met Little Eric, Auntie Emmy's son. He had been christened Eric after me but in order to differentiate between us he was called Little Eric. In fact although he had been little when I brought him a German helmet from Normandy, now I was the little one.

In the course of our conversation, he told me that his mother was in a nursing home just round the corner. My heart leapt – my dear old Auntie Emmy. I grabbed his arm and we made our way to the nursing home. Groups of old people sat round a table in a corner and in a wheelchair alongside was Auntie Emmy. She didn't seem to have changed much in all the years since we'd last met. She greeted me with a pale shadow of her old smile as it had always been. I kissed her on both cheeks but she didn't respond. 'How are you, Auntie?' I said. Her smile remained but she didn't utter a word. I glanced at Little Eric. He shook his head. 'She won't recognise you,' he whispered. I looked again at her dear face. I was very close to tears: I desperately wanted to thank her for all the kindness she had shown me in my adolescent years and now the chance was gone. Had my time been so valuable in the last fifty years that I could not have spared a few moments to say thank you?

Twelve months later John joined Irene to be buried in the same cemetery; Auntie Emmy had passed away shortly after my last visit. A door in my life had been slammed shut for ever.

Many of my fellow thespians have their own particular favourite venue. My heart lies not in the West End of London but in a little provincial theatre in Lincoln, the Theatre Royal. It is not imposing, brassy and glitzy; on the contrary, it is old, small and familiar. Entrances and exits I have made in this theatre too numerous to remember, in pantomimes, comedy plays and farces. On one rare occasion I even tried out my one-man show and I still believe that had I been able to transport that Lincoln audience with me on a short tour it would have been a sell-out.

In other theatres I rarely visit the green room, but at Lincoln it is one of my first ports of call. The warm-hearted atmosphere is largely due to Chris Moreno, who amongst all his other theatrical interests manages to keep a watchful eye on what is perhaps one of his favourites too. He also owned or part-owned with Paul Elliott the Grand Opera House in York. On one of my appearances at this venue Chris came to my dressing room just before the doors had opened for the evening performance, and asked me if I would accompany him up to the circle. On arriving, he handed me a pair of scissors and invited me to cut a ribbon across a door. I did so and looked up at the lettering saying 'The Eric Sykes Bar'. To say I was astonished is an understatement. I felt humble, knocked out and several other emotions which occur to many people but not all at once. Chris was beaming and from his expression I knew there was more to come. The walls of the bar were lined with pictures of me at various stages of my career, most of which I hadn't even seen myself, and the whole bar was decorated with memorabilia of my life. How Chris had managed to come by this collection – even my army boots which had marched me through the war – is beyond me. I couldn't find the words to express my gratitude. It was a red-letter day in my life that I shall never forget. When Chris eventually gave up his tenure of the Grand Opera House, he took the collection with him and installed it in the Theatre Royal at Lincoln.

Kafka's Dick, a play by Alan Bennett, was Bill Kenwright's next venture and would you believe it, there was a part in it for me, as an elderly man moving about the stage with the help of a Zimmer frame. I didn't mind the Zimmer, but why must I always be cast in elderly parts? I wasn't yet eighty and could walk up and down stairs without any assistance at all and, what's more important, I could remember why. Apart from this small gripe, I had the pleasure of working with the delightful Julia McKenzie, John Gordon-Sinclair, Michael Byrne and Dennis Lill. We never saw Alan Bennett – not before, during or after the play – and being a paid-up paranoiac I have always assumed that when he learned that I was in the cast he took a year's sabbatical in Tahiti.

I was in the make-up room in the film studios in Madrid, where we were about to begin the production of a film called *The Others*. Naturally the first day of shooting is always an adrenalin-pumping time, and I was both excited and a little apprehensive. The make-up girl was busy with my face, which didn't take too much ageing, when a tall, elegant lady entered the room and put out her hand. 'I'm Nicole Kidman,' she said. It was delivered in a voice that put me at my ease straight away. I told her my name and she replied, 'I know. I saw you in *School for Wives* at the Piccadilly Theatre.' She not only broke the ice but dispelled any misconception I might have had about high-flying screen idols. From that moment I was wholeheartedly one of her acolytes and in the many months it took to complete the film nothing in her character destroyed my illusion. Alejandro Amenabar, the director of the film, a young man of only twenty-six already a legend in the film world, was a perfect guide and mentor for Nicole. Both spoke in soft voices and it was obvious that they had each other's total respect.

NEWSFLASH

Two of my grandchildren, Thomas and Sophie, discovered one day that I did other things besides being a granddad: I was in the *Tellytubbies*. Not strictly true, of course – my only contribution, along with Penelope Keith, was to introduce the programme. However, when Thomas and Sophie recognised my voice I was elevated to the ranks of stardom by my only but most important, treasured fan club.

Shortly afterwards, Thomas was at his primary school when the teacher asked the class to name famous people. Winston Churchill was the first name and the teacher chalked it up on the blackboard. 'Anyone else?' she asked, and a little boy at the back yelled out, 'Florence Nightingale.' The teacher squeaked this on to the blackboard under Winston Churchill.

It was then that Thomas's hand shot up. 'Yes, Thomas,' said the teacher expectantly.

Thomas, bless him, replied, 'My granddad's famous.'

'Oh,' replied the teacher. 'What is he called?'

'Eric Sykes,' said Thomas, and my name was chalked on the board underneath two of the most revered people in our history, for which honour I thank my little grandson.

And to avoid a split in the ranks, here's an anecdote about Sophie. Their mother was about to appear in a commercial, and in one of the shots, inside a busy supermarket, Laura was directed to walk past the camera holding the hand of a little girl. There will be no prizes for guessing who the little girl would be. Who else but Sophie, who was then only four years old? She immediately adopted the mantle of an actress, so much so that when during one of our family lunches I suggested we should have a meal at a restaurant when we were all free, poor Sophie she declined, and with an explanatory gesture the late, great Sarah Bernhardt would have applauded, she wailed petulantly, 'No, not next week . . . I'm working.' Leaving me in no doubt into which career she was heading.

I know that most other ordinary grandparents have the same feelings of pride and we could fill a book about our little treasures, but this happens to be my book and I am not ashamed to write about them – and if anyone thinks their grandchildren are better than mine, step outside.

NORMAL SERVICE WILL BE RESUMED

As if he had been waiting for my arrival from Spain, Bill Kenwright stepped forward with another short tour in a well-known classic, *Charlie's Aunt*. Much as I had enjoyed my education in the film world of Madrid, I was glad to be back on stage again in front of a live audience, having left one of my fields fallow according to my philosophy.

When I was in *Rough Crossing* in Liverpool, Bill Kenwright took me home and introduced me to his mother and father, and I was made an honorary member of his family. Incidentally *Rough Crossing* was produced by Bill's brother Tom, and although Bill is teetotal whenever Tom and I meet we toast each other and the Kenwrights with a glass of Glenfiddich.

Just one more year and I would be an octogenarian, which doesn't mean I would give up meat but simply gives away my age: seventy-nine and still available to play cardigan-and-slipper roles on stage, film or television. Once more Bill Kenwright had plans for me. His approach had varied little over the years. He would ask how did I feel about doing a play and, knowing that he had already vetted it, I invariably replied that I'd be delighted. This new venture at the Vaudeville Theatre in the Strand was a farce called *Caught in the Net*, written by Ray Cooney. My heart sank. It is no official secret that Ray and I are poles apart. Although neither of us speaks the language, in Ray's method performers act by numbers: that is, bedroom door opens, someone emerges in vest and pants, other member of cast centre stage whips his head round, one two three to observe this scantily clad entrant, turns his head to face the audience wide-eyed, mouth agape, another one two three when vest and pants says 'Sorry' and pops back into bedroom. Ray's interpretation of comedy is that all the laughs should be achieved only by the lines he has written, which leaves little scope for actors – they are virtually automatons, although to be fair a short run in one of Ray's farces improves one's mathematics. On the opposite side of the coin, my understanding of humour is to make audiences laugh, the more hysterical the laughter the more successful the evening will be.

During a meeting in my office with Bill, Ray and Norma, most of the talking was between Ray and myself, quietly sensible to start with and growing to a heated argument as Ray showed me how to act the part like a ventriloquist's dummy being manipulated by some unfortunate suffering from St Vitus's dance, and I must confess that my pointing finger was within an inch of his nose as my voice rose in anger. It was obvious that Ray didn't want me in the cast. He need not have bothered, as I didn't want any part in it either. When the meeting finally broke up, with no decisions, we all dispersed in gloomy silence. Back in his own office Bill telephoned Norma and, still shell-shocked, said, 'I've never seen Eric like that before.' I felt I'd let the side down.

A couple of days later Ray telephoned me to apologise for our set-to and I apologised to him for behaving like a child of ten who knows his rights. He said he was sorry that I didn't want to play the part of the old father and I said I was sorry to have to let him down, but behind all this waffle we were both glad I wasn't in it. Bill Kenwright had other ideas. He has always understood the infantile tantrums of people who act out their careers by pretending to be somebody else, and he didn't attain his eminence as one of our leading impresarios by backing risky productions. He had a quiet word in Ray's ear. On the following Monday morning, I was wondering whether to sit down and relax or stand up when Ray telephoned me to ask me where I was. I said I was at home. He told me it was the first day of rehearsal and could I get over to join them as soon as possible? I did so, with a nagging feeling that Bill in his inscrutable way had had the posters printed even before the meeting in my office. That's one of the things I like about him.

So there I was playing the part of Russ Abbott's dad in *Caught in the Net*. However, instead of a walking stick, which Ray had used as a prop when he played the part, I replaced it with a Zimmer frame. I fail to see much humour in a stick but with a Zimmer frame the possibilities are endless. I won't explain further in case Ray is taking this down.

I must say that my part was a doddle. My first entrance opened the second half, so when I made my appearance all the groundwork had been done. But my old dad portrayal was hectic, physical and exhausting. I was making a rod for my own backside simply in order to hear the audience's reaction. It wasn't very clever of me, but neither was diving off the high board at Blackpool's Derby Baths while pickled.

Before the play opened, Russ insisted that I take the number-one dressing room. I was touched by this gesture and I thanked him, but as he was top of the bill number-one dressing room was his right and I was quite comfortable where I was. I have never forgotten his most generous offer and as I got to know him better I realised that it was typical of him.

On 26 February 2002 one of the jewels fell from the comedy crown. It was the day Spike Milligan, with whom I'd shared an office for over fifty years, passed away. I use the phrase 'passed away', for that is exactly what he did. Spike will never die in the hearts of millions of us who were uplifted by his works. For me and Norma, his manager, he still prowls the building in unguarded moments. He will always be welcome. As Hattie was my sister, so he was my brother. Rest in peace, Spike, and say hello to Peter and Harry.

To be successful in our profession is sometimes as simple as being in the right place at the right time. Sadly this is not as easy as it sounds. It is purely a matter of coincidence and when it happened to me, I wasn't even there.

Jeff Pope and Bob Mills were writing a television series called *Stan the Man*, starring John Thompson. As my television set is mainly ornamental these days and the screen a collector of dust – in fact I only keep it in order to pay the licence fee – it's not too surprising that Jeff and Bob and their work had escaped my notice. That is the status quo from now – I can only write what I learned later.

Jeff and Bob had written a gem of a part for an elderly gentleman called Stafford, but they were having trouble with casting. For several days they trawled through *Spotlight*, the actors' *Yellow Pages* – they must have pored over every old character actor's photo, but most of them were unsuitable as they were dead. They hadn't come up with anyone to fit the part and time was now in short supply. During all this I was still appearing at the Vaudeville Theatre in *Caught in the Net* content to bask in the laughs and blissfully unaware that events were in hand to pour cream over my bowl of strawberries.

Jeff Pope was in London, still no nearer to putting a face on his Stafford, and as he left Charing Cross station old character actors paraded through his thoughts. Moving slowly along the Strand in a taxi, he gazed dispassionately at the passing scene, the Adelphi Theatre, restaurants, shops and eventually the Vaudeville Theatre, and here he jerked upright, unable to believe what was before his eyes: a large photo of yours truly above the entrance. He whooped in triumph, 'We've got our Stafford.'

At about the same time I was standing over a three-foot putt on the first green at Fulwell Golf Club for a seven, which explains why I was somewhere else when I became Stafford. There was another slight hiccup: I was busy with *Caught in the Net*. When Norma told Bill of the offer, he readily agreed to release me for a week in order for me to play John Thompson's father alongside such distinguished company as Gaynor Fay, Kay Mellor playing Gaynor's mother, Joe Absalom and for afters a very juicy emotional scene with George Costigan. I mention the whole cast because of the way they looked after me: they were a fur coat on a cold night.

I returned to the Vaudeville rejuvenated, having enjoyed my working holiday in Manchester and especially Thomas's Chop House – if it wasn't so far from London I'd be lunching there every day.

Russ Abbott was still carrying the banner for *Caught in the Net*, the cast Carol Hawkins, Helen Gill and Robert Dawes welcomed me back as if I was a born-again Henry Irving and I slotted back into my dad's role as if I'd never been away.

One evening Chris Moreno, together with three colleagues, came to see *Caught in the Net* and afterwards Chris invited me to supper, where I was introduced to his party, who were not just ordinary theatre goers but the producers of *Chitty Chitty Bang Bang*, which was due to open at the London Palladium. It was a very enjoyable meal and it wasn't until the coffee that I realised that there was more to it than just putting on weight. I was invited to take part in *Chitty Chitty Bang Bang*. I was tempted to accept, remembering my old dressing room and the prestige of being at the Palladium again. It was then that I came down to earth – I was thinking back to over forty years ago. Reluctantly I turned the part down. It is difficult to accept that you are no longer a spring chicken, but sadly, sadly, sadly, my decision was to prove correct: after a few more weeks at the Vaudeville my curtain came down with a resounding crash.

Matinées made for a long day, though a pleasurable one because between shows we went for a meal at Il Paradiso, just round the corner in the Strand. On this occasion after the final curtain came down on the matinée we left the stage, and the young'uns rushed up the steps to the dressing rooms yelling and whooping, like children let out of school, while the rest of the cast followed more sedately. But something didn't quite fit . . . to me the steps seemed eminently steeper and interminable. I remember putting my foot on the bottom one when suddenly I was on a scenic railway thundering down the slope at breakneck speed, and as far as I could see there was no up at the end of it. Despair was about to lurch into panic when, as if a switch had been thrown, all was peaceful – the eye of the hurricane . . . I was sitting in a chair in my dressing room; nothing seemed to matter and I felt strangely light-headed. I sensed other people in the dressing room from the rustle of subdued conversation, interrupted by the ringing of a far-off telephone, which was odd in itself because the telephone was only a yard away from me. When I tried to rise, my right leg refused to obey my brain; it was numb and mocking in mute rebellion. At that moment two burly figures entered and I was lifted bodily on to a wheeled contraption, carried up another flight of stone steps and finally pushed out of the stage door and into the back of an ambulance. One thing will remain in my mind for ever: just before the doors of the ambulance closed on me, I saw the lone figure of Bill Kenwright with a look of deep concern on his face. I still don't know how he managed to be there. Of course time had no meaning for me – an hour may have elapsed between my discovery of my disobedient leg and my transfer to St Thomas's Hospital, where I was placed on a gurney, still in my stage costume, still aloof from the world. I was pushed into a gloomy space behind a large curtain of sorts, very likely for privacy. Then the curtain was lifted and Bill was again by me. I wasn't well enough for coherent thought; I just accepted his presence. Bill stood by my gurney until eleven o'clock that night – over five hours, in which we exchanged no words. Only when a hospital porter entered to take me away did Bill leave. Friends like Bill are really worth having.

It must have been near midnight when I was ambulanced from St Thomas's down to the New Victoria Hospital in Kingston, where I was immediately lifted into a wheelchair and taken to a bed in a private room. With a great surge of relief I was greeted by Edith and Kathy with my pyjamas, dressing gown and slippers. What a joy it was to see them! In the morning the first person I saw at the foot of my bed was dear old Bill Cullings and my spirits rose. When one is lost, helpless and above all sick, it is a great boost to meet a doctor in whom one has great faith. For the first time since the onset of the stroke, I began to live again; at the sheer sight of him optimism crept into my consciousness.

After a couple of weeks, still unable to move without the aid of a wheelchair, I was again transported by ambulance, this time to Unstead Park in Godalming, Surrey, for the therapeutic part of my cure. Dr Al-Memar travelled with me in the ambulance and his cheerful demeanour and positive attitude convinced me once again that I would come out of this horrifying experience whole.

Unstead Park is situated in pleasant countryside, but for all that it is still a hospital, where shattered minds and bodies are nursed back to health. The staff were without doubt diligent, skilful and caring. This was my second stroke and a little more serious than the first one. For a time most of my weight was carried by my left leg while the right one struggled to keep up. It is so irritating when your legs don't get on with each other.

Once again it was a subtle warning from my mother that time

waits for no man. Without waiting for the show at the Vaudeville to close, she had once more taken me off to an enforced rest before my next hair-brained attempt at being middle-aged . . . And while I am on the subject it would be remiss of me not to pay my respects to someone on my shortlist of people I admire, Derek Griffiths, comedian, the most outstanding villain in pantomime, guitarist, singer – his accomplishments are far and beyond most people's ambitions. I have worked with him on many occasions, mainly in *Run for your Wife*, in which he played the role that would have been mine years ago, while I played the avuncular, incompetent detective, which gave me a ringside seat from which to observe at close quarters Derek's extraordinary talent. He roars rapidly from here to there on a very snazzy, high-powered motorbike, travelling from the Aldwych to Esher in less time than it takes me to get out of my stage costume. And what about his periods of relaxation? He sails his own yacht and owns a restaurant in Paris. How he manages to find the time to sleep is beyond me. In this schedule of a man possessed he still found time to visit me when I was in hospital. Half an hour with Derek was worth more than six months on the National Health.

About to begin rehearsal for Chekhov's *The Three Sisters*, directed by the much-respected Michael Blakemore, I was introduced in the rehearsal room to Kristin Scott Thomas, Madeleine Worrall and Kate Burton, who were playing the title roles. I only knew Kate by proxy, she being the daughter of Richard Burton, whom I'd met but once in a bar off Times Square in New York. He wasn't famous then and we were just two Englishmen abroad. I didn't even know he was Welsh, but I was captivated by his melodious voice and I couldn't understand why he hadn't yet been discovered. We parted in high spirits – it had been a great afternoon. I went again to the bar on the following day but he wasn't there. The barman didn't remember him and I don't even remember the barman. That was the one and only time I met Richard, but I will always treasure the memory.

Anyway back to Chekhov. Most of my scenes were with Douglas

Hodge, a charming impressive young actor. We had little dialogue together for most of our scenes. I was merely standing about the stage, endeavouring to be invisible. The only hardship in the play had nothing whatever to do with Chekhov: it was the physical effort of getting to the stage from my dressing room, which was buried deep underground. I had about forty steps to climb in order to reach the stage, and obviously the same to get back to my dressing room, which is eighty steps in all; and as I had five appearances in the show that amounted to approximately four hundred steps in every performance. This doesn't include the steps from the street down to my dressing room and back up again after the show. I may have exaggerated a little but the mere fact of writing this has left me breathless.

Backstage has always attracted visitors after each show. Some nights at the Playhouse Theatre during the run of *The Three Sisters* the well between the dressing rooms was a *Who's Who* of the theatrical profession waiting to offer congratulations, criticise or in some cases to get out of the rain. One evening as I sat in my dressing room after the show, footsore and weary, the babble of conversation outside my door decreased suddenly to a whisper. Immediately I was curious. Could it be that Michael Blakemore had arrived? Perhaps it was some international bimbo or – in a moment of mad optimism – royalty who had caused the hush. I was about to see for myself when there was a knock on the door. Good grief, it was my old pal Ken Dodd with his wife Ann. What a lovely surprise! It was indeed royalty – the king of vaudeville himself. He and Ann didn't want a drink, so I had theirs while Ken regaled me with the reason for their visit. They had come down from Liverpool with the express purpose of seeing *Tommy*, a play featuring a man in a fez giving an impression of the great Tommy Cooper. However, on leaving the station they'd passed a billboard advertising *The Three Sisters* and, taking Ken's breath away, there was my name amongst the cast list. Straightaway they forgot *Tommy* and made their way to the Playhouse to see if someone else was using my name – after all, it was Chekhov. In the unlikely event of it being me, was I ill, had I lost my marbles or, worse, had I been forced into the play against my will? As he put it, 'It was as if the Archbishop of Canterbury was appearing in *I'm a Celebrity Get Me Out of Here*.' I was in hysterics as Ken related this to me. When Ken finally took his leave, the crowd were still in the well outside my dressing room, waiting to catch another glimpse of the great man.

There are thousands of actors in our profession but there is only one Ken Dodd.

For me to work on the stage of the Playhouse Theatre was not just another venue. It was much more than that: it was a pilgrimage. It was there, over fifty years ago, that Bill Fraser had taken me into his number-one dressing room and rescued me from an untimely exit, which in turn kick-started my career under the bright lights.

On my eightieth birthday I felt no different from when I was seventy-nine. Having spent your allotted three score years and ten anything after is bonus, so when reaching the ripe old age of eighty one tends to creep furtively by that milestone, feeling slightly guilty of having stolen more than your share. But my birthday did not go unnoticed. During the interval of *The Three Sisters*, the whole cast assembled outside my dressing room in order to present me with a very elaborate birthday cake. Obviously fire regulations did not permit candles, but the icing was rich and plentiful, 'Happy Birthday' was sung and champagne sparkled the occasion. Everyone made a fuss of me and all I'd done in return was get older. The show ended – curtains, bows, applause – and the best surprise was about to happen: from the wings John Williams walked on to the stage with his guitar. In a welter of emotions, I was ushered forward and the audience and cast sang 'Happy Birthday' again, accompanied by the greatest classical guitarist, who made that simple melody sound like a salute to Strauss. When the final curtain came down, John and I embraced. I was too choked to speak; I couldn't see him properly as my eyes were glistening, so moved was I by his most generous gesture. Indubitably it was the highlight of my sojourn at the Playhouse Theatre.

*   *   *

My performance in *School for Wives* was beyond my wildest nightmares but Peter Hall must have been satisfied because he invited Norma and me to lunch as before – same restaurant, same table and once again Peter was late, only the waiter was different. Peter bustled in, apologising for his tardiness – how were we, had we ordered, all these queries delivered as if he had a train to catch. We were at the pudding stage before he mentioned Shakespeare. My compote of fruit lost its flavour, but Peter didn't appear to notice and regaled us with the wonderful story of how William Shakespeare had only ever appeared in one of his own plays, and that was when he took the part of Adam in *As You Like It*.

In a pause I interjected, 'And you are directing *As You like It* at the moment?'

'Yes,' he replied, 'at the Bath Festival, and I wonder . . .'

I finished off the sentence for him. 'If I could play the part of Adam, and the answer Peter is no, no, no. Molière was a salutary lesson to me but Shakespeare has never been on my "things to do" list.'

I was adamant and I was about to thank him for the lunch when he leaned across the table, as he was wont to do, and hissed, 'Before you say a word, you can do it,' stressing the word 'can'. But I was determined, which will give you some idea of how weak was my determination, because when the coffee arrived I had already agreed to do a three-week season at Bath with the Peter Hall Company in his production of *As You Like It*. And for those of you who prefer a happy ending and a touch of déjà vu, I was lumbered with the bill for lunch again.

Lunches aside, being directed by Peter Hall was a lesson in psychology. Some directors gain reputations by yelling, screaming and generally drawing adverse attention to themselves. I maintain that behaviour of this kind is counter-productive, childlike and a substitute for talent. In all the time I watched Peter's handling of well-established temperamental actors, I never once heard him raise his voice. If he had any admonishments or criticisms to pass on to members of the company, he delivered them quietly and personally. He had the ability to reach people's minds, to treat everyone as individuals by instinctively knowing which buttons to press. I was a pushover; my mind was no more complicated than an old edition of *Beano*.

Knowing that I learned my parts by listening to a tape on cassette, he personally recorded my lines in *As You Like It* in order to instil in me the rhythms and nuances of old Will's writing. Without this recording I would no more have understood the old bard than a book on quantum mathematics.

As I sat in rehearsals not understanding a word that was being said, I idly rummaged in my memory box, musing on how the feisty rumbustious knockabout days of vaudeville had given way to the rediscovery of drama. The transition was furtive but definitely educational, through the universities of Stoppard, Ayckbourn, Bennett towards the higher reaches of Molière, Chekhov and now incredibly the top banana, Shakespeare. A long march from the German at the French windows with a scar over one eye in Accrington.

I eagerly await Peter's next invitation to lunch, but if it turns out to be the title role in *Aida* I'll not only be paying the bill again but for weeks I'll be having singing lessons.

Before my dalliance with Chekhov and Shakespeare, I made three television appearances, the first being as an old man living in a tower block in an episode of *The Bill*. Number two was as an old man visiting his wife in hospital and having trouble with his middle-aged daughter in an episode of *Holby City*, and for my next I was an old man, again living in a tower block also having problems with his middle-aged daughter in *The Doctors*. Three similar performances – different cardigans and choice of slippers. I have almost given up hope of being the next James Bond.

I'm satisfied now to play some of the charity golf matches, but for pure relaxation I'm perfectly content to get around nine holes with Julie or David, and now my grandson Thomas. When they are otherwise engaged, Nigel Turner, Steve Burridge or Rodney Hutton share a few laughs and nine holes with me. These are the club professionals at Fulwell, Subroke Park and Hersham Village. With regard to the last one, the president elect is my long-time buddy Kenny Lynch.

Bruce Forsyth had for years possessed a buggy in which to transport himself round the west course at Wentworth, but from what I hear, he is now trolling around in a golfing Rolls-Royce. The seats are more comfortable, and it has receptacles for drinks and Isinglass curtains that you can roll right down in case there's a change in the weather (compliments of *Oklahoma*), but that's only for starters. Stepping out of the buggy at the first tee, you drive off. Back into the cart and you make a luxurious ride up the fairway to your ball – and here's the surprise: the buggy has been programmed, yes, programmed, and an instrument on the dashboard gives you the exact yardage from your ball to the green. How's that for an optional extra? Innovation marches on or, to be more accurate, it's broken into a trot. I fear it won't be long before the buggy will be programmed to hit the shot as well . . . Far fetched? With the bounds of technology out of control, don't be on it.

Before you go, I would like to recall an incident that happened one beautiful early evening in Normandy 1944, when a mass flight of Lancasters approached Caen, then still held by fanatical German troops.

Now over fifty years later I have learned that a rear gunner in one of the Lancasters was Warrant Officer First Class Jack Toulson-Clarke, who, when peace was finally declared, had completed fifty-seven missions as 'tail end Charlie'. He is now a close friend. Very rarely do we talk about the war, but on this occasion we were both in the frame, as it were. How did we come to meet in more civilised surroundings? He is Norma's partner. They are a great couple and two's company, as the old adage goes, but I'm happy to make it a crowd.

✻   ✻   ✻

This is only my own supposition but I think the word 'freelance' must have been derived from medieval times, when some poor devil in a suit of homemade armour and a borrowed nag would enter the lists, taking his life in his hands in the hope of getting paid. Having been a freelance all my life I know that I am one of the lucky ones, which makes me so proud of Kathy and Julie taking the same rocky path along the edge of a precipice. Kathy was a production co-ordinator, working on films such as *Absolute Beginners* and *Shanghai Surprise* – good groundwork for her future promotion to production manager – and on moving higher up the ladder she became production supervisor on *Captain Corelli's Mandolin*. Unless she is abroad on some project or other she never fails to eat her Sunday lunch with us at home for what she is happy to call joined-up meat.

At the same time Julie is still making her way up the ladder of television. She is now assistant director and her assignments are worthy of note: *My Hero, Coupling, The Vicar of Dibley* and Rory Bremner – in fact it seems that most of the good stuff on television bears her name in the credits. The climate has changed from the days when Julie was asked if Eric Sykes was her dad; now the boot is moving over to the other foot and people often ask me if Julie is my daughter. Incidentally, whenever I am in a film I have to admit proudly that yes, Kathy is my daughter.

Susan, a lady of above-average height, now has to look up to her children, who are taller. In fact when I talk to Matthew, the eldest, conversation is usually limited in order to avoid getting a crick in my neck. William, the youngest, is a teenager, computer literate, a wizard on the internet, fax, emails and texting – his knowledge of modern technology places him in a different world from mine, so much so that I feel sometimes as if I've just walked out of my cave to look for a stray dinosaur. Every time we have a family gathering he and Thomas disappear to play their complicated computer games. Eleanor, a very snazzy young lady, is still at college and will obviously graduate in something or other that will make me want to go back into my cave and pull a skin over my shoulders, which leaves Matthew. As if being tall isn't enough, he is now twenty-three and a dubbing mixer in Soho, and what's more, he's building up his credits on numerous programmes – all this inside one year. I can only touch my forelock. Now that her children are self-sufficient Susan has decided to go back into nursing, and having trained as an aroma-therapist she is at present installed at Frimley Park Hospital.

David, Laura, Thomas and Sophie live in a house renovated and decorated by David. There are also other mouths to feed: two Jack Russells, or to be more precise one Jack Russell and a Jill, named Trumpet and Maisie respectively. I believe they have a cat, although every time I visit it decides to prowl somewhere else. Whenever Edith, Kathy, Susan or Julie encounter problems in their homes, be it a washing machine that's packed up, TV on the blink, an angry boiler or whatever, the cry goes up, 'Send for David,' and either before he goes to work or on his way home he pops in and puts whatever is wrong to rights. For a self-confessed non-achiever he has turned himself into a top-of-the-market Jack of all trades and, although this may embarrass him, to my mind one of his most endearing qualities is his modesty.

My greatest bouquet, however, must go to my wife Edith. With me being so busy with my job, which never stops, the main burden of bringing up the family has rested largely on her shoulders and for the most part all I've done is to stand aside and admire the results. She rules the home like a benevolent despot whom we are all proud to serve.

ALL DOWN FOR THE GRAND FINALE

The writing of this book has been a rollercoaster ride in my mind. Some passages opened up nostalgic memories stored away for future reflection; on the other hand, I've had to turn over many stones I'd hoped I'd forgotten. On the whole, I grew up in a world of wonder, where summer sound was punctuated by the clip-clop of horse's hooves on cobbled streets, a time when the sky was strictly a domain for the birds whose excited, exuberant twittering heralded the early day. In all my young life the only aeroplane to invade their privacy was but a dot in the sky, writing the word 'Persil', an advert for washing powder.

Oldham, my birthplace, was but a tram ride from the country-side, meadows, dandelions and buttercups. Lying in the lush sweet grass, gazing up at the heavens, was one of my favourite diversions; lulled by the somnolent buzzing of a bee, butterflies just as busy but silent, and sometimes the distant bark of an inquisitive mongrel – traffic a word as yet unknown – that was my world.

Coincidences are commonplace and happen to all of us, but miracles are rare, and as I have been the recipient of these blessings I believe fervently that my mother is the source. Throughout my career she has guided my journey in mysterious ways.

To me this book has been a romp down memory lane, during which I stopped every few paragraphs to relive happy times with some of my old mates.

I dislike the term show business – it lacks grace, it is careless and plastic. Theatre, ballet, orchestral concerts and fast-disappearing vaudeville are now pigeonholed under the even worse heading 'showbiz'. What a sad indictment of a once proud profession, now overloaded with 'celebrities'!

To my mind I liken a career in theatre to an ornate gilded palace several landings high, culminating in the ballroom on the top floor. Just inside the imposing entrance doors a cocktail party is in progress. After sipping champagne between exchanging banalities, some collect their coats and leave. The rest move up the staircase to the first landing. Same banalities, more champagne. Inevitably again some of them walk down the staircase into the night, and the rest, now smaller in number, make their way up to the next landing. All this is repeated until only a handful reach the top floor, but only one or two enter the ballroom, where they attain the stars . . . For my own part, the lure and the dazzle up the staircases under the sparkling chandeliers have never appealed. I preferred to make the trip to the ballroom up the servants' staircase, lit only by a forty-watt bulb. I'm on the top floor and my journey is almost done. I can see a bar of light under the doors to the ballroom, but now I am here I'm not sure I want to dance.

My mother, however, is still the artificer and I the tool . . . I have been cast as Frank Bryce in the latest Harry Potter film.

My mother, Harriet

INDEX